# NEGOTIATING NATIONAL IDENTITIES

# Research in Migration and Ethnic Relations Series

*Series Editor:*
Maykel Verkuyten, ERCOMER
Utrecht University

The Research in Migration and Ethnic Relations series has been at the forefront of research in the field for ten years. The series has built an international reputation for cutting edge theoretical work, for comparative research especially on Europe and for nationally-based studies with broader relevance to international issues. Published in association with the European Research Centre on Migration and Ethnic Relations (ERCOMER), Utrecht University, it draws contributions from the best international scholars in the field, offering an interdisciplinary perspective on some of the key issues of the contemporary world.

Forthcoming

The Bosnian Diaspora
Integration in Transnational Communities
*Marko Valenta and Sabrina P. Ramet*
ISBN 978 1 4094 1252 6

*Other titles in this series at back of book*

**EUROPEAN RESEARCH CENTRE
ON MIGRATION & ETHNIC RELATIONS**

# Negotiating National Identities

## Between Globalization, the Past and 'the Other'

CHRISTIAN KARNER
*University of Nottingham, UK*

**ASHGATE**

Published by
Ashgate Publishing Limited
Wey Court East
Union Road
Farnham
Surrey, GU9 7PT
England

Ashgate Publishing Company
Suite 420
101 Cherry Street
Burlington
VT 05401-4405
USA

www.ashgate.com

**British Library Cataloguing in Publication Data**
Karner, Christian.
Negotiating national identities : between globalization, the past and 'the other'. – (Research in migration and ethnic relations series)
1. Nationalism–Europe. 2. Ethnicity–Europe. 3. Nationalism–Austria–History. 4. Nation-state and globalization–Europe. 5. Globalization–Social aspects–Europe.
I. Title II. Series
303.4'82-dc22

**Library of Congress Cataloging-in-Publication Data**
Karner, Christian.
Negotiating national identities : between globalization, the past and 'the other' / by Christian Karner.
  p. cm. – (Research in migration and ethnic relations series)
Includes bibliographical references and index.
ISBN 978-0-7546-7638-6 (hardback : alk. paper) – ISBN 978-0-7546-7639-3 (ebook)
1. National characteristics, European. 2. Nationalism–Social aspects–Europe. 3. Group identity–Europe. 4. Identity (Psychology)–Social aspects–Europe. 5. Globalization–Social aspects–Europe. 6. National characteristics, Austrian. 7. Nationalism–Social aspects–Austria. 8. Group identity–Austria. 9. Identity (Psychology)–Social aspects–Austria. 10. Globalization–Social aspects–Austria.
I. Title.
D1055.K365 2011
320.54094–dc22

2011002284

ISBN 9780754676386 (hbk)
ISBN 9780754676393 (ebk)

Printed and bound in Great Britain by the MPG Books Group, UK

# Contents

# Acknowledgements

This book is the culmination of nearly a decade of research, reflection and writing. Needless to stress that the people who – and the institutions that – have supported me during this extended period of time have been many, perhaps too many to be named individually. Nonetheless, I would like to express special gratitude to the following. I was enabled to build the foundations for my research on (Austrian) national identity negotiations by a Leverhulme Trust post-doctoral fellowship from 2002 to 2004, for which I am deeply grateful. Early publications arising from this 'Special Research Fellowship', on which I build in parts of the following analyses, included articles in *National Identities* 7 (4) (www.tandf.co.uk/journals/titles/14608944.asp), *Nationalism and Ethnic Politics* 11 (2) (www.tandf.co.uk/journals/titles/13537113.asp), *Ethnicities* 7 (1) (www.uk.sagepub.com/journals/Journal200776), and *Social Identities* 14 (2) (www.tandf.co.uk/journals/carfax/13504630.html). I would like to thank Taylor & Francis for permission to re-use some of those materials for the purposes of this book. Further, I would like to thank the School of Sociology and Social Policy at the University of Nottingham for providing a supportive, intellectually stimulating environment. More particularly, special thanks must go to my colleagues Esther Bott, Davide Però, Nick Stevenson, Elizabetta Zontini and especially David Parker for their time, expertise, support and friendship over the years. My thinking for this book was helped by many hours of stimulating discussion with Alan Aldridge and Bernhard Weicht. Whilst all responsibility for what follows is of course mine alone, Alan's and Bernhard's time and help were and are much-appreciated. Most of all, the greatest debt of gratitude is due to those closest to me, whose help – both practical and, especially, emotional – has been humbling, unswerving and inspiring: this book is dedicated, with love and gratitude, to them – first, my parents Christa and Peter Karner, and, second, Chrysanthi Lekka. Danke and Ευχαριστώ!

# Introduction

For the past few years I have woken up to the same song every morning. My CD-playing alarm clock marks each new day with a song by Wolfgang Ambros, one of Austria's best known singer-songwriters. Its title translates as *I'd like to stay human*; its lyrics include lines to the effect of 'I do not want to be sold like a commodity, not everything of value needs a price'. First released in 1974, the song is more than a contribution to a musical genre, Austro-Pop, little known outside the Alpine Republic. It arguably needs to be seen in what was then a new social and historical context – distinctly transnational and increasingly global in scope.

A year previously the beginning of a new, 'post-industrial' age (Bell 1973) had been announced. A leading sociologist (Castells 1996; 1997; 2000) would subsequently identify the 1970s as the beginning of a new 'mode of development': a watershed in human history, beyond which communication and information technologies and the now globally inter-connected worlds of business and finance cut across national boundaries, creating a transnational 'network society', a 'space of flows' between the world's metropolitan areas and dominant economic actors; alongside, however, inequalities and social exclusions have continued and often deepened. In the comparatively privileged 'Western world' the 1970s and 1980s also saw the growing cultural dominance of consumerism and structural changes of de-regulation and privatization associated with neo-liberalism. The collapse of Soviet-style communism and the end of the Cold War in 1989 led some to enthusiastically proclaim the 'end of history' (Fukuyama 1992), the ultimate victory for democracy, laissez-faire capitalism and global markets. With the benefit of hindsight, the naivety of such prognoses is now apparent. Ethnic conflicts, resurgent nationalisms across and far beyond Europe, and the 'war on terror' are but the most prominent examples of ideological antagonisms and of the significance of group boundaries in our globalizing era. Similarly, the current global economic crisis has led some economists to declare the 'end of neo-liberalism' and has seen governments trying to re-assert their long lost primacy over the market.

Whilst Wolfgang Ambros could not have anticipated this in 1974, his song nonetheless raises questions that have preoccupied much of the world – and certainly much of his and my native Austria – ever since. Returning to his haunting lyrics, one may ask what kind of human being Ambros wants to remain. How does he define humanity, or, rather, in opposition to what? The market seems to be at the forefront of his concerns. Putting this another way, what are the threats he is alluding to? How significant is commodification, given his insistence that things valuable and monetary values are not the same thing? There is a sense of far-reaching historical change I hear Ambros bemoan every morning, a nostalgia for the recent past prior to the onset of some perturbing transformations. This raises questions about the relevance of our interpretations of the past to how we make sense of the present and confront the future. Moreover, the category of 'the human' requires more careful discussion. Historical and anthropological records show that humans rarely think of all of humanity when invoking their humanity (though there is nothing in Ambros' song suggesting that he might not be thinking universally). We still live in a world of borders and boundaries, constant crossings and negotiations notwithstanding, in which categories of identification often only stretch far enough to include those we consider – by almost invariably arbitrary criteria – to be 'most like us'. We belong, for better or worse, to collectives. Of course we are made to belong and consider ourselves as belonging to different groups, depending on context (or sometimes self-interest). Amongst these, shared citizenship to a nation-state is amongst the most consequential types of collective for the overwhelming majority of human beings.

Ambros' wish to 'stay human' in the face of profound changes he saw unfolding in the 1970s inadvertently resonates with key themes explored here. This is a book about national identities and their negotiation in the context of the current phase of political, social, cultural and economic globalization – the now inescapably global markets and their effects on regions, localities, biographies, and everyday lives. It is a book about some of our era's defining tensions between the global and the local or national, about individuals' and groups' use of various cultural resources to understand and respond to rapid change. This is also a book about the relevance of the past, of sometimes strongly contested interpretations of history, to and in the present. And crucially, this is a book about the construction, reproduction *and* contestation of group boundaries, about collectives *and* individuals, about exclusions *and* political struggles against them, about institutions *and* social agency. Importantly, this book is also about people's struggles to maintain their humanity – however defined and experienced, in their particular social locations, to their particular historical backdrop, and in a contemporary context widely felt to be extraordinary, unsettling, challenging or anxiety-inducing.

The following chapters strike a balance between understanding context-specific particularities and extrapolating more generally, transnationally applicable insights into defining contemporary dilemmas. This book is the culmination of nearly ten years of research into the contemporary negotiation of Austrian national identities; as such, the crux of the book is empirically and historically focussed and geographically delineated, presenting a series of analyses centred on Austria as a part of the European Union. However, this book also reveals pan-European and even wider tendencies behind their Austrian manifestations. Each chapter begins with a conceptual discussion regarding key questions: these variously relate to the study of nation-states, nationalism, national identities and the politics of their negotiation, and the relevance of cultural symbols and historical memories in times of crisis; globalization and its (perceived) localized effects; civil societies, social exclusion and political struggles; discussions surrounding migration, integration and 'cohesive communities'; and cultural representation. Each chapter then proceeds to examine Austrian manifestations of these wider issues. I draw on a wide variety of data, including Austria's ideologically heterogeneous media and forms of cultural signification, sports, discourses about the environment and food, political manifestos, literature, street magazines, everyday language, historiography, readers' letters to newspaper editors, civil society initiatives and public debate, as well as 'ordinary' social practice. The analysis of such wide-ranging data is informed by a critical engagement with relevant social and cultural theory. Moreover, each chapter then develops its analysis further by discussing empirical parallels in other European countries. In other words, each chapter will start conceptually, then focus on Austria in order to extrapolate and work towards comparative, pan-European observations about national identities and globalization.

This movement from the conceptual to the empirically and historically specific and from there to the transnationally recurring and significant has obvious limitations and raises questions about the relevance of my central case study to its wider contexts. Any understanding of contemporary specificities is beset by an inevitable dilemma: the inescapability and pace of further change, which relegates our analysis of today's current affairs to recent memories and already outdated historical snippets almost before the ink on our pages has dried. In this particular context this means that recent Austrian, European and global changes have overlaid and continue to overlay my analyses, which are therefore best regarded as snapshots taken at different times over the last decade. At the heart of each chapter lies an analysis of a particular aspect of contemporary Austrian society first offered and published at different times since 2002. Whilst I have updated, refined and significantly added to these analyses, their original contexts need to be born in mind. In almost every case elections have been fought, won and lost since, political figureheads have died or retired and others appeared, controversies have unfolded, been half-forgotten and sometimes subsequently remembered, old crises have been overtaken by more recent, more global and seemingly more threatening new ones, national and international contexts have changed and continue to do so. Although it may be impossible to keep apace of constantly changing social realities, this need not result in intellectual paralysis. Instead, I here attempt to employ careful contextualization and – as already suggested – to extrapolate the general from the specific in order to facilitate discussion and to encourage further research. All of this said, Austria's relevance to a wider understanding of national identity negotiations in the contemporary world still needs to be established. On one level, this is of course a main task in this book and a complete and coherent answer will only emerge over subsequent chapters. However, a preliminary illustration of Austria's significance to our key concerns must form our starting point.

## Austria: context and relevance

The European Union has been described as a 'network' of states whose supra-national sharing of authority constitutes a defensive reaction to the globalization of the economy (Castells 1998). The contemporary European project is thus partly premised on the realization that a pan-European market provides individual member-states with a competitive advantage in a now inescapably global economy. At the same time, the rise and salience of neo-nationalist politics, the rejected EU-constitution and, more recently, widespread grassroots scepticism about the 'Lisbon Treaty' show that this 'network state' struggles to connect with many European citizens' lived identities, solidarities and histories. Meanwhile, anxieties about immigration have led to Europe's increasing 'fortification', which has in turn triggered civil society initiatives and much political discussion about the human rights of excluded or marginalized 'strangers'. This book presents an empirically detailed and theoretically wide-ranging analysis of these political and cultural struggles to be understood in the context of national histories, the contemporary tensions between global market forces and localized everyday lives, and the negotiation of boundaries in multicultural spaces and encounters.

There can be few, if any, more fitting settings in which to examine these questions than contemporary Austria. The controversial Austrian Freedom Party (FPÖ), its rise to political prominence during the 1990s and subsequently to power have been interpreted as paradigmatic of the renewed salience of nationalist politics observed in numerous contexts, both in and beyond the European Union, since the end of the Cold War. This has crystallized in conceptualizations of recent European shifts to the political right as evidence of 'Haiderization' (e.g. Wodak 2006), thus named after the FPÖ's former and highly controversial populist head – the now deceased Jörg Haider. After several years in coalition governments with the Austrian People's Party (ÖVP) – and a series of initial 'sanctions' temporarily imposed on the Alpine Republic in 2000 by her then 14 EU-partners – the FPÖ split into two now competing parties in 2005, the FPÖ and the initially Haider-led *Bündnis Zukunft Österreich* (BZÖ, or Alliance Future Austria). Following the parliamentary election in 2006 both found themselves in opposition to a 'grand coalition' between Austria's Social Democrats (SPÖ) and the ÖVP, which in turn collapsed following the publication of a letter to Austria's most widely read newspaper by then-Chancellor Alfred Gusenbauer (SPÖ) and his successor and then-Minister of Infrastructure Werner Faymann in June 2008. In this letter they announced that future amendments to the EU reform treaty, which had already been ratified by the Austrian parliament to the backdrop of considerable public debate, should be subject to a national referendum, if such amendments were 'consequential' to Austria (*Kronen Zeitung* 27 June 2008). The ensuing election in September 2008 led to a new though now weakened grand-coalition-government of SPÖ and ÖVP, though 28.2 per cent of votes cast for either FPÖ or BZÖ showed that the conditions underpinning the earlier mobilizing success of nationalist discourses of belonging and exclusion are still in place and require detailed and urgent examination. We shall see that nationalism indeed needs to be understood in relation to its 'surrounding' social and political fields.

This book demonstrates that in Austria as across the European Union these 'fields' are wider and more contested than commonly acknowledged: they subsume civil societies, the realm of cultural production, as well as diverse and competing ideological reactions to a period of far-reaching structural transformations and perceived crises, many of which are – or are widely interpreted as – symptoms of globalization and as such indicative of the contemporary tensions between nation-states and transnational forces and 'flows' (Appadurai 1990). Put differently, this contextualization of Austrian and other European identity politics in the wider processes and pressures associated with globalization will show neo-nationalism to be one among several competing reactions to contemporary challenges and perceived dislocations. Alternative, inclusive notions of identity and belonging have emerged particularly, though not only, from the realms of civil society and cultural production. To understand contemporary developments and such ideologically diverse reactions to them, a range of conceptual questions in the sociology of culture, identity and globalization need to be raised: those include the significance of history and contemporary economic contexts to the construction and negotiation of social identities; the contested boundaries between dominant majorities and groups of perceived and excluded 'others'; the politics of representation; the apparent tensions between global forces and resurgent localisms; emotional and ethical investments in competing visions of social order and political entitlements.

In addressing such issues, this book shifts the study of national identities from the party-political into various social, cultural and economic realms. Building on existing work on 'banal nationalism' (Billig 1995a) and the relevance of popular culture and the everyday (Edensor 2002), I detect and examine complex and contested national identity negotiations in a wide range of empirical 'settings'. As already hinted, their analysis will selectively draw on various contributions to social and cultural theory. The resulting discussions will combine detailed empirical research with theoretical insights into late modern identities and exclusions, the politics of culture and language, and the social contexts to the contemporary economy.

Any discussion of contemporary Austria must engage with its darkest historical chapter: the horrors of World War II and the Holocaust. At the same time, the turns and controversies of Austria's more recent history also teach lessons of more general significance (also see Wodak and Pelinka 2002). More accurately, in positioning Austria in relation to other European contexts throughout, this book draws attention to a multitude of contemporary tensions: between rival understandings of national identity; between global market forces and local histories, attachments and solidarities; between regional-, national-, European- and global power structures; between competing ideological forces in civil societies that are simultaneously local, national and at times transnational; and, crucially, profound disagreements within ethnic majorities about the presence and rights of 'the stranger' (see Bauman 1990) in their midst, about group boundaries and social inclusion, about justice, political entitlements and responsibility – in short, about social cohesion in Europe at the beginning of the twenty-first century.

In the autumn and winter 2007, the Austrian public began to witness a controversy as relevant to the issues examined here as it is paradigmatic of 'Fortress

Europe' at the beginning of the twenty-first century: the 'case' in question was that of a then fifteen-year old Kosovo-Albanian girl who temporarily disappeared to avoid deportation following her family's unsuccessful application for asylum. On one level, this was one among countless comparable instances across the EU and a reflection of increasingly restrictive asylum acts that respond to the anxieties among European populations and the exclusionary politics to which they give rise. At the same time, however, this case also re-ignited long-standing public debates about Austria's asylum-legislation, with people polarized in their opinions on how the state should handle this 'case'. There were recurring calls – emanating from parts of the political spectrum as well as from the readers' letters pages in Austria's most widely read newspaper – for the girl's and her family's deportation. However, there was also very considerable support for and political activism on behalf of the family (as there has been in a range of similar cases across the country), and the girl was ('illegally') sheltered by a succession of individuals – most notably by an outspoken priest – during her disappearance. Moreover, protest against existing legislation and deportations culminated in a demonstration organized by Austria's Green party in Vienna and attended by intellectuals, celebrities and between 5,000 and 10,000 people (http://www.orf.at 10 October 2007).

Such examples raise more general questions about human rights, social exclusion, and political struggle in our globalizing era. They also make simplistic, monolithic accounts of national identities untenable. Instead, they alert us to the contested nature of Europe's political realms and civil societies, in which existing configurations of power and exclusion are both reproduced and challenged. This book reveals, examines and analyzes such complexity, as well as its specific historical and wider structural contexts, in a part of the world widely – and too simplistically – associated with merely one of the several competing ideological currents currently shaping it. To fully understand Austria's relevance to discussions of how national identities are negotiated and struggled over at the beginning of the twenty-first century, external representations and images of the country also need to be considered. Such portrayals of the Alpine Republic simultaneously act as a point of reference and departure for the following chapters: rightly emphasizing Austria's historical particularities and responsibilities, relevant external representations also illustrate that the country is frequently seen to be typical of a wider and renewed salience of nationalist sentiments and politics. At the same time, however, many such representations also over-simplify and distort considerably more complex social realities, which call for more finely nuanced analyses.

**The 'world's gaze' and traces of the past**

Lyn Spillman's study (1997) of the role of (bi-)centennial celebrations in the construction of American and Australian national identities draws attention to the 'symbolic repertoires' underpinning the discursive crystallization of national 'comradeship'. Whilst ideas about land, history and founding moments, shared values and institutions, prosperity and internal diversity have shaped dominant understandings of 'American-ness' and 'Australian-ness', Spillman also draws attention to more general pre-occupations: first, 'internal integration' and, second, 'world position'. As classic 'countries of immigration', the US and Australia look back on histories of debate concerning cultural pluralism within an over-arching 'national community'. The historical backdrop in Europe is – of course – different and yet, as shown by recent political developments and regular media headlines, questions and widely perceived challenges of 'integration' are also key to understanding contemporary European societies. The much-debated politics of integration is a recurring issue over the following chapters. The second broad issue Spillman highlights – a pre-occupation with one's standing in the world – similarly continues to shape discourses of 'the nation' across the globe. More accurately, national identities are in part negotiated in response to outsiders and in interaction with external perceptions. The 'world's gaze' (Spillman (1997, 62) is indeed a crucial reference point, variously used to corroborate or contrast with existing self-definitions, for so-called domestic 'elites' and 'ordinary social actors' alike.

Austria does not make international headlines often. When it has done over recent decades, it has tended to be in the context of controversy, perceived upheaval, shocking cases of crime and in relation to contemporary 'responses' to World War II and the Holocaust. A widely discussed political controversy was provided by the presidential election of former UN general secretary Kurt Waldheim in 1986. Waldheim's war-time past triggered national and international debate about the highly problematic post-war construction of Austria as Hitler's 'first victim' (e.g. Uhl 2006), as well as an anti-Semitic backlash in parts of the national press (see Mitten 1992). More recently, the above-mentioned temporary 'sanctions' against Austria following the FPÖ's inclusion in a coalition government with the ÖVP in 2000 reflected European disquiet about Jörg Haider's xenophobic populism and a series of infamous statements he had made about World War II. The 'world's gaze' and concerns manifested, for example, in *The Guardian*'s headlines of 'Europe in turmoil over far right pact in Austria': published the day Austria's ÖVP-FPÖ government was formed, the article quoted Ehud Barak, then Israel's Prime Minister, saying that 'the inclusion of an extreme rightwing party … in the government of Austria should outrage the free world'; then German Foreign Minister Joschka Fischer observed that 'it is the first time that a political movement with a declared anti-European and xenophobic stand and a very dubious relationship to the Nazi era is coming to power' (Black and Connolly 2000). Following Haider's deadly car accident in October 2008, *The Observer* offered a similar summary of his politics:

> [T]he son of two Austrian Nazi sympathisers and a brilliant law student, was one of Europe's most controversial politicians. He based his career on a relatively explicit admiration for German National Socialism, aggressive Euroscepticism, persistent attacks on immigrants, and an instinctive ability to subtly but effectively tap into a long local history of anti-semitism. … Haider, along with

… France's Jean-Marie Le Pen, was … one of the pioneers of the new European extreme-right populism of the past two decades. In 1991 he provoked fury after praising the 'orderly employment policy' of Nazi Germany, in 1995 he dismissed Nazi concentration camps as 'the punishment camps of National Socialism', and said that the Nazi Waffen-SS 'deserved every honour and recognition'. (Burke 2008)

The infamous statements quoted here explain Haider's pariah-status both internationally and amongst his Austrian opponents and critics. At the same time, as shown by recent scholarship (e.g. Gingrich 2002; Sickinger 2008), Haider's political success relied on his employment of different, context-specific registers, he appealed to different audiences for sometimes different reasons, and his ideological emphases and political strategies changed over time, important continuities notwithstanding. The sociologically more relevant question addressed in this book pertains to the wider conditions and changes that have granted increasing appeal to Europe's far-right populist parties over the past twenty years.

A few months prior to Haider's death, the world's gaze had turned to Austria in the more jovial context of the European football championship the country co-hosted with Switzerland. The past and Austria's relationship to it again caught up with the Alpine Republic when the British tabloid *The Sun* reported tracking down 95-year-old Milivoj Asner – the third most-wanted on the Simon Wiesenthal Centre's list of suspected Nazi war criminals – in the city of Klagenfurt, where he had been protected from extradition to his native Croatia on the grounds that he was allegedly not fit to stand trial (Flynn 2008). This case was also subsequently highlighted in the Simon Wiesenthal's annual report for 2009, in which Austria was criticized for its inefficiency in prosecuting suspected Nazi war criminals: unlike in Germany, the report noted, Austrian courts have not passed a single relevant sentence in 30 years (http://derstandard.at/druck/id=1240297879283).

Traces of the Nazi past were also detected in the context of one of the most notorious crimes of recent decades: the case of a 73-year-old Austrian who – in the spring of 2008 – was discovered to have locked up his daughter for 24 years in a dungeon, sexually abusing her and fathering seven children, one of whom had died of neglect and three of whom had never seen daylight until they were discovered. Soon thereafter, *The Sun* relayed the following account by a criminal allegedly 'inspired' by Hitler:

Adolf Hitler had been given a rapturous welcome in F.'s home town of Amstetten … in 1938, around the time of the cellar fiend's third birthday. F. … said he took his belief in 'strict discipline' and 'the need to be controlled' from Hitler's evil regime … 'I grew up in the Nazi times and that meant the need to be controlled and the respect of authority. I suppose I took on some of these old values. It was all subconscious of course.' (Flynn et al. 2008)

It is not at all clear why F. would suddenly unearth the 'sub-conscious' underpinnings of his actions. Worryingly, this account seemingly wants to 'explain' a horrendous crime as history's causal effect on an individual, thus denying the latter's agency and failing to see his crime as his unique and uniquely abominable actions. Whilst it may be tempting to interpret this as F.'s self-serving rambles, another external journalistic observer also claimed to see the root causes of this crime in the enduring and psychic legacy of Austria's past:

> Austria is … a 'look-away' society … Marc Dotroux, a Belgian, held schoolgirls captive … and abused them. Germany has had its cannibal and countless cases of infanticide. There is no monopoly on cruelty. But Austria is a society that nurtures its secrets, that suppresses its history … There is a consensus mentality, an aversion … to open conflict, that has reached almost neurotic proportions … Perhaps there is something Habsburgian about this; an echo, too, of Sigmund Freud's Vienna. The tone politically was set in the 1920s by the feuding Austro-Marxists, national and Christian socialists, and then in the 1930s by the sense of relief – enthusiasm even – felt by many Austrians when Nazi Germany incorporated Austria into the Third Reich. The ignoble fact is that 40 per cent of the staff … of concentration camps were of Austrian origin … After the war many Nazis were swallowed up into democratic party structure … Far longer than in Germany, Waffen SS veterans met to chat about old times. The central question for post-war Germans has been: how many facts do I need to know about my father to know myself? It is a good question, rarely posed in Austria … [A] cod psychologist might draw the conclusion that 73-old Mr F, whose early childhood was spent in Nazi Austria, came to accept certain modes of behaviour … [I]t is the interlocking circles of secrecy that make Austria special in the way that it deals with, or ignores, individual tragedies. (Boyes 2008)

This account contains well-known and appalling historical facts. It also echoes the frequently made observation (e.g. Lebow 2006, 18) that post-war Austria and Germany showed contrasting (dominant) responses to their shared responsibilities for Nazism and the Holocaust. Alongside, however, Boyes' account also offers a flawed and disconcerting form of stereotyping. Let us spell out what it suggests: that a nation is a collective with shared psychic properties that are grounded in its history and shape present actions, dispositions and institutional structures. There are good reasons to be sceptical and concerned about the stereotyping, agency-denying and de-contextualizing facilitated by such accounts. Before elaborating, however, similar portrayals of Austrian society and politics that have variously been offered by academic observers and external as well as domestic commentators warrant discussion. They not only corroborate the existence of the 'world's gaze' but also reveal comparably problematic assumptions guiding what 'it sees' or, more accurately, how the observed is interpreted. Moreover, some such accounts show that similar assumptions reappear in influential narratives of 'the nation' articulated from within its boundaries. What they have in common is a gaze that *reifies*. As later chapters of this book show, sociologically untenable reifications of 'Austrian society' – as, for example, allegedly monolithically secretive or conflict adverse – cannot capture or analyze the struggles and contradictions of (recent) Austrian history and its complex politics of national identity negotiations.

## Questioning metonymy: *'homo austriacus'*...?

The journalistic accounts summarized above focus on social and political phenomena – ranging from Waldheim to Haider, from the horrendous 'Amstetten-case' to the fact that much more should have been done to bring Nazi war criminals to justice – that have been prominent aspects of recent Austrian history. Each of these facts and phenomena requires urgent, ongoing and detailed discussion, criticism and reflection. At the same time, the *format of their portrayal*, rather than their content, and the *inferences drawn* from it are at times deeply problematic. Many such accounts employ what the cognitive linguist George Lakoff (1987, 77–79) terms 'metonymic' reasoning and defines as the 'extremely common [tendency] for people to take one well-understood or easy-to-perceive aspect of something ... to stand ... for the thing as a whole'; a particular part – 'some sub-category or member or submodel' – is thereby used to characterize and 'comprehend the category as a whole'.

One manifestation of such metonymic thinking emerges from the following account of the effects of the Waldheim-controversy:

> [The controversy] marked a turning-point ... in the Austrians' perceptions of themselves and in the perception of Austria by the outside world ... *The Austrians*, like Waldheim, had got used to thinking of themselves purely as victims of Nazism, with no regard for the part they had played in its regime of evil ... For four decades after achieving independence, Austria had again become, to most foreign eyes, the sweet land of The Sound of Music; of Strauss and Mozart; of Danube steamers and alpine ski-runs. That outside vision had now been shattered, at least temporarily, and *the Austrians* themselves had been brought up once more against the challenge which had always threatened their sense of identity – the German complication in race, in allegiance and in ideology. *They* finally emerged from the Waldheim years not so much transformed as strengthened in some of their less admirable qualities. *They* tended to be more anti-Semitic than ever and – ironically for a people who flourished on tourism – more enclosed. (Brook-Shepherd 1997, 439, italics added)

This account contains much that is important and continues to be of relevance to an understanding of *certain aspects of* contemporary Austria. At the same time, however, this portrayal is remarkable in its essentializing tone: a country of more than eight million is reduced to a stereotype of 'the Austrians'; a – as we shall see – pluralistic and intensely contested political field is overlooked and hidden behind a monolithic narrative of allegedly all-embracing collective emotions, delusions and dispositions; a partial truth, a depiction of what is one cultural and political stream among others, is wrongly presented as a singularly sufficient historical analysis. As this book will show, a convincing analysis of contemporary Austria needs to be more nuanced, fine-grained and willing to capture contradictions, ambivalences and struggles.

Metonymic and hence reductive narratives are common. Ruth Wodak and her co-authors show this in their discussion of 'five major thematic areas' enabling *The Discursive Construction of National Identities* across a range of public, semi-public and semi-private Austrian settings: 'the linguistic construction of the *homo Austriacus*'; 'the narration … of a common political past'; 'the linguistic construction of a common culture', of a 'common political present and future' and of a 'national body' (Wodak et al. 1999, 30). Whilst each of these matters to the following analyses, the first discursive dimension – 'stereotypical image[s] of *homo Austriacus* and the concepts of a "typically Austrian national character" … "typically Austrian behaviour" and a "specific Austrian mentality"' (Wodak et al. 1999, 193) – provides a conceptual point of departure. Importantly, Wodak and her colleagues observe that stereotypes inform not only portrayals of 'the other' but also prominent constructions of the 'national self'; put more simply, they reveal discursive processes of 'self-stereotyping' within the nation. Before returning to these, it is worth mentioning another recent instance of an essentialized notion of *homo austriacus* being invoked in an external portrayal of Austria: in a commentary on the then recent collapse of Austria's previous SPÖ-ÖVP coalition government, the German paper *Welt am Sonntag* linked Austrian politics both to globalization and to what it portrayed as allegedly Austrian particularities. Entitled 'Austria has never been as Austrian as it is now', the article in question imputed an 'Austrian-ness' allegedly defined by a refusal to acknowledge the benefits globalization has brought to the country. Writing before the global financial crisis spread to Eastern Europe and from there – via loans provided by Austrian banks – to the Alpine Republic itself, the article argued that although Austria had benefited from the EU's easterly expansion more than most countries, Austrians refused to see themselves as an example of successful globalization; on the contrary, it was suggested, such economic gains had exacerbated a sense of national narcissism; Austria's 'motto', it was postulated, was to 'act global, think Austrian' (Alexander 2008).

Such essentializing, often psychoanalytically framed accounts appear not only in external media representations of Austria. Political scientist John Bunzl accounts for Haider's political appeal through the notion of a historically shaped – and, problematically, seemingly all-embracing – collective psyche:

> [T]he womb is still fertile – fed by a deep resentment that Austrians, after belonging to the elite of a grand empire, have been reduced, twice in the twentieth century, to a small and relatively unimportant existence. Monumental changes in the surrounding world have re-awakened slumbering demons. In a broader sense, these resentments, together with the weakness of a collective ego,

*predispose Austrians* to hostility towards the 'other' – the stranger – which is
an apparent displacement of their anxiety over losing their own shaky identity.
(Bunzl 2002, 65, italics added)

Suggestive though this may appear to be, the following chapters show that ideas
about historically determined, collective psychic dispositions fail to illuminate
– or even acknowledge – what are more complex, ideologically heterogeneous
and contested social and political realities.

The most famous application of psychoanalytical concepts and insights to an
analysis of Austrian society and politics was contained in a series of speeches and
essays in the 1980s and early 1990s by Austrian psychoanalyst Erwin Ringel. Ringel
coined the term 'Austrian soul', which bore the neurotic scars of authoritarian,
emotionally depriving child-rearing practices of the post-war era and manifested
in hierarchical, patriarchal structures, a widespread amnesia of Austrians' shared
responsibility for the Holocaust, sexual repression and social conformity, as well
as xenophobia as an outward projection of deep-seated feelings of inferiority (see
Ringel 2005). Ringel applied psychoanalytical insights in the service of some
much-needed social and political criticisms, some of which continue to be timely
and extremely relevant. Yet, and the value of psychoanalysis to social analysis
notwithstanding, there are several reasons – from a sociological perspective – to
be wary of the reifications such applications can entail.

First, as already implied, some such interweaving of psychoanalysis with
historical analysis provides problematic essentialisms, denying agency and ignoring
evidence of ideological disagreements and contestation. Unlike psychoanalytical
work of a more universalist orientation (e.g. Žižek 1989), which detects the affective
conditions of possibility underpinning racism in the human psyche common to us
all, notions of a 'national psyche' often project such sentiments, politics and their
psychologies onto a particular and monolithically conceived grouping. Second,
questions concerning the actual verifiability of some such suggestions need to be
raised: what would count as empirical evidence that a particular politics is indeed a
manifestation of a corresponding but generally unrecognized psychic 'condition'?
And could such evidence not potentially allow for alternative interpretations?

Third, the concept of a 'national psyche' appears unsuited to an era of global
connections and influences, constant boundary-crossings and transnational
dynamics. Whilst not unique to our era, cross-border flows and experiences of
globalism have undoubtedly intensified over recent decades. Just as yesteryear's
'container theory' (Beck 2000) equating social with national boundaries is ill-
equipped to illuminate the transnational complexities of contemporary life, it is
doubtful that the idea of 'national psyches' captures or illuminates its psychological
ramifications. Fourth, and most crucially, there is a wealth of empirical evidence,
only a fraction of which is examined below, that reflects a diversity of ideological
leanings, competing political preferences and practices shaping contemporary
Austria (and indeed Europe). It is not at all my intention to question the general
psychoanalytical validity of the concepts invoked by some of the portrayals

mentioned above. However, the material examined in what follows demonstrates that if certain psychodynamic conditions and processes are indeed common to a given population, different individuals and groups display strikingly different and sometimes diametrically opposed ways of responding to and living with them.

This book demonstrates that civil society – broadly defined as the organizational and discursive realm of mobilization, debate and politicization between the levels of individuals and families and the structures of the state and political parties respectively – is crucial to the negotiation of local, regional, national or indeed European identities and hence to the politics of inclusion, exclusion, rights, responsibilities and entitlements. As such, I also present material that challenges another cliché of Austria: that of a steeply hierarchical, paternalistic, traditionalist and conflict-adverse society (e.g. Mappes-Niedik 2002). Writing in the Austrian quality daily *Der Standard*, the *Neue Zürcher Zeitung*'s correspondent for Austria recently invoked this cliché in attempting to explain the horrendous 'Amstetten case': this unprecedented crime, it was suggested, could only have happened in the context of general disinterest and inattention as well as an underdeveloped civil society – all allegedly 'Austrian peculiarities' (Ritterband 2008).

There are indeed important factors that contributed to the relatively late development of Austria's civil society (e.g. Bruckmüller 1996, 42–43; Pelinka 1990, 24), to which such arguments allude. However, as in the instances of metonymic stereotyping mentioned earlier, one particular aspect, in this case a historically outdated and since superseded aspect, is here wrongly taken to represent larger, more complex and more diverse social realities and to also allegedly 'explain' particular occurrences. Neighbourly inattention may indeed have been a necessary precondition for this horrific, 24-year long crime. However, projecting this onto a national scale and interpreting it – in seemingly circular fashion – as corroboration for a civil society assumed to be weak fails to provide an analysis and, as this book will show, is out of touch with contemporary Austrian realities. The latter are multi-faceted, complex, internally ideologically contested, often defined by profound disagreements and heated political debates. It is on such terrain that the meaning and boundaries of national identities are negotiated. Moreover, such negotiations are also about social inequality, exclusion and about rival understandings of ethics, entitlements and rights. And most importantly, such polarizing debates and negotiations are no longer, if ever they were, confined within national boundaries: they unfold – especially in our era of global connections and inter-dependencies – in a wider European framework, to a backdrop of global challenges and in a climate of transnationally shared crises and anxieties. Whilst all of these dimensions form the inescapable and vital backdrop to the later chapters of this book, the more immediate European context requires some still preliminary comments.

## European dimensions

Condensing a key point developed above, national identities are partly articulated and negotiated in conversation and interaction with outside perceptions and narratives. At the same time, such identity negotiations also need to be understood in relation to structural changes and wider phenomena that are transnational or global in character. In this section, by way of conclusion to this introduction, I further develop my rationale for relating Austria to other comparable European case studies: the three dimensions crucial to my analyses – concerns with *globalization*, with *the past* and with '*the other*' – matter not only in contemporary Austria but indeed across (and of course beyond) Europe.

The significance of the European project can hardly be overstated. Integrating nation-states previously divided by centuries of antagonism, competition and periodical warfare ranks amongst the most outstanding political achievements in human history. At the same time, this project is clearly ongoing and incomplete. Whilst the accession of ten formerly communist, Central and Eastern European countries since 2004 has added to the EU's historical importance and impressive record, it has also presented individual member states, ordinary citizens and transnational European structures with new challenges. Responses to some of those challenges are yet to be found and anxieties 'on the ground', some of which feature prominently in later chapters, need to be taken seriously. The effects of the financial crisis and economic recession have further added to the difficulties faced across Europe. Writing shortly before the subsequent global economic down-turn, Montserrat Guibernau expressed concern (2007, 115–116) as to how a 'still embryonic' and 'non-emotional' European identity and the in some ways 'still fragile' institutions of the EU would withstand a 'major economic crisis'. Now in the midst of such a crisis, Guibernau's pessimism seems to have been partly justified. At the European elections in June 2009, the almost pan-European weakness of the political left – arguably the very politics one may have expected to benefit from the widely proclaimed end of neo-liberalism – was striking; this was accompanied by a significantly strengthened position for Europe's dominant centre-right block and very significant gains for anti-European or EU-sceptical rightwing and populist parties (e.g. Hoffmann-Ostenhof and Müller 2009). At the same time, however, pro-European Green parties also gained and there is evidence suggesting that EU approval rates can rise in times of economic crisis: thus, the generally widespread EU scepticism in the Alpine Republic notwithstanding, surveys conducted prior to the 2009 EU elections revealed that more than three quarters of Austrians supported continued EU-membership, which amounted to one of the highest approval rates since Austria's accession in 1995; significantly, 70 per cent of respondents pragmatically agreed that individual states would be less able to cope with a recession than the EU as a supranational collective (*Profil* 29 May 2009, 36).

Such pragmatism, the 2009 election results and current trends all need to be seen in the wider context of the EU's recent enlargements and ongoing debates about structural changes, most notably as envisaged by the much-debated Lisbon Treaty designed to ensure a more efficient institutional functioning of a European Union of now 27 member states. At the time of writing (autumn 2009), and despite its parliamentary ratification across most of the EU, there have been widespread concerns the Treaty would further shift power from individual nation-states to Brussels. Grassroots opposition to the Lisbon Treaty has, albeit to varying degrees, been articulated across Europe, including in Austria, Germany, the Czech Republic, Poland, the UK and Ireland. The latter, notably, is the only member state to have held referenda on the Treaty, which resulted in its initial rejection in June 2008 and its subsequent approval in October 2009. It should be remembered that the Lisbon Treaty was also intended as a somewhat 'diluted' substitute for the European constitution previously rejected by the French and Dutch electorates. This more than symbolic blow by two countries at the historical core of the European Union raised questions about the perceived tensions or complementarity between the historically entrenched structures of the nation-state and the more recent European 'network state'. Later chapters of this book examine these questions in more depth and demonstrate that the issues involved are complex and cannot be reduced to a presumed clash between deep-seated attachments to the nation-state and a European project driven by elites and lacking grassroots legitimacy respectively. A closer look and analysis will reveal that the question as to *which kind of Europe* citizens want is debated widely and intensely (chapter three) and that much political anxiety is underpinned by concerns about the *local effects of global markets* and about the scope for social solidarity and the meaning of political entitlements in our globalizing era (chapter four).

In a still preliminary and descriptive sense, the findings on Austria contained in the 2004 Euro-barometer spring survey are worth mentioning: conducted at a high-point of EU scepticism, when many Austrians felt alienated by the temporary 'sanctions' put on Austria by her 14 EU-partners in 2000, the survey suggested that only 30 per cent of Austrians still considered EU membership to be 'generally a good thing', with 29 per cent seeing it as a 'bad thing', and 36 per cent expressing ambivalence; moreover, the findings pointed at a relative lack of identification with the European Union, with 50 per cent of respondents defining themselves as 'Austrian, not European', and a further 36 per cent as 'primarily Austrian, and only secondarily European' (http://derstandard.at/standard.asp?id=1725913). These findings need to be seen in the context of the year 2000 and its aftermath. And as the more recent figures quoted above illustrate, EU approval rates fluctuate significantly and have risen to the backdrop of the current economic crisis. Beyond country-specific particularities, the 2004 survey also contained pan-European relevancies: thus, whilst ranking alongside the UK, Sweden and Estonia amongst the most EU sceptical member states,[1] Austrians' concerns clearly resonated then

---

1    The summer 2009 Euro-barometer showed further fluctuations: whilst many Austrians still showed  considerable EU scepticism, the survey corroborated that the economic crisis had led to higher EU approval rates in the Alpine Republic; moreover,

– and have continued to do so since – with many other European citizens: these were/are concerns about EU enlargement, about unemployment (due to companies relocating), about crime, declining social welfare, the pension system, and the rising costs of EU membership.[2] Some of these undeniably pan-European anxieties reflect experiences of (economic) globalization as a catalyst for job insecurity, potential redundancy, downward social mobility or permanent social exclusion. Leading sociologists (Bauman 1998; Beck 2000) corroborate these assessments in defining our current era of globalization by a general 'disempowerment' of individual nation-states, which find themselves in a permanent state of competition with each other over vital foreign investment in their respective territories and its populations; a new and decisive feature is the fact that major economic players have become transnational businesses, with the ability – and often the inclination – to relocate their sites of production and assembly to areas with a cheaper work force and lower taxes; this not only makes many jobs temporary and uncertain, but also results in a loss of important tax revenue for nation-states, whose welfare systems consequently become harder to finance. Important parts of the analyses presented in this book address the question as to how individuals and groups live with such fears and uncertainties and how discourses of identity and belonging relate to them.

Globalization does not only manifest in the economic realm. On the contrary, the European Union is the arguably best example of transnational political structures, cultural exchanges, social and institutional interconnections, and an emerging sense of a supra-national source of identity. That said, the EU is also clearly a 'work in progress' and assessments of its achievements to date as well as visions for its future trajectory differ hugely. Whilst some of these diverging interpretations and blueprints will be analyzed in due course, two important areas of debate are worth mentioning at this stage: first, some of the most vocal advocates of closer European integration (e.g. Busek 2008) identify the present lack (or at best weakness) of a pan-European public sphere, also reflected in the relative absence of pan-European media, as an obstacle a better functioning European Union will need to overcome. The second area of debate relates to the above-mentioned issue as to whether EU citizens define themselves as only citizens of their country, as Europeans, or as both (and if both, how they negotiate such complementary identities). Whilst critics and sceptics of the European project tend to portray different national histories as continually divisive or refer to some sobering Euro-barometer findings (see above), others (Cram 2009, 101) stress

---

Austria was no longer amongst the most sceptical member states – a position now occupied by the UK, Latvia and Hungary (http://oe1.orf.at/inforadio/112625.html).

2   Another survey, conducted in June/July 2005 (Haupt 2005), showed that EU scepticism is *not* automatically tantamount to opposing EU membership: whilst the survey revealed the highest level of EU scepticism recorded thus far, a majority of 66 per cent of respondents – the same proportion that had voted for Austria's EU accession in 1994 and including some of the sceptics – nonetheless favoured continuing membership.

that 'the relationship between European and national identities … need not be a conflictual, either/or trade-off nor a simple … co-existence but may be synergistic, producing an outcome which is greater than the sum of its parts'. Elaborating on such synergies premised on diversity rather than a single, 'homogenous European identity', Cram suggests that certain identifications may be taken-for-granted but are nonetheless important:

> As Billig argues … identification is not always passionate … but mundane, even banal. For EU citizens, identification may equally be based on daily low-level engagement in unremarkable ways (carrying passports driving licences, conforming with legislation, walking past EU flags) which nevertheless remind citizens of their involvement in the larger EU system. (Cram 2009, 104–105)

Such 'banal Europeanism' does not answer the question as to how different Europeans relate to 'the other', to the world beyond what has come to be referred to – amongst some of its critics – as 'Fortress Europe' and to the non-Europeans who are trying to get access to 'it'. Widespread and pan-European concerns about immigration and unemployment were recorded in the autumn of 2003, prior to the EU's two most recent rounds of enlargement and long before the current economic crisis:

> 33 per cent of Europeans feel threatened by immigration … This is shown by a survey by the Italian 'Nord-Est' Trust. 81 per cent of the population of the [then] 15 EU countries consider the fight against illegal immigration to be of utmost importance … Italian sociologist Ilvo Diamanti stresses that there are similar fears of immigration across all EU countries. 36 per cent of respondents consider immigration to constitute a danger to security … 35 per cent fear that immigrants could take their jobs. Germans, in particular, expressed this anxiety. 28 per cent of respondents are concerned about Europe's cultural and religious identity. Anxiety about immigration is particularly high amongst low-income respondents. (http://www.diepresse.at/Artikel.aspx?channel=p&ressort=eu&id= 381404)

There is much about these findings that is remarkable, including their pan-European dimensions and the fact that they record widespread anxieties at a time of relative economic stability. Moreover, the different responses – 33 per cent reporting feeling threatened by immigration, 81 per cent declaring the fight against 'illegal immigration' to be a priority – relate to different types of migration: labour migration widely perceived to result in additional competition on the job market on one hand, and the much-debated phenomena of human trafficking and undocumented migration on the other. Issues of migration and associated fears have further gained in urgency and intensity since 2003: there are important differences across the EU concerning the employment rights of nationals of recent Central and Eastern European accession countries; most divisive of all, there are ongoing debates and profound disagreements concerning the distribution and rights of – as well as the responsibility for, and the country-specific systems faced by – asylum-seekers in the European Union. Indeed, few issues are as topical or as directly related to Europe's response to 'the other' as that of asylum: at the time of writing, as the EU continues to debate different asylum-systems and potentials for increasing coordination, citizens are regularly reminded of the plight and suffering of African would-be asylum-seekers who have died at sea or are turned back to lives of destitution and hopelessness before they can make a claim for asylum on European shores (e.g. *Euronews* 2 September 2009). Later chapters of this book will demonstrate that debates surrounding migration in general, and asylum in particular, revolve around competing political discourses that centre on *citizen-specific entitlements* and *universal human rights* respectively. My analyses will draw attention to different social realms – including party politics, civil society activity and cultural production – involved in these defining debates of our time.

Migration and asylum involve my three central analytical dimensions: globalization, 'the other' and the past. The relevance of the first two is self-explanatory and written into the experience of cross-border movements and ensuing inter-cultural encounters. To understand the relevance of the past, however, one must consider the reasons behind contemporary (forced) migration, which implicate wider structural contexts. These wider political contexts are in turn decisively shaped by profound inequalities – whether on local, regional, national or global levels, or on all of those. Such inequalities manifest in relation to people's relative access to, or exclusion from, vital resources and decision-making power, in their highly variable life chances, standards of living, or mere ability to live in dignity. Moreover, such inequalities have historical roots. Our global system is characterized by staggering inequalities, the various and complex origins of which also include the history of European imperialism and colonialism. Put another way, the past – which is also, in part, a European past – is vital for an understanding of present and global migratory flows. What holds in relation to migration, also applies to issues concerning national and European identities: memories and the past matter. In Griffin and Bollen's words (2009, 609), 'memories of important past events are systematically … correlated with what people believe about pressing national issues'. There is a growing and important body of literature (e.g. Müller 2002; Bell 2003) that distinguishes between individual memories of things personally experienced, and collective/national memory or 'mythology' respectively. The latter refers to a social, culturally transmitted, identity-bestowing but also internally contested[3] framework for interpreting the past and also, through analogy, the present. Several of the following analyses (particularly chapters two and three) build on existing work on collective, national memories, their political appropriation and contestation. More immediately, such debates are also relevant to European memories and a possibly unifying European identity.

---

3    The notion of 'counter-memories' is crucial in this respect and will resurface in later chapters.

Ideological contestation and competing memories notwithstanding, national 'mythology' and national identities are, in part, 'mutually constitutive' (Müller 2002, 21). This raises the question if a supra-national European identity can or already has been generated through a particular form of historical consciousness (see Pakier and Stråth 2010). More accurately, the centrality of memories of the Holocaust to processes of 'Europeanization' has come to be the debated in the literature (e.g. Bet-El 2002; Grunwald 2010). However, analyses of the question as to whether a common European identity has emerged from collective remembrance of the Holocaust reveal a complex picture. Grunwald points out (2010, 298) that memories have the power to unite *and* to divide, with Europe emerging as a 'space of particularly dense and contested collective ... memories'. His analysis of 'Holocaust memorialization in postwar Europe' reveals how the Cold War led to divisive instrumentalizations of the past:

> [T]he experience of National Socialist occupation and persecution, while providing for homogeneous experiences of victims regardless of their nationality, did not feed directly into a unified European consciousness. On the contrary, the memory of these experiences was harnessed to bolster projects of national reconstruction, as well as being utilized by both East and West in the emerging Cold War confrontation. (Grunwald 2010, 310)

The period since 1989, Grunwald shows, has seen a 'surge in Holocaust memorialization' (as well as infamous and deeply troubling examples of its contestation), the increasing importance of transnational contexts, and well-known initiatives to institutionalize Holocaust remembrance and research. The latter have included the Stockholm conference of January 2000 and the establishment of the 'International Task Force for Holocaust Education, Remembrance and Research' (ITF). Significantly, the ITF is 'open to all countries' but is also presently 'overwhelmingly European': 18 of the 24 current ITF members are EU member states (including Austria), the remaining six being Switzerland, Norway, Croatia, Argentina, Israel and the US (Grunwald 2010).

Clearly, memories and the past matter to the negotiation of identities both on national and European levels. Later analyses presented in this book corroborate that – and explore how – collective memories are subject to appropriation, negotiation, and potential contestation by individuals and groups in particular contexts. Collective memories, present identity politics and their structural settings will be shown to be closely intertwined.

*Globalization*, *the past* and '*the other*' are the three central dimensions, around which the identity negotiations examined below revolve. As anticipated earlier, each of the following analyses begins with, and centres on, a key conceptual question or set of questions. In their central sections, each chapter then proceeds to analyze Austrian data relevant to its respective conceptual/theoretical focal point. And each chapter concludes by examining other relevant European examples, in order to illustrate both country-specific particularities and pan-European commonalities. The conceptual foci of the following chapters are as follows: chapter one examines the difference between nationalism and national identities; the latter are shown to be ideologically considerably more diverse and to draw on a range of alternative frameworks of (national) self-definition. Chapter two centres on national memories and symbols of identity and the consciousness-raising effects of perceived crises. Chapter three examines interpretations of change and perceived problems as well as selective invocations of the past in debates concerning the nation-state in the European 'network state'. Chapter four analyzes discourses of national belonging as reactions to the dislocations of globalization; more accurately, it shows that various forms of contemporary identity politics are indicative of widely felt tensions between markets and 'the nation'. Chapter five moves the discussion on to more 'open' conceptualizations of identity and 'community', as they are articulated – in criticisms of existing structures of power and exclusion – across civil society. Chapter six focuses on some of the complexities and ambivalences of everyday life, where rigid discourses of belonging sit alongside – and in seeming contradiction to – lived experiences of 'hybridity', as well as daily boundary-crossings and negotiations. Finally, chapter seven offers an analysis of select cultural representations *of* and *by* 'the other', in order to further examine the politics of difference and complex identity negotiations in (one of) Europe's multicultural societies.

# Chapter 1
# Paradigms of Identity

## Introduction

This chapter draws a crucial distinction: between national identities and nationalism. Nationalism, it will be shown, does not exhaust – or exercise an ideological monopoly over – national identities. Put differently, national identities are the larger, more complex and diverse phenomenon of the two. National identities are subject to processes of (re)construction, (re)interpretation, and (re)appropriation. They are in continuous flux, comprising an ideological force-field contested by competing notions of inclusion and exclusion, rights and entitlements. National identities are, in short, subject to ongoing negotiations involving competing visions of social order, alternative interpretations of history and delineations of a national self that differ in their relative inclusiveness or exclusivity vis-à-vis 'the other'.

The notion of a 'positive nationalism' may indeed be a paradox (Aftenberger 2007, 215), at least from the vantage point of a universal ethics of human rights and if independence struggles inspired by more positively connoted nationalisms are bracketed out. Negative judgments of nationalisms are due to their rigid separation of 'self' and 'other' (Aftenberger 2007, 99), shaping visions and demands for an *unequal* allocation of resources, rights and entitlements according to perceived membership in – or exclusion from – the 'imagined' (Anderson 1983) national community. However, one cannot project such rigidity from nationalism to the more heterogeneous and complex domains of national identities and their negotiability. Whilst nationalist ideologies are prominent parts of such domains, the latter also include discourses that propose more inclusive definitions of 'the national community' or even question the differentiation of the in-group from certain outsiders. There is no shortage of discourses that regard the nation-state as the most consequential political unit and as a significant source of identification, whilst also opposing nationalism and criticizing existing exclusions. There is, in other words, much between the two opposing ends of an ideological spectrum that stretches from rigidly exclusive, externally hostile nationalisms to utopian discourses of post-national global belonging. With regard to the former in particular, and however objectionable nationalist discourses may appear to observers, sociological analysis must strive – in the first instance – for contextualization: rather than condemning nationalism *a priori*, its conditions of possibility, appeal and plausibility to many need examining and analyzing. Only from a position of informed understanding can differences between nationalism and other identity discourses be gauged and, if appropriate, a convincing ethical response be formulated.

The concept of national *identities* implicates social processes, institutions and historical change. Stuart Hall (1996) conceptualizes identities as *routes* or ongoing projects of becoming rather than as static *roots*. Such routes are shaped by institutions and discursive practices, which speak to and make demands of social actors, constraining their possible courses of action and life chances. Identities are thus in part the subject-positions structures of power provide us with or impose on us. However, they also involve individuals *interpellated* or 'hailed into place', recognizing or accepting – in a given context – a place in the world with its constraints and opportunities. Such an understanding of identities involves power and its manifestations in institutions and language. It also recognizes individuals' (constrained) agency in responding to or contesting their interpellations, in recognizing or potentially transcending some imposed subject-positions. Whilst emphasizing the highly variable impact of power and inequality on differently positioned individuals and groups, Hall's framework also allows for psychologically complex individuals whose negotiations may effect ideological resistance and structural change. Translated into our terms, national identity negotiations occur within the institutional parameters provided by nation-states, their histories and legislation related to – for example – citizenship and immigration. Moreover, such identity negotiations occur in the context of representations of boundaries defining and separating 'self' and 'other', as well as through social practices and civil society activities that variously help reproduce or challenge existing power structures. Nationalism, then, is one amongst several competing discursive regimes that aim to speak to and interpellate groups and individuals, who in turn variously accept or contest their claims and constructions.

I begin with an outline of theoretical debates underpinning my subsequent analysis of relevant empirical materials. My central claim that nationalisms and national identities are conceptually and empirically separate – albeit often interrelated – entities draws on Anthony D. Smith's (2008) 'historical sociology of nations and nationalism'. This is followed by a discussion of the politics of social classification as manifest in the institutional and discursive delineation and reproduction of group boundaries. This is followed by a mention of seminal conceptualizations of 'hybrid' experiences – those of inhabiting and speaking from within the spaces *between* categories – that occupy a more central role in later chapters. Its theoretical apparatus in place, the present chapter then turns to its main focus: an analysis of different discourses of national identity that have shaped Austrian history since the late nineteenth century. The purpose of this analysis is, first, to provide a historical overview crucial for an understanding of Austria in the twentieth and twenty-first centuries and, second, to present empirical evidence of the politicization and negotiability of Austrian national identities in and across different contexts. My main empirical finding and conceptual point in this chapter thus concerns the discursive diversity and contestability of national identities. The chapter then traces similar complexities through existing research on three other European contexts: Ireland, Sweden and the UK.

## Theoretical context

Modernism, a major paradigm in the study of nations and nationalisms, insists on the relatively recent origins of nationalism as an ideology of legitimation for (modern) nation-states. That said, the dating and decisive symptoms of modernity postulated by different theorists vary. Most famously, Benedict Anderson (1983) traces nationalism to the dual forces of the invention of the printing press and capitalism – or 'print-capitalism', which through novel cultural products such as novels and newspapers published in a newly dominant vernacular language facilitated the 'imagining' of a comradeship transcending intra-group divisions and the lack of social interaction amongst the vast majority of co-nationals. Ernest Gellner (1983), meanwhile, saw the origins of nationalism in industrializing society's demand for a culturally homogenized workforce consisting of 'mutually substitutable' workers, who possessed a minimum of numerical and literacy skills in order to service the rapidly modernizing and urbanizing social formations of the nineteenth century. This in turn required a standardizing educational system that achieved cultural homogeneity by transmitting the 'high culture' of emerging national elites.

Anderson's and Gellner's are by no means the only modernist analyses of nations and nationalisms, but they illustrate the main thrust of the modernist project: they level a powerful challenge against some academic work (e.g. van den Berghe 1995, 2005) and much commonsensical 'knowledge' and political rhetoric about the taken-for-granted – but rarely if ever empirically demonstrated – ancient or 'primordial' origins of nations. Nations, such widely held beliefs assume, are perennial units of social and political organization and nationalism, such discourses continue, is the 'natural' feeling of belonging to such seemingly inevitably entities. Clearly, the gulf between such primordial accounts and modernist scholarship is wide, though not necessarily insurmountable. An alternative approach referred to as 'ethno-symbolism', and widely associated with the work of Anthony D. Smith, successfully bridges the gulf between the two (Özkirimli 2000) by offering a synthesis: it echoes the modernist insistence on the relatively recent social transformations underpinning the genesis of an international order based on the institutions and ideologies that define nation-states, whilst emphasizing that national identities and nationalisms have had to, in order to be generally recognized and appealing, tap into and utilize pre-existing traditions, symbols, myths and practices.

Smith's most recent contribution to these debates, entitled *The Cultural Foundations of Nations* (2008) continues along similar lines. It offers a 'historical sociology' of 'cultural traditions' rooted in antiquity – those being ideas about hierarchy, covenant and the civic republic – that subsequently influenced the genesis of nations and nationalisms. Smith insists (2008, 184) that the categories of 'nations' (and national identities) and 'nationalisms' have to be kept separate. He defines nationalism (2008, 15–17) as '*an ideological movement for attaining and maintaining autonomy, unity, and identity on behalf of a population, some of whose members deem it to constitute an actual or potential "nation"'*. Smith identifies a number of core nationalist beliefs: the notion that 'the world is divided' into historically distinctive nations; that 'the nation is the sole source of political power' and 'must possess maximum autonomy'; that 'a just and peaceful world must be based on a plurality of nations'; and 'to be free, every individual must … give primary loyalty to the nation'. Smith also provides a more fine-tuned definition of 'the "ethnic" variant of nationalism' as emphasizing 'genealogical ties', 'vernacular culture … indigenous to the land', 'nativist history – a belief in the virtues of indigenous history' and popular mobilization. Conversely, he offers the following ideal-typical definition of nations and national identities:

> [T]he 'nation' [is] *a named and self-defined human community whose members cultivate shared myths, memories, symbols, values, and traditions, reside in and identify with a historic homeland, create and disseminate a distinctive public culture, and observe shared customs and common laws* … '[N]ational identity' [refers to] *the continuous reproduction and reinterpretation of the pattern of values, symbols, memories, myths, and traditions that compose the distinctive heritage of nations, and the identification of individuals with that pattern and heritage* … [There is a] centrality of social process and symbolic resources in the formation and persistence of nations, giving them their distinctive but flexible character. (Smith 2008, 19, italics in the original)

Two dimensions of this are crucial. First, Smith's analysis of vast historical stretches and geographical terrains enable him to demonstrate (2008, 15–16) that 'the assumption that only nationalists create nations is questionable' and that, on the contrary, 'some conceptions of the nation, which may well differ from modern conceptions of the nation, antedate by several centuries the appearance of nationalism'; the nation can therefore not be simply 'derived from the ideology of nation*alism*'. Second, Smith's insistence on the 'flexible character' of nations, the 'centrality of social process', and ongoing symbolic 'reproduction *and reinterpretation*' as defining features of national identities is echoed in the following analyses.

In a quantitative and comparative study, Kunovich (2009, 574) defines 'national identity as a socially constructed sameness resulting from nationalism'. This is problematic and contradicted by the argument made here: Smith's historical sociology shows that national identities and sentiments often predate nationalism. In chronological terms, then, national identities cannot 'result from' nationalism; instead, Smith reveals that modern nationalisms and many 'present-day nations' developed out of, built on but also significantly transformed older traditions and solidarities best understood as national sentiments (Smith 2008, 184–185). Moreover, and this is an argument crucial to this book and will be developed over successive chapters, there is evidence of vastly different discourses of national identity, some of which do not insist on 'sameness'. Instead, they define 'the nation' as inherently pluralistic. At the same time, this does not mean that such inclusive discourses do not also draw external boundaries or regard the nation as the crucial unit of political organization. Put differently, there are pluralistic, multicultural conceptions of national identity that are not automatically tantamount to an ideology of postnational utopia.

This discussion is also about the politics of social classification, about the power to draw and institutionalize boundaries, as well as about the everyday experience of negotiating boundaries. This is, in short, also a discussion about the state, the construction and reproduction of groups, social inclusion and exclusion, and about individuals' agency and their sometimes hard-to-classify lived realities. Two theoretical strands that resurface in later chapters are worth mentioning here, for they jointly provide a conceptual framework for thinking about processes and experiences of social classification. The first strand is derived from Zygmunt Bauman's analyses (1990; 1993) of the modern nation-state's promotion of cultural homogeneity. Bauman describes how 'the stranger', defined by Georg Simmel as 'a person who comes today and stays tomorrow', is perceived as an embodiment of difference and a political challenge by nation-states, which respond to such heterogeneity with a combination of 'methods' first differentiated by the anthropologist Claude Lévi-Strauss: *anthropoemic* strategies of segregation and *anthropophagic* strategies of enforced assimilation. Whilst these strategies respond to difference with contrasting methods of permanent exclusion and coercive 'ingestion', they are both distrustful of – and opposed to – diversity or classificatory ambivalence (see Karner 2010a).

This latter phenomenon, the experience of inhabiting and speaking from within the *ambivalent spaces between* categories, relates to the second theoretical strand: analyses of 'syncretism', 'liminality' and 'hybridity'. Though not identical, these terms overlap in capturing social realities that are 'messy', hard-to-classify unambiguously, positioned in the interface or at the threshold between categories, and defined by an inherent pluralism. Homi Bhabha, a key theorist of hybridity, argues that 'ambivalence' and an 'impossible unity' are intrinsic to 'the idea of the nation':

> The 'locality' of national culture is neither unified nor unitary … nor must it be seen simply as 'other' in relation to what is outside or beyond it. The boundary is Janus-faced and the problem of outside/inside must always itself be a process of hybridity, incorporating new 'people' in relation to the body politic, generating other sites of meaning … What emerges … is a turning of boundaries and limits into the *in-between* spaces through which the meanings of cultural and political authority are negotiated. It is from such narrative positions between cultures and nations … that *Nation and Narration* seeks to … extend Frantz Fanon's revolutionary credo: 'National consciousness, which is not nationalism, is the only thing that will give us an international dimension'. (Bhabha 1990a, 4)

Classification, boundaries and hybridity are key conceptual themes explored in this book. Bhabha also adds weight to the argument developed in the present chapter: that nationalism and national identities (or 'national consciousness') are not necessarily the same thing. I now turn to an overview of different, to some extent co-existing yet also often competing discourses of national identity that have shaped different eras in Austria's recent history. Not only have dominant understandings of 'the nation' changed, but their criteria of inclusion also differ significantly. The conceptual point I develop through the following historical analysis is simple but crucial: even within a given national context, national identities are not ideologically monolithic but are defined by heterogeneity, disagreement and discursive struggle.

## Competing discourses of Austrian identity

In *Language and Solitude*, Ernest Gellner (1998) terms two diametrically opposed discourses that circulated on the territories of the decaying Habsburg Empire the 'universalistic-atomic' and the 'romantic-organic' vision respectively. The former was associated with an individualistic world-view based on the Enlightenment notion of Universal Man and a 'bloodless[ly] cosmopolitan' *laissez-faire* liberalism (Lukes 1998, xiii). Its discursive rival conceived the individual to be intrinsically part of a linguistic-cultural collective. Such 'holistic' romanticism provided the 'rationale' underlying the ethnic nationalisms that contributed to the disintegration of the Habsburg Empire. The same ideological configuration informed the negotiations at Saint Germain after World War I, resulting in the redrawing of the borders in Central Europe and several newly legitimated nation-states. Austria – according to Karl Renner, its Socialist representative at Saint Germain and first Chancellor – was 'what was left' of the former Austro-Hungarian Empire. Reduced by two-thirds in territory and three quarters in population, the First Austrian Republic was – from its creation until its infamous *Anschluss* to Hitler Germany in 1938 – unsure of its cultural identity and political destiny (e.g. Brook-Shepherd 1997). Following World War II and the horrors of the Holocaust, post-war reconstruction, decades of political neutrality and consensual democracy on the Western side of the Iron Curtain, the revolutions of 1989 and Austria's EU membership in 1995, national identity is being negotiated, to a profoundly different historical and ideological backdrop, in contemporary Austria. The earlier-mentioned temporary 'sanctions' by Austria's then 14 EU-partners in 2000 following the formation of a coalition government between the centre-right ÖVP and the controversial FPÖ also testified to this.

In this section, I analyze competing constructions of national identity articulated in Austria throughout the twentieth and at the beginning of the twenty-first centuries. Taking Gellner's archaeology of thought as a conceptual point of departure, I contextualize these different identity frameworks that have varied in prominence and political impact across successive eras. I trace these discourses across a range of data encountered in Austria's public sphere at different points in her recent history, with emphasis on the media[1] – the country's main newspapers and its national broadcasting network (ORF) between August 2001 and April 2002, as well as September 2003 and January 2004, which saw intense debates concerning (definitions of) national belonging/exclusion and Austria's past, present and future. The material analyzed also includes (more recent) statements by politicians, writers, commentators and academics. Moreover, while discourses of national identity are often articulated explicitly, they also resonate in the minutiae of language and taken-for-granted everyday activities (see Edensor 2002). The data discussed therefore ranges from the politicization of 'Austrian-ness' to instances of implicit or 'banal nationalism' (Billig 1995a; also see de Cillia et al. 1999). My underlying premise is broadly discourse analytical in orientation: language is seen as a 'social practice' (Fairclough 1989) that helps to uphold or subvert existing power relations; discourse is language that is both 'structured' by social systems and crucial to their reproduction *or* transformation (Weiss and Wodak 2003, 10). In Antonio Gramsci's terminology, ideological struggles between the forces of hegemony (i.e. social reproduction through intellectual/cultural leadership) and counter-hegemonic contestation are reflected in written and spoken language (e.g. Fairclough 1992).

The first framework of national identity construction amounts to a nowadays peripheral and de-legitimated pan-Germanic ethnicism ideologically rooted in the organic romanticism discussed in *Language and Solitude*. The second, now hegemonic but politically heterogeneous framework has been crucial to the 're-imagining' of Austria's national community since the end of World War II. Defining Austria as different and distinct (from German and other 'others'), this discourse came to underlie the reconstructed Austrian nation-state after 1945. Thirdly, I discuss discourses of identity that insist on Austria's intrinsic European-ness and thus on the complementarity between the nation-state and the European Union. Fourthly, I examine an identity discourse that equates 'Austrian-ness' with ethnic pluralism/'hybridity' and traces this multiculturalism to the history of the Habsburg empire. Finally, I prepare the ground for argumentative strands crucial to later chapters by drawing attention to counter-hegemonic constructions of the (national/post-national) 'self' and, briefly, to social actors' manoeuvring amidst different identity discourses.

---

1  My present purpose is to historically trace competing discourses of Austrian identity, but not to assess their demographic/quantitative spread or their relative prominence in the country's different – and ideologically very differently positioned – newspapers. Instead, I propose a qualitative discussion of distinguishable, historically grounded, more or less widely shared yet contested definitions of the national 'self'. For a relevant discussion of the media as a 'one of the main realms in which the national community is "imagined"', see Yadgar (2002).

*Traces of pan-Germanic ethnicism*

The first, now distinctly marginal discourse of national identity recognizes little distinction between Austria and Germany but presupposes the existence of a single 'German(ic) nation'. Its 'logic' resembles organic-romanticism and its essentializing ideology of 'blood, soil and people'. Such a discursive formation underlies a particular, nowadays de-legitimated construction of Austrian history as part of a pan-Germanic entity and the latter's juxtaposition to perennially excluded 'others'.

*Historical precedents*
Hitler's arrival in Vienna in March 1938, with thousands cheering on the *Heldenplatz* (literally 'heroes' square'), testified to the earlier-mentioned identity crisis that had plagued many Austrians between 1918 and 1938. The viability of the First Republic had been questioned across the political spectrum ever since Saint Germain, with only (former) monarchists, some in the conservative Christian Social Party and Austrian communists asserting Austria's political and cultural distinctiveness (e.g. Thaler 2001, 72–74; Bukey 2000, 22). Calls for an amalgamation with Germany were 'ubiquitous' – though contextually/regionally variable in 'vehemence' – in Austria of the inter-war period (Hanisch 1994, 126–127),[2] a context characterized by economic crises, political polarization and a gradual descent into authoritarianism (e.g. Kleindel 1984; Hanisch 1994, 263–333).

Engelbert Dollfuß' Austro-fascist *Ständestaat*, following the dissolution of the Austrian parliament in 1933, advocated a hierarchical and distinctly Catholic social order. Dollfuß was initially assured of Mussolini's support and from the start opposed by both Hitler and the growing Nazi movement on Austrian territory. The latter staged an unsuccessful coup in 1934, resulting in Dollfuß's assassination and his succession by Kurt Schuschnigg, who initially continued his predecessor's politics and insistence on Austrian independence. However, when confronted by an increasingly hostile Adolf Hitler in 1938, Schuschnigg conceded to demands for a Nazi minister of the interior (Arthur Seyss-Inquart) and eventually to the *Anschluss* to Germany. Schuschnigg's explanation, he did not want 'German blood to be spilled' (Brook-Shepherd 1997, 318), revealed a widespread assumption of a shared 'racial' or ethnic essence common to both Germans and Austrians that

---

2   The pan-Germanic discourse among German-speakers in the Habsburg monarchy can be traced to 1848 (and beyond) and the support among the liberal bourgeoisie for 'the efforts of the Frankfurt Parliament to unify Germany into a nation-state' (Bukey 2000, 6). Austria's defeat at the hands of Bismarck's Prussia in 1866 and her expulsion from German political affairs 'led to the intensification of [many Austro-Germans'] until-then largely self-evident but not necessarily urgent sense of German identity' (Thaler 2001, 68). In the late nineteenth century a radical pan-Germanism was articulated by Georg Ritter von Schönerer who synthesized it with opposition to the Habsburg monarchy (and the Catholic clergy) and rabid anti-Semitism (e.g. Schiedel and Neugebauer 2002).

goes some way to explaining many Austrians' enthusiasm over their incorporation into Hitler's *Reich*. The ease with which Austria was transformed into a German province, the rapid increase in Austrian Nazi party membership in the immediate aftermath of the *Anschluss*, the scale and intensity of the anti-Jewish pogroms in Vienna during the *Kristallnacht* in November 1938 (e.g. Bukey 2000, 131–152; Brook-Shepherd 1997, 344), confirm that Hitler's message found a large and susceptible audience in Austria. Though never uncontested,[3] the 'organic-romanticist' idea of Austrians as part of the German *Volk* constituted an already widespread 'interpretative repertoire' (Potter and Wetherell 1998) during and before the 1930s. Following the *Anschluss*, this pan-Germanic discourse was transformed from its previously oppositional status in the *Ständestaat* into the hegemonic self-understanding serving to perpetuate Nazi rule over Austria.

The pan-Germanic paradigm was pushed back beyond the margins of political respectability and displaced by a distinctly Austrian national 'imagining' after 1945. Yet, occasional traces of a Germanic (*deutschnational*) discourse of identity can be detected in the history of post-war Austria. Among those, we must distinguish between the explicit (de-legitimated and marginal) re-politicization of pan-Germanic sentiments, and implicit (non-reflexive) articulations of ethnic/national proximity between Austria and Germany respectively.

*Sub-cultural extremes*
Some of the most explicit articulations of nationalism in contemporary Austria echo pan-Germanic discourse, often refusing to acknowledge the now dominant discourse of a distinct Austrian identity. Extremists of this far-right variety seemingly regard current political entities and boundaries – between Austria and Germany – as obstacles to the realization of an assumed 'racial' 'Germanic destiny'. Part of a numerically insignificant, xenophobic, historically revisionist, not infrequently law-breaking[4] sub-culture, advocates of this extremist pan-Germanism use several channels of mobilization (Aftenberger 2007) including demonstrations, websites and newsletters.[5]

---

3    See Bukey (2000) for a summary of the realms (e.g. parts of the [lower] Catholic clergy and the rural population, political 'underground' activity, regional aloofness to Nazism particularly in Tyrol) and motivations (e.g. anti-Prussian sentiments, a persisting 'economic gap' between the *Ostmark* and the *Altreich*, food shortages, war casualties and later allied aerial bombardment) of anti-German, Austrian patriotic sentiments between 1938 and 1945.

4    Recent convictions for *nationalsozialistische Wiederbetätigung*, or revival of Nazism, included sentences passed against five young men in Innsbruck in January 2004 (http://tirol.ORF.at 20 January 2004).

5    The *Dokumentationsarchiv des Österreichischen Widerstandes* ('Archive of Austrian resistance') reported an increase in the number of such publications, demonstrations and contacts between German and Austrian extremists for example in 2002 (http://www.orf. at 13 June 2003).

The role of the 'ordinary (German) soldier in World War II' constitutes a site for competing narratives of the nation(s) and its/their history/-ies both in Germany and Austria. Questions of obedience and 'duty' or, alternatively, of knowledge of and responsibility for war crimes are evoked by the historical figure of the soldier who served in the German *Wehrmacht*. Proposed answers have varied from the apologetic to the highly critical (see *Profil* 3 August 2009 and 17 August 2009), regarding 'ordinary soldiers' as passive, innocent pawns or responsible agents and perpetrators of genocide respectively. The 'myth of the untainted Wehrmacht' (Pollak 2008) was critically deconstructed by two exhibitions (with different emphases) on its role in Hitler's 'war of annihilation', which were organized by the *Hamburger Institut für Sozialforschung* and toured German and Austrian cities between 1995 and 2004, attracting much interest and triggering widespread debate (Heer et al. 2008). The exhibitions also rekindled discussions about the responsibility, role – and its (il)legitimacy – of Austrians fighting for Hitler's *Reich*. Shortly after the second exhibition opened in Vienna in 2002, two diametrically opposed understandings of history clashed in a confrontation between 100 neo-Nazis and some 4,000 'counter-demonstrators' supporting the exhibition's aim to rethink (Austrian) history self-critically. The neo-Nazi minority's pan-Germanic discourse was epitomized in their signs thanking the *Wehrmacht* for its 'deeds of heroism' and declaring that 'we are all Germans' (*Kleine Zeitung* 14 April 2002; Uhl 2008, 264).

The weekly *National Zeitung* provides a further illustration of explicit, decidedly counter-hegemonic pan-Germanism. Published in Munich, it operates a website and epitomizes an unashamed organic-romanticism of the Germanic *Volk*. Discursively subsuming Austria in the 'German people', it articulates a conspiratorial worldview based on the recurrent motives of encroaching American hegemony, the threat of 'illegal' immigration and allegedly anti-Germanic misconstructions of World War II. Declaring it to be the 'nation's conscience', its editor defines the *National Zeitung* (5 April 2002, 1) as 'our voice for truth and justice for the German people'.

*The politically controversial*
Traces of an ideologically very different and implicit form of pan-Germanism have resonated in some controversial political rhetoric on a 'linguistically microscopic' level, where boundaries are delineated through 'familiar habits of language' invoking notions of national identity often 'beyond conscious awareness' (Billig 1995a, 94). One such instance occurred in the context of the controversy surrounding Kurt Waldheim, former UN general secretary, who was the ÖVP's presidential candidate in 1986. His ultimately successful candidacy gave rise to heated transnational debates concerning his role during World War II and triggered public discussion and some critical soul-searching concerning the darkest chapter in Austrian history (e.g. Pick 2000). While the details of the controversy including a disconcerting anti-Semitic backlash in the tabloid press have been analyzed most comprehensively by Richard Mitten (1992), Waldheim's

alleged 'amnesia' concerning his past was – according to numerous commentators (e.g. Pick 2000; Uhl 2006) – paradigmatic of a previous and widespread (though never all-embracing[6]) reluctance to confront Austria's role in World War II. In terms of the pan-Germanic historical narrative, one of Waldheim's most widely quoted statements was particularly revealing: his declaration that his role in World War II had simply been that of the 'ordinary soldier doing his duty'. As argued by Josef Haslinger (1995, 26–27), this statement by the Austrian President at the time is remarkable for it presupposed the 'naturalness' of an Austrian serving in the German army and fulfilling his 'duty' for a dictatorship that had eradicated Austria as a separate political entity. Waldheim's statement could only make sense in a context where Austria's assumed (historical) German-ness constituted a still available, though now marginal and of course strongly contested, 'interpretative framework'.

Arguably less implicit and more consciously ideological were some of Jörg Haider's statements in the early part of his political career. His occasional invocation of pan-Germanism during the 1980s was most clearly revealed in a highly controversial reference to the Austrian nation as 'an ideological miscarriage' (Haslinger 1995, 48; Auinger 2000, 52). Haider's politics were of course the major reason behind the then 14 other EU member states' temporary imposition of 'sanctions' on Austria in 2000 (see Merlingen et al. 2001). Haider's rhetoric derived considerable energy from the construction of an antinomy between German-speaking Austrians and 'culturally alien', allegedly encroaching 'foreigners' (Wodak 2000). Yet, the FPÖ's rise to political prominence and success was not only due to its xenophobic nationalism articulated in the context of rapid social change but also a symptom of a power vacuum left by increasingly de-legitimated political configurations formerly dominated by the Social Democrats and the ÖVP (see Pelinka 2000; Fillitz 2006). Widespread discontent with the old *Proporz* system of consensual politics, the systematic power-sharing within the country's large public sector among the two big parties of the post World War II era,[7] was another major factor contributing to the FPÖ's gradual rise to power between the mid-1980s and the year 2000 (Morrow 2000). Haider's political career was thus significantly aided by wider structural factors (rather than mere ideological appeal) and after the 1980s his rhetoric clearly distanced itself from earlier echoes of pan-Germanism, opting for a discourse of Austrian nationalism instead (e.g. Auinger 2000, 30).

---

6   For earlier, pre-1986 instances of self-critical engagement with Austria's World War II history, see Adunka (2002, 19, 32–33).

7   For a critical discussion of Austria's post-war system of 'consensual democracy' and social partnership, see Menasse (2000). For a summary of the FPÖ's demographically complex electoral support base in 1999, including its appeal to (particularly male) voters under the age of 30, the unemployed, and female pensioners, see Amesberger and Halbmayr (2002, 237).

However, Haider continued – on a regional Carinthian level – to tap into a history of conflict[8] relatively widely understood in terms of a divide between the 'German(-speaking) self' and the Slavic/Slovenian 'other', in the context of revived debates about bilingual 'village-signs' enshrined in the State Treaty of 1955. According to a compromise designed by the Socialist Chancellor Bruno Kreisky in the 1970s, villages with a Slovenian minority population of 25 per cent or more were required to provide bilingual signs at all in- and outgoing roads (e.g. Portisch 1996, 385). In late 2001, the issue re-emerged in a row between Haider – who voiced his intention to raise the demographic benchmark for bilingual 'village-signs' or possibly to get rid of them altogether (*Die Presse* 20 December 2001, 1) – representatives of the Slovenian minority, and the then president of the Constitutional Court. The latter found the 25 per cent benchmark to be anti-constitutional, granting one year for the full implementation of minority-rights for bilingual signs as envisaged in the State Treaty.[9] Haider subsequently postulated a continuing Slovenian conspiracy to steal territory from Carinthia (*Die Presse* 20 December 2001, 1, 7). Several years on, the conflict was yet to be resolved, after a series of at best highly controversial delaying tactics by the regional BZÖ (e.g. Klenk 2009; http://www.orf.at/ticker/338265.html). What is significant to the present discussion is that some local discourse continues to interpret past and present struggles (over language and/or territory) between Slovenians and German-speaking Austrians in 'organic-romanticist' terms. Language is thus still seen by some as a surface marker for an assumed underlying ethno-linguistic (i.e. 'German-national') essence. A regional study (Obid et al. 2002, 145–149) confirms that this history of conflicts continues, in parts of Carinthia, to be conceptualized in essentialist terms that presuppose mutually exclusive, 'Germanic' *or* 'Slavic', identities, amounting to a continuing – though of course now strongly contested – '*deutschnationale* hegemony' in certain localities. The 'village-sign' controversy therefore reflects local traces of pan-Germanism in a part of Austria with a long history of ethno-nationalist conflict and 'organic-romanticist' identity politics.

Another recent controversy revealing discursive traces of pan-Germanic thought was triggered by an interview in *Die Presse* with Martin Graf (FPÖ), a deputy speaker of the Austrian parliament and one of the country's most controversial[10] politicians. Asked about South Tyrol, the now autonomous and affluent Alpine province annexed by Italy at the end of World War I, Graf made a series of statements premised on an 'organic-romanticist' understanding of language as a surface marker of an assumed underlying ethnic essence:

---

8    For a summary of the armed territorial struggles in Carinthia in the aftermath of World War I, see, for example, Hanisch (1994, 272).

9    Two years later, the Austrian Greens criticized the then government for further delays in implementing this (www.orf.at 15 December 2003).

10    For a discussion of Graf's political career, his membership in a far-right fraternity, and his involvement in a series of recent controversies, see Linsinger and Zöchling (2009).

> Martin Graf: South Tyrol is part of the whole Tyrol … South Tyrol has a German-speaking majority population … and is currently Italian territory … I am still a firm believer in national self-determination. The South Tyroleans have been deprived of that … since the end of World War I … There are still many, many Tyroleans, both in the South and in the North who favour this. But one does not know this until the population gets asked … I am generally under the impression that for political considerations the *German* population of Europe gets fewer rights granted than other peoples … Austria's role as a protector of the *German* majority of South Tyrol should be strengthened … I believe the reason why the South Tyroleans are well off in Italy is because they are a hard-working people. No matter which state they belong to, this is the people's achievement, and not due to … a state. (Nowak 2009, 7, my translation, italics added)

Much of this is noteworthy, particularly the persistent invocation of an assumed 'German-ness', which is presented as an enduring tie of ethnic solidarity spanning across the Italian-Austrian border and as an alleged source of political disadvantage. The following statement further emphasized this assumption, whilst using a rhetorical strategy that is discussed in greater depth in chapter three: the 'analogical' (mis)use (see Müller 2002) of 'other historical cases' as alleged points of comparison:

> Martin Graf: I support the peaceful right to national self-determination. If this results in shifting borders, because the population decides that way, I don't see a problem … in times like these. The same thing happened during the collapse of Yugoslavia. And the rights the Slovenes, the Croats and other peoples were granted, why are the South Tyroleans deprived of those? This question needs to be posed. Unless … one believes that these right apply to all but *the Germans*. (Nowak 2009, 7, my translation, italics added)

Concerned by these statements, major Austrian politicians (e.g. Reuters 2009) and the country's media strongly opposed and rejected Graf's views. Writing in *Der Standard*, one of Graf's most vocal critics argued that such *Deutschnationalismus* was disturbing and raised the constitutional question if the role of a deputy speaker of the parliament was compatible with Graf's ideological leanings (Baier 2009). Graf's ethnic self-understanding subsequently surfaced again in another interview (with the Viennese *Falter*), in which he defined himself – in opposition to the majority of contemporary Austrians' self-identification – as 'a member of the German ethnic and cultural community'[11] (quoted in Apfl and Klenk 2009).

---

11   In the same interview Graf suggested that, in stressing the assumed ethnic ties between Austria and Germany, his own 'political community' had always insisted on Austria's co-responsibility for the period 'before 1945'; proposing a problematic argument (Manoschek in *Falter* 34/09, 6), Graf suggested that this was a more honest approach to

*'Austrian-ness': Heterogeneous hegemony*

The second, now dominant discourse of national identity is premised upon Austrian distinctiveness. Like all identity constructions, it relies on the delineation of various 'others', which include – depending on context and ideological 'preference' – Germans, Eastern Europeans, 'immigrants' and, in some articulations, the European Union. Importantly, this dominant discourse of national belonging includes a diverse range of political positions. What they have in common is a shared assertion of Austria's historical and cultural uniqueness, what de Cillia et al. (1999) term the 'discursive construction of national sameness'.

*World War II and beyond: Germany becoming 'other'*
Widespread receptivity to pan-Germanism aided Austria's *Anschluss* to Hitler Germany in 1938. As the war wore on however, ideological resistance and counter-hegemonic activity by Austrians increased. Although never as organized as the French *resistance*, Austrian contestation of its (continued) inclusion in Nazi Germany took various forms (Bukey 2000, 209): linguistic differences, economic disparities, food rations and the trauma and casualties of war contributed to growing discontent and rekindled stereotypes of the Prussian 'other' as 'the arrogant *Piefke*'.[12] Political activism included the resistance group O5 and its graffiti calling for Austrian independence (e.g. Hanisch 1994, 389), and individual Austrian participants in the unsuccessful 1944 plot to assassinate Hitler (*Operation Walküre*). This is to say nothing of the tens of thousands Austrian Jews, Roma, Communists, homosexuals and other ideological 'undesirables' murdered in Hitler's death camps.[13] Many more thousands had escaped, resulting in the mass exodus of Vienna's intellectual and artistic elite.

With the defeat of Hitler Germany and the creation of the Second Austrian Republic (in the context of allied military occupation until 1955), previously marginal or counter-hegemonic imaginings of Austria as culturally distinctive were transformed into the new official identity narrative. This ideological project of (re-)conceptualizing Austria as distinctive – with a unique history and place in the post-war 'order' – derived considerable discursive 'energy' from the Moscow declaration of 1943 (e.g. Thaler 2001, 27), which had defined Austria as 'Hitler's first victim' before stating that future Austrian governments would, due to widespread Austrian participation in the war, have to bear part of the responsibility for the horrors committed by the Hitler regime. However, in the post-war years this verdict was appropriated selectively, stressing the notion of Hitler's 'first victim'

---

the past than the 'myth of victimhood' (see below) advocated by Austria's other parties for much of the post-war era.

12 Derogatory Austrian term for Germans.

13 See Bukey (2000, 227): '128,000 Jews banished from their home and country; 32,000 outcasts and dissenters driven to death in Gestapo jails or concentration camps; 65,459 remaining Jews slaughtered in the Holocaust, 2,700 patriots executed for resistance'.

and formulating a myth of Austrian World War II passivity and innocence (e.g. Hanisch 1994, 480; Uhl 2006). Germans thus gradually came to be constructed as a significant ethnic 'other' – a prominent theme also in Austrian post-war cinema (e.g. Mappes-Niedik 2002, 38). This highly selective construction of World War II history challenged the pan-Germanic discourse and facilitated widespread amnesia concerning Austrian contributions to the Holocaust (e.g. Wassermann 2002), which has been contrasted to German attempts to confront her past (*Vergangenheitsbewältigung*) and to mourn the victims of the Holocaust (e.g. Pelinka and Weinzierl 1987; Rauscher 2000).[14] Meanwhile, the now hegemonic re-imagining of Austria as ethnically distinctive took place in the context of post-war reconstruction and the creation of a consensual politics intended to avoid rekindling the centrifugal forces that had thrown the First Republic into civil war (e.g. Sully 1990; Fitzmaurice 1991).

Austrian post-war 'nation-building' was significantly driven by political elites, succeeded against the backdrop of Austria's 'economic miracle' and was supported by the education system and 'the widening of legal restrictions on Germanist discourse' also enshrined in the 1955 State Treaty (Thaler 2001, 121). Regular surveys since 1945 suggest a steady increase in the demographic spread of the idea of Austria as a separate nation. The proportion of Austrians who thought of themselves as 'a separate people' – rather than ethnically German – was 49 per cent in 1956, 66 per cent in 1970, 75 per cent in 1987 and has continued to rise since (Bruckmüller 1992, 262). These percentages indicate the increasingly widespread articulation of, and commitment to, the post-war narrative of national identity premised on Austrian 'distinctiveness'.

Yet, conceptions of Austrian nationhood vis-à-vis Germany vary from the out-rightly oppositional to a more graded perspective, which – whilst asserting Austrian identity – also assumes relative cultural proximity. The first variant, which postulates radical otherness, is echoed in Wodak et al.'s (1999, 192–193) interview and focus group data revealing their participants' emotional investment in the construction and maintenance of clear boundaries separating Austria from her northern neighbours. More famously, the World Cup in Argentina in 1978[15] provided a moment of continuing significance to the discourse of Austrian distinctiveness. Austria faced Germany and managed, in contrast to many defeats Austrian football has suffered at the hands (or feet) of the German national team over the years, a 3:2 victory (see Ingrao 2001). The style of the victory was perhaps even more significant, with Hans Krankl – a much-celebrated striker – scoring two spectacular goals. TV-footage of his second and decisive goal, and of a commentator screaming himself into a celebratory frenzy, is still broadcast

---

14    According to a recent study, the prosecution of Nazi war criminals was between 1945 and 1955 more rigorous in Austria than in Germany; however, this trend was markedly reversed after 1955 (http://derStandard.at 2 December 2003).

15    For a discussion of football as conducive to emotionally charged national imaginings, see Stroeken (2002, 9).

by the ORF (and appreciated by the audience) on some occasions to this day. No other victory in the history of Austrian football meant nearly as much to the Austrian public and no other opponent could elicit the same 'spell' of national identification. Against the backdrop of linguistic and geographical proximity, the significance of German tourism to the Austrian economy and a large 'degree of Austro-German cooperation in the sphere of media' (Thaler 2001, 38), everyday discourse also asserts national difference through concepts as vague and varied as Austrian *Gemütlichkeit* (conviviality), 'cultural sophistication' and a sense for 'the good life'. Contrasting clichés of German rigidity, formality, efficiency but lack of enjoyment resonate in such stereotypes. However, hegemonic 'Austrian-ness' can also be compatible with the discursive maintenance of cultural affinity to Germany: national differences therefore also appear, on occasion, to be conceptualized as graded phenomena and hence a matter of degree. Thus, in surveys between the 1970s and 1990s between 60 and 70 per cent of Austrians named 'Germany as the country most similar to their own' (Thaler 2001, 79; Reiterer 1988; Ulram and Tributsch 2004). This alternative understanding premised on assumptions of relative cultural proximity also occasionally manifests on the level of non-reflexive everyday discourse, such as when a weekly magazine identifies Germans as 'our favourite neighbours' (*TV Woche* 20 December 2003, 4).

*Identity and Boundaries*
De Cillia et al.'s analysis of Austrian national identities (1999, 158–160) reveals five areas of identity construction: notions of '*homo austriacus*', 'narratives of a collective political history', the 'discursive construction of a common culture', of a 'collective present and future' and 'national body' (spanning landscape, architecture and sports personalities). Clearly, this implies the delineation of boundaries between the 'self' and various excluded 'others'. The nature and permeability of these boundaries in turn raises the question as to which 'model of the nation' dominates in public discourse.

It has been suggested that contemporary Austria adheres to a territorial, assimilationist or 'French' concept of the nation (e.g. http://www.orf.at 26 October 2001) – rather than the 'German' (organically-romanticist) model based on unchangeable ethnic belonging (Kohn cited in McCrone 1998, 8). German writer Mappes-Niedik (2002), for example, induces from his experience in rural Austria that assimilation is encouraged and expected of immigrants. On a policy level, some recent legislation, such as an Integration Act seeking to define compulsory German language courses as a pre-requisite for renewing immigrants' residence permits (http://www.orf.at 17 February 2002),[16] indeed suggests an *anthropophagic* model assimilation. A similarly 'demanding' version of integration is advocated by an Austrian academic and journalist arguing that

---

16   According to a subsequent report, during the first year of this legislation only 951 people had completed the language course, whereas more than 75,000 had successfully claimed exemption (http://www.orf.at 26 January 2004).

'Austria only has space for immigrants willing to integrate' (Stiegnitz 2000, 14).[17] However, a closer look at relevant legislation and public discourse reveals that contemporary Austria combines elements of both the 'French' and the 'German' ideal types of national belonging. Such blurring of, or changes to, dominant models of identity and exclusion are by no means unusual. Recent changes in German citizenship laws thus represent an 'assimilationist turn' (Brubaker 2001), whilst France returned from a period of relative 'differentialism' to its traditional civic nationalism, as reflected in controversial plans to prohibit public displays of religious symbols (e.g. http://www.orf.at 17 December 2003[18]). In wider structural terms, demands for assimilation such as the ones mentioned above can sit alongside mechanisms of exclusion: similar to other EU countries, residence permits in Austria have historically not automatically conferred work permits (see Krzyżanowski and Wodak 2009, 46). Exclusion from the job-market (plus the resulting cycle of dependency and relative deprivation) at one point constituted the most frequently voiced complaint by (non-EU) 'foreigners in Austria' (*Kleine Zeitung* 23 December 2001, 2–3).

Alongside pan-European commonalities, Austrian citizenship legislation arguably provides an arena of relative particularism, though one subject to ongoing discussion: after Germany partly modified her historical principle of conferring citizenship on the *anthropoemic* basis of descent (*ius sanguinis*) by introducing legislation according to which citizenship is attributed 'to children born in Germany to foreign parents, one of whom has resided legally in Germany for at least eight years' (Brubaker 2001, 538), Austria continued to broadly adhere to *ius sanguinis*. Yet, recent amendments to Austrian citizenship law combine its historical emphasis on descent with assimilationist clauses pertaining to the conferral of citizenship to foreign nationals: as before, the most common route for non-Austrians to apply for citizenship is after ten years of legal residence in the country[19]; however, applicants now also need to be economically secure, they are required to pass a German language test and – as in several other European countries – a 'citizenship test' (e.g. http://www.orf.at 6 December 2005; Karner 2007a, 111). There has been considerable political disagreement and debate about the issue. In 2003, for example, SPÖ and the Greens – Austria's then party-political opposition – voiced their support for proposals to replace *ius sanguinis* with *ius soli* (i.e. place of birth conferring citizenship) (http://derStandard.at 21 November 2003), thus

---

17  This argument sidesteps profound ethical and logical dilemmas, not least how – and by whom – integration is to be assessed.

18  Debates in France concerning assimilationism, secularism and cultural pluralism were already raging months before Chirac's controversial announcement; see, for example, *Le Nouvel Observateur* 15 May 2003.

19  2003 saw 'record numbers' of naturalizations, with 18,420 'new' Austrian citizens in Vienna alone (http://wien.ORF.at 28 January 2004). Those numbers have decreased considerably since the above-mentioned citizenship legislation amendments in March 2006 (http://www.orf.at/ticker/338499.html).

underlining that citizenship legislation is subject to discursive contestation and, possibly, future legislative redefinition.

The shockwaves of the French headscarf controversy reached Austria in 2003, after the German region of Baden-Württemberg prohibited teachers from wearing the Islamic *hijab* at school (whilst exempting Catholic nuns). On the question of the public expression of Islamic identity, Austria constitutes a contrast – comparable to Britain's traditional multiculturalism (Baumann 1999) – to both the French and the German examples. This is reflected in Austria's *Islamgesetz*, passed in 1914 to protect the right to 'free and public Islamic worship', and 'rediscovered' since the 1960s and with the introduction of Islamic religious studies to schools in 1982 (http://dieStandard.at [sic] 29 October 2003). While this 'Austrian model' of religious autonomy and pluralism has been praised by Muslims across Europe, it has not been uncontested. For example, the FPÖ has called for 'more assimilation' (http://dieStandard.at [sic] 29 October 2003), and a controversial 2009 study suggesting that 21.9 per cent of Islamic religious education teachers in Austria 'reject democracy because it is irreconcilable with Islam' (quoted in Apfl 2009, 10–11) led to public debate about the merits and potential dangers of the current legislation. With regard to this discussion, however, the *Islamgesetz* illustrates that pluralism co-exists both with *anthropophagic* trends (e.g. the Integration Act) *and* with a differentialist, descent-based definition of citizenship.

Returning to everyday language, the ideological reproduction of boundaries also emerged from an annual survey of Austrians' 'favourite and most disliked words' by the *Kronen Zeitung*, Austria's biggest newspaper,[20] in 2001. It suggested that the majority of Austrians evaluated the terms 'security', 'home/roots', 'order', 'stability', 'independence', 'work/productivity' and 'political neutrality' most positively. Their negatively connoted discursive opposites, or 'Austria's most disliked word[s]', were 'nuclear energy' and 'genetic engineering' (Gnam 2002). The positively evaluated terms arguably reflect a conservative discourse of national belonging (see Rauscher 2000), and are – in semiotic terms – meaningful only in relation to 'that which they are not' amongst the defining debates at the time. Such implicit contrasting signifiers include change (seemingly opposed to 'order' and 'stability') associated with EU expansion and the problems, including unemployment and a national identity crisis (as the opposites implied by 'work' and 'roots'), widely feared as likely consequences. Nuclear energy – the allegedly most negative term – resonated with a major controversy of 2001 centred on a nuclear power plant in the Czech town of Temelin, near the northern Austrian border. Widely feared to be unsafe, Temelin came to be interpreted through an environmentalist discourse and rekindled memories of the nuclear disaster in Chernobyl. This time, according to widespread fears, an accident could occur on the Austrian doorstep and the consequences – for Austria – would be disproportionately higher. Temelin and the Czech Republic thus provided the 'connotative domain' (Hansen 1999,

---

20   With some 40 per cent of Austrians reading the *Kronen Zeitung* (e.g. Thaler 2001, 39), it has been termed the 'world champion in circulation' (Mappes-Niedek 2002, 167).

43) to 'nuclear energy', whose negative associations implied a delineation of the national 'self' threatened by an environmentally irresponsible 'other'.

The second discursive formation and its core notion of Austrian distinctiveness constitute the now dominant identity paradigm. However, this discourse contains a variety of ideological positions. The sometimes profoundly antagonistic stances taken by the five main parties – SPÖ, ÖVP, FPÖ, Greens and BZÖ – on, for example, asylum and immigration, citizenship (see above), or the future of the EU[21] show that the same discursive framework of 'Austrian distinctiveness' accommodates heterogeneous ideas concerning the nation and its history (past, present and future), and competing definitions of boundaries, their salience and permeability. While a discussion of differences within the dominant framework of a historically and culturally distinctive Austrian community will be developed over subsequent chapters, two concluding points about the hegemonic framework of Austrian particularism warrant mentioning now. The first re-emphasizes how pervasive the definition of Austria as politically, culturally and historically unique and distinctive has become. In a recent interview Jörg Haider's sister and BZÖ politician Ursula Haubner, whose family history has been described as steeped in pan-Germanism (e.g. Sickinger 2008, 120–128; Zöchling 2009a), insisted upon Austria's particularism. Asked about far-right claims that Germany and Austria are part of the same ethnic nation, Haubner's response was as follows:

> Austria has a very special identity, culturally, socially and also in terms of its scenery. And it is precisely this special identity that we must preserve in a large Europe. I am very proud of my homeland, I am very proud to be Austrian. (Haubner in Theiss 2009, 33, my translation)

Secondly, parts of this discussion have shown that common descriptions of national 'communities' as defined by *either* 'civic' *or* 'ethnic' criteria can distort and oversimplify more multifaceted and contradictory realities. In the Austrian case, Wodak et al. (1999, 6) have shown that 'strictly disjunctive and static concepts such as *Staatsnation* and *Kulturnation* [are] analytically insufficient'. Working in a comparative framework, Anthony D. Smith (2008, 145) similarly demonstrates that 'it is difficult to distinguish the two kinds of loyalty, with many members, mainly of the dominant *ethnie*, having little regard to the analytic distinction between a state and its political community and the nation as an ethnocultural community.' Kunovich (2009, 575) also reveals the distinction between *Staats-* and *Kulturnationen* as a false dichotomy in summarizing 'research on contemporary national identities … [which] suggests that both ethnic and civic conceptions of the nation are found within most national states'.

---

21   A useful sense of the five main parties' notions of national inclusion/exclusion and their sometimes very different stances on Austria's past, present, and future can be gleaned from their respective websites (http://www.bzoe.at, http://www.fpoe.at, http://www.gruene. at, http://www.oevp.at, http://www.spoe.at).

There is indeed much evidence, some of which we encounter in later chapters, that many Austrians define themselves *both* by their attachment to the Austrian state, its territory, history and institutions, *and* by a more or less deeply felt sense of belonging to a community defined in cultural and symbolic terms. As chapter two shows in more detail, key symbols of contemporary Austrian identity convey cultural/ethnic particularism – rather than 'only' political attachment to the Second Republic. Such symbols of Austrian cultural identity, which include food and scenery amongst others, directly contradict older, pan-Germanic – and these days only to far-right extremists still convincing – self-understandings. Weigl (2009, 93–94) further corroborates the hegemonic status of the discourse of Austrian distinctiveness: whilst older regional identities provided a template for self-definitions based on 'communities of descent', the history of the Second Republic has been, in part, a history of 'cultural homogenization that also excluded Germans more or less categorically'.

*Austrian 'Europeanness'*

At a 1994 referendum, following months of heated debate between the proponents and opponents of European Union membership, 66.4 per cent of Austrians voted for the country's EU accession, which took place on January 1 of the following year. EU membership has transformed the political, economic and legal structures of which Austria is now a part, whilst also altering the discursive parameters within which (national) identities are being negotiated. Fifteen years later, the Alpine Republic has come to be associated with widespread Euro-scepticism, notwithstanding a recent increase in Austrians' EU approval rates that is arguably indicative of a pragmatic concession that the European Union provides some security in times of global economic crises (see *Profil* 29 May 2009, 36).

Austrian EU-scepticism is crucial to this book and forms the object of a separate analysis in chapter three. A key point of crisis affecting Austrian-EU relations unfolded around the already mentioned temporary 'sanctions' on the Alpine Republic by her then 14 EU partners in early 2000 – as a reaction to the FPÖ's inclusion in a coalition with the ÖVP. Then, as before and since, Austrians have been divided in their attitudes towards the EU and their relative embrace or rejection of a European identity alongside their national identities. A question debated across a range of media and public settings thus concerns the actual and desired relationship between the nation-state and the European 'network state'. Stating the obvious, there is a wide spectrum of answers stretching from outright opposition to the EU on one end, to EU enthusiasts and a 'banal Europeanism' (Cram 2009), which considers European and national identities to be compatible (and the former to be part of the everyday), on the other. This echoes Smith's following observations that are directly relevant to the re-negotiation of (Austrian) national identities in the new structural and historical circumstances created by EU membership:

[N]ations have … been subject to considerable conflict and change … their 'destinies' … the locus of elite rivalries and public contestation. Like all communities and identities, nations and national identities are subject to periodic reinterpretations of their meanings and revolutions of their social structures and boundaries, which in turn may alter the contents of their cultures … [N]ational identities are … continually challenged by other kinds of collective identity – of family, region, religion, class, and gender … by supranational associations and religious civilizations. (Smith 2008, 24)

As we will see in chapter three, such reinterpretations and ongoing negotiations centre, in this case, on the question as to 'which Europe' is to be created and how close current realities approximate or how far they diverge from the competing visions on offer. Once again, my key finding will be one of plurality and discursive struggle: debates about the relationship (and its future) between Austria and the EU are defined by sometimes profound disagreements, competing loyalties, and alternative interpretations of the past and present. Within such ideological heterogeneity, there are of course particular actors or media that are more or less coherent in their political leanings. For example, the already mentioned *Kronen Zeitung* has recently been amongst the most outspoken EU critics (for a full discussion, see chapter three). And yet, even on its pages and amongst its readers' letters to the editor, there are occasional 'counter-discourses', such as the following reader's letter by the Austrian vice president of the 'European seniors' union':

It is true – the European Union does suffer a big democratic deficit. For example, the European parliament cannot – unlike the Austrian parliament … – initiate legislation. And it is difficult to know what the European population really wants, as there is no such thing as a European referendum. Not yet, that is! And it is time we created that tool! The question is sometimes posed whether us Europeans actually exist. Well, I am Viennese! Vienna is the most beautiful city in the world! And I am of course Austrian! That's obvious from the way I speak. Austria is the most beautiful country in the world! But of course I am a European! And I am very proud of that! Never before in history have 500 million people declared peace. Countries with the death penalty cannot join the European Union. … And never before in history have 500 million people enjoyed our levels of social security, nobody in Europe dies of starvation, nobody needs to fear being abandoned if they fall ill. Us Europeans can be very proud. And I believe that we have the duty to act as model for other parts of the world. All the more reason to address those democratic deficits in the EU … A European referendum … needs to become reality. (*Kronen Zeitung* 22 July 2009, 19, my translation)

This is noteworthy as an example of counter-discourse on the generally highly EU-sceptical pages of the *Kronen Zeitung*. It is all the more remarkable as it combines a clear sense of regional belonging, a pronounced Austrian patriotism, *and* a celebration of European-ness. In other words, it does not conceive of local, national and supranational identities as mutually exclusive but, on the contrary, as compatible and complementary. Moreover, as a celebration of Europe it is not uncritical but focuses on a crucial question: which kind of Europe we want to live in and how this differs from current realities.

*Austrian pluralism*

Smith summarizes the impact of immigration on older notions of national identity, and a resulting multicultural national consciousness thus:

> We have ... become much more accustomed to think of the nation as an overarching community housing, but also binding together, through a common symbolism and institutional network, different ... ethnic communities ... [T]he hierarchical nation may have pointed the way to a looser, 'post-modern' type of national community. (Smith 2008, 106)

Later chapters of this book analyze evidence of such open, pluralistic and inclusive understandings of Austrian national identity that are articulated, in particular, in the spheres of cultural production and civil society activity and in opposition to nationalist discourses of narrow belonging and ethnic exclusion. I will contextualize these diametrically opposed self-understandings with reference to the lived experiences and widely debated effects of immigration to Austria since the 1960s and particularly over the last two decades. In demographic terms, Austrian society has during this period been transformed at least as much as – and in many cases considerably more than – other European countries.

With regard to pluralistic definitions of national identity, Austria is particularly relevant as it demonstrates that multicultural discourses are not inevitably tied to the current era of globalization and heightened mobility. An alternative paradigm of Austrian identity defines it by an inherent pluralism, which it historically grounds in – and traces to – the cultural heterogeneity of the multi-ethnic Habsburg Empire. Wodak et al. summarize this multicultural conception of Austrian identity as a historical antidote to the pan-Germanic discourses discussed earlier:

> The question of the ... origin of an 'Austrian people' is answered by two different myths of ancestry, the 'Germanic' and the 'multicultural' ... The idea that present-day Austrians are primarily of German descent is opposed by the multicultural myth, 'according to which the Austrians brought elements from all sides and thus unified German orderliness, the Slavic soul, Hungarian cuisine and Italian musicality' ... This multicultural myth emphasizes Austria's ethnic, linguistic and cultural plurality. (Wodak et al. 1999, 67)

This multicultural understanding provides a further framework of interpretation and political positioning available to academic and journalistic observers, to politicians and artists, and – of course – to the public at large. The multicultural discourse also resurfaces in Brook-Shepherd's account of Austria's potential role in a united Europe:

> If the Austrians still have a special role to play … it is a cultural one … helping to bond together the many races and creeds of the region. As in the days of the Monarchy, this supra-national role will not help them to define their own nationhood more sharply, however far they succeed in distancing themselves from their German cradle … They are, after all, like a brew of Germanic tea-leaves, on to which, for centuries, Danube water has been poured. And as all the streams of Central Europe feed into the Danube, there are Magyar and Slav currents which flow incessantly into that great river, and into Austrian consciousness. There is no pure essence which can be distilled out of this. The mixture is the essence. (Brook-Shepherd 1996, 454)

This conveys a convincing account of how syncretism and hybridity have shaped Austrian history. On a 'deeper' argumentative level, however, this account also contains some problematic assumptions: Brook-Shepherd misleadingly presents Austrian identity as atypical in its inherent pluralism, whilst reifying the other 'races and creeds' it alludes to as supposedly less internally heterogeneous; in invoking an unquestioned 'German cradle', Brook-Shepherd seemingly reintroduces 'organic-romanticism' through the backdoor. The assumption that other 'nationhoods' can be 'defined more sharply' is strongly contradicted by the theoretical work reviewed above, which points to the 'multistranded character' of all nations, 'which can be read as so many palimpsests of different collective pasts and cultural traditions' (Smith 2008, 187). Moreover, empirical studies discussed below corroborate that other national identities are – just like Austrians' – also internally diverse and subject to historical construction, negotiation, disagreement, struggle and change.

Another invocation of the discourse of Austrian multiculturalism avoids drawing misleading contrasts between different national contexts. A contribution to the musical genre of Austro-Pop, the song in question takes a political stance in opposition to nationalism. Entitled *I bin aus Österreich*, which translates as 'I am from Austria', its lyrics (STS 2000) begin by opposing the renewed appeal of slogans about 'blood, soil, people and race'. It then celebrates what it portrays as Austria's historically engrained cultural diversity, by tracing the singer's family history to ancestors who were variously German-speaking Alpine farmers, ethnically Hungarian and Roma; the result is a cultural hybridity embodied by individuals, whose biographies and ethnic backgrounds challenge simplistic group classifications and allegedly monolithic identities (see Karner 2010a). To the backdrop of Austrian history and contemporary multiculturalism, *I bin aus Österreich* presents 'mixed' family histories as the rule rather than the exception. Multiple identities and cultural syncretism are celebrated and used to deconstruct rigid self-other distinctions. In the process, nationalist obsessions with purity are portrayed as ethically bankrupt and historically inaccurate.

*Counter-hegemony*

*I bin aus Österreich* provides an apt conceptual bridge to a range of discourses, cultural genres and initiatives that can be subsumed under the concept of counter-hegemony: ideas and practices that challenge existing structures of power, inequality and exclusion. Whilst counter-hegemonic politics and understandings of national identity are discussed in depth and detail in later chapters, a brief overview of some relevant examples helps complete the present 'archaeology' of different Austrian identity discourses.

Discursive struggles over national identity can be divided into three ideal types: first, critical narratives – articulated particularly through various genres of cultural and artistic production – that challenge some of the premises, particularly those related to World War II and the Holocaust, underlying certain versions of the discourse of 'Austrian-ness' summarized above; second, grass-root political opposition to existing policies and dominant ideological trends; and, third, new imaginings of what we may tentatively term the 'post-national self'. Although it is impossible to do justice to the range of such counter-hegemonic activities (many of which query the notion of static/unitary identities) in the space available here, mention must be made of some of them and in anticipation of later analyses.

Literature constitutes the best-documented arena of ideological resistance and cultural critique in post-war Austria (e.g. Chalmers 2002; Fliedl 1998). Some of her most widely acclaimed novelists and playwrights, notably Elfriede Jelinek and the late Thomas Bernhard, have found themselves at ideological loggerheads with dominant paradigms of identity and historical interpretation. The earlier-mentioned post-war 'amnesia' concerning Austria's role in World War II as well as contemporary xenophobia and anti-Semitism have provided the raw material for these (and other) authors' critical reflections (Hanisch 1994, 476–481). Their literary works, most famously Bernhard's play *Heldenplatz* (1988), have resulted in public debate and controversy. Challenging the assumption of Austrian 'World War II victim-hood'[22] and taking issue with all forms of nationalism, several authors – including the recent Nobel-Price winner Jelinek (see Kosta 2003) – have been accused of 'national defamation' in the tabloid media and beyond (e.g. Saville 1999). Other articulations of counter-hegemonic narratives of the nation and its history are encountered in essays written by left-wing writers, intellectuals and poets (e.g. Haslinger 1995; Roth 1996). Many of these constitute critical responses to Austria's politics of the last three decades (also see Menasse 2000). There is also, as has already been mentioned, evidence of *Austro-Pop*, Austrian popular music, occasionally serving as a vehicle for critical, inclusivist, and counter-hegemonic readings of Austrian history and national identity (Karner 2002).

---

22    A speech given by Franz Vranitzky, then Austrian Chancellor, in 1988 has been widely interpreted (e.g. Sully 1990, 114) as an important watershed insofar as it officially emphasized Austria's 'dual role' – as both perpetrator and victim – in World War II.

Regarding grass-root political opposition, the most conspicuous recent examples of a clash between the (then) forces of hegemony and ideological resistance were provided by ritual demonstrations starting in February 2000 against the ÖVP-FPÖ government. Prior to its official formation, thousands had protested against the then imminent inclusion of the FPÖ and its anticipated consequences for Austria and the EU (*The Guardian* 3 February 2000, 1). Subsequently, protests involving more than a quarter of a million people were organized in Vienna on 19 February 2000 (see Rabinovici 2000). Their critical message continued to be articulated by weekly Thursday night demonstrations in the Austrian capital. Opposing the FPÖ's nationalism, the demonstrations created a shared space for a variety of social movements, organizations and 'resisting individuals'. This form of ideological resistance reflected the contentiousness of discourses of exclusive national identity and belonging. More recently, controversial changes to asylum-legislation have been the object of continuous criticism, voiced most consistently by the Green Party, NGOs and charitable organizations. One amongst many protests involved the public reading of the names of homeless asylum-seekers in front of the Interior Ministry in December 2003 (http://derStandard.at 19 December 2003). The problems and exclusions faced by asylum-seekers have also become the focal point for a range of civil society organizations and initiatives to be analyzed in chapter five of this book. Finally, oppositional voices are also encountered in well-known local and regional papers (to be analyzed in chapter five), which take a vocal and critical stance concerning (local, national and transnational) inequalities and exclusions.

Austria's EU accession in 1995 has also made discourses of central-[23]/pan-European- or transnational identity more salient – notwithstanding, and often in diametrical opposition to, a prominent, continuing and at times deepening EU-scepticism. One example of what we may term 'post-national' imaginings, has been articulated by Wolfgang Zinggl (2002) in a critical commentary on certain representations of Austria as a 'cultural nation' (*Kulturnation*). Zinggl describes such representations as premised on the assumption that Austria's artistic legacy determines today's national identity, as though contemporary Austrians were 'responsible for' – or innately predisposed to emulate – the country's cultural history. Zinggl suggests that this ignores omnipresent complexities (e.g. diversity within collectives) and is particularly unsuited to the contemporary era. The latter, he argues, is a time of multiple 'communities of interest' that crosscut national boundaries and their legitimating ideologies. Illustrating this, Zinggl argues that feminist animal rights campaigners from Sweden will identify with like-minded sub-Saharan Africans rather than with co-patriot lorry-drivers transporting livestock across the EU. While it seems – in light of recent history – sociologically impossible to agree with Zinggl's conclusion that 'flags and anthems belong to

---

23　Articulations of a central European identity also at times occur through artistic media, such as in a (pre-EU-enlargement) season of performances and exhibitions of Hungarian, Czech, Slovak and Slovenian art in Vienna (http://www.orf.at 18 November 2003).

a by-gone era', the publication of his article in a reputable national newspaper illustrates that the centrality of the nation, as an identity-bestowing concept in the contemporary world, is questioned by some.

Before turning to the similarly heterogeneous character of national identities in other European contexts, a point concerning the complex relationship between individuals and discourses, which will be developed in greater depth in due course, needs to be made. Later analyses in this book examine how individuals and groups *negotiate* different frameworks of identity. Competing discourses of (national) belonging construct different subject-positions, which are variously appropriated or contested by social actors whose 'practiced' or 'experienced' identities often elude the neatness of ideological categories and boundaries (see chapter six). There are, of course, obvious limits to such identity negotiations – as most powerfully illustrated by the constraining and enabling power of a person's citizenship, which in a world of nation-states defines rights and entitlements.

Within these parameters, however, there is evidence to suggest that individuals' articulations and experiences of national identity can indeed be discursively 'fragmented' and contextually variable. Taken from different historical contexts, the following brief examples suggest that the phenomenon of identities being (re)negotiated predated postmodern consumerism, with which 'unstable selves' are frequently associated. Hanisch (1994, 156–161), for example, shows that for much of the early twentieth century the 'boundaries between German and Austrian identities were constantly moving' and that such shifts occurred 'within individuals'. Summarizing Austrian attitudes and identities during World War II, Bukey similarly argues (2000, xi) that 'many individuals held split-minded views, looking in opposite directions at the same time'. And as a more contemporary and well-documented example, it has already been noted that Haider distanced himself, in the course of his political career, from the pan-Germanic discourse he still occasionally invoked in the 1980s. More recently, a – due to its encoded anti-Semitic undertones (see Bering 2002; Pelinka 2002; Wodak and Reisigl 2002) – highly controversial speech given in February 2001 also revealed noticeable discursive manoeuvres amidst different frames of reference and identification.[24] A year after the imposition of the above-mentioned temporary 'sanctions', Haider criticized several Austrian and European politicians, immigration policy, as well as – most infamously – the head of the Viennese Jewish community. Alongside the dominant discursive framework of the (beleaguered) Austrian nation, there were also traces of a European(-oriented) discourse. Characteristically oppositional, and also addressing the defining 'which Europe' issue to be discussed in chapter three, Haider claimed that his political mission included the transformation of

---

24    While many such manoeuvres (the present examples included) may be explicable by self-interest, the latter cannot account for every individual's ideological articulations all the time. Instead, analysis should allow for psychologically complex social actors and their context-specific uses of different frameworks of meaning not always and inevitably for reasons of economic/political instrumentalism (see chapter six).

a bureaucratic Europe into 'a Europe of citizenship and democracy' (quoted in Pelinka and Wodak 2002, 229).

## Other European settings: 'clashing epistemes', 'superordinate' national identities, 'fragmentary' patriotism

The key argument developed here is that national identities are subject to ongoing definitional negotiations, discursive struggles and ideological contestation. So far, this chapter has examined different paradigms of Austrian identity and traced their respective histories. In the remainder of this chapter, I discuss comparable discursive diversities and complexities as examined by existing research on three other European contexts: Ireland, Sweden and the UK.

Markus Kornprobst's analysis (2005) of the historical 're-construction of Irishness' throughout the twentieth century, provides a highly relevant point of comparison to the analysis presented above. Kornprobst's Irish case study corroborates that dominant national identities change over time and as a consequence both of ideological struggles within the nation and of external influences. His analysis unfolds around a focus on the role played by political (and intellectual) elites in articulating and disseminating (competing) notions of national identity. Conceptually, Kornprobst's understanding of national identities (2005, 409) is informed by Michel Foucault's notion of the 'episteme', defined as a taken-for-granted 'background capacity that consists of a shared set of interrelated ... beliefs on the basis of which social actors construct the world'. In other words, discourses of national identity imply that a group of people share a set of assumptions about themselves and the world, which are held on a semi-conscious or unconscious level and have tangible political consequences. Kornprobst continues in terms that complement my earlier discussion of *the other* and of memories of *the past* as key dimensions in the ongoing construction of national identities:

> First, national identity is identification ... an ongoing, never-ending process. Second, national identity is a non-essentialist category. It is a historically and socially contingent construct. Third, national identity is relational. Part of what gives meaning to a nation is the relationship between itself (Self) and other nations (Other). Fourth, national identities are constructed through telling stories about Self and the relationship between Self and Other. Identity is a narrative category. It is constructed through communicative acts that, by connecting events of past, present as well as desires and expectations about the future, tell stories about Self and Other. These narratives are not objectively true or false, but they are intersubjectively plausible or implausible ... The episteme delineates which identity narrative is plausible and which one is not. (Kornprobst 2005, 409)

Kornprobst proceeds to examine identity narratives articulated by Irish elites at different points in the twentieth century and to extrapolate their underlying 'epistemic' assumptions. The first framework of Irish identity, decisively shaped by a colonial discourse that defined nations as self-contained and homogenous units, dominated in the early twentieth century and constructed Irishness in terms that resemble Smith's (2008, 16–17) earlier-mentioned definition of (ethnic) nationalism. Kornprobst shows (2005, 410–413) that Ireland's 'nation-builders' articulated a discourse of 'exclusive Irishness' premised on several axiomatic beliefs: that Ireland was an 'ancient nation', ethnically homogenous, 'distinctly Celtic', thus clearly demarcated from outsiders and, in particular, defined in opposition to Britain. This, in turn, underpinned the political struggle against British colonial rule. Moreover, Ireland's literary and political elite discursively emphasized an 'authentic self' and 'true Ireland', which celebrated its 'mythical Gaelic roots' and was defined as Catholic, rural and anti-modern.

Kornprobst then shows (2005, 413) that the first sustained challenge against this episteme of ancient and exclusive 'Irishness' started to be formulated from the 1930s on by critical historians. They opposed nationalist historiography, deconstructing its narrative of Irish history as a perennial struggle of 'the Gaelic nation against an external enemy … [and instead] traced the origins of the Irish nation to the nineteenth century'. Another alternative and more influential paradigm for defining Irish identity emerged in the late 1940s and 1950s, to gather pace in the 1960s to the backdrop of Ireland's application to join the then European Economic Community. This alternative episteme took inspiration from 'the Idea of Europe' and its premises of 'integration, co-operation and the overcoming of Europe's splintering into nation-states'; defining Ireland as a modern European nation, this new paradigm emphasized 'plurality' and 'integration' instead of an assumed ethnic homogeneity and national 'demarcation' (Kornprobst 2005, 413–414). Kornprobst's historical analysis concludes by tracing how this newer, inclusive discursive framework eventually achieved hegemonic status. The two epistemes of exclusive- and inclusive Irishness clashed throughout the 1970s and 1980s, being articulated by different sections of the country's elite. In the 1980s, however, film and literature joined the debate, critically deconstructing ideas of national homogeneity and authenticity underpinning the exclusivist episteme. Soon thereafter, the idea of Ireland as inclusive and positively European was clearly dominant:

> By the 1990s, the identity discourse by Irish elites showed a distinct Europhilia … [and] all political parties … relevant to decision-making in the Republic had adopted a pro-European stance … Both aspects of the inclusive Irish identity – integrative vis-à-vis Europe and respect towards Unionist aspirations – were endorsed by the Republic's three national newspapers. (Kornprobst 2005, 416)

Recent events, most notably the initial Irish rejection of the EU's Lisbon Treaty in 2008 (and its subsequent approval by a second referendum in October 2009), showed that in Ireland – as elsewhere – national identity negotiations are ongoing, dominant epistemes subject to continuous contestation, and that the extent of Europhilia 'on the ground' fluctuates considerably over time.

The Irish case complements my analysis of recent Austrian history and shows that the emergence and co-existence of – and the struggle for ideological hegemony between – different discourses of national identity are by no means country-specific particularities. In very general terms, such similarities call for further research on the different definitions of the national 'self', its 'others', its past and its advocated future available in any national setting. In more specific conceptual terms, historical developments and discursive shifts of the kind examined in my analysis of Austria or in Kornprobst's discussion of Ireland suggest that an understanding of national identity negotiations requires – in any setting – an 'archaeological' approach capable of unearthing different paradigms of national self-understanding.[25]

Less concerned with diachronic change, a second recent study shows that another key dimension in my analysis of Austria – the relative inclusiveness or exclusiveness of different conceptualizations of national identity – is of similar transnational relevance. Hans Lödén's quantitative study (2008) of everyday attitudes and definitions of Swedish national identity, discusses the significance of inclusive notions of 'Swedishness' to the successful integration of migrants. The context to Lödén's research (2008, 257–258) is provided by recent demographic changes: Sweden, not unlike Austria, has become a 'country of immigration', particularly due to 'work force immigration' since the 1950s and asylum-immigration since the 1980s, with some 20 per cent of its population of nine million now 'of foreign origin'; both the relative unemployment figures amongst immigrants and across the Swedish population as a whole and several other socio-economic indicators reveal considerable social inequalities.

Against this backdrop that Lödén discusses the important question as to how 'feelings of belonging' and democratic political participation can be encouraged among immigrants statistically more likely to suffer structural disadvantages and who 'often com[e] from non-democratic countries with strong authoritarian traditions' (2008, 258). Lödén argues that the forms of national identity, 'creation' of which is a 'constantly ongoing process', on offer are crucial. More exactly, Lödén shows that successful integration requires the availability of inclusive, 'superordinate' national identities, capable of minimizing the differences and competitiveness between different subgroups. Moreover, superordinate national identities are seen to be defined by fairness, encouraging trust in the law and respect for the country's political institutions. Crucially, superordinate national identities are achievable for former outsiders:

---

25   For a relevant, quantitative analysis of changing patterns of national attachment in Spain since the end of Francoism and the country's transition to democracy, see Muñoz (2009). Muñoz analyzes changes at the individual level in the context of a transformation of 'traditionalist national-Catholicism of the [former] regime … [into] a new, democratic and inclusive conception of nationhood' (2009, 620).

[A] superordinate identity in order to be attractive to outgroups should be devoid of ingroup prototypicalities impossible to meet for [outsiders]. Skin colour, birthplace and religious faith are such prototypicalities. And, on the other hand, to the extent a superordinate identity is characterised by criteria possible for anyone to appreciate (e.g. fairness) and meet (e.g. language) it ought to attract the interest of the potentially excluded. (Lödén 2008, 259)

Lödén's study involved 1000 secondary school students, from eight municipalities across the country and broadly representative of national demographics, completing a questionnaire on 'ethnic self-identification, importance of specified criteria for Swedishness, sense of belonging to Sweden and preparedness for political engagement' (Lödén 2008, 261). Most crucially, the survey asked respondents to rank the importance of three inclusive criteria of Swedishness (i.e. ability to speak Swedish, respect for Swedish law and institutions, feeling Swedish) and three exclusive criteria (i.e. having been born in Sweden, having lived there most of one's life, Christian faith). Analysis of his findings showed that a majority of some 55 per cent of his student respondents favoured inclusive definitions of Swedishness, with 45 per cent articulating an exclusive understanding of national identity. By way of contextualization, Lödén points to Swedish data from other European-wide social surveys that have revealed – compared to other European countries – lower levels of xenophobia and more positive attitudes towards immigration.

As an indicator of Swedish attitudes towards migration and pluralism, such findings are encouraging. However, as reflected in persisting social inequalities, relatively widespread endorsement of an inclusive discourse of Swedishness does not automatically translate into structural 'openness'. In Lödén's own words, an inclusive national identity is a 'necessary but not sufficient condition' for migrants' identification with – and successful integration into – Swedish society. Equality regarding living standards, social mobility and security, or 'factual societal integration', thus remains the 'overriding concern' and hope for 'immigrant youth':

A superordinate, inclusive national identity … is an important vehicle for reducing bias among subgroups … decreasing intergroup conflict and creating a common sense of belonging. Experiences of fair treatment seem to be decisive for feelings of attachment to a superordinate national identity. Inclusive criteria of nationhood can be understood as expressions of fairness. Swedish and non-Swedish students to a large extent express similar attachment to inclusion. But this is not enough in order to make non-Swedes' feeling of belonging to Sweden reach the same levels as those expressed by Swedes … In order to be viewed as trustworthy the rhetoric must be complemented by material and substantial evidence from the society at large concerning fair chances to establish oneself as a full member of society. (Lödén 2008, 263)

Therein lies, of course, a crucial, distinctly pan-European, indeed global, lesson: a truly successful multicultural future will not be measured by ideological commitments or discursive hegemony, significant though they are; the ultimate litmus test is provided by social structures and their manifestation in discrimination or equality.

The third other European context to be mentioned here, in order to further illustrate the discursive negotiability of national identities and their potential symbolic 'openness', is the UK. Contemporary British society has been profoundly shaped by inward migration since the end of World War II. This included, most notably, labour migration from parts of the British commonwealth, in particular from South Asia and the Caribbean, that played a vital role in the context of the 'post-war boom'; starting in the 1960s, economic decline led both to legislative restrictions for commonwealth migrants and to family reunions and permanent settlement for many already in the UK (see, for example, Castles 2000). The combined effects of South Asian and Afro-Caribbean settlement with migratory flows from many other parts of the world have led to descriptions of parts of contemporary Britain as 'super-diverse' (Vertovec 2007). In terms of material realities, the British picture is complex: considerable structural disadvantages and persisting inequalities suffered by some groups sit juxtaposed to upward social mobility enjoyed by others (e.g. Modood et al. 1997). It is against this backdrop – and particularly in the context of events since 9/11, the 'war on terror', and 7/7 – that recent years have seen public debate concerning the meaning of Britishness and the future of multiculturalism.

Tim Edensor's examination (2002) of the significance of popular culture and the everyday to national identities is highly relevant to such debates. Edensor's analysis unfolds around four dimensions that shape national identity negotiations anywhere: the ideological significance of particular spaces and places (e.g. landscapes considered to symbolize the nation); ritual performances of national identity; material culture and commodities associated with the nation; cultural representations of the nation and its history (e.g. film and literature). This is followed by a discussion of an exhibition of contemporary British identities in London's millennium dome (Edensor 2002, 171–189). The exhibition in question was termed the 'self-portrait' and consisted of five parts: display boards presenting quotes on a series of topics including 'diversity', 'fair play', 'public spirit' and 'language'; a collection of satirical sculptures; audio-recordings of local children talking about their hopes and of different British 'soundscapes'; the 'national portrait' – a collage of some 250,000 images of people and of objects, landscapes and artworks associated with Britain; and finally, the 'Andscape' – a selection of more than four hundred responses, from people across Britain, to 'leaflets left in Marks and Spencer stores [i.e. the 'self-portrait' sponsor] and in public spaces … [asking] the question: "What one thing best represents something good about Britain to you and why?"' (Edensor 2002, 175). Crucially, the 'positive signifiers of Britain' thus collected conveyed – as did the 'self-portrait' as a whole – British national identities as defined by internal heterogeneity. This is illustrated by a sub-selection of some of the suggested symbols of Britishness included in the 'Andscape', which Edensor (2002, 175) groups into the following categories: things (e.g. the Union Jack, black cabs), food and drink (e.g. marmite, a pint of beer), geographies (e.g. canals, Tower bridge), institutions and abstract qualities (e.g. the royal family, tolerance, sarcasm), people (e.g. the Beatles, Tony Blair), animals and plants (e.g. dogs, thistle, rose, shamrock, daffodil), popular cultural forms (e.g. James Bond, British newspapers), technology and innovation (e.g. the Eurostar train, the mini cooper), cultural practices (e.g. pantomime, village cricket, bingo, Sunday morning football). Not surprisingly, each category contains some of 'the obvious' signifiers of 'quintessential Britishness' known to international audiences thanks to global media and tourist industries: for examples, red phone boxes, fish and chips, red double-decker buses, Big Ben, Robin Hood and the annual boat race (between Oxford and Cambridge). Other symbols named in the 'Andscape' – such as teapots, ice cream vans or the traditional 'fry-up' breakfast – relate to various realms of everyday life. British Euro-scepticism notwithstanding, inclusion of the 'UK/EU passport' may be interpreted as evidence of the earlier mentioned phenomenon of a growing 'banal Europeanism' (Cram 2009). At the same time, various other symbols relate to key episodes in recent British, or English, history (e.g. war memorials, the white cliffs of Dover, Wembley's twin towers) and articulate a narrower national focus. Alongside all of this, symbols of urban youth subcultures – such as graffiti or skateboard parks – and, for example, the controversial footballer Lee Bowyer were also included. Most crucially for our purposes, however, the 'Andscape' clearly reflected – and in part celebrated – British multiculturalism: kebabs, Chinese takeaway, chicken tikka masala, the Balti, mosques, Hindu temples, the inter-faith network, Notting Hill carnival, news presenter Trevor MacDonald, and 'a mixed-race couple' thus all made the list of 'positive signifiers of Britain'.

Overall, as Edensor summarizes (2002, 188–189), national identities emerged from the 'Andscape' as 'continually dynamic', displaying symbolic 'flexibility', offering new 'links' in a 'vast, shared cultural matrix' and 'opening up multiple points of connection'. Also commenting on the millennium dome's 'self-portrait', Les Back observes that – despite a contemporary climate of renewed nationalisms – many people's life-worlds now display a patriotism that is multicultural and 'fragmented':

> The debate on multiculturalism is dominated by material metaphors. Commentators often invoke the idea of a 'mosaic' with hard … edges … [between] discrete pieces … Alternatively, [there is] the notion of the 'melting pot' … in which the heated encounters liquefy difference and produce fusion … [T]he notion of a fragment that refuses to represent some inherent difference … offers another kind of metaphor … There can be no assemblage of these fragments into some stable coherent national identity. Rather nationalism remains shattered regardless of the efforts … to put it back together. What endure are pieces that can be shared and combined … without requiring a stable identity … This patriotism

in fragments breaks with the longing for … whole identities and foregrounds that such grand national identities are forever in pieces. The affinities that result are loose, changing and open, yet powerful like the photographs collected in the Millennium Dome exhibit. (Back 2007, 148)

## Concluding remarks

Rainer Bauböck argues (quoted in Kaloianov 2008, 3) that if 'the persistence of racial segregation is the American dilemma, the integration of immigrants may very well be the European dilemma'; he elaborates that this tension consists of reconciling 'the fact that European countries have become societies of immigration with dominant ideas about national identity that rule out the American self-conception as a nation of immigrants'. Perceptive though this is, such exclusive European conceptualizations of national identities are by no means uncontested. As later chapters illustrate, national identities are not monolithic, but discursively fought over. Exclusive, culturally homogenizing definitions find themselves challenged by alternative self-understandings that regard 'the nation' to be inherently pluralistic and ethnically heterogeneous. What is more, such alternative discourses celebrate internal diversity, in outright opposition to and subversion of the 'dominant ideas' summarized by Bauböck.

At the beginning of the twenty-first century, nationalisms are a prominent and consequential force in and beyond Europe. As this chapter has begun to argue, however, a fuller understanding of nationalisms must locate them within 'deeper' historical contexts and within broader social and political arenas, in which *national identity negotiations* unfold. The former, nationalism, is thus a sub-category of the latter. National identity negotiations, in turn, are internally contested and ideologically diverse. They are the political and cultural terrain, on which boundaries are continually (re)produced, crossed, redrawn, but also questioned and at times 'dismantled' (see Wodak et al. 1999, 4, 33).

This chapter has developed these conceptual points through an analysis of different discursive frameworks – and their recent histories – of Austrian identity: a once dominant but now peripheral and de-legitimated ideology of pan-Germanism; the hegemonic and itself ideologically heterogeneous paradigm of Austrian particularism; celebrations of Austria's 'European-ness'; a discourse that defines Austria as inherently multicultural and syncretistic; various forms of counter-hegemony critiquing existing structures of power and exclusion and directed against nationalism in particular. The co-existence of these different discourses provides empirical corroboration of Anthony Smith's observation (2008, 187) of the 'multifaceted nature of most nations and nationalisms, the often layered character of their cultural traditions, [that are] the result of gradual evolution or of drastic change'. Moreover, discursive struggles between different frameworks of self-understanding are by no means a contemporary particularity: this is shown by, for examples, Gellner's above-mentioned analysis (1998) of the clash between cosmopolitanism and romanticism in the final decades of the Habsburg Empire.

Moving from Austria to Ireland, Sweden and the UK, this chapter has traced comparable ideological heterogeneities and identity negotiations in these other European contexts. The Irish case study provided further insights into historical shifts in dominant national self-understandings. Lödén (2008), meanwhile, examines exclusive and inclusive versions of 'Swedishness' as manifest in the everyday setting of secondary schools. Finally, Edensor's analysis (2002) of the national 'self-portrait' zone in London's millennium dome provides additional insights into the lived experience and (relative) symbolic openness or 'fragmentation' of contemporary, distinctly multicultural national identities. This paves the way for the analysis presented in the next chapter: we now turn to an examination of national symbols in times of perceived crises.

# Chapter 2
# National Symbols and Histories in Crisis

## Introduction

> In the old days it made no sense to ask whether the peasants loved their own culture: they took it for granted … But when labour migration and bureaucratic employment became prominent features within their social horizon, they soon learned the difference between … a co-national, one understanding … their culture, and someone hostile to it. This … taught them to be aware of their culture, and to love it (or, indeed, to wish to be rid of it) … In stable self-contained communities culture is often quite invisible, but when mobility and context-free communication come to be of the essence … the culture in which one has been *taught* to communicate becomes the core of one's identity. (Gellner 1983, 61, italics in the original)

Building on the previous discussions, we now examine national symbols and memories in the identity negotiations that partly define contemporary Europe. I will show that key to understanding many such negotiations are widespread experiences and perceptions of *crises*, in response to which previously commonsensical markers of identity, rarely examined memories and historical narratives come to be critically re-examined and widely debated. As such, Gellner's observations opening this chapter of the effects of the industrializing processes of the nineteenth century are also highly relevant for an understanding of the collective and individual responses to the (perceived) dislocations that define the post-industrial societies of the late twentieth and early twenty-first centuries.

McCrone (1998, 182) detects in contemporary nationalisms a 'cultural defence', the 'pursuit of political resources' and 'vehicles for social identity … when conventional state structures premised on their sovereignty over cultural, economic and political aspects seem to be on the wane'. Whilst this encapsulates crucial parts of the following analysis, my focus is wider: I locate nationalism in broader social fields undergoing rapid change on the levels of both social structures and everyday life-worlds; nationalism is one amongst several competing and mutually contesting ideological reactions to such (perceived) change. This chapter again proceeds from an outline of relevant theoretical leads to a focus on Austria as my central case study and, from there, to a discussion of other comparable European contexts. The latter examines recent disagreements over memories and narratives of the national past in several European countries and the effects of personal crises on 'national sentiments' (Mann and Fenton 2009).

**Theoretical context**

Nationalism and the politicization of cultural identities are defining characteristics of the contemporary world. Variously interpreted as 'neo-tribal' yearnings for community in postmodern times (Bauman 1992), as 'resistance identities' against exclusion from the information age (Castells 1997), and as reactions to the 'denationalization shock' and individualism in a globalizing 'risk society' (Beck 2000; 1992), such developments raise questions concerning the construction and contestation of social/national identities and the relationship between culture and politics. Related challenges include how to account for the transformation of the not-so-long-ago enthusiastically proclaimed 'end of history' (Fukuyama 1992) into an age of ethnic and national reassertion and, often, outright antagonism.

However, national identities are not only articulated in fiery speeches and explicit identity politics but they are also constructed, reproduced and experienced in a seemingly more 'trivial' and less reflexive everyday manner. Michael Billig's groundbreaking work on *Banal Nationalism* (1995a) established a distinction between 'hot-' and 'cold nationalism'. The latter, Billig argues, provides part of the taken-for-granted backdrop to people's lives, discursively manifested in a range of practices including the 'national deixis' – a rhetorical 'pointing' through, for example, the use of the pronouns 'we', 'us' or 'our' in the national press and beyond – as well as the constant (albeit largely non-reflexive) waving of national flags. The very social fabric to life inside modern 'nation-state containers' (Beck 2000, 23–25) thus contributes to the ongoing delineation and maintenance of boundaries separating the national 'self' from excluded 'others'. Tim Edensor (2002) has developed this further, arguing that national identities infuse everyday life and popular culture, as manifest in shared understandings of space, the performance of national rituals and emotional investments in national symbols and material culture (e.g. car industries).

This chapter aims to bridge cold national identities and hot nationalism. In doing so, I explore the analytical utility of a set of concepts already invoked in parts of the literature on nationalism and ethnicity (e.g. Billig 1995a, 42; Edensor 2002, 20, 71, 88–98; McCrone 1998) and initially contained in Pierre Bourdieu's *Outline of a Theory of Practice* (1977). At the heart of Bourdieu's (early) sociology lies his concept of the *habitus*, or the 'structuring structures' provided by shared categories, dispositions, practices, assumptions and tastes that enable and constrain (though without fully determining) social action and furnish a taken-for-granted, rarely reflected on and hence predominantly unconscious cultural common sense. This concept has been employed to analyze a range of phenomena in the area of ethnic studies (see Karner 2007a). Steven Vertovec (2000, 64–73), for example, interprets a 'process of ideologization' brought about by experiences of migration and settlement among diaspora communities as the transformation of previously 'largely non-conscious' cultural phenomena and practices, or *habitus*, into an ideological and reflexive ground of self-definition and political mobilization. For my present purposes, the theoretically and empirically most relevant application of

Bourdieu-ian theory is contained in a seminal study of the 'discursive construction of [Austrian] national identities':

> *[N]ational identity* can be regarded as a *sort of habitus ... a complex of common ideas, concepts or perception schemes*, (a) *of related emotional attitudes* intersubjectively shared within a specific group of persons; (b*) as well as of similar behavioural dispositions*; (c) all of which are internalized through 'national' socialization. In the case of the Austrian nation, the ideas and schemata in question refer to the imagination of the 'homo austriacus' ... the Austrian 'as such', to a common national culture, history, present and future as well as to a type of 'national body' or national territory. At the same time, the national habitus also has to do with stereotypical notions of other nations and their culture, history, etc. (De Cillia et al. 1999, 153, italics in the original)

The 'suffusion' of 'ordinary ways of speaking and experiencing the world' with nationally specific meanings (Billig 1995b, 93) is also captured by a former Austrian Vice-Chancellor who indirectly summarizes his own experience of the national *habitus* in describing places, food, memories and feelings 'beyond conscious awareness' (Busek 2001).

In what follows, I develop this theoretical trajectory by employing Bourdieu's (1977, 164–173) closely related concept of *doxa* – or the cultural 'universe of the undiscussed ... seen as self-evident and undisputed' – and its transformation into a 'universe of discourse (or argument)' as a result of crises:

> [T]he tradition is silent ... about itself as tradition ... The adherence expressed in the doxic relation to the social world is the absolute form of recognition of legitimacy through misrecognition of arbitrariness ... The truth of doxa is only ever fully revealed ... by the constitution of a *field of opinion*, the locus of the confrontation of competing discourses ... The practical questioning of ... a particular way of living ... brought about by 'culture contact' or by the political and economic crises correlative with class division is not the purely intellectual operation ... [of] the deliberate, methodical suspension of naïve adherence to the world. The critique which brings the undiscussed into discussion ... has as the condition of its possibility objective crisis, which, in breaking the immediate fit between the subjective structures and the objective structures, destroys self-evidence practically. It is when the social world loses its character as a natural phenomenon that the question of the ... conventional character ... of social facts can be raised ... Crisis is a necessary condition for a questioning of doxa but it is not in itself a sufficient condition for the production of a critical discourse. (Bourdieu 1977, 167–169, italics in the original)

Bourdieu's account of crises triggering a general questioning of a previously taken-for granted cultural commonsense and social order resonates in Gellner's above-quoted account of the consciousness-raising effects of industrialization.

However, Bourdieu stresses that the formulation of social critique is not an inevitable outcome, that the resulting 'field of opinion' is not monolithic but a terrain of ideological contestation between the 'dominated' and the 'dominant'. In what follows I demonstrate that, building on the notion of *habitus*, the *doxa-crisis-discourse* schema enables a historically contextualized analysis of the transformation of 'cold' or everyday national identities (on the level of taken-for-granted *doxa*) into 'hot' nationalism and various reactions against it (on the level of politicized opinions/discourses) triggered by the dislocations experienced in the context of contemporary globalization. This theme recurs in later chapters as it relates to Castles' (2000, 179) 'hypothesis … that globalization leads to fundamental societal changes, which are experienced as crises of the national economy and social relations … of culture and identity, and as political crises' and that this 'general crisis of modernity' is linked to 'contemporary racisms'. Krzyżanowski and Wodak's (2009, 2) analyze the latter as a form of post-industrial 'xeno-racism', which has replaced older ideologies of biological superiority with discourses about 'protecting jobs, concern about welfare benefits … or cultural incompatibilities or differences'. In addition to such contextualization, the following account also underlines the internal heterogeneity of the 'universe of discourse' in contemporary Austria and other parts of Europe.

A second theoretical line explored below relates to national memories or 'mythologies' and their (recent) interrogation and questioning in many European contexts. In a seminal essay on the relevance of the past to national identities that I also return to in chapter three, Duncan Bell (2003) draws a conceptual distinction between memory – defined as a property of individual minds and thus tied to personal life histories – and 'collective remembrance' or 'mythology' respectively. Closely related to the latter is Bell's notion of a 'mythscape' – a contested terrain of competing narratives and interpretations of the national past (including events personally experienced and others predating 'us'):

> '[O]rganic' forms of collective remembrance can actually run against the grain of the dominant narrative (or 'governing mythology') of the nation … Memory can thus function as a counter-hegemonic site of resistance, a space of political opposition … we need to separate out the concepts of memory and myth rather than subsuming them under the monolithic notion of collective memory. I consequently introduce the notion of a mythscape, the temporally and spatially extended discursive realm wherein the struggle for control of people's memories and the formation of nationalist myths is debated, contested and subverted incessantly. The mythscape is the page upon which the multiple and often conflicting nationalist narratives are (re)written; it is the perpetually mutating repository for the representation of the past for the purposes of the present. (Bell 2003, 66)

Three insights can be extrapolated from this that resonate with crucial parts of the following analyses. First, 'collective remembrance' is shared and transmitted and its time-span thus much longer than a person's individual memories. Second, collective memories are contestable and subject to alternative interpretations that jointly constitute an ideologically heterogeneous 'mythscape'. Third, the national past is not truly past but its rival interpretations are invoked and utilized for, in Bell's words, 'the purposes of the present'. The return of – or to – the national past in the present, and ensuing contests over the meanings of history and its relevance to the here and now, are defining themes in chapters two and three of this book: whilst I initially focus on often polarizing debates about the nation's history triggered by particular controversies or crises, I subsequently turn to more mundane invocations of a variety of historical 'analogies' (see Müller 2002; Karner 2010b) as rhetorical devices purporting to make sense of the present or to 'predict' the future.

Having outlined the theoretical strands guiding the analysis in this chapter (and parts of chapter three), I now return to my central case study to trace the effects of (perceived) crises on Austrian national identity negotiations over the past three decades. This is followed by a discussion of comparable phenomena elsewhere: ideological contests over national memories in France, Switzerland and Germany. The chapter concludes by tracing the consciousness-raising effects of the experience of crises to the level of individualized life histories as recorded in research on British 'national sentiments'. The perception or experience of crises is thereby shown to impact on both collective and idiosyncratic national identity negotiations.

## Returning to Austria

International perceptions of Austria have changed over the last 25 years. Previously associated with consensual democracy and social peace (e.g. Fitzmaurice 1991, 122) and stereotypically identified with *The Sound of Music*, Mozart, and winter sports, the Waldheim controversy of 1986 and Jörg Haider's subsequent rise to political prominence triggered transnational debates concerning the Alpine Republic's World War II past and its version of right-wing populism. The FPÖ's inclusion in a coalition government by the centre-right ÖVP in February 2000 led to the earlier-mentioned temporary imposition of a series of 'sanctions' on Austria by her then 14 EU-partners[1] and constituted the controversial high-point in a process that has altered external perceptions of Austrian history and politics. I here analyze internal perceptions of, and responses to, this process, which started in the 1980s, climaxed at the beginning of the new millennium and has continued since. I argue that, firstly, the experience of a number of (political, socio-economic, and

---

1    For an analysis of the sanctions and some of the underlying motivations for Austria's EU partners, see Merlingen et al. (2001). The sanctions were lifted following the recommendations of a report compiled by the so-called 'three wise men' mandated by the EU-14 and the European Court of Human Rights.

cultural) crises lies at the heart of recent controversies in and surrounding Austria; secondly, that these perceived crises have affected prominent self-definitions in contemporary Austria, altering the salience and mobilizing potential of discourses of national belonging and exclusion; thirdly, that the responses to these crises have been more varied than commonly acknowledged, thus giving rise to discursive struggles over and against nationalism. Such ideological diversity challenges a common homogenizing tendency encountered in studies by some Austrian- and non-Austrian academics and journalists alike. This tendency manifests, for example, in the subtitle of an edited collection on right-wing populism (Eisman 2002) that raises the questions whether this is a peculiarly 'Austrian sickness or part of European normality'. Similarly, Ron Scollon reviews a seminal analysis of anti-Semitic prejudice (back-cover to Reisigl and Wodak 2001) as an 'important book for anyone with interests in … today's Austrian/European crisis'. Elsewhere, Nick Ryan (2004, 249) captures some but by no means all Austrian discourses about the country's World War II past, when he wonders 'if they're suffering from some form of collective amnesia'. As is well known and confirmed in this and later chapters, right-wing populism, anti-Semitic and racist prejudice and some deeply troubling historical narratives continue to be a part of Austrian society and politics that demand urgent and ongoing attention. However, they are also subject to ongoing political contestation and intra-Austrian criticism and therefore should not be metonymically misrepresented as an assumed essence of a varied and diverse social field. An understanding of the latter demands broader contextualization, both historically and in relation to the competing ideological responses triggered by recent and contemporary crises.

The majority of data analyzed below was derived from a qualitative reading of the *Kronen Zeitung* between 2002 and 2004, the country's biggest newspaper with a – by international standards – staggering circulation of some 40 per cent (see, for example, Thaler 2001, 39; Mappes-Niedik 2002, 167; Reisigl and Wodak 2001, 102) in a country of over eight million people. This is complemented by additional and more recent coverage across Austria's other, ideologically heterogeneous newspapers and coverage by the public broadcasting network ORF. An ongoing and inherently contested process of national self-definition and re-assertion can be observed in several discursive arenas that include sport, language and other national symbols, nature/landscape/the environment, debates surrounding immigration and the national past. Power struggles within the European Union and anxieties and perceived uncertainties suffuse debates in these discursive realms. Drawing on the theoretical strands outlined above, this chapter illustrates that a sociological understanding of national identities in contemporary Austria and other parts of Europe requires an analysis of crises transforming previously (largely) taken-for-granted cultural meanings, the 'doxic' national *habitus*, into varied ideological positions.

*A national habitus, critical (of) memories*

If our understanding of contemporary Austria and its widespread (external) association with a nationalist revival is to be advanced by an application of Bourdieu's model outlined above, the existence of a 'national habitus' and *doxa* and their transformation in periods of crises must be established. However, a preliminary question needs to be posed: Can a country that still ranks amongst the relatively most stable and affluent worldwide, growing internal inequalities and insecurities notwithstanding, be said to be experiencing the kind of 'objective crisis' that Bourdieu defines as a 'necessary condition' for the 'questioning of doxa', for 'bring[ing] the undiscussed into discussion' (1977, 168–169)?

Krzyżanowski and Wodak (2009, 68) raise a similar issue, writing prior to the global financial crisis that started in the autumn of 2008, by pointing out that 'the Austrian economy remains in relatively good shape' and that 'no particular "disruptions" or "crises" have occurred … in the recent past'. Their suggestion is that there is no real economic hardship that could account for the rise of populist neo-nationalism over recent decades. However, the arguments I develop in the present and next chapters show that crises need to be conceptualized differently in the Austrian context. Comparisons, it will be shown, are not being made synchronically – with other, less well-off countries in the here and now – but diachronically: with 'oneself' in the past. The assessments thus made tend to be negative and nostalgic, setting up a contrast between present ills and anxieties and an assumed 'golden age' in the allegedly not-so-distant past. Krzyżanowski and Wodak (2009, 69) themselves provide evidence of negative change as reflected in Austrian unemployment rates that, whilst still relatively low compared to some other European contexts, rose considerably between 2000 and 2005 – a trend that has continued since. Emerging narratives of loss and nostalgia, it will turn out, 'suit' exclusivist politics that appeal to growing numbers fearing 'downward social mobility, loss of status and loss of identity' particularly in the 'small, affluent countries of Western Europe' (Gingrich 2006, 47, 37). The point about crises I develop below is largely a point about *perceived crises*, about the effects of changes widely decoded as changes 'for the worse' and felt as deteriorations when compared to 'oneself' of not very long ago. A period of such locally perceived crises can be traced to long before the more global and systemic financial and debt crises that have unfolded since 2008. Before developing this argument, Austria's recent history and the national *habitus* associated with it need to be discussed.

Austrian twentieth-century history (e.g. Kleindel 1984; Hanisch 1994; Brook-Shepherd 1997) can be broadly schematized by the following successive periods: The gradual disintegration of the Habsburg empire prior to, during, and following World War I; economic instability and crisis, political antagonism and turmoil in the 1920s and 1930s; the rise of fascism and the infamous *Anschluss* to Hitler Germany in 1938; the horrors of World War II (e.g. Bukey 2000) and the Holocaust; the reconstruction of the Austrian state and the continuing occupation by allied forces until 1955 and the signing of the State Treaty; the post-1955 period as characterized by economic recovery, increasing affluence, social partnership, political neutrality and power sharing between Austria's socialists (SPÖ) and the ÖVP, and – as discussed in chapter one – by the increasingly successful project of 'nation-building' and growing hegemony of distinctly Austrian self-understandings in opposition to the pan-Germanism that had dominated in the first half of the century (e.g. Thaler 2001). By the 1980s and 1990s a distinctively Austrian patriotism was firmly established and also relatively more salient than in other countries: prior to the referendum on EU accession in June 1994 Austrians expressed an exceptionally prominent 'national pride' that was only surpassed by US citizens; in a European context, and as early as 1990, Austrians emerged as the second most patriotic behind Poles, which changed by 1995 when Austria topped the European ranks in national pride; furthermore, by 1998 the salience of a chauvinistic, 'negatively connoted' patriotism even overtook that recorded in the US (Rathkolb 2005, 25–26).

In our theoretical terms, the question arises which ideas, categories, tastes, practices and symbols – (predominantly) encountered on the pre-conscious level of *habitus/doxa* – had come to underlie the dominant discourse of Austrian nationhood. Existing data concerning 'objects of national pride' identified by a (representative) sample of 1999 Austrians interviewed in the mid-1980s sheds some light on this question: More than 80 per cent declared their pride in the country's 'scenic beauty', whilst 67 per cent were proud of Austria's 'historical treasures' and 64 per cent greatly valued their country's sporting (i.e. skiing-) achievements (Reiterer 1988, 118–119). These and other parameters of routinely experienced national identities – some of the dispositions and associations that constitute the national *habitus* – also emerged from another survey conducted in 1980, which revealed widespread attachment to a range of national symbols and stereotypes: On this occasion, 97 per cent declared great pride in Austria's 'scenic beauty', 96 per cent in her political stability and social peace, 94 per cent stated their attachment to friends, families and 'likeable people' living in the country, 93 per cent emphasized shared language, 87 and 79 per cent valued Austrian neutrality and her artistic history respectively, while 74 per cent expressed a particular affinity to government policies and Austrian food (Bruckmüller 1996, 70). The following analysis revisits some of these dimensions of national self-identification (more than) twenty years on. Methodologically different, my qualitative reading of relevant media coverage between 2002 and 2004 reveals that several of these core dimensions of the national *habitus* – particularly those related to national history, sport, language, landscape/the environment – still take centre-stage in prominent discourses of national identity. What has changed, however, are widespread perceptions and experiences of crises, which have transformed previously often taken-for-granted objects of 'national pride' into much-valued assets now considered to be under threat and erosion. It is this element of crisis that is crucial to an understanding of contemporary Austrian society and key to a fruitful application of Bourdieu-ian theory.

Nick Crossley argues (2004, 101) that the 'doxic level of culture is society's "unconscious"' and that 'the sociologist can and should delve into the repressed history of contemporary societies, bringing previously doxic assumptions, which serve the interests of elites, to the level of reflective argument'. Though not for the first time but on a previously unknown international scale, and not due to academic 'delving' but as a result of historical contingencies and electoral politics, Austria's previously largely doxic and arguably repressed World War II history became the object of public controversy and reflection in the mid/late-1980s. 1986 can be identified as a watershed in recent Austrian history, as the year when, in the run-up and aftermath of former UN general secretary Kurt Waldheim's presidential election, the country's wartime past became the object of international scrutiny. Debates concerning Waldheim's role in the *Wehrmacht* in the Balkans and Greece during World War II followed by his own declaration to only have 'done his duty' as a soldier in the German army (e.g. Haslinger 1995, 26–27) provided the backdrop to an anti-Semitic backlash (in parts) of the country's tabloid press and beyond (e.g. Mitten 1992; chapter three in Reisigl and Wodak 2001). The period prior to 1986 is often portrayed with reference to a widespread amnesia concerning Austria's role in World War II and the Holocaust (e.g. Pelinka and Weinzierl 1987; Sully 1990; Fitzmaurice 1991; Rauscher 2000). In the aftermath of the Waldheim-controversy, the ensuing internal ideological polarization and transnational debate, Austria's previous (international- and self-) image of an 'island of the blessed' became increasingly difficult to sustain. A long overdue process of historical reflection came to be most widely associated with a speech given by (then) Chancellor Franz Vranitzky in 1988, fifty years after Austria's *Anschluss* to Hitler Germany, which has been interpreted (e.g. Sully 1990) as the first official acknowledgement of the country's dual historical role – as both perpetrator and victim[2] – during World War II. While the importance of Vranitzky's position is undeniable, even more significant to the present discussion were the various, often polarized reactions to the 'crisis of 1986'. In Bourdieu's terminology, the Waldheim-controversy transformed a previously largely non-reflexive and 'undiscussed' national *doxa* pertaining to Austria's recent history into a 'universe of discourse and opinion'. The latter was from the start heterogeneous: the widely observed nationalist and anti-Semitic backlash was thus strongly opposed by, for example, well-known contributions to Austrian popular culture (e.g. popular music), which articulated a self-critical discourse aimed at debating Austria's past, at mourning the victims of the Holocaust, and at challenging (contemporary) exclusionary, nationalist politics (Karner 2002).

Historical scholarship documents a shocking reluctance to prosecute Nazi war criminals in post-war Austria (e.g. Zöchling 2009b), a wider reluctance to confront

---

2   There is much literature concerning the construction and maintenance of a public myth of (Austrian) WWII victimhood based on a selective reading of the Moscow declaration of 1943: see, for example, Bischof (1993), Hanisch (1994), Embacher et al. (1999), Uhl (2006).

the Holocaust (e.g. Stadler 2004; Uhl 2006), and more or less 'encoded', or 'secondary', forms of anti-Semitism (e.g. Pollak and Eger 2002) – some of which cut across the political spectrum (Reiter 2002) – prior to the 1980s. However, there were also moments and currents of earlier resistance and some reflexive engagement with the Holocaust. In 1955, for example, a demonstration calling on the public 'never to forget' and for 'Nazis to go' prevented a right-wing politician from giving an anti-Semitic speech in Vienna; and when the anti-Semitic outbursts by a professor of economic history in the mid-1960s led to violent clashes between sympathizers and opponents and the tragic murder of a concentration camp survivor by a neo-Nazi student, the 'Anti-fascist student committee' and the 'Austrian resistance movement' responded by organizing a march of silence attended by some 20,000–25,000 people (see Adunka 2002, 17–19, 29–33).

Such earlier confrontations notwithstanding, it was only in the aftermath of the Waldheim-controversy that the formerly largely repressed was brought to wider public consciousness and the previously widely taken-for-granted myth of World War II victimhood (*Opfermythos*) came to be debated and officially rejected. As 'predicted' by Bourdieu's theory, however, an emerging 'universe of discourse' has been internally heterogeneous:[3] The most troubling reactions have included vandalism at Jewish cemeteries in Vienna and Eisenstadt in the early 1990s, an 'anti-Semitism without Jews' among groups of football hooligans (John and Marschik 2002), and a well-documented instance of encoded political rhetoric tapping into latent anti-Semitic prejudice (Pelinka 2002; Mitten 2002; Wodak and Reisigl 2002). On the other hand, successive Austrian governments have put 'new emphasis on education to achieve greater knowledge and awareness of the Holocaust ... political and church leaders have made great efforts to set the historical record straight, school books[4] have been re-written, anti-Semitism has been decried, a national fund was established for ... Jewish survivors, the law was amended so that Austrian refugees ... were able to have dual nationality. Restitution claims are handled expeditiously' (Pick 2000, 201).

For all the historical consciousness-raising since 1986, there are still some troubling sub-cultural currents that periodically surface. Since 2009 there have been several scandals indicative of a continuing reluctance amongst some sections to acknowledge Austria's role in the Holocaust, let alone mourn its millions of victims. These incidents variously involved a regional FPÖ politician lashing out against the director of a Jewish museum in the Western province of Vorarlberg (Ortner 2009a); an anti-Semitic Tyrolean hotelier refusing to provide accommodation to Jewish visitors (http://diepresse.com/home/panorama/oesterreich/478066/print. do); in another extremely worrying incident four teenagers violently interrupted a ceremony commemorating the liberation of an outpost to Mauthausen concentration

---

3   Highly relevant to this are the analyses in Heer et al. (2008) of the debates triggered by the exhibitions on the Wehrmacht's 'war of annihilation' between 1995 and 2002.

4   For a more critical analysis of Austrian history school-textbooks, see Loitfellner (2008).

camp in the upper Austrian town of Ebensee (see Enigl 2010) and the outer walls of Mauthausen itself have been defiled by racist graffiti on two separate occasions (http://ooe.orf.at/stories/441047/). Elsewhere, the 2010 FPÖ presidential candidate Barbara Rosenkranz, whose affinity to the extreme right (see Lackner 2010b; Zöchling 2007a) caused much public outcry, was pushed to sign a declaration of oath condemning the crimes of national socialism in order to publicly distance herself from historical revisionism (http://www.orf.at/100308-48803/index.html). Rosenkranz subsequently received some 15 per cent of votes at the presidential election; her candidacy arguably further corroborated what Pelinka terms the 'x-factor' of Austrian right-wing populism: unlike otherwise comparable phenomena in other parts of Western Europe, it is partly defined by a 'sloppy' relationship to the Nazi-past, a reluctance at times to unambiguously condemn and categorically distance itself from it (see Gärtner 2009, 58, 160).

Right-wing populism, extremism and historical revisionism are of course widely condemned. Most recently, this manifested in much opposition to Rosenkranz's candidacy, including an internet campaign and demonstration entitled 'dance of lights against Rosenkranz' that galvanized a broad alliance of individuals and organizations (www.orf.at 24 March 2010). The point is this: over the last 20 to 25 years Austria's post-war 'myth of victimhood' and co-existing tendencies to uncritically reify 'dutiful' Wehrmacht soldiers (Uhl 2006) have been subject to public debate, controversy and introspection. A previously widespread (though never universal) reluctance to examine Austria's recent history self-critically has given way to public reflection. Whilst the reactions have not been uniform but – in line with Bourdieu's notion of an internally contested 'universe of opinion' – heterogeneous, a previously predominantly doxic 'national mythology' has been transformed into a politicized terrain of historical debate and national soul-searching: in short, into an ideologically contested 'mythscape' (Bell 2002).

*Further crises*

The late 1980s and 1990s saw further crises unfolding in and around the Alpine Republic. Corruption scandals added to discontent with (and a growing crisis of legitimacy affecting) the long-established system of consensual democracy and *Proporz* – the sharing of Austria's large and influential public sector between SPÖ and ÖVP. The collapse of communism right beyond Austria's doorstep and the fall of the Iron Curtain that had constituted her eastern borders for decades, the war in former, neighbouring Yugoslavia in the early 1990s, and demographic changes brought about by an influx of immigrants and refugees, all contributed to a widespread sense of social and political uncertainty. The decision to join the European Union on 1 January 1995 (e.g. Bieler 2000), supported by 66.4 per cent of Austrians at the 1994 referendum, fundamentally altered the wider parameters, within which national identity and some of its traditional moorings – such as neutrality enshrined in the State Treaty of 1955 – have since had to be re-negotiated. The period spanning the late 1980s and 1990s also coincided with Haider's rise to political prominence, culminating in the FPÖ's earlier-mentioned, controversial inclusion in a coalition government in 2000. As already mentioned, Haider's success during the 1990s had different reasons, including his articulation of increasingly widespread dissatisfaction with established power structures (e.g. Pelinka 2000; Fillitz 2006) but also the disconcerting appeal to some of some of his most controversial statements[5] made in the earlier stages of his career, and a discourse constructing a nation under threat by 'encroaching foreigners'(e.g. Wodak 2002; Reisigl 2002) that acquired increasing mobilizing potential in a context of demographic and structural changes. Haider's political success, like populist/nationalist discourses and parties in other parts of the world, must thus be understood as a form of identity politics made plausible, in part, by the dislocations, uncertainties, anxieties and crises experienced by many in times of globalization (e.g. Camus 2002; Hainsworth 2000; Morrow 2000).

In 1990, political scientist Anton Pelinka (1990, 147, 151) made two arguments relevant to the present discussion: First, Pelinka reminded us, identities cannot be reduced to the nation-state, but are also continually experienced and constructed on sub-national (e.g. localities, regions, provinces, political groupings) and supra-national/pan-European levels; second, Pelinka observed that Austria's traditional elites were no longer able to successfully define and disseminate a hegemonic national identity, thus giving rise to a 'vacuum' to be filled by grass-root identity re-negotiations. Pelinka subsequently painted an even clearer picture of the structural and ideological changes sweeping across Austria. Not only was the country bidding farewell to its traditional joint domination by the 'subsocieties' of catholicism and social democracy, but Pelinka observed 'the party state and the corporate state los[ing] some of their grip on the political system, ... increasingly volatile voting behaviour, ... media systems getting out of (political) control, a degree of political deconcentration, new actors enter[ing] the political arena, and the political process los[ing] its predictability' (Pelinka 1998, 96). Inadvertently corroborating Castells' definition (2000, 338–365) of the European Union as a 'network state' formed in accommodation to the forces of the 'information age', Pelinka (1998, 138, 155, 172; also see Haller 1996) also argued that Austria's EU membership reflected a concession that economic independence had become untenable. Pelinka further suggested that social partnership and political neutrality – two defining pillars of post-war Austrian society – had become debatable: strong cartels of interest were perhaps no longer required and neutrality could be redefined in light of changing, transnational security concerns. The latter two assessments are arguably out of step with many people's sentiments, as demonstrated by an opinion poll suggesting that the majority of Austrians, in times of widespread political discontentment, continues to trust the institutions of social partnership (www.orf.at 23 January 2004). Similarly, debates about possible

---

5   The most infamous statements included references to the Austrian nation as an 'ideological miscarriage' and the 'orderly' employment policies of the Third Reich (e.g. Haslinger 1995, 48).

future 're-definitions' of Austrian neutrality tend to be received with considerable scepticism. Writing in the *Kronen Zeitung*, for example, the late Günther Nenning (2004a) – newspaper columnist and former politician – called for renewed political commitment to Austria's neutrality, claiming that 80 per cent of the population continued to support it.

The last twenty years can thus be described as a period of increasingly widespread uncertainty triggered by, on one hand, (historical) controversies and, on the other, by profound and rapid structural changes in and surrounding the Alpine Republic. If as late as 1980 few Austrians professed a lack of confidence in national politics (Ulram and Tributsch 2004, 37), more recent opinion polls paint a very different picture: Against the backdrop of rising unemployment, anxieties concerning EU expansion and the partial erosion of the welfare state, surveys conducted in late 2003 suggested that 60 per cent of Austrians expected the then imminent EU enlargement to bring few or no advantages, 52 per cent feared a decline in living standards (www.orf.at 3 December 2003), and a mere 39 per cent approved of the country's political trajectory (http://derstandard.at 4 November 2003). A subsequent survey, conducted against the backdrop of the then still recent memories of the 'sanctions' of the year 2000, revealed a profound and increasing disenchantment with the European Union and the relative weakness of a European discourse of identity (http://derstandard.at 13 July 2004).

More recently, the weekly *Profil* related the continuing appeal of right-wing populism to an endemic state of perceived and experienced crises defining the life-worlds of growing numbers of Austrians:

> Why do aggressive politics penetrate into the hearts and minds of more and more Austrians? ... Günter Ogris, who heads the social research institute SORA, interprets his own data thus: 'We live with a constant awareness of crises: the climate is changing, the social welfare system is crumbling, pensions are insecure ... planning ahead is increasingly difficult. There is a chronic lack of direction.' In such contexts, he argues, a politics of fear, such as the FPÖ's, is particularly effective. (Lackner 2010a, 21, my translation)

The perception and experience of recent crises affecting the everyday experience of national identities emerges from the following qualitative, thematic analysis of Austria's main daily newspapers (and the national broadcasting network) over a two-year period. In a striking example of 'national deixis' (Billig 1995a), the rhetorical delineation of the 'national self' from excluded 'others', the *Kronen Zeitung* of 26 November 2003 reflected on a 'dark week for us Austrians'. The article in question argued that a disastrous week had begun with the allegedly unjustified disqualification of an Austrian skier; this was followed by the suggestion that the EU's decision not to penalize French and German financial deficits constituted a discrepancy favouring the big and powerful; the article then criticized the anticipated detrimental effect of new (domestic) policies on pensioners and job-seekers, and concluded with a disillusioned reflection on the European parliament's regulations concerning lorry traffic across Austria: henceforth, it was predicted, lorries would be 'thundering across' the country without restrictions (http://wcw. krone.at 26 November 2003). Sport, social change, (pan-European) politics, and environmental concerns thus emerged as some of the discursive realms conducive to the continual (re-)production of national identities. In what follows, I discuss the now explicit articulation and reflexive negotiation of previously non-reflexive, 'cold' or 'banal' forms of national identity through an examination of the discursive treatment – in *Kronen Zeitung* and other press coverage – of sport, language and other symbols of the nation, a well as nature/landscape/the environment. This analysis therefore revisits several 'objects of national pride' (and the perceived effects of European policies and politics on them) identified in the earlier-quoted surveys conducted prior to the period of change and crises that has been unfolding since the mid-1980s. In theoretical terms, I argue that a continuing period of crises has transformed previously largely taken-for-granted assumptions, dispositions, categories, tastes, symbols and practices – in short, a more or less widely shared, national version of (the related phenomena of) *habitus* and *doxa* – into a universe of debate and competing discourses.

*Sport*

The 'intrusion' of sport into political discourse tends to involve what Billig (1995a, 11, 119–127) describes as the 'routine "deixis" … continually pointing to the national homeland' encountered in the media and beyond. The celebration of 'our' sporting heroes and achievements constitutes a powerful, though largely non-reflexive way of reproducing and naturalizing national boundaries, stereotypes and identities. Edensor summarizes its cultural pervasiveness as follows:

> Probably the most currently powerful form of popular national performance is that found in sports … Sport is increasingly situated in the mediatised matrix of national life, is institutionalised in schools, widely represented in a host of cultural forms and is an everyday practice for millions of national subjects. (Edensor 2002, 78)[6]

In an Austrian context, a sporting performance of lasting significance, and one already mentioned in the previous chapter, was provided by the national football team's 3:2 victory over Germany on 21 June 1978 during the World Cup in Argentina. A more recent manifestation of football serving as a discursive medium for the articulation of national identities was encountered after Austria and

---

6    While many such national performances in and through sport tend to occur beyond conscious reflection and hence on the level of *habitus*, Edensor adds that dominant representations and interpretations are certainly 'open to negotiation and contest'. This also echoes the Bourdieu-ian argument adopted here of the undiscussed and taken-for-granted (i.e. *doxa*) being subject to transformation into a heterogeneous 'universe of opinion'.

Switzerland had been announced as the co-hosts for the European Championship in 2008, edging out – among others – a joint application by Ireland and Scotland. A regular columnist in the *Kronen Zeitung* responded, in a comment entitled 'bad losers', to an article published in the Scottish *Daily Record*, which had lamented the decision favouring Austria and Switzerland. The resulting rebuff reproduced a range of national stereotypes contained in the precipitating Scottish article, while inverting their ideological evaluation. In the *Kronen Zeitung* response, the 'passion' of Austrian classical music and 'stylish' *Lederhosen* were juxtaposed to contrastingly connoted Scottish bag-pipes and kilts; the article concluded by responding to the *Daily Record*'s disparaging remark that no other nation had named a football stadium after a movie star (i.e. Arnold Schwarzenegger)[7]: 'why not', the columnist queried, followed by an intertextual 'hasta la vista, Scotland' (Pohl 2003). Although ostentatiously humorous, both articles provided but two of near daily (and global) instances of sport and discourses about sport being conducive to the articulation of self/other stereotypes as repertoires of national identity construction.

The lasting presence in popular memory of the events of June 1978 (and the general popularity of football) notwithstanding, it is hardly surprising that skiing provides the primary sporting realm of Austrian national imaginings. The country's geographical location, her history of skiing achievements, the significance of winter tourism to Austria's economy and international image, the general popularity of the sport, and practices such as institutionalized skiing trips for secondary school children all suggest that the 'embodied practices' of skiing form part of the national *habitus* and *doxa* – the 'unnamed' 'structuring structures' that inform (everyday) life and are (largely) accepted 'without argument or scrutiny'. As postulated in Bourdieu-ian theory, however, crises can transform the 'undiscussed' into an object of debate and controversy. Reiterer's earlier-mentioned survey of the mid-1980s inadvertently revealed such a transformation reflected in a then-pronounced version of 'down-hill nationalism': asked whether 'all possible efforts' should be made for Austria to regain her status as the dominant nation in winter sports, 43 per cent of respondents expressed their complete agreement, 35 per cent agreed in part, 19 per cent expressed scepticism, and three per cent did not comment. However, Reiterer's survey revealed considerable variation in responses to this question, the strongest support for 'down-hill nationalism' had been articulated by the rural population in the west and south-east of the country, among working class respondents, and among people aged 51 years and older (Reiterer 1988, 80–81). In our theoretical terms, this again suggests that 'universes of opinion' – here concerning Austrian skiers and brought about by a period of relative underperformance widely decoded as a form of national crisis – are internally contested and heterogeneous.

---

7    The stadium in question is located in Graz, Austria's second city, and is no longer named after Schwarzenegger who grew up in the north-western outskirts of the city.

General interest in Austrian skiers[8] continues to be very strong (see Langer 1996[9]) and is reflected in the broadcasting of nearly all races in any given season on the national television network and in (during the winter) near-daily newspaper articles in the tabloid papers and beyond. The country's most successful skiers are widely-recognized icons and media celebrities, none more so than Hermann Maier nicknamed – in another instance of intertextual reference to Schwarzenegger, the country's most famous recent 'export' – 'the Herminator'. When, following a motorcycle accident in which he had nearly lost a leg, Maier managed a highly unlikely comeback and celebrated his first post-accident victory in Kitzbühel in January 2003, enthusiasm for an apparent moment in 'skiing history' was articulated by the tabloid and broadsheet press alike. The reputable *Der Standard*, for example, declared that 'there can only be one' Herminator (http://derstandard. at 27 January 2003).

De Cillia et al. (1999, 165) point out that the linguistic means employed in the discursive construction of national 'sameness' and identity include the 'three tropes of metonymy, synecdoche, and personification'. These rhetorical strategies all point at a common phenomenon in discourse about sporting personalities and achievements: the 'sliding' between, or semantic conflation of, the individuals or groups described and the larger (national) entity they are constructed as the epitome of. Synecdochal projection, whereby the part comes to symbolize the whole, was typically articulated at the skiing world championship a week after Maier's unlikely triumph. The first race of the competition was won by Austrian skier Eberharter (with Maier and the American Miller sharing second place) and subsequently hailed as a 'dream start for Austria' (http://sport.orf.at 3 February 2003). The significance of skiing to widespread discourses of national belonging, and their articulation with 'the aid of' personal pronouns as a form of 'national deixis', again emerged the day after the end of the world championship, when the *Kronen Zeitung* (17 February 2003, 1) front-page displayed photographs of the nine Austrian medal winners in the competition and a caption declaring that 'we are particularly proud of them'. Returning to the perception and experience of crises, which take centre-stage in the following sections, another *Kronen Zeitung* front-page of a few months previously (*Kronen Zeitung* 15 December 2002, 1) is worth mentioning, as it highlights the wider context of conflict and perceived uncertainty mentioned earlier as well as the discursive co-existence (and mutual 'intrusion') of sport and politics. Referring to disagreements between Brussels and

---

8    While skiing takes centre-stage, media interest in Austrian achievements in other winter sports is also pronounced. Relevant illustrations during the main period of data collection for this chapter included coverage of the national ice-hockey team's largely unprecedented successes and keen interest in (Austrian) ski-jumping (e.g. Unverdorben 2003).

9    Based on research among Austrian students aged 17 to 19, Langer argues that even though the significance of 'the nation' to young people's social identities is declining, sport (and skiing in particular) has the continuing power to evoke collective/national emotions.

Vienna over (the safety of) a Czech nuclear power plant and the quota of lorries allowed to cross Austria,[10] the paper's headline declared that there was a 'deep divide between the EU and Austria', thus mis- portraying intra-EU disagreements as a clash of seemingly separate political entities; interestingly, this headline connoting political disappointment and pessimism was juxtaposed to a picture of three celebrating Austrian skiers who had come first, second, and third in a downhill race the day before.

*Language and (other) symbols of the nation*

As mentioned earlier, the delineation of the 'Austrian self' from the 'German other' formed a core aspect of the post-war project of national re-'imagining'/re-construction (e.g. Thaler 2001). The increasing acceptance of the discourse of Austrian particularism in the second half of the twentieth century came to be reflected and articulated in a range of cultural spheres including language. Although internally/regionally highly heterogeneous, Austrian German – with its distinctive intonation, pronunciation, idiomatic expressions and idiosyncratic vocabulary – provided a particularly germane mechanism of boundary maintenance between Austrians and their German(-speaking) neighbour(s). The salience of this boundary is documented in Wodak et al.'s discourse analytical revelation (1999, 192–193) that for their research participants 'an emphasis on differences between Austria and Germany … [satisfied] an emotional need within the realm of everyday culture' and that 'Austrian German was stressed in particular contexts … as an important criterion of difference'. My analysis of (*Kronen Zeitung* and other) press coverage shows that, more recently, a discourse pessimistic about the continuing viability of this criterion of difference has emerged. There are calls proclaiming an erosion of Austrian German as a significant identity marker and suggesting two underlying causes: the increasing inter-penetration of the Austrian and German media and a more general process of cultural standardization relatively widely associated with the European Union.

In September 2001, the *Kronen Zeitung* published an article warning that 'television German', by which it meant German spoken in the (linguistically more alien) northern regions of Germany and widely disseminated via satellite TV, was 'ruining our language'. Citing Austrian linguists' expert opinions, the article postulated that 'our children are losing the Austrian [language]' and hypothesized that the popularity of German TV series and soap operas among Austrian audiences bore a large part of the responsibility. However, the article went on to suggest that the forces of identity-eroding linguistic change were varied and complex: a 'further danger', the author postulated, was posed by the adoption of English words leading particularly children to 'mix different languages, such as German, English, Austrian and Viennese [*sic*]' (Pommer 2001). Another *Kronen Zeitung* article – critical of

10    Known as the 'Transitstreit', this intra-EU conflict will re-appear in subsequent sections.

the adoption of 'German-German' on restaurant menus and in colloquial language – reported the stirrings of linguistic resistance, a self-conscious revival of Austrian German in opposition to linguistic homogenization (Schrems 2002). This counter-discourse of linguistic re-assertion received additional support from the *Kronen Zeitung*'s then arguably most eminent columnist – the late Günther Nenning,[11] previous (SPÖ and subsequently Green) politician, intellectual and journalist. In August 2002, Nenning argued that dialect constituted Austrians' actual mother tongue and that official- or dictionary-German was no more than a secondary and artificial medium of communication (Nenning 2002a). Nenning subsequently wrote of an unfolding 'war of liberation' against linguistic standardization, citing a publication that listed nearly a thousand peculiarly Austrian words unknown in standard German (Nenning 2003a).

The most controversial recent case in linguistic identity contestation, widely interpreted as a necessary response to the forces of cultural homogenization within the European Union and hence deflected onto Brussels, unfolded around the labelling of jam jars in the autumn of 2003. The controversy, in which the *Kronen Zeitung* and several Austrian politicians were particularly vocal, constituted a clear example of what can be analyzed – in Bourdieu-ian fashion – as (previously) taken-for-granted and undiscussed 'linguistic *doxa*' becoming the object of debate and politicized discourse. The precipitating 'crisis' was brought about by the introduction of (EU-wide) standardized labels on jam jars. In Austrian German, both jam and marmalade are denoted as *Marmelade* – in contrast to the (German-) German term *Konfitüre*. Henceforth, only citrus-fruit based marmalade would be designated as *Marmelade* on the corresponding jars sold in Austria, with other jams being labelled *Konfitüre*. Eight years previously, Austria's treaty of EU accession secured the 'protection' of 23 food-related 'Austriacisms' that somewhat arbitrarily excluded the term *Marmelade*. While parts of the media acknowledged that more extensive negotiations in 1994–1995 would have enabled Austria to join Greece and Denmark as 'jam exceptions' within the EU (e.g. Tanzer 2003), the dominant discourse postulated that resistance against the external encroachment by the forces of European 'sameness' was needed. This was epitomized in a reader's letter to the *Kronen Zeitung* editor (23 October 2003, 34) inspired by the paper's *Marmelade*-campaign, which declared it necessary and 'inspiring to defend one's dialect and mother tongue' as a 'part of culture'. Not dissimilarly, a comment published in *Der Standard* called for 'hands to be taken off *Marmelade*' and to put a stop to 'EU linguistic impositions' (Hintze 2003). Austrian campaigning bore fruit (pun intended) when in March 2004 the EU commission passed a further

---

11    Summarizing Nenning's various ideological incarnations (informed by socialism, environmentalism, 'a version of Catholicism', and self-critical patriotism), Reiterer (1996, 318–319) describes Nenning as an intellectual who 'has understood that the nation constitutes a[n ongoing] political project … and has attempted to provide it with [discursive/political/ethical] content'.

resolution re-allowing jam jars to be labelled *Marmelade* on the Austrian market (www.diepresse.at 6 March 2004).

Other recent crises resulting in the transformation of parts of a previously undiscussed 'universe of doxa' into a 'universe of argument' have involved key figures of Austria's cultural and 'historical legacy' (i.e. another 'object of national pride' discussed earlier), the local effects of economic globalization and the power of multinational companies.

In the summer of 2003, the German broadcasting network ZDF and the German newspaper *Bild* conducted surveys on the 'greatest historical Germans'. Using the various and frequently shifting political boundaries since the Middle Ages as defining (and flexible) criteria of German identity (http://derstandard. at 8 August 2003), the individuals suggested in the surveys also included some of the historical personalities many contemporary Austrians take greatest pride in and, unambiguously, consider to be one of 'their own', including Wolfgang Amadeus Mozart, Joseph Haydn, and Sigmund Freud. Perhaps not surprisingly, their inclusion on ostentatiously German lists triggered controversy and outcry in the Austrian media (e.g. Kopt 2003). A *Die Presse* article thus implied that the surveys in question had taken significant parts of Austrian national pride hostage: 'We all know', the article conceded, 'that Austria is not a big country – but only few seem to know that Austria has produced great historical figures' (www. diepresse.at 8 August 2003). It did not take long for the weekly *News* magazine to respond by conducting its own survey on 'Austria's greatest', which was soon 'led' by Mozart ahead of the country's former Chancellor Bruno Kreisky; not only were Freud, Egon Schiele, the late rock star Falco, the earlier-mentioned icons Schwarzenegger, Krankl and Maier competing for a place on the 'podium', but – interestingly – German-born composer (and later resident of Vienna) Ludwig van Beethoven was also receiving large numbers of votes (*News* 2003).

Edensor argues (2002, 103–137) that certain commodities, industries (particularly 'national car cultures') and other aspects of material culture constitute repertoires of national identity construction heavily invested with symbolic, emotional and economic significance. The closure of the tyre production factory *Semperit* in the Lower Austrian town of Traiskirchen in July 2002, decided upon by its multinational owners, confirmed the ideological salience of some such commodities and industries and – again in Bourdieu-ian fashion – the consciousness-raising effects of crises. The closure would cause, according to the mayor of Traiskirchen, the loss of some 2,300 local jobs; moreover, previous re-location plans by the factory's multinational owner in 1996 had been averted by the intervention of Austria's then government; it was only in the changed political climate and due to the 'inactivity' of the then ÖVP-FPÖ coalition, the mayor argued in a letter to the *Kronen Zeitung* (19 July 2002, 22), that the closure had been allowed to happen. Aside from the economic implications of, and political controversy surrounding, the factory closure, a recurring account in the emerging 'universe of discourse' spoke of a direct affront by the forces of globalization on a symbol of Austrian national identity: The front-page of the regional daily *Kleine*

*Zeitung* (20 July 2002, 1), for example, showed the picture of two factory workers carrying the last tyre – the words 'the last real Semperit tyre' written on it – coming off the Traiskirchen production line; the previous day, the *Kronen Zeitung* (19 July 2002, 23) had published a full-page obituary to 'the Semperit tyre', praising its quality over a proud 102-year history, thanking its Austrian customers, and blaming the factory closure (or symbolic death) on the 'capitalist arbitrariness of a multinational company'.

## The environment and natural/national resources

The earlier-mentioned surveys revealing Austria's 'scenic beauty' as a celebrated 'object of national pride' should also be understood in the context of the historical rise of citizenship initiatives, environmental politics and the Green movement. The widespread appeal and resonance of the anti-nuclear movement emerged in a referendum in November 1978, when 50.47 per cent of voters stopped an already-constructed nuclear power station in Zwentendorf, in Lower Austria, from coming into use (e.g. Portisch 1996, 412–429). The salience of environmental concerns was once again demonstrated in December 1984, when a crowd of demonstrators prevented the deforestation of the *Hainburger Au* – the dense woodlands along the Danube east of Vienna; what was then intended to become the site of a power station has meanwhile been granted nature reserve status. The period of the early- to mid 1980s coincided with the evolution of the Greens from a social movement into a political party with increasingly widespread mobilizing power and electoral appeal. More than twenty years on, environmental concerns have further intensified. Significantly, a widely circulating discourse conceptualizes issues related to environmental degradation and sustainability as global concerns requiring transnational dialogue, co-operation and solutions: For example, prior to the 2004 European elections Austria's Green party emphasized that environmental threats required pan-European/international responses (www.orf.at 14 May 2004). However, an alternative narrative in public debate frames environmental crises as national issues – as the depletion of national resources, as threats to 'our' population, health and future generations.

Yet, corroborating discourse analytical insights, individual social actors can manoeuvre in and out of different 'interpretative repertoires' (Wetherell and Potter 1992) in a context-sensitive manner (also see chapter six). Such discursive 'switching' was demonstrated by the earlier-mentioned *Kronen Zeitung* columnist Günther Nenning, whose credentials as an environmentalist are undeniable. After nearly four decades in the party, Nenning was expelled from the SPÖ because of his leading role in the above-mentioned demonstrations in the *Hainburger Au* in 1984 and became a founding member of the Green party (Nenning 2002b); further disillusionment with party politics precipitated Nenning's switch into journalism; having acquired a prominent voice in the media, Nenning continued his dedication to environmental causes, albeit in terms that not infrequently crossed the boundaries separating global/pan-European- and national/Austrian discourses of environmentalism.[12] August 2002 saw a series of disastrous floods in Germany, the Czech Republic and northern parts of Austria. As an environmental and – to hundreds of thousands affected citizens – personal crisis of hitherto unknown proportions, the floods led to considerable public soul-searching concerning the causes and effects of climate change as well as political responsibility in a period of collective suffering and tragedy. Four days after the *Kronen Zeitung* (14 August 2002, 1) had called on the government to direct much-needed finances to the aid of flood-victims instead of investing in controversial new military jets, Nenning's column offered a decidedly transnational/global interpretation of the floods, and of human responsibility for environmental change. Anticipating further 'man-made climatic and environmental catastrophes', Nenning stressed that 'we are all part of a Europe' dedicated to economic growth and hedonistic consumerism; as such, he argued, the floods had been a timely reminder of the need for self-reflection and a new, inclusive environmental consciousness (Nenning 2002c). In later columns, Nenning articulated similarly pan-European or global critiques directed at, for example, the widening socio-economic gap between the rich and poor and continuing environmental degradation in times of globalization (Nenning 2002d), as well as the allegedly global lack of political interest in environmental concerns; significantly, the latter criticism was not only directed at the global dominance of neo-liberal politics but also at Nenning's former party colleagues among Austria's Greens (Nenning 2003b).

There have, however, also been controversies widely interpreted – by Nenning and others – as involving environmental hazards and injustices imposed on Austria by 'outsiders'. One of these revolved around the planned privatization, and hence likely future ownership by 'foreign companies', of some of the country's hydroelectric power stations. *Kronen Zeitung* coverage portrayed the plans to privatize a power plant in the Alps as a threat to local jobs and, significantly, as the dispossession of 'our' (i.e. national) water facilitated by EU policies aimed at turning water into a commodity for the international market (Salzmann 2003). This was followed by one of Nenning's columns tellingly entitled 'Our water' and framed in a discourse of nation-centred environmental consciousness. It was shameful, he suggested, that property rights over Austrian water might be sold to international companies; accusing the latter of trying to 'cash in' on water shortages in parts of the world less fortunate than Austria, he argued that 'our water, our greatest treasure, is under greater threat than ever before. The *Kronen Zeitung* … along with all conscientious Austrians, will fight with all means necessary for our water' (Nenning 2003c).

---

12 If interpreted as examples of 'thinking globally, acting locally', there may be no contradiction between these discourses. However, their analytical separation serves the purpose of drawing attention to the tendency to define natural resources – such as air, water and food – as collectively owned national 'possessions'.

Two other controversies similarly centred on changes and decisions widely understood as entailing environmental crises, through which previously largely undiscussed natural assets – such as water, food and air – were transformed into national objects to be defended against perceived external threats. The first of these crises was triggered by the European Commission's decision to block Austrian intentions to install agricultural 'zones' free of genetically modified fruits and vegetables. Less than two years after a survey revealed that the term 'genetic engineering' triggered (along with 'nuclear energy') the most negative connotations among a representatively chosen sample of Austrians (Gnam 2002), a *Kronen Zeitung* article postulated that the decision made by 'bureaucrats in Brussels' was difficult to understand and meant that '"contaminated" food would end up on our plates' (Budin 2003). The second controversy was similarly complex and long-standing; given constraints of space, it can here only be summarized; the controversy in question was the already-mentioned *Transitstreit* – a dispute between Vienna and Brussels over the quota of lorries permitted to cross Austria en route within the European Union.

Concerns in the early to mid-1990s that Austria's EU accession in 1995 would lead to a drastic increase in the number (and environmental impact) of lorries crossing the country were temporarily assuaged through an interim agreement. Designed to control the number and types of lorries allowed to drive through Austria per year, this agreement expired on 31 December 2003. Already a year earlier, however, environmental and health concerns were firmly back on the agenda. Reporting that carbon dioxide emissions had increased by 42 per cent over a ten-year period (in contrast to a 19 per cent increase in the EU overall), a *Kronen Zeitung* article declared that 'Eastern European lorries are poisoning the air' and that the then imminent EU enlargement would cause a further 'explosion' in lorry traffic (Schönauer 2003). Several months on, Günther Nenning entered into the debate in terms that sought to redress the balance between a European consciousness and the articulation of a discourse focussed on, and critical of, damage to the Austrian environment in particular. While 'we, the peoples of Europe', Nenning declared, would like to be fully participating Europeans, 'we' keep being confronted by 'bureaucracy and brutal capitalism' emanating from Brussels; he argued that an uncompromising 'freedom of traffic' resulting in an anticipated 'avalanche of lorries' sweeping across Austria as of January 2004 was tantamount to a human-rights violation; echoing a then widely debated possible strategy, Nenning concluded that road blocks would become justified and necessary (Nenning 2003d).

When, in late 2003, EU ministers and the European parliament voted against Austrian objections for a new agreement concerning lorry traffic crossing the country, reactions in and beyond the Alpine Republic differed sharply. Considered to be an exceptional concession to Austrian demands by some EU politicians, the new agreement was portrayed as a 'declaration of ecological bankruptcy' by Austria's Transport Minister and sections of the national media (http://derstandard. at 26 November 2003). According to the new regulations, only the oldest models of lorries would be prohibited from travelling across Austria, while the number of 'intermediate' types would continue to be limited and the most commonly used and environmentally least 'unfriendly' lorries would have unrestricted access to Austrian roads (http://derstandard.at 19 December 2003). In an instance of the earlier mentioned phenomenon of 'rhetorical pointing' or national *deixis*, the *Kronen Zeitung* responded by setting out 'what *we* can do against the lorry avalanche': echoing some politicians' suggestions, the article argued that the case should be taken to the European Court of Justice and that rigorous 'lorry controls' on Austrian roads constituted possible tactics of national resistance against the 'encroachment' and environmental impact of European traffic (http://wcm.krone. at 27 November 2003). The dispute between Brussels and Vienna soon escalated when the Austrian government announced that it would not implement the new, costly and – in its eyes – ineffective regulations; the EU commission, on the other hand, still considered the compromise to be a concession to Austrian environmental demands and in turn threatened, if it was not implemented, to take Austria to the European Court of Justice (http://derstandard.at 6 January 2004).

This lengthy *Transitstreit* constituted an example of struggles over power, in this case fought on a pan-European level, transforming parts of a previously taken-for-granted national *doxa* – or universe of undiscussed cultural commonsense – into a discursive battleground of competing positions. Austria's self-image of an 'environmentally friendly' and 'health-conscious' nation taking great pride in its 'scenic beauty' has had to be called into question, in light of worrying environmental statistics, over recent years. In 2004 environmental reports had already confirmed the earlier-mentioned increase in carbon dioxide emissions between 1990 and 2002; while the *Kronen Zeitung* offered a firmly nation-centred account of this drastic rise in air pollution, declaring that 'our air keeps getting dirtier' (http://wcm.krone.at 9 July 2004), the European Court of Justice criticized Austria for failing to adhere to the relevant EU-wide guidelines (http://www.orf.at 9 July 2004). Whether looked at from a national perspective or in a wider European context, recent environmentalist debates are also indicative of ideological struggles over the structures of power and decision-making that have changed enormously since Austria's EU accession in 1995. 'The environment' has thus become another symbol of national self-definition and identification many perceive to be under threat in times of globalization and its concomitant, far-reaching changes. The argument presented here has been premised on a Bourdieu-ian reading of contemporary Austria as shaped by the transformation of a previously 'undiscussed' national *doxa* into a 'universe of opinions' triggered by the experience of crises. I have already drawn attention to the struggle between competing positions in the emerging universe of discourse. It is this ideological heterogeneity, itself a challenge to unduly monolithic accounts of contemporary Austria, that I turn to – albeit relatively briefly – in the next section.

**Discursive diversity**

Nationalism is, of course, far from uncontested in contemporary Austria. This was perhaps most powerfully demonstrated by the Viennese protests, mentioned in the previous chapter, in the months following the FPÖ's inclusion in a coalition government in 2000. It is also evidenced by the fact that the main political parties – SPÖ, ÖVP, FPÖ, Greens and BZÖ – position themselves on very different points along the ideological spectrum and embody competing definitions of national identity as well as a heterogeneous range of political stances in relation to globalization, the European Union, the future of the welfare state, neutrality, and a long list of other highly pertinent issues. Moreover, and as mentioned earlier, outright ideological opposition to nationalism (see Charim and Rabinovici 2000) as well as a (self-) critical engagement with Austrian (World War II and post-war) history have been powerfully articulated in a wide range cultural spheres including art, popular music, and most famously the literature of Thomas Bernhard, Elfriede Jelinek, Peter Turrini and others (e.g. see Lamb-Faffelberger 1992; Lichtmann 1993; Fliedl 1998; Turrini 2001). And as shown particularly in chapter five, there is now also a prominent and outspoken counter-hegemonic press, including quality dailies, regional papers as much as street magazines, and a now vibrant civil society that reflect the ideological heterogeneity – and contested nature – of the 'universe of discourse' in contemporary Austria. However, returning to the transformation of 'cold' national identities into politicized discourse in times of crisis as the focus of this chapter, analytical rigour demands an analogous demonstration of a *diversity of opinions* surrounding the particular controversies discussed above. At closer inspection there is indeed strong evidence that reactions to national sporting performances, to debates about linguistic/cultural identities and to environmental concerns reflect – even in the more narrowly delineated discursive field of the national print media – a diversity of (competing) accounts, which make reifying descriptions of 'Austrian society', as gripped in its entirety by a nationalist revival, impossible to sustain. Given constraints of space, I restrict myself in the remainder of this chapter to specific examples illustrative of more widely circulating discursive alternatives to the data analyzed above.

As mentioned earlier, the link between sporting achievements and 'national pride' was as early as 1988 demonstrated to vary significantly by age, class and region. Bearing in mind the sociological axioms that identities are negotiable and discourses contestable, it should come as little surprise to discover opposition to the 'politicized opinions' concerning the widely proclaimed threats to Austrian German, to historical symbols of the nation, and to her natural resources examined above. A counter-hegemonic take on the alleged erosion of linguistic identity bemoaned in the *Kronen Zeitung* and beyond was articulated in a commentary published in *Die Presse*, which argued that the 'jam controversy' was a negligible issue compared to the omnipresence of German-German in the media and the increasingly common adoption of English terminology: while concern for Austria's linguistic identity, the author thus conceded, was justified, a focus on the labels displayed on jam jars overlooked far more powerful agents of linguistic change and was expressive of little more than a 'linguistic inferiority complex' (Male 2003). Subsequently, linguistic self-assertion also began to unfold around a 'spelling reform' jointly adopted by Germany and Austria. Years after school curricula and textbooks had been brought in line with the new spellings, the *Kronen Zeitung* opposed what it portrayed as another instance of identity-eroding bureaucratic imposition, claiming that between 62 and 85 per cent of Austrians favoured the old spellings (Kindermann 2004). Nenning followed suit, arguing that many Germans sympathized with the growing movement of Austrian linguistic particularism (Nenning 2004b). However, calls for a(n Austrian) return to the old spellings were firmly opposed by, amongst others, then Chancellor Wolfgang Schüssel and his Education Minister. Writing in *News*, the weekly magazine that had first published survey findings suggesting that 62 per cent of Austrian opposed the spelling reforms, journalist Peter Pelinka (2004) described resistance to the new spellings as potentially costly and an 'absurd' distraction from more important issues. Competing discourses surrounding linguistic self-assertion were given another twist with the publication of a 'linguistic manifesto' signed by five Austrian writers and a linguist. Unlike many of the opinions expressed in the context of the 'jam controversy', the manifesto portrayed EU legislation as potentially conducive to the maintenance and institutional strengthening of Austrian linguistic particularism in opposition to 'German German'; the demands articulated in the manifesto included the 'development of Austrian and European linguistic consciousness', the long-term aim of creating a written version of Austrian that would reflect its spoken particularities, the constitutional re-definition of Austria's official language as – instead of German – 'Austrian in a European context' *or* 'Austrian German' *or* 'German and Austrian'; finally, the manifesto declared, the government should strive for the recognition of Austrian as an 'independent EU-language' (http://www.orf.at 13 August 2004).

Outcry over Mozart's inclusion in the above-mentioned list of 'great historical Germans' did not go uncontested either. A *Die Presse* article quoted historian Brigitte Hamann's verdict of the entire debate as 'anachronistic nonsense'; reflecting on her own biography (Hamann was born and trained in Germany but has been resident in Vienna for 35 years), she pointed out that all social identities are contingent and multi-dimensional; unlike most of the earlier-quoted headlines, this *Die Presse* article thus gave space to an alternative discourse critical of reified national identities that ignore the complexities of social life and the ongoing negotiations of all identifications (http://www.diepresse.at/default.asp?channel= k&ressort=k&id=370338). This also (inadvertently) echoed Busek's scepticism (2001, 20), given the multiple forces shaping all biographies, concerning nationalist attempts to claim or unambiguously 'position' Mozart or anyone else. Cultural theorist Wolfgang Zinggl (2002) has similarly challenged the nationalist postulate of a cultural or genetic continuity between celebrated historical figures, artistic treasures and scientific achievements of the past on one hand, and the contemporary 'national community' on the other.

At the height of the *Transitstreit*, *Der Standard* again provided space for a – on a national level – counter-hegemonic discourse, which shifted much blame for the environmental impact of lorries travelling across Austria away from Brussels and onto the domestic economy:

> Only slightly more than ten per cent of lorries on our roads are foreign. Austrian lorries are, on average, older and hence less environmentally friendly. Austria relies on it exports, which in turn adds to other country's lorry traffic. And Austria is one of the main beneficiaries of EU enlargement, which will cause a further increase in traffic. (Spudich 2004, my translation)

Lest it be objected that commentaries published in the country's broadsheet press constitute predictable channels for the articulation of critical opinions and that, in general, ideas can with relative statistical reliability be ascribed to ideologically fixed social actors, mention must again be made of the discourse analytical counter-argument: recurring themes, interpretations and persisting political preferences notwithstanding, social actors inhabit – in Austria as elsewhere – internally contested and ideologically heterogeneous discursive fields and may draw on different interpretative repertoires in a context-sensitive fashion. Some historical fluidity has also been exhibited by the *Kronen Zeitung*. Its former affinity with Haider's opposition to the effects of globalization and the old system of power sharing between SPÖ and ÖVP (Morrow 2000, 50–52) subsequently gave way to its apparent self-definition as a political agent in its own right, which – for example – took a leading role in the Austrian protests against the nuclear power station in the Czech town of Temelin (Ulram and Tributsch 2004, 119–120) or in the protests against the EU's Lisbon reform treaty to be discussed in the next chapter. In addition to Nenning's switches between global and nation-centred discourses of environmentalism discussed above, the *Kronen Zeitung* has also engaged in some well-known political u-turns, reflected in its increasingly hostile attitude towards EU-membership since the mid-1990s for example, and has withdrawn its support for previously favoured politicians (see Thurnher 2010). Moreover, despite its generally hostile attitude towards the European Union (more and more recent evidence of which is analyzed in chapter three), there have even been occasional acknowledgements in the *Kronen Zeitung* (e.g. 7 December 2002, 4) of some of the benefits of EU enlargement to the Austrian economy.

This discussion has shown that crises can indeed disrupt the previously commonsensical or *doxic* terrain of a national habitus. Moreover, analysis of Austrian materials has revealed – and thus corroborated Boudieu-ian theory – that crises-induced reflexivity has resulted not in ideological agreement but in internally contested fields of competing political positions. Analogous transformations and resulting diversities can be detected in several other European countries and, particularly, in their World War II memory politics.

## Contested histories in France, Switzerland and Germany

We have seen that the national *habitus* includes dominant interpretations of key historical episodes, the shared interpretative frameworks that 'nationally conscious individuals use to organize ... history' (Snyder 2002, 39). The importance of such shared 'frames' to national identity politics notwithstanding, Bell's concept of the 'mythscape' emphasizes the co-existence of competing historical narratives:

> The governing myth of the nation – of a fundamentally decent and moderate Britain, an eternal and heroic France – is contested continually, and it usually gains ascendancy at the expense of other dissident voices. Such narratives ... should be seen in the context of relations of power and logics of dominance. There is no singular, irreducible national narrative ... [T]here always exist counter claims and alternative readings ... The governing myth [is] thus ... contested by subaltern myths.' (Bell 2003, 73–74)

In the Austrian context then, a particular controversy unsettled doxic assumptions about the national past and brought previously largely taken-for-granted narratives to the forefront of public consciousness and disagreement. Historical scholarship documents comparable processes resulting in the interrogation of previously dominant conceptions of national history, as part of the respective national *habitus*, in several other European countries. Also, many of these discussions have gathered pace since the mid-1980s. Not surprisingly, their focus has been on the key episode in twentieth-century (European) history: World War II and the Holocaust.

In his analysis of the 'legacy of World War II' in France, Richard Golsan (2006, 85) builds on previous scholarship to distinguish between three successive phases of French responses to the trauma of the Nazi occupation and the Vichy regime: 'myth-building, amnesia and deheroization'. The first was closely associated with the immediate post-war era and De Gaulle's two periods of leadership, who promoted 'the myth of a quasi-universal and undivided resistance' – though one primarily attributed to the (during the war exiled) Free French Forces rather than the 'internal', leftist resistance. Ultimately however, in a step towards 'national recovery' and inclusiveness, De Gaulle promoted a 'collective vision of the French struggle for liberation, pass[ed] over ... the role of Vichy and ... the allies, and nationaliz[ed] the contribution of the resistance movement' (Lagrou quoted in Golsan 2006, 79). Whilst the strikes and student revolts of 1968 began to cast doubt on this national mythology of universal resistance against Nazism, the subsequent presidencies of Pompidou and Giscard d'Estaing 'fostered a ... forgetfulness or "quietism" that sought ... to put the past behind' or 'defuse' it (Golson 2006, 81). This period of relative amnesia in the 1970s gave way to a further paradigm shift in dominant French narratives of World War II. Much of this is closely tied to François Mitterrand. After Mitterand had in the early 1980s 'revitalize[d] the legacy of resistance', subsequent developments cast a different light on his own and the collective past: having controversially 'disavowed any responsibility on the part of Republican France for Vichy, its anti-Semitism and ... participation in the Final Solution', the extent of Mitterrand's rightwing activism and 'service to Vichy' – prior to his later role in the resistance – were revealed in a 1994 biography that triggered heated debate and intense national soul-searching (Golson 2006, 84). Whilst particular moments and controversies thus also disrupted previously firmly entrenched historical narratives in the French context, Golson shows that literature and film acted – by problematizing the myth of universal resistance or thematizing French anti-Semitism – as critical counter-weights within each of the three successive eras in France's politics of the past. Moreover, and in further inadvertent corroboration of Bourdieu's notion of crises creating internally divided discursive fields, Golson (2006, 98–99) summarizes the post-Mitterrand period as follows:

> Jacques Chirac publicly acknowledged the role of the Vichy regime in backing up the 'criminal insanity' of the Nazis ... and spoke of a 'collective sin' on the part of his countrymen ... Chirac's statement marked a sharp break with the attitudes of his predecessors ... and [was] greeted with satisfaction by the great majority of the public ... [I]t is possible to argue that by the late 1990s the haunting memory of Vichy was ... being put to rest. But this is perhaps too optimistic ... In ... 2002 Jean-Marie Le Pen's ... first-round victory in French presidential elections demonstrated ... that xenophobia and racism are very much alive ... [T]he denial of the Holocaust is still a ... rallying cry for many on France's extreme right.

Such polarized historical attitudes corroborate the 'nation as a contested terrain', on which 'groups with competing memories struggle to generalize their ideal conceptions of society' (Levy and Dierkes 2002, 244). Moreover, similar moments of historical reflexivity transforming previously firmly embedded discourses of a nation's history and identity have been documented in other parts of Europe.

Regula Ludi (2006), for example, reports a Swiss crisis and subsequent diversification of national memory since 1989. The first major trigger was provided by the end of the Cold War, depriving staunchly anti-communist Switzerland of its main ideological 'other'. Even more significant, however, was the 'Holocaust-era asset scandal' in the wake of Jewish restitution claims against Swiss banks since the mid-1990s. Switzerland's previously dominant 'myth' of wartime resistance and humanitarianism had to be critically re-examined in light of the realization that neutrality had not prevented a series of 'entanglements' – mainly economic, through the infamous 'gold transactions' by the Swiss national bank, but also ideological – with Nazism:

> The findings of the international historian commission, appointed in 1996 to examine the history of the Nazi-era past, shattered the remaining foundations of popular assumptions. Its reports on gold transactions and refugees ... showed that all agents – officials as well as the business community – were well aware

of the consequences of their actions and much better informed about Nazi atrocities than they had made believe. The commission ... [concluded] that the Swiss authorities, with their restrictive asylum policy that discriminated against Jewish refugees, had helped the Nazi regime achieve its genocidal goals. (Ludi 2006, 237).

The outcome of the Swiss 'memory crisis', Ludi observes (2006, 238), was a polarized public pitting 'nationalist reflexes', on one hand, against growing numbers of people willing to critically re-think 'morally inflated' ideas of (wartime) neutrality, on the other.

Crucial to any discussion of World War II and Holocaust remembrance, the case of (West) Germany provides further evidence of periodical shifts in dominant understandings of national history and of internally contested 'mythscapes'. The dominant mood of the 1950s has been described as a 'communicative silence' accompanied by 'lamentations of German victimhood' (Kansteiner 2006, 108), although the same period also saw the first acknowledgements of German guilt by parts of the political elite, particularly the Federal Republic's president Theodor Heuss (Herf 2002, 190–192). Starting in the 1960s, and with the aid of West Germany's critical media, a younger cohort of historians, the coming-of-age of the first post-war generation, and some well-known literary works, a more honest and self-critical 'memory culture' began to take hold; West German *Vergangenheitsbewältigung*, attempts to confront the Holocaust and 'contain its legacy', reached their 'most active phase ... both in terms of intensity and social depth' in the 1980s (Kansteiner 2006, 124). The same decade, however, also witnessed the much-discussed 'historians' dispute': a clash between conservative and left-liberal historians – with the former alleging similarities between Nazism and communism and the latter stressing the 'singularity of the Holocaust' (Berger 2006, 212) –, which resulted in a 'fragile consensus' about the 'profound ramifications' of the Holocaust for 'German identity and politics' (Beattie 2006, 153). The next watershed in German memory politics occurred in the 1990s following re-unification. The 'Kohl-era' witnessed a sometimes problematic resurrection of the 'topos of German victimhood for building a post-unification national identity', initially by parts of the political spectrum[13] and subsequently also in sections of the media and cultural production (Niven 2006, 5–8). Crucially, and lest this rough schematization be misinterpreted in absolutist term, Ruth Wittlinger (2006, 73) reminds us that 'collective memory is not homogenous' and that 'different memory discourses' can and do co-exist. For example, (West) Germany's hugely important official and public commitments to *Vergangenheitsbewältigung* were not necessarily matched by private counter-memories:

---

13　Disconcerting political instrumentalization of this topos needs to be distinguished, of course, from a simultaneous increase in serious historical scholarship on 'ethnic cleansing of Germans' and the bombing war (see Berger 2006, 218).

> [R]ecent research has shown that German victimhood by far outweighs
> German culpability in German family memory. A study … into the way
> historical consciousness is passed on to the next two generations suggests that
> the 'victimisation discourse' has always been very prevalent … even outside
> … specific victim groups such as the expellees and the prisoners of war …
> [T]here is a dominant perception … that relatives were not Nazis … [T]here
> is a vast discrepancy between the official commemoration culture and private
> remembering. (Wittlinger 2006, 74)

The cases of Austria, France, Switzerland and Germany confirm that different
European memory politics, and their previously *doxic* assumptions, transformed
significantly – due to generational changes and in response to moments of
introspection and contextual factors – between the 1960s, the 1980s and since (see
Fogu and Kansteiner 2006). This discussion has also shown, however, that the
resulting fields of historical reflexivity and memory politics have been internally
heterogeneous and contested. Indeed, the eventual 'revenge of history … remains
partial' (Judt 2002, 169).

## Personal crises, individual politics

What, then, propels different individuals towards different positions in the
ideologically diverse fields that surround them? This is a complex question
that can only be raised for now, through Mann and Fenton's research into the
biographically specific experiences informing personal 'articulations of national
identity' (2009, 518). Importantly, they also confirm the relevance of Bourdieu's
sociology, particularly of the experiences of *personal* crises.

Attachments to nationalist or pluralist visions of society cannot, Mann and
Fenton demonstrate, simply be reduced to collectively shared structural positions.
Based on four detailed biographical case studies of individuals' responses to
social change in the British city of Bristol, they reveal more complex 'lives within
milieus' where class intersects with 'different personal circumstances' and life-
stories. The starting point to their discussion is the interpretation of 'racist neo-
nationalism' as 'grounded in the anger and social resentments of petit bourgeois …
and working-class populations who see their livelihoods and once-protected social
institutions being threatened' (Mann and Fenton 2009, 530). Shared dispositions
and expectations that partly constitute a (class) *habitus* provide individuals with
a sense of entitlement, an interpretative grid and anticipations of what life *should*
entail. However, and to state the obvious, lived realities are affected by structural
changes and biographical contingencies. Hence, culturally shared expectations
and lived experience diverge for many individuals and across class divides:

> As Bourdieu … argue[s], one cannot understand one's position in the macro
> social order without reference to the directly experienced effects of social

interaction within different social microcosms ... [E]xpressions of national belonging, particularly emotional or resentful expressions, need to be understood not simply in terms of objective social differences but with reference to more nuanced ... personal dimensions ... [N]arratives of personal experience (such as frustration, satisfaction etc.) will be influenced by a socially embedded "habitus" of expectations, self-understandings and values which are themselves shaped by ... class position. Consequently, personal unease and resentment emerging from unfulfilled expectations and status frustrations can be found amongst both middle-class and working-class segments. (Mann and Fenton 2009, 520)

What matters, then, is the relative fit or discrepancy between inherited expectations and biographically specific 'micro-experiences'. Mann and Fenton's case studies illustrate this in revealing a set of person- (rather than class-) specific emotional responses – such as resentment and anxiety or optimism and contentment respectively – tied to contrasting experiences of frustration or social mobility. Individuals' very different notions of identity and belonging, described as a contrast between 'resentful nationalism' and 'indifferent cosmopolitanism', are thus related to 'differences [in] the sense of autonomy and control over key personal decisions and over one's social situation, against a sense of having been affected ... [by] disappointments' that are interpreted as signs of social decline (Mann and Fenton 2009, 522, 529).

Chapter six of this book explores similar issues in more detail and, in doing so, asks whether in fact individuals' ideological leanings are themselves consistent or potentially more ambivalent and contradictory. For now, however, Mann and Fenton's work makes several crucial contributions. First, it emphasizes the significance of local and biographical contexts for an understanding of identity negotiations. Second, it corroborates the relevance of Bourdieu-ian insights into crises and the *habitus* in collective and individual contexts. Third, and in anticipation of a key theme explored in chapter three, they capture discourses of perceived 'social decline'.

## Concluding remarks

Contemporary nationalism constitutes a form of resistance (e.g. Castells 1997) against the consequences of globalization: the dominance of multinational capital resulting in the partial erosion of the (territorial) monopoly of power previously exercised by the modern nation-state; the hegemony and consequences of neo-liberalism and increasingly individualized (and risk-prone) life-courses (e.g. Beck 1992; 2000; Bauman 1998). The recent rise of the populist right in several European countries can thus be partly attributed to its ability to speak to many among the victims of globalization or those fearing future marginalization (e.g. Hainsworth 2000; Morrow 2000; Camus 2002). Exclusion or the mere anticipation thereof, existential anxiety brought about by far-reaching structural changes – in short, a sense of perceived or imminent crisis – lie at the heart of the nation-centred revival currently witnessed in many parts of the world. If nationalism is thus partly seen as an ideological antidote promising community (and hence exclusion), order, and meaning in response to the (socio-economic) uncertainties accompanying globalization, this analysis has highlighted a further dimension to the experience and articulation of national(ist) discourse in contemporary Austria as a part of the world frequently associated with such populism: based on an analysis of (tabloid- and other) media coverage, I have argued that many debates about 'the nation in crisis' unfold in areas related to previously 'banal' or everyday national identities, including the discursive realms pertaining to history, sport, language and national symbols, nature and the environment. Bourdieu's model of crises transforming a previously non-reflexive national *habitus* and *doxa* (i.e. the cultural universe of 'the undiscussed') into discourses articulated for the purposes of identity politics provides a framework, through which to view contemporary Austria. Whilst the main building blocks of a national *habitus* were extrapolated from surveys conducted in the early 1980s, I argued that a period of successive crises since the mid-80s has transformed previously largely taken-for-granted national identities into objects of reflection and dispute. While some of these (perceived) crises were triggered by (trans-)national debates concerning Austria's World War II history, many others can be attributed to the direct or indirect effects of contemporary globalization; the closure/relocation of long-established factories decided upon by their multinational owners can be counted among the former, whereas policies implemented on the level of the European Union, itself a 'network state' formed in accommodation to the forces of globalization (Castells 2000), provide examples of indirect/mediated effects. Crucially, the emerging universe of discourse in contemporary Austria is characterized by internal ideological heterogeneity. Whilst Bourdieu's *doxa-crisis-discourse* model thus captures much that has happened in and surrounding the Alpine Republic over recent decades, nationalism is but one of several competing discursive responses to the experience of crises. In theoretical terms, this keeps with Bourdieu's observation (1977, 168–170) that crises 'awake' political consciousness and create 'competing possibles', whilst it empirically challenges simplistic meta-narratives of an allegedly total and all-pervasive nationalist revival. Nationalist discourse, as has been widely recognized, constructs clearly delineated 'in-' and 'out-groups'. An application of Bourdieu's model to the data analyzed above adds to this by contextualizing such processes of identity construction in wider experiences of change and crisis, and by drawing attention to competing arguments in the resulting (and ideologically contested) universe of discourse.

Extending its glance from Austria to other European contexts, this chapter has shown that experiences of crises or 'disruptions' have also crucially affected national identity politics elsewhere. This was illustrated by a discussion of the contemporary 'mythscapes', now comprised of competing historical narratives pertaining to memories of World War II, in France, Switzerland and Germany. In each of these contexts there is evidence that over the last two decades previously firmly established narratives of the nation's recent past, and thus parts of a 'commonsensical' national *habitus* and largely unexamined terrain of doxic assumptions, have come to be debated and contested. This was followed by a move from national memory politics to individual biographies: Mann and Fenton's British research (2009) was used to illustrate that the experience of personal crises is also key to understanding the relative exclusivity of national sentiments articulated by specific social actors. Such a grounding of national identity politics in very specific 'micro-experiences', concerns and anxieties is a recurring theme in the following chapters. For example, we now turn to an examination of the argumentative strategies used by individuals as they make sense of social change and the relationship between local lives, national- and supra-national (i.e. European) politics.

# Chapter 3
# The Past, The Present, Nation-states and Europe

## Introduction

This chapter is being written in the context of a deep debt-crisis, which – having started in Greece – threatens to engulf the Euro-zone and possibly the European Union in its entirety. Structural weaknesses inherent to the Euro-zone and persisting divisions internal to the EU are debated, with the most outspoken sceptics questioning the viability of the Euro and even the future of the European network state. Competing assessments of the relationship between the EU and its member-states are currently 'tested' by daily developments: are European institutions insufficiently grounded in emerging European identities to withstand the economic crises currently unfolding (Guibernau 2007, 115–116)? Alternatively, do Europeans' life-worlds now display a 'banal Europeanism' (Cram 2009) capable of counteracting entrenched nationalisms and the fragmentary forces generated in these difficult times? Manuel Castells anticipated much of this already a decade ago:

> Faced with the whirlwind of globalization … European countries came together … to unify their currencies, and thus their economies, around the turn of the millennium. However, the cultural and political dimensions, essential to … European unification, are still unsettled, so that the fate of Europe will ultimately depend … on solving the historical puzzles posed by … the shift from the nation-state to … the network state. (Castells 2000, 3)

The present crisis has brought a tension defining contemporary globalization to the fore: between nation-states (and the European network state) and market forces, particularly the power of financial markets, respectively. Whilst this is the focus of chapter four, I here build on a discussion presented elsewhere (Karner 2010b) to examine how some 'ordinary European citizens', rather than political elites, make sense of recent developments and current crises. The following analysis of everyday 'grassroots' rhetoric and media discourse reveals three characteristics: first, the establishment of ideological linkages between disparate concerns and issues, which reduce complexities in the act of interpretation and articulate a defensive politics of national(ist) exclusion; second, a pre-occupation with perceived disparities between European 'ideals' and 'realities'; third, 'bottom-up' uses of various memories and narratives of the past (see Karlsson 2010; Müller

2002) that reveal disquiet and anxiety about rapid and far-reaching changes. Following an outline of pertinent theoretical leads, this chapter focuses on relevant Austrian data indicative of these discursive features, whilst contextualizing them in political fields of disagreement and contestation. I then trace similar phenomena across several other European contexts.

## Theoretical context

The first conceptual question addressed below concerns the manifestations and workings of ideologies of belonging and exclusion. My working-definition of ideology, a notoriously contested term, regards it as language and 'behavioural practices' that are political insofar as they contribute to the reproduction or transformation of power relations (Augoustinos 1998). Two points follow. First, ideology thus defined alerts us to the ubiquity of power, the politics of the everyday; in this chapter this translates into an examination of the opinions and interpretations offered by so-called 'ordinary social actors' in the media, particularly through readers' letters in Austria's most popular newspaper. Second, this definition of ideology resonates with discourse analytical approaches to the study of language in context, as a form of social practice that reflects *and* acts on structures of power (e.g. Weiss and Wodak 2003).

Focusing on the workings of power on and through language, discourse analysis offers conceptual leads crucial to this chapter. Most fundamentally, discourse analysis detects larger social forces in the minutiae of language, in recurring themes, 'vocabularies, phrases, tropes and instances used in argument' (Grillo 2005, 245). Related to this is the key concept of the *topos* – those 'parts of argumentation that belong to … either explicit or inferable premises … the content-related warrants … that connect the argument … with the conclusion, the claim' (Reisigl and Wodak 2001, 74–75). Argumentative frameworks discussed in the literature and relevant to this analysis include, amongst others, *topoi* of 'threats' and dangers, of 'usefulness' or disadvantage, of authority and humanitarianism (Reisigl and Wodak 2001). Equally relevant are the 'Duisburg group' and its studies of German media coverage of crime and a tendency to discursively connect it to ethnicity; central to their work is 'the analysis of "*collective symbols*" … tied together in "*discourse strands*" … [and] described as thematically interrelated sequences of homogenous "*discourse fragments*" (Jäger quoted in Krzyżanowski and Wodak 2009, 19). Similarly, Krzyżanowski and Wodak explore symbolic associations – or 'thematic interconnections' – between topics that emerged in their focus groups with migrants in Austria:

> [P]rimary topics developed into secondary topics, inasmuch as discussion themes triggered by general questions led to the unplanned appearance of secondary topics … [This reveals] ways in which the general issues affecting … immigrants in Austria (reflected in the primary topics) are perceived by the

migrants in the study, and what kind of less general associations and elements of social reality these are typically associated with. (Krzyżanowski and Wodak 2009, 154)

Building on such 'discursive strands' and 'thematic associations', my analysis opts for the term *discursive chains* to capture emerging series of signifiers, which are discursively linked by socially circulating frameworks of interpretation and political argumentation.[1] Such interlinked signifiers (e.g. crime–immigration–open borders–EU) articulate – and thereby frequently mis-construct – separate phenomena in close association with one another.

The second core issue relates to ordinary citizens' perceptions of the European Union or, more accurately, to the above-mentioned question: is the European network state able to connect with Europeans' everyday life-worlds and are the latter therefore beginning to experience the former as a meaningful source of identity? Whilst Euro-barometer surveys generate a wealth of quantitative information on this issue, my analysis offers a thematic, qualitative reading of relevant data. Emerging themes centre on two inter-related issues: first, the (differences between the) perceived and desired relationship between the EU and its member-states; second, perceived discrepancies between European ideals and realities. Jointly, these debates revolve around the question as to *which Europe* ordinary citizens want.

My third key question pertains to the role of memory, or the uses of the past (see Karner 2010b; Karlsson 2010), in such negotiations of national and European identities. This extends Bell's notion (2003, 74), discussed earlier, of national 'mythscapes' as ideological terrains contested by 'governing myths' and 'subaltern myths': my analysis shows that everyday identity politics utilize, on the micro-level of interpretation and argumentation, a wide range of historical reference points, both national and global. Many such 'analogical' (mis)uses of history (Müller 2002; 2010) are problematic – politically, ethically and historiographically. Yet, as rhetorical devices they need to be taken seriously, for they express speakers' disquiet about perceived negative changes. Some invocations of the past indeed qualify as what Karlsson (2010, 47) terms the 'existential use of history' encountered in post-industrial societies and indicative of 'post-materialist values related to belonging, self-expression and the quality of life'. More generally, this analysis therefore also seeks to address a relative absence in existing literature, the fact that we thus far 'know too little about how people actually remember, let alone how elite discourses might or might not affect individual memories … what is missing are the audiences, the "consumers" of collective memory' (Müller 2010, 26).

---

1   Also very relevant to this notion is Volf and Bauböck's concept (quoted in Markom and Weinhäupl 2007, 152, my translation) of 'chains of associations'.

**Everyday politics in Austrian media**

The bulk of the data examined in this chapter is comprised of news coverage and readers' letters in Austria's most widely read paper – the already discussed *Kronen Zeitung* (or *Krone*), between 2008 and 2010. This period of data collection saw the *Krone* assume an ever more prominent role in the articulation of anti-EU sentiment or, at least, deep-seated EU-scepticism. It also coincided with numerous key events and controversies: parliamentary, presidential and European elections; the ratification of the EU's Lisbon Treaty; financial and debt crises on European and global levels; (trans)national debates on a range of issues including the rights and treatment of asylum-seekers inside 'fortress Europe', concerns about crime, the welfare state, and rightwing populist politics against Europe's alleged 'Islamization'.

The *Kronen Zeitung*'s extraordinary reach was confirmed by a readership of nearly 3 million – some 40 per cent of Austrians – in 2007 (*Der Standard* 28 March 2008, 33) and 2008/09 (*Kronen Zeitung* 2 October 2009, 5), making it the in percentages of the population most widely circulating paper worldwide. The *Krone*'s political significance is well-known (e.g. Thurnher 2008) and recently manifested in the circumstances triggering the collapse of the previous SPÖ-ÖVP coalition: in a letter to the *Krone* on 27 June 2008, then Chancellor Gusenbauer and his successor, then Infrastructure Minister Faymann, announced that amendments to the EU reform treaty should – if consequential to Austria – be subject to a national referendum. This SPÖ u-turn was widely perceived (e.g. Lackner 2008a; http://derstandard.at/druck/?id=3395006) as a concession to the *Krone*'s opposition to the Lisbon Treaty.

A longitudinal study (Rittberger 2009) of the *Kronen Zeitung*'s political stances between 1968 and 2008 has revealed a shift away from an initial benevolence towards 'guest-workers' towards an increasingly prominent xenophobia; Rittberger contextualizes this change in the economic shift from Keynesianism to neo-liberalism, from full employment to growing unemployment and associated insecurities, arguing that the *Krone* reflects and helps shape common sentiments. Other research (Plasser quoted in Lackner 2010c) into the paper's coverage of the candidates and parties at the 2008 general election reveals two significant dimensions: first, the co-existence of seemingly contradictory positions – support for SPÖ-candidate and now Chancellor Faymann, alongside ideological preferences for the rightwing populism of FPÖ and BZÖ; second, many readers letters reflected or exacerbated these (ambivalent) affinities.

The paper's coverage of national and European politics and the responses by readers on its popular 'letters to the editor' pages therefore provide relevant and near daily insights into prominent identity negotiations. A methodological focus on media discourse and readers' letters has the additional advantage of capturing 'naturally occurring' national identity talk, bypassing problems of 'impression management' and of interviewers' complicity in the construction of national identities reported in the literature (Condor 2000; Mann and Fenton 2006).

Readers' letters, though edited and selected, provide a valuable perspective on the life-worlds, everyday experiences, and ideological leanings of some 'ordinary citizens'. As a 'site within which people ... articulate their views in public', readers' letters 'afford ... analysts the opportunity to examine how the writer uses argument to express their opinion or concerns on a sensitive topic' (Lynn and Lea 2003, 430).

However, the *Krone* and its readers' letters of course only reflect parts of the spectrum of positions concerning the relationship between the nation-state and Europe. A wider and accurate understanding of contemporary Austria demands broader contextualization. The data examined below therefore also includes relevant coverage in Austria's other, ideologically heterogeneous print media (i.e. local and national, daily and weekly, tabloid and broadsheet) and in the national broadcasting network. The analysis of all this material was guided by the following questions (also see Karner 2010b): *which issues and anxieties recur in this data and how are they presented and interpreted? Which boundaries and self-other category relations are constructed and negotiated? How is the relationship between Austria and the EU defined? Which rhetorical strategies underpin the discourses used?* As this thematic, qualitative analysis of a large body of data shows, there is evidence of recurring concerns and positions (expressed through particular 'discursive devices') *and* of important 'counter-discourses' (Lynn and Lea 2003).

*Discursive chains*

A close reading of the *Krone* and its readers' letters over a two-year period and extrapolation of recurring themes and 'discursive strategies' (Wodak 2007) from this data[2] reveals that key issues and concerns tend to be discussed in close association with one another. In the process, discursive connections between disparate phenomena are constructed; terming such emerging, assumed (and often sub-culturally entrenched) links between often unconnected issues *discursive chains*, this analysis examines their interpretative uses as sense-making aids, and their ideological effects as speakers/writers position themselves politically in the process of invoking them. The following list is not exhaustive but draws attention to the most prominent assumed connections. Moreover, their analytical separation should not distract from inter-connections – on the level of rhetoric and sense-making – between these discursive chains; talk about criminality and borders, for example, thus itself easily 'spills over' into complaints about asylum-seekers, 'Islamization' or the so-called liberal 'do-gooders'.

---

2   All extracts quoted below are my translations and are representative of frequently recurring claims, sentiments and narratives.

*Criminality and borders*

Readers' letters between 2008 and 2010 provided near-daily insights into a key concern, especially in Austria's eastern regions, with rising crime (particularly burglaries). These fears are widespread and were – at least for some time[3] – grounded in increases in crimes that had previously indeed been relatively uncommon. What is significant for our purposes is not the understandable fear and condemnation of such criminality, but the kinds of interpretations offered and circulated. The following are select examples that epitomize the dominant narrative on crime encountered in the *Krone*. Several discursive features stand out as defining characteristics of many relevant readers' letters. First, the rhetorical *deixis* (Billig 1995a) of – or pointing at – the national 'in-group' in opposition to equally clearly delineated 'out-groups':

> We have often shown our humanism, but we cannot host any more refugees. Moreover, there is a rising tide of crime, mostly committed by gangs from the east, which is tormenting our population and police. Austria's 'boat is full'. Other European countries now need to take in new refugees, as Austria has done for so long. (*Kronen Zeitung* 25 September 2009, 29)

Similar strategies of 'positive self- and negative other-presentation' (Wodak 2007, 662) define the following:

> This crime-wave cannot be stopped and the gangsters are getting ever more brutal … Simultaneously, self-defence is made harder by new restrictions on handgun-ownership for us law-abiding Austrian citizens. (*Kronen Zeitung* 14 October 2009, 23)

The discursive result is the construction of what Krzyżanowski and Wodak (2009, 82–83) term the topoi of 'criminality of migrants' and of 'threat and anxiety':

> Austria ranks amongst the most popular destinations for illegal immigration … [which] often starts a life of crime … burglary, prostitution, undocumented work… (*Kronen Zeitung* 22 October 2009, 32)

A further disconcerting variant of this topos and the discursive linking of migration with crime were articulated – in particular – by a series of *Krone* headlines in 2005 that 'nearly equated [sub-Saharan] Africans with drug-dealing' (Rittberger 2009, 56).

---

3    A subsequent decrease in crime (e.g. *Kleine Zeitung* 10 April 2010, 14; *Krone* 10 April 2010, 12) and the revelation (Lackner 2010d) that a very substantial proportion of crime had been committed by German citizens – rather than by Eastern Europeans more widely 'scapegoated' – has so far received less attention. Similarly, there is comparatively little public interest in migrants' own experiences of insecurity: as shown by a recent study, their fears centre on precarious residence statuses, poverty and xenophobia (see Braun 2010).

Crucially, criminality is often thematized in connection – and hence attributed – to other phenomena, particularly the expansion of the Schengen area in December 2007, resulting in open borders between Austria and her easterly neighbours. Whilst an assumed link between crime and 'eastern gangs' (*Ostbanden*) has a longer genealogy, it emerged as a widespread anxiety in a survey conducted before successive EU expansions and the Schengen enlargement in the winter of 2007 (http://www.diepresse.at/Artikel.aspx?channel=c&ressort=w&id=392950), the opening of borders has made such a link seemingly more tangible for many *Krone* readers:

> Dear anti-Austrian politicians and EU-servants! Given that you hospitably opened our borders to eastern criminals, why didn't you also fax your addresses to those countries? (*Kronen Zeitung* 18 October 2009, 27)

> To the detached and blind EU-politicians and particularly Austria's politicians: Have you not noticed how important protection, security and the fight against murderers, thieves and other criminals are for our country? Austria is the last bastion against the former East. And all those criminals come particularly from the former Eastern block. Have they not noticed this in Brussels? … So re-instate our border controls. We Austrians have the right to sleep peacefully again … (*Kronen Zeitung* 27 January 2010, 27)

Again, the outrage at, and trauma of, being a victim of crime is of course understandable. What is most significant, however, is the lack of contextualization: such xenophobic accounts and stereotypes do not allow for an acknowledgement or discussion of intra-European inequalities and the consequences of the structural exclusions suffered at or beyond Europe's margins.

*On asylum-seekers*
After 1945 Austria became, relative to the size of her population, Europe's primary country of refugees' (initial) destination/transit, which most memorably manifested in widespread Austrian solidarity with refugees from Hungary in 1956/57 and – to a slightly lesser extent – from Czechoslovakia in 1968 (Weigl 2009, 33–34, 82–83). Starting in the 1990s, after the collapse of communism and with rapidly increasing numbers of asylum-seekers, much of this changed. Shifting attitudes and growing xenophobia began to take root, parts of the media and the populist right constructed asylum-seekers as a pariah (Gärtner 2009, 151–154), and – symptomatic of Europe's increasing 'fortification' – increasingly restrictive immigration and asylum legislation was passed (Krzyżanowski and Wodak 2009, 41–53).

The dominant tone concerning asylum-seekers in *Kronen Zeitung* readers' letters between 2008 and 2010 was one of fear and danger – though not of (past, present of future) dangers faced by asylum-seekers but of the alleged dangers posed by them. Such interpretations are profoundly political, for they position readers and those they write about and their discourses help legitimize particular configurations of power. Notably, 'the topos of danger and threat' Krzyżanowski and Wodak (2009, 115) have extrapolated from FPÖ parliamentary discourse on, or rather against, immigration recurs in many claims and narratives concerning asylum-seekers on the *Krone*'s readers' letters pages:

> How long will our politicians watch those 'poor' asylum-seekers commit crimes …? I don't think there is another country that permits this and even supports such foreigners financially … In return, crime is rising, and people don't dare go out, fearing to be burgled or mugged. (*Kronen Zeitung* 16 October 2009, 28)

Krzyżanowski and Wodak show (2009, 115) that the topos of threat is tied to several other topoi, including a 'topos of numbers – the argument that large numbers … are coming to Austria and thereby threatening it'. Several readers argue similarly in relation to asylum:

> People's experiences with immigrants … have been negative … One wonders how long this madness will continue. Instead of accepting more refugees, we should stop this. Austria isn't responsible for all the world's problems. Austria's population has done enough for … migrants in the past, if things continue, we'll soon be victims ourselves. We shouldn't build new reception-centres, but shut existing ones and close the borders. (*Kronen Zeitung* 4 January 2010, 20)

Also tied to the topos of threat is a 'topos of burden' (Krzyżanowski and Wodak 2009, 115), the postulate that asylum-seekers are not only dangerous but also costly:

> [T]he asylum-problem in Austria costs tax-payers huge amounts every day and only causes theft, burglary, violent crime and rape. (*Kronen Zeitung* 21 October 2009, 28)

Discourses of economic scarcity (as opposed to legal and humanistic commitments to protecting the vulnerable and persecuted) are thus tied to a 'topos of criminality – the suggestion that most or all … asylum-seekers are criminal' (Krzyżanowski and Wodak 2009, 115). This is epitomized in *Krone* readers' constructions of 'Austria [as], an EU-paradise for criminals and pretend-asylum-seekers' (e.g. 11 November 2009, 29), which echo the 'differentiation between bogus and genuine asylum-seekers' Lynn and Lea (2003, 433) detect in readers' letters in British national newspapers. The same interpretative template defines the following reader's position:

> Lorries-full of immigrants – from Turkey, the future hope amongst EU-dreamers – cross our open borders … These are largely economic migrants and criminals we don't need. If caught, they shout 'asylum' – which gives them legal and social rights … (*Kronen Zeitung* 15 October 2009, 38)

These different claims and topoi frequently intersect and overlap, as in the following reader's opposition to plans, which were announced in late 2009 and subsequently scrapped, for an asylum-seeker induction-centre in Eberau, in Austria's most easterly region of Burgenland:

> Austria is no longer on the EU's periphery and therefore shouldn't need to take any more asylum-seekers! … This government should work in Austria's interest, instead of wasting millions in tax-payers' money for a new asylum-seeker reception centre. Unbelievable! … This money should be spent on the many Austrians living on the poverty-line … Instead, our politicians allow work-shy bogus asylum-seekers into Austria, who abuse our welfare system without ever having contributed to it. Only asylum-seekers with particular skills, technicians and scientists should be let in, that would be positive for our country. (*Kronen Zeitung* 19 January 2010, 24)

As in the earlier examples of everyday discourses about criminality, what is also significant about such arguments and claims about asylum is what is *not* being said. The dominant positions on asylum articulated by *Krone* readers' have little to say about the structural exclusion and hardship faced by asylum-seekers inside 'Fortress Europe'. Similarly, obligations of the world's relatively affluent and secure regions in relation to the UN 1951 convention relating to refugees – people who because of a 'well-founded fear' of persecution 'for reasons of race, religion … membership of a particular social group' in their country of nationality seek protection by another state (Moorehead 2005, 28) – remain unacknowledged in such discourses.

*Citizen entitlements threatened by 'do-gooders'?*
'[P]olarisations, black-and-white portrayals and manichean divisions into good and bad' (Reisigl and Wodak 2001, 56, 96) indeed define some prominent discourses on the nation-state and its 'others'. Moreover, loyalties are frequently portrayed as a zero-sum game in accounts that pit migrants' interests in diametrical opposition to citizens'. One side is thus constructed as necessarily gaining at the expense of the other:

> Immigration rules are totally wrong, turning Austrians into foreigners in their own country, providing us with fewer rights than migrants. (*Kronen Zeitung* 26 November 2009, 41)

Much of this revolves around notions of entitlements, with citizenship[4] being seen as both the 'natural' unit of political organization and as threatened by current

---

4    In the area of work, for example, there is a long Austrian genealogy to such thinking connecting entitlements to citizenship: in 1925 the primacy of citizens' job security over foreigners' was legally enshrined (Herzog-Punzenberger 2009, 20).

developments. There is another category – part of 'us' but constructed as siding with the other – integral to this discursive chain:

> Do-gooders are demanding better medical and psychological support for failed asylum-seekers awaiting deportation. Yet, Austrians who are pushed into poverty, get ill, lose their job, are not getting medical and psychological support and need to cope by themselves. (*Kronen Zeitung* 18 September 2009, 25)

Akin to Lynn and Lea's findings (2003, 444–445) concerning 'white liberals', as a target for disenfranchised readers writing to British newspapers about the alleged ills brought about by 'the other' and their supposedly privileged British sympathizers, the figure of the 'do-gooder' (*Gutmensch*) recurs in relevant *Krone* readers' letters:

> The do-gooders' currently dominant *Zeitgeist*, demanding unrestricted … immigration, is wrong and creating Europe's next catastrophe. (10 November 2009, 22)

'Do-gooders'' loyalty is portrayed as lying elsewhere, supporting the 'other', and hence as working to the alleged detriment of the clearly delineated national 'in-group':

> For our pensioners, families and homeless there is not enough money, but the state helps finance the EU, foreign cultural associations, the UN, asylum-seekers, the unemployed and artists … And according to the do-gooders tax-payers should pay for asylum-seekers and the work-shy. (*Kronen Zeitung* 14 January 2009, 30)

There is little if any space for mutually supporting, 'bridging' (Putnam 2000) relationships between self and other in such accounts. Furthermore, actual power relationships are misrecognized and discursively inverted: the comparatively secure are portrayed as victims of marginalization and those outside and excluded are seen as the alleged beneficiaries in a situation of scarcity and competition; in a *Krone* columnist's words:

> People are tired of how this government has recently only been interested in the well-being of asylum-seekers, illegals, immigrants etc. They have been won over by organizations seeking to privilege foreigners over citizens. (*Kronen Zeitung* 12 January 2010, 3)

Similar assessments recur in readers' letters:

> I am also saying this in the name of well-integrated immigrants: those foreigners who criminally abuse our welfare- and health-systems and the prosperity we've worked hard for must be stopped. (*Kronen Zeitung* 9 October 2009, 30)

As mentioned, discursive chains are themselves frequently discursively interwoven, with one set of grievances being tied to the interpretation of another: for example, complaints about 'do-gooders corroding citizens' rights' can turn into accounts of another alleged danger unrecognized by the supposedly more privileged: the spectre of Islam.

### The dangers of 'Islamization' and the Swiss example

Since 9/11, Wolfgang Kaschuba argues (2010, 72), a 'narrowly constructed chain of association has been propagated that puts migration and terrorism into a causal relationship'; 'increased Islamist activity' is juxtaposed to 'concurrent Christian-Occidental ... cultural defences', the latter manifesting in the 'formation of angry citizens action committees in almost all European cities in which new ... mosques are being built. Such groups regard future minarets as army flags of a foreign cultural infiltration, and thus they seek to defend "the Occident" in their neighbourhood.'

Austria is no exception. Recent years have seen local (Kübel 2009) and regional (Hafez and Potz 2009) opposition to the building of new Islamic community centres or minarets, Islamophobic sentiments have been politically instrumentalized by rightwing populism (Hafez 2009, Gärtner 2009) and become prominent in parts of the discourse on migration, pluralism and integration. Many *Krone* readers' letters are symptomatic of this, revealing discursive 'chains of association'[5] that view and construct Islam through a topos of danger or 'invasion':

> Previous immigrants integrated, they originated in Christian Europe and not in oriental, exotic countries. Today's immigrants are only here because of our higher living standards compared to their home countries ... If this continues, us Austrians will be the minority in 30 years. (*Kronen Zeitung* 28 October 2009, 24)

Manifestations of the much-feared 'Islamization' of Europe or Austria are detected in diverse settings, ranging from everyday markers of cultural difference to alleged religious-political subversion:

> The number of Turkish Muslims is growing disconcertingly ... they want to dictate things in Europe. Daily confrontations ... make a Christian fear for

---

5   In the context of the controversy around Danish caricatures of the prophet Muhammad in 2005, Sonnleitner (2009, 194) detects a similar 'discursive web', presenting a monolithic account of Islam associated with war and violence, in parts of the broadsheet press. For a relevant analysis of Islamophobia in British broadsheets, see Richardson (2004).

the future … The smallest incident, caricature or objection, makes Muslims aggressive and hateful … in our [Viennese] district former shops have been turned into subsidized (!) Muslim prayer-rooms. Instead of being grateful for being able to live in a beautiful country like Austria, they refuse to integrate and demand that we … remove our crucifixes … and stop serving pork … This is a Christian Europe and shall remain so. (*Kronen Zeitung* 25 November 2009, 22)

There are also recurring demographic anxieties, with readers projecting from current birth-rates that the Turkish minority could at some point become the majority:

The first baby born in the new year in Lower Austria is called Azra Öcel, in Styria Moamer Duceliz … We will soon need refugee-camps for the last remaining Austrians with German names … Just look at Vienna and other cities where German names are already the exception. Even in smaller towns the proportion of Muhammeds, Aishas etc. is increasing … When are we going to be an Islamic Republic? (*Kronen Zeitung* 4 January 2010, 19)

Particular controversies, such as the one triggered by an earlier-mentioned study claiming to detect a democratic deficit amongst a substantial proportion of Islamic religious education teachers in Austrian schools, are interpreted through a schema of external danger:

I am surprised that only a fifth of Islamic religious-education teachers consider Islam and democracy to be incompatible. For the Muslim [sic] law resides in God. Islamic countries work by a different logic. It gets dangerous when different systems, religions and people mix. (*Kronen Zeitung* 3 February 2009, 25)

A further recurring complaint concerns linguistic diversity at Austrian schools, which readers frequently interpret[6] as reflecting lack of integration and 'parallel lives' lived by Austria's Turkish community. Cross-references to the discursive chain around 'liberal do-gooders' are established in narratives of class suggesting that the privileged are removed from – and thus ignorant of – everyday tensions and conflicts in the life-worlds of 'ordinary people' living alongside Muslim migrants:

Self-declared 'experts' … will now assess [the FPÖ's political success in the region of Vorarlberg] … Particularly Austria's smallest region has seen disproportionate rates of immigration, with all the well-known problems. Clearly, not everyone is happy with such 'multiculturalism' … this is why the FPÖ is now the second-strongest regional party. (*Kronen Zeitung* 24 September 2009, 30)

---

6   As with the other discursive chains, such accounts leave little room for discussions of historical context or the effects of structural inequalities and exclusions.

Wider European dimensions, interpreted through siege-metaphors and cultural/religious essentialisms, also feature:

> In fact, Christianity in Europe is being pushed aside by Islam. In France every third child is born to a Muslim family. In twenty years Vienna, too, will have fallen. Brussels, London, Amsterdam or Stockholm will follow. (*Kronen Zeitung* 13 January 2010, 23)

> Turkey's accession would be tantamount to the EU's end, particularly concerning human rights. (*Kronen Zeitung* 12 January 2010, 21)

> A German study of religiosity and social behaviour amongst 14–16-year-olds … [shows that whilst] religiosity translates into less violence amongst young Christians, aggression increases with growing devotion amongst Muslims … [O]nly 28 per cent of young Muslims have German friends and 21 per cent feel German. Anyone thinking that the situation here is any different is a dreamer unable to face reality. (*Kronen Zeitung* 11 June 2010, 26)

Particular notice was taken of the controversial Swiss referendum in late 2009, at which a majority voted for a ban on further minarets. The dominant response amongst *Krone* readers was one of understanding and support:

> Again, the Swiss have proven to be European pioneers in (direct) democracy. With a remarkable majority of 57 per cent they voted for a ban on minarets and thus for a defence of Christianity. (*Kronen Zeitung* 1 December 2009, 22)

> Switzerland is the last real democracy, whose population is still empowered to determine its way of life. The recent rejection of minarets was … a defence against growing subversion and unwillingness to integrate shown by all kinds of immigrants across Europe. (*Kronen Zeitung* 11 December 2009, 28)

Another component in this discursive chain – the notion of 'Switzerland as a model' Austria ought to emulate – articulates profound EU-scepticism. Switzerland, so this frequently made claim goes, is better off because unlike Austria is has stayed outside the EU:

> Though comparisons are difficult, Switzerland didn't have to experience world wars and is a 'golden island' for investors, we should learn from its prudent politics demonstrating that one can do without the EU … Had we stayed with our Schilling, we now wouldn't have to bail out Greece … we would still be neutral and enjoy peace and stability. Let's emulate Switzerland, this smart country, we can only win. (*Kronen Zeitung* 27 May 2010, 36)

*Counter-discourse*

Whilst this chapter's main purpose is to examine the rhetorical workings of certain prominent discourses of national identity and exclusion, these must be contextualized more widely. The narratives of interpretation examined here are of course subject to widespread debate and contestation in, for example, Austria's quality press. For instance, *Profil* editor Rainer challenges common xenophobic topoi:

> A central prejudice: asylum-seekers … are held responsible for … burglaries allegedly experienced by everyone. Question: when has the Interior Minister last pointed out that such crimes are overwhelmingly committed by Eastern European gangs that leave the country as quickly as they arrived? And generally not by asylum-seekers, refugees … or immigrants![7] … Another widely documented prejudice: Foreigners allegedly abuse the welfare-state. When … has the government pointed out that foreigners pay much more in tax than they receive in benefits, making the 'sponging-off-argument' untenable? … Politicians seem to fear being denounced as 'do-gooders' in the *Krone*. (Rainer 2010a, my translation)

But even within the narrower remit of *Kronen Zeitung* readers' letters there are occasional 'counter-discourses' refuting the 'topos of threat and danger':

> The word foreigner is often negatively connoted, one rarely reads about positive experiences, although they also happen. Some time ago my daughter caused a car accident, the injured party was a Turkish man who, instead of blaming my daughter, comforted her … [He] even phoned subsequently to ask if she was OK. (*Kronen Zeitung* 23 February 2010, 26)

> Religious buildings are symbols of openness … Rejecting Muslims' calls for mosques with minarets … reflects a lack of information and intelligence. Their calls should be seen positively, reflecting a willingness to engage and integrate. (*Kronen Zeitung* 1 December 2009, 22)

Similarly, as chapter five illustrates, Austria's critical media and civil society dedicate much of their energies to countering nationalist exclusions. One example relevant to the present discussion is provided by Gamze Ongan (2009), head of an advisory organization – and editor of a magazine – for and by migrants in Vienna. Writing about public outcry about 'forced marriages', she argues that those most vocal about the ills of Oriental patriarchy are much less interested in migrant women's rights – if they were, they would need to address the more widespread

---

7    SPÖ and Green politicians have similarly criticized the discursive linking of asylum-seekers to criminality/burglaries in a recent statement by the Interior Minister (http://www.orf.at 23 July 2010).

problems posed by poverty and immigration legislation – than in presenting a politically motivated and strongly reified picture of Islam.

Whilst European dimensions feature in the discursive chains discussed above, more explicit discussions and frequent complaints about – or opposition to – the EU are a further defining element of the data examined for this chapter.

*Which Europe?*

Europe is an important reference-point for the parties and ideological currents that constitute the 'new right' across different national contexts: first, as allegedly threatened by the culturally imperialist forces of American hegemony; second, European nation-states are seen as facing a further shared danger in the shape of 'Islamization', calling for a 'Christian defence of the Occident'; third, such perceived pan-European interests and dangers notwithstanding, current EU structures are portrayed as subverting national identities and imposing an unnecessary centralism (Aftenberger 2007, 175–193). Austrian rightwing populism has derived considerable discursive energy from its projection of diverse anxieties and perceived ills onto Brussels. Whilst it rarely propagates dropping out of the EU, de-centralization and a re-strengthening of Europe's nation-states (*Europa der Vaterländer*) are amongst its defining demands (e.g. Gärtner 2009, 21–22). However, criticisms of existing European structures recur more widely and amongst considerably broader stretches of the ideological spectrum. Successive Euro-barometer surveys have thus shown Austria to rank amongst the most sceptical EU member-states, although approval rates have increased in the context of the financial crisis since 2008 (Gärtner 2009, 160–161). The now strongly EU-critical *Kronen Zeitung* as the country's most popular paper and its readers' letters are highly relevant for an understanding of the rhetoric and claims of EU-scepticism. Analysis of this data between 2008 and 2010 reveals several key characteristics: the association of the EU with a number of emotive issues; disgruntlement with what are seen as unnecessary bureaucratic impositions emanating from Brussels; debates about perceived discrepancies between European ideals and realities, between desired and actual relationships between the European Union and its individual member-states; pessimistic predictions about the EU's ability to respond to current crises.

The *Krone* and its readers' letters provide near daily insights into various critical positions on the EU, ranging from mild concern and annoyance to disillusionment and outright hostility. Given constraints of space, I here present only select examples that illustrate frequently recurring claims and sentiments. The first set of 'EU-opinions' relates to some key concerns in Austrian public debate, including the earlier-mentioned dispute between Brussels and Vienna about the impact of lorries crossing Austria *en route* within the EU, as well as widespread anxieties surrounding nuclear energy or genetically modified food (see chapter four):

[We] were considerably better off in the 1960s than today. There were fewer
existential uncertainties and environmental problems … News about our
politicians were largely positive … whereas today they just make up the numbers
at EU-summits. There were no concerns about … genetically modified food [or]
nuclear accidents … (*Kronen Zeitung* 31 May 2008, 31)

Environmental concerns are associated with the European Union. Dangers are
thus constructed as emanating from outside the nation:

Globalization and particularly our EU membership are the reasons we are not
meeting our climate targets … Open borders increase lorry traffic. (*Kronen
Zeitung* 23 November 2009, 21)

In cross-reference to discursive chains discussed earlier, the following reader's
account characteristically blames the EU for the assumed dangers posed by open
Schengen borders and associated demographic changes, with no acknowledgement
of the historical significance of such changes or concomitant benefits:

In my neighbourhood there have been several recent burglaries … demonstrably
committed by foreigners … I am not scared yet, as I own a gun – as long as the
EU and our do-gooders allow me to … We've got … politicians supporting an
EU-constitution [sic] and keen on removing border-controls to thank for this.
(*Kronen Zeitung* 3 March 2009, 26)

If such is the tone of many a reader's commentary on the EU's allegedly sole
responsibility for a variety of ills and dangers, another recurring discourse
associates European politics primarily with bureaucracy considered unnecessary
and intrusive. EU regulation is portrayed as out-of-touch with, or even hostile to,
the life-worlds of ordinary citizens:

This EU wants children no longer to use the world 'mother' (only parent), it gets
rid of our Christian symbols … let's not allow Brussels to burden us any longer
with regulations on the shape of cucumbers, light-bulbs, or this stupid gender-
neutrality. (*Kronen Zeitung* 23 June 2010, 27)

*Krone* readers' have detected recent instances of such perceived European
intrusions in the phasing-out of traditional light-bulbs, as well as in relation to
the feared removal of crucifixes from classrooms and to rumours of potential
health restrictions on a culinary symbol of Austrian identity – her salt-crusted
rolls (*Salzstangerl*). Such concerns reflect the inverse of Cram's notion (2009)
of 'banal Europeanism', defined as the everyday complementarity of European
and national identities; instead, we here encounter perceptions of a clash between
European decisions and local/national lived experience. Objects of taken-for-

granted material culture or symbols of collective identity are portrayed as being under unnecessary and legalistic 'attack from Brussels'.

Several important, inter-related questions arise from this: first, how is the relationship between 'ordinary citizens' and political elites defined in such discourses? Second, what relationship between nation-states and the European network state is advocated and (how) does this differ from perceived realities? Third, in postulating a clash between Brussels and 'us', who does this discursively constructed in-group include? Co-nationals only or also other European citizens presumably affected by the same problems? These questions were illuminated by heated debates surrounding the Lisbon Treaty (Karner 2010b); designed to facilitate the EU's more efficient functioning with now 27 member-states, the Treaty was met with much grassroots- and some political opposition in Austria and other European countries – including an initial rejection at a first referendum in Ireland, the only country to hold referenda on the Treaty – prior to coming into force in December 2009. In the spring of 2008, when the Treaty was approved by Austria's lower and upper houses of parliament and the federal president, the *Krone* and many readers were amongst its most vocal opponents. The paper supported a citizens' initiative called 'Rescue Austria'[8], with the most frequently voiced objections to the Lisbon-reforms revolving around fears of a loss of national sovereignty and of Austrian neutrality. Moreover, readers' articulated their disenchantment by postulating a deep division between political elites, in Vienna and even more so in Brussels, and ordinary people. Worryingly, readers frequently detected a profound 'democratic deficit' at the heart of the EU, which they saw worsening further with the Lisbon Treaty:

> As every 'ordinary citizen' knows, this Treaty is only designed to further strengthen the EU-dictators' power. (*Kronen Zeitung* 29 November 2009, 37)

Recurring, near daily calls for an Austrian referendum on the Treaty and, in general, for more 'direct democracy' reflected populist 'anti-elite rhetoric' and its characteristic discourse of 'hyper-democracy' (Guibernau 2007, 143; Gärtner 2009, 23). However, a closer look at the category relations between 'us' and 'them' postulated in *Krone* readers letters reveals different positions (see Karner 2010b). In inadvertently addressing the question as to who exactly 'we' are, some readers clearly invoked a national in-group defined in outright opposition to the EU:

---

8　This topos of calling for a collective rescue builds on a long genealogy (Karner 2010b, 391): in the 1920s, the Christian-Social party campaigned to 'rescue Vienna' and, in doing so, tapped into anti-Semitism (Hanisch 1994, 120). More recently, the FPÖ's 1993 anti-immigration petition 'Austria first' (see Reisigl and Wodak 2001, 151–165) invoked similar notions of an external danger calling for a rescue of the allegedly threatened in-group. It should also be noted that reactions to the latter included a 'procession of light', the largest demonstration in the history of the Second Republic (Weigl 2009, 85), which articulated a counter-discourse of tolerance and pluralism.

Austrians want to remain Austrian and do not want to become servants to European elites. (*Kronen Zeitung* 10 April 2008, 34)

Beautiful Austria, not Europe, is my homeland. (*Kronen Zeitung* 11 April 2008, 29)

However, in other readers' letters a different, non-national 'deixis' (Billig 1995a) was at work, pointing at a pan-European citizenry. In a discourse of cross-border solidarity, 'ordinary *European* citizens' across the EU were defined as sharing a common fate, as collectively abandoned by their respective and equally self-serving political elites:

Almost all Europeans want a democratic EU … but we don't want to become servants to the US, we want to … stay true to our roots. (*Kronen Zeitung* 15 June 2008, 63)

When will those arrogant politicians realize that they can't treat European citizens like this? (*Kronen Zeitung* 17 June 2008, 26)

I am for Europe and value being part of its culture and civilization. But Europe is not the same as the EU … EU-politicians have no right to take possession of Europe, yet they do so … Europe belongs to us all, not just to the bureaucrats in Brussels. (*Kronen Zeitung* 21 May 2010, 26)

Another crucial assumption recurs across multiple letters: the diagnosis that current realities and developments deviate from Europe's founding vision and raison d'être. Put differently, the claim is often made that Europe is not, or not any more, what it ought to be:

The idea of a peaceful Europe after World War II was noble … However, today a centralized European state, deprived of soul and culture, is being propagated … Europe needs free trade, financial control … and a socially responsible capitalism … Only a federal and truly democratic Europe can benefit Austria and the other member-states. (*Kronen Zeitung* 28 October 2009, 23)

I am a committed European, but a firm opponent of the undemocratic EU-dictatorship in Brussels. (*Kronen Zeitung* 27 June 2010, 33)

Assessments of divergences between European ideals and realities also defined the positions of some key actors in the debates surrounding the Lisbon Treaty. Their respective pronouncements on the gap between what is and what ought to be (Karner 2010b) included calls for stronger regions, critical MEP Hans-Peter Martin demanding a new and 'exemplary citizens' democracy in Europe' (*Krone* 24 June 2008, 4–5) as well as then Chancellor Gusenbauer and his successor envisioning a 'truly social union' (*Krone* 27 June 2008, 4). Such alternative visions for the EU's future also crystallized a key function of all forms of rhetoric, offering interpretations whilst, crucially, enabling speakers to argue for one of at least two competing positions or courses of action.

The inter-related rhetorical functions of interpretation and political self-positioning emerged again in recent *Krone* readers' responses to the Greek debt-crisis. Not only, so a recurring narrative went, would the EU be unable to solve the crisis but the time for some drastic national decisions had come:

> Greece will certainly not be expelled from the Euro-zone. Instead … countries like Austria will be dragged down along with the rest … Since the EU can't be improved, as it is fundamentally flawed, there is no alternative for Austria but to exit this project of non-peace. (*Kronen Zeitung* 10 April 2010, 27)

> Greece is bankrupt, Portugal, Spain and Italy will follow; the former communist countries have had to be supported since their accession, and the UK enjoys a generous special status … Austria, Germany, Holland, Finland and Luxembourg will have to contribute even more towards gigantic EU-bailouts for financially struggling member-states … The achievements of hard-working earlier generations are sacrificed in the name of greed – only exploitation and quick profit matter. A more social capitalism, values such as patriotism, honour, solidarity, reliability and family are being discredited. Austria's political puppets lied to get us into the EU … The solution: to leave the Eurozone or, even better, the EU. (*Kronen Zeitung* 11 February 2010, 35)

Echoing a suggestion previously made in a *Krone* column (1 May 2010, 3), another reader concurred that there was another, more viable European model, one smaller and grounded in the history of the Habsburg empire:

> The EU's end will not be pleasant but it does not imply Europe's end. On the contrary! It means a new beginning! New, but over centuries naturally grown alliances will re-form – perhaps exactly as recently implied here: as a new Danube-alliance with entirely different rules. Because the EU will collapse, but Austria remains. (*Kronen Zeitung* 7 May 2010, 31)

As with the discursive chains discussed earlier, such claims and interpretations invite counter-claims and are contested by alternative accounts. On occasion, and the paper's generally highly EU-critical line notwithstanding, some *Krone* readers offer a counter-discourse that is at least moderately pro-European and rejects divisive, de-contextualized and simplistic scape-goating. The following letter by a German reader is a case in point:

> I am concerned about … many readers' letters. Instead of constructively debating the current crisis, they blame everything on the EU … I can't understand why some people are disappointed by what has happened since Austria's EU

accession: the country has experienced an economic upturn, for which Austria is widely envied. (*Kronen Zeitung* 1 August 2008, 24)

A similar counter-discourse seeking to provide a transnationally co-operative answer to the 'which Europe?' question emerges in a 'pro-EU case' made by former Austrian Chancellor Franz Vranitzky (2008, 4, 6, my translation) in the *Krone*:

> The Lisbon Treaty does not dis-empower Austria. Strange claims that it would end our neutrality, deprive us of our water or our sovereignty … are false. Austria is not threatened by this … Clearly, today's gigantic problems – concerning energy, the environment, migration, knowledge transfer, global economic competition and many more – cannot be tackled by a single, small country.

Looking beyond the *Krone* and its readers as my main units of analysis in this chapter, Austria's wider press also includes vocal and prominent pro-European voices. For example, the present debt crises have also been interpreted through calls for closer European integration (as opposed to national re-entrenchment):

> Emerging tensions between Germans and Greeks … could strike a fatal blow to Europe, both economically and politically. The only alternative is a big leap towards the political union many consider to be impossible. [This] would ultimately determine budgets, taxes, pensions and social welfare systems. Economic uncertainties won't disappear. But a united Europe, without member-states working against one another, will be able to tackle instability much more effectively … Somebody should dare face reality: the United States of Europe have become an economic necessity. (Löw 2010a, my translation)

> In the midst of the financial crisis, addressing Europe's future is an absolute necessity … Reality has already given the answer. If the EU doesn't turn into a kind of United States of Europe, it will collapse. The economy determines this. (Hoffmann-Ostenhof 2010b, my translation)

*Analogies and nostalgic contrasts*

Reflecting on the 'existential', 'moral', 'political' and 'scholarly' uses of history in the context of an attempted 'cultural Europeanisation', Klas-Göran Karlsson (2010, 45) observes that 'history is made use of … in a communicative process so that certain groups can satisfy certain needs or look after certain interests'. Two sets of questions follow from this, which can only be meaningfully addressed in empirical context: which history is being used? And who are the groups or individuals utilizing 'it', what are the 'needs' they are addressing and the interests they are pursuing? The first question is also debated by Konrad Jarausch (2010, 313), who argues that national histories constitute the dominant frameworks of interpretation and that, unlike sections of Europe's political establishment, 'the overwhelming majority of ordinary Europeans can hardly be supposed to be framing their recollections in a European fashion'. Building on an analysis published elsewhere (Karner 2010b), I now turn to rhetorical invocations of different historical memories and narratives by *Krone* readers in the period 2008–2010. Two main insights pertaining to the discursive uses of the past emerge from this: first, whilst distinctly national memories are indeed the most prominent, 'ordinary Austrians' also draw on a wider range of European and global historical reference points in the micro-contexts of interpretation and argumentation. Second, the apparent 'need' being satisfied by such invocation is the nostalgic – and strongly politicized – articulation of narratives of loss, crisis and anxiety.

A recent manifestation of the rhetorical invocation of particular memories, or a specific historical narrative, occurred following EU concessions to the Czech Republic in the context of the Czech ratification of the Lisbon Treaty and concerning the controversial Beneš decrees and the expulsion the Sudeten Germans after World War II:

> In agreeing to a clause that accepts the Beneš decrees and thus should not be condoned by any civilized European people, the European governments … have betrayed the victims of heinous crimes … In light of this, it is not surprising that there are calls to leave the EU. (*Kronen Zeitung* 12 November 2009, 35)

Such letters articulated their opposition to the Lisbon Treaty by, first, accusing the EU of ethical double-standards and, second, by invoking a discourse of (German/Austrian) historical victimhood (see Niven 2006). Such arguments show that 'ordinary social actors' can and do look beyond national borders for historical reference points; crucial, however, is the interpretative work performed by the memories and narratives in question and the rhetorical uses – here the articulation of opposition to the EU – to which they are put.

*Krone* readers' opposition to the Lisbon Treaty and European integration indeed make frequent reference to various historical contexts *constructed* as alleged points of similarity and meaningful comparison with perceived present ills. Disconcertingly, the alleged common denominator between closer European integration and the historical contexts invoked in the following claims can be summarized as a 'democratic deficit' and perceptions of political elites as self-serving and out-of-touch with ordinary citizens:

> Today's situation of the EU diluting democracy is strongly reminiscent of the Weimar Republic! And we all know what happened subsequent to that. Surely, post-war achievements including freedom [and] democracy … mustn't be lost due to the stupidity and decadence of the political elite. (*Kronen Zeitung* 6 January 2010, 21)

> Like many past empires the EU, originally a great idea, has mutated into an uncontrollable, alien and money-sucking giant, which in its current form is destined to die. (*Kronen Zeitung* 19 May 2010, 29)

The initial Irish rejection of the Lisbon Treaty in a first referendum in June 2008 was welcomed in the *Krone* and interpreted through an essentialist discourse on Ireland's past and present premised on the supposedly enduring legacy of the Irish anti-colonial struggles (e.g. 8 June 2008, 2–3; 17 June 2008, 16).

In other contexts, readers develop arguments against European integration further by, worryingly, likening present European structures with historical examples of dictatorship:

> EU-commissioner Olli Rehn wants to restrict member-states' budgetary sovereignty ... [W]e've gradually been deprived of our rights ... unrestricted lorry traffic ..., rising criminality, unrestricted immigration ... EU-regulations that make life harder and only benefit big corporations ... If budgetary decisions are now also handed over the EU, then the only thing missing will be a 'strong man' and we'll be precisely where we were 80 years ago. (*Kronen Zeitung* 17 May 2010, 23)

Several observations can be made of such typical claims that recur on the *Krone* readers' letters pages: first, readers clearly cast their web widely – in both time and geographical space – in their search for points of alleged historical comparison. Second, and disconcertingly, such accounts reveal that the European Union suffers from a deep crisis of legitimacy amongst sections of its population. Third, the kinds of rhetorical comparisons drawn in these and other accounts are defined by a large dose of historical de-contextualization. Fundamental dissimilarities and defining differences in political systems, social structures and ideological contexts are overlooked and ignored in the service of rhetorical claims whose purpose is to make straightforward sense of complex scenarios and to express political disgruntlement (Karner 2010b). Such accounts are defined by what Jan-Werner Müller describes as 'resort[ing] to analogy instead of argument'; 'analogical reasoning', he shows, 'serve[s] to reduce complexity and short-circuit critical reflection [and] also to create instant legitimacy' (Müller 2002, 8, 27). As with some of the claims discussed in the previous section, the rhetorical purpose of such alleged historical analogies is two-fold and seemingly unaffected by the historical distortions they contain: to make sense of a present situation and to position oneself politically in relation to it:

> [D]espite current turbulences, the EU-commission recommends Estonia's inclusion in the Euro-zone ... [and] Austria pushes for EU-membership for the remaining Balkan countries ... How about Israel, Palestine, Egypt, Lybia ... so that we've got another 'Roman Empire'...? I'd suggest Istanbul as capital ...

> Get out, who can! … History has shown that things that don't work on a small
> scale, fail spectacularly in larger structures. (*Kronen Zeitung* 27 May 2010, 37)

Another controversy, the aforementioned 'case' that divided the Austrian
public of a Kosovo-Albanian girl who spent her formative years in Austria and
was fighting deportation for many months following her family's unsuccessful
asylum-application, was also commented on by a *Krone* reader in terms that made
analogical use of a particular chapter in (Austrian) history and, in doing so, made
a case for her deportation and for restrictive asylum legislation:

> There can only be one solution … Kosovo needs to be rebuilt. That is what
> our grandparents did in Austria. So why should the [Interior Minister] not send
> the rest of the family … back to THEIR country? (*Kronen Zeitung* 27 May
> 2008, 22)

The experience of Austrian post-war reconstruction is here (mis)used as a political
yardstick to judge an individual case shaped by altogether different historical –
and of course idiosyncratic – circumstances. In addition to the political opinion
articulated on this particular issue, such letters contain traces of another key
feature of many accounts offered by *Krone* readers – a strong sense of nostalgia
that juxtaposes a negatively perceived present to an earlier 'golden age' (Karner
2010b):

> After the state treaty we had our economic miracle … There was full employment,
> little criminality, no problems with asylum-seekers or mass migration …
> a functioning welfare system … [W]e made our own decisions. Those were
> the best years for … Austria … Things have gone downhill … since our EU
> accession. (*Kronen Zeitung* 11 April 2008, 29)

Time and again *Krone* readers portray Austria's EU accession as a fall from grace,
a historical turning point allegedly reached under false pretences:

> They blatantly lied to us when promising a stable Euro… One should ask all EU-
> enthusiasts why we lived a good life during the post-war decades and why, since
> 1995, we've had many more problems. (*Kronen Zeitung* 18 May 2010, 31)

Since 1995, such arguments claim, things have gone downhill. Moreover,
suspiciously simplistic causal connections are postulated between EU-membership
and a diversity of perceived dangers:

> A propaganda-campaign deceived Austrians to join the EU … Our currency
> and neutrality disappeared, as did our borders and sovereignty. The EU has
> had an negative effect on employment and prosperity … Multiculturalism and
> unrestricted immigration are presented as normal, without acknowledging the

costs of integration and lack of cohesion ... future conflict is inevitable ...
People are turned into hedonistic nomads, forgetting that happiness and success
require continuity and sustainability. Speculation is replacing serious economics
... (*Kronen Zeitung* 12 November 2009, 34–35)

Several conceptual insights follow from the discussion presented in this section.
The data presented here corroborates and further refines Bell's (2003) notion of
the national 'mythscape'. This terrain of competing, 'dominant' and 'subaltern'
memories and narratives of the national past has here been shown to be interspersed
– in micro-contexts of ongoing sense-making and daily political argumentation
– by a multitude of historical analogies. The latter reflect the geographical and
temporal breadth of reference points – national, European and global – utilized
by social actors as they interpret the present and position themselves ideologically
within it. At the same time, such 'analogical reasoning' tends to be self-interested,
politically motivated, de-contextualizing and thus often distortive. All this
having been said, the postulated analogies and contrasts unearthed here clearly
reflect some deeply felt disgruntlements and anxieties. Articulated in one of the
world's still most stable and affluent countries, growing insecurities and internal
inequalities notwithstanding, such sentiments need to be taken seriously – both
by the observing sociologist and from the perspective of a common European
project. The Austrian materials analyzed here show that relative affluence and
deep anxieties are not mutually exclusive but seemingly inter-related (Karner
2010b, 406). Recent nostalgic memories of Austria as an 'island of the blessed'
(Liessmann 2005) yield themselves as an interpretative framework that sees
current structural and cultural changes as deteriorations, chronic crises and steep
decline. The transformations typically encountered in post-industrial societies
then come to be seen as avoidable changes for the worse, and political elites – on
both national and European levels – are turned into the culprits for present ills and
insecurities; and the more tightly 'sealed' nation-state of the not-too-distant past
is constructed as both a now lost haven of former security and as the proposed
answer to contemporary uncertainties and dangers. All of this confirms Gingrich's
observation (2006, 44–47) of 'economic chauvinism' and 'cultural pessimism' as
defining characteristics of neo-nationalisms in the 'small and affluent' countries
of Western Europe, where they reflect 'concerns and fears about downward social
mobility, loss of status and loss of identity ... among the majority population'.

   However, as with the discursive chains and discussions about the relationship
between Europe and its member-states examined earlier, there are prominent
counter-discourses challenging the kinds of historical narratives outlined here.
For example, the following reflections on the EU – proposed prior to the current
economic crises in Austria's quality weekly *Profil* – view European structures in a
very different historical light:

[T]he EU has integrated a dozen poverty-stricken countries from the former
Eastern block ... it has avoided the United States' economic and political mistakes,

has turned the Euro into the world's strongest currency ... and has enormously benefited the economies of countries like Austria and Ireland. Criticism ... can only start once these incomparable achievements are acknowledged ... Of course there are weaknesses, but how a-historical can one be to be to expect anything else? ... How can the EU's achievements be ignored? (Lingens 2008, my translation)

Similarly, a *Falter* commentary on the initial Irish rejection of the Lisbon Treaty argued that today's challenges could not be handled by nation-states individually, yet there was perhaps a case for a smaller though more committed EU: 'There is no compulsion to be part of the European project. The EU might then be smaller but less paralyzed' (Horaczek 2008, my translation). More recently, against the backdrop of the Greek debt-crisis, Raimund Löw selected historical analogies entirely different from the ones typically utilized by *Krone* readers, in order to call for closer European integration:

[W]hen ... the nationalist cacophony [was] almost unbearable, Europeans have tended to take new integrative steps. Today's politicians must attempt the same feat. Yet, the circumstances are even more challenging, now that governments' hesitancy has strengthened the nationalist populists. (Löw 2010b, my translation)

## Opposing pluralism, Brussels and change in other parts of Europe

The analysis above has revealed three discursive features defining everyday argumentation contained in the readers' letters of Austria's most popular newspaper. These features, which were also shown to be resisted by counter-discourses both within and outside the paper in question, offer both interpretations and political positions. All three features – the *discursive linking* of disparate phenomena and concerns, a pre-occupation with the question as to *which Europe* is the most desirable and as to how far this departs from current realities, and invocations of *nostalgic memories* and historical narratives to make sense of the present – are equally detectable in political debates and many other social settings across Europe. Whilst it is hoped that future research will provide detailed investigations of these discursive characteristics in other contexts, the remainder of this chapter provides select snapshots of other European settings where debates informed by sentiments and rhetorical patterns similar to the Austrian material examined above are at work.

A noteworthy articulation of a discursive chain linking a deeply reified portrayal of Islam with various perceived social ills, whilst nonetheless refuting critical assessments of such accounts as xenophobic, emerged in a recent *Profil* interview with the Dutch populist Geert Wilders:

> Wilders: The large majority of Muslims in the Netherlands are law-abiding
> citizens ... But we believe that their culture and ideology contradict our values
> and identity. This is why we demand that a stop be put to Islamization and mass
> migration from Islamic countries ... Although ... Islam possesses religious
> symbols ... it bears much closer resemblance with totalitarian ideologies: after
> all, Islam wants to govern every aspect of life and society, which is why I compare
> it to communism and fascism ... Look at what happens to Muslims wanting to
> convert to another religion. Their lives are in danger! Honour killings, genital
> mutilation – all this is part and parcel of Islamic culture, which Islamization has
> brought to us ... Dutch statistics also show that crime [and] dependency on the
> welfare state are higher amongst Muslims. (*Profil* 22 March 2010, 82–83, my
> translation)

Several of the rhetorical strategies examined above are at work here. First,
Wilders engages in 'positive self- and negative other-presentation' (Wodak 2007,
662), pitting 'us' against 'them', and presenting the former as superior to, yet
threatened by the latter and its alleged 'Islamization' of its 'host society'. Second,
Wilders' monolithic understanding of Islam and 'topos of threat' utilizes utterly
de-contextualized historical analogies, likening Islam to 'other totalitarian
ideologies'. Third, and in equally de-contextualized fashion, Wilders discursively
ties Islam to criminality and welfare-dependency. Later in the interview, Wilders,
whose 'Party for Freedom' is now the third largest in the Dutch parliament, also
commented on another 'node' in the discursive chain surrounding the perceived
threat of 'Islamization' discussed earlier:

> *Profil*:    [A US foreign office human-rights report] criticizes the Swiss ban on
>            new minarets.
> Wilders:   That is ridiculous. I welcomed the result of the Swiss referendum.
>            I don't want Islamic symbolism here. That is not discrimination, it
>            is every country's right to reject things like that ... Look at the new
>            mosque in Rotterdam: what an imperialist minaret! People hate those
>            minarets for good reasons. I am not calling for the closure of existing
>            mosques. But neither do I want even more to be built, and the public
>            does not want this either. Are we democrats or not? (*Profil* 22 March
>            2010, 83, 85)

Wilders' question bears the hallmark of populist 'hyper-democracy' (Guibernau
2007), in which the will of the majority trumps minority rights.

   In a different European context, writing about contemporary experiences of
racist discrimination and violence endured by Hungarian Roma, Éva Kovács argues
that under different socio-political circumstances their experiences of exclusion
and poverty could have evoked widespread solidarity. As it is, however, structural
marginalization is further compounded by inter-related racist stereotypes, through
which many amongst the ethnic majority have come to view the Roma:

Although these citizens have little if any social and economic capital, dominant discourses has stigmatized them: through the culturally-racist generalized suspicion of 'Gypsy criminality', the biologically-racist fear of 'uncontrolled Gypsy birth-rates', and 'welfare-racism' that regards Roma as 'parasitically living off benefits'. (Kovács 2009, 100, my translation)

We here again encounter prominent discursive chains, which resonate on the content-level with some of prejudices and argumentative patterns extrapolated from the materials examined above, linking a particular ethnic 'other' with crime, fearful demographic projections and ideas about welfare entitlements or alleged 'abuses'. The wider context to the Hungarian example is provided by the recent rise of rightwing extremism across parts of post-communist Central and Eastern Europe. In a review of a recent book on this issue, Anton Pelinka summarizes its specific features as follows: anti-Semitism and hatred of Roma, 'as if the Holocaust had never happened'; the construction of 'the West' and 'America' as a conspiratorial pariah that appeals particularly to young male workers disappointed and marginalized by the capitalist transformation but also, more so than elsewhere, to some amongst the young and educated (Pelinka 2010, 16, my translation).

The second discursive feature emerging from the above discussion, criticisms of the EU in its present structures, reappears and is examined in Abts et al.'s (2009) recent quantitative study of the 'sources' of Belgian Euroscepticism. This consists of statistical analyses of a 2007 survey, of 1,004 randomly sampled respondents, on 'the changes in the scope, nature and characteristics of citizenship … as an effect of the process of deepening and enlargement of the European Union' (Abts et al. 2009, 7). Two contextual points need to be noted. First, Belgian levels of Euroscepticism have been comparatively low. This was also reflected before the recent Belgian elections, when the eventually victorious Flemish separatists defined their goals as further regional empowerment *within* the European Union (Euronews 12 June 2010). Second, Abts et al. (2009, 19) conceptualize Euroscepticism as a multi-dimensional, 'multifaceted' phenomenon. In the survey data they analyze this was measured by respondents' various attitudes towards Belgium's EU membership, towards European integration, European enlargement, and the possibility of Turkey joining the EU.

Abts et al. frame their analysis through several hypotheses that fall under three established paradigms for explaining Euroscepticism: 'utilitarian approaches' that regard EU-scepticism as a negative assessment of membership arrived at through (individual or collective) 'cost-benefit' calculations; 'cultural attachment' theses regarding nationalist sentiments and distrust of (European or non-European) 'others' as key; and approaches that see 'institutional distrust' of the EU as the decisive determinant of Euroscepticims. It is also noteworthy that each of these dimensions is present in the *Krone* readers' letters examined earlier: beliefs that Austria and hence individual tax-payers help finance the EU without deriving substantial benefits, strongly nation-centred discourses of identity, and profound discontent with the structures and workings of the European Union. In the Belgian context, and from amongst 13 more specific hypotheses, Abts et al.'s statistical analyses reveal three major determinants of Euroscepticism. First, 'negative evaluations of the egocentric benefits of EU membership' (Abts et al. 2009, 20) – or personal assessments that *individually* one has gained little if anything from being a citizen of an enlarging and increasingly integrated European Union. Second, 'social distrust in European fellow citizens' is shown to be consequential, strongly suggesting that social capital building across the EU's internal, national boundaries is key to the European project's future. The third major determinant of Euroscepticism confirmed by Abts et al.'s analyses is the afore-mentioned distrust in EU institutions (rather than national politics). Moreover, Abts et al. (2009, 20) show that low levels of education correlate with Euroscepticism and, crucially for our purposes, that citizens with exclusively national identities are 'the most hostile to Europe … [whereas those] who see themselves in terms of … multiple identities that include an element of supranationalism are more favourable to the European project'.

Put differently, the various suggested answers to the question as to how the relationship between nation-states and Europe is or should be defined indeed matter. Exclusive national identities – as opposed to more open, inclusive and multi-dimensional self-understandings – tend to translate into higher levels of Euroscepticism. With regard to the latter, Abts et al.'s Belgian research corroborates an important point. Whilst Europe 'seems to act as a screen onto which some groups … project their general feelings of threatened interests, identity and power', such sentiments include different meanings, a broad array of 'critical dispositions', disbeliefs and doubts about Europe and European integration: from 'hard Euroscepticism' or 'outright rejection' on one end of the spectrum, to 'soft Euroscepticism' implying 'contingent or qualified' concern on the other (Abts et al. 2009, 21, 8). In other words, the *which-Europe*-question matters, in Belgium as in Austria and elsewhere, and Euroscepticism is itself not an ideologically monolithic phenomenon.

The final other European context to be mentioned in parallel to my discussion of Austrian materials is comprised of various British settings.

Lynn and Lea's analysis of the 'social construction of asylum-seekers' in British newspapers and, in particular, readers' letters in 2001, a context the authors describe as characterized by a 'reawakening of national identity' (2003, 426), reveals several similarities with my earlier discussion. Adopting a discourse analytical framework, Lynn and Lea extrapolate various defining rhetorical features from a series of readers' letters. First, there is a recurring tendency to construct a difference between 'genuine' asylum-seekers deemed in need of protection and alleged 'bogus' asylum-seekers. The latter are constructed – by a frequently recurring assertion – as a drain on national resources, allegedly resulting in UK citizens 'being denied a "birth right", [or] taken-for-granted entitlement[s] that come with their citizenship' (Lynn and Lea 2003, 434): particularly the nation's weaker and already marginalized citizens, according to such claims, loose out further due to the support given to allegedly undeserving asylum-seekers. Second, there is a recurring conflation of asylum-seekers with other issues and perceived dangers. Thus, in another example of a discursive chain linking disparate phenomena as though they were causally related, asylum-seekers are in some readers' letters discursively tied to the threat of terrorism (Lynn and Lea 2003, 440). Third, Lynn and Lea reveal a repeated preoccupation with another alleged 'enemy in our midst': 'white liberals', whose inclusive, human-rights centred 'counter-discourse' sympathetic with asylum-seekers' plight, is constructed as elitist and out-of-touch with ordinary people's concerns and hardships. In this we therefore encounter a discursive strategy reminiscent of *Krone* readers' hostility towards 'do-gooders' perceived to side with 'the other' in opposition to the ethnic majority.

A nostalgic discourse focused on a by-gone 'golden era' and opposed to recent social changes was shown to constitute a defining feature of the *Krone* readers' letters pages. Such anxiety and unhappiness with some of the structural transformations typical of life in post-industrial societies are encountered in numerous settings across and beyond the European Union. Moreover, such sentiments are not confined to particular localities caught out by recent changes. More accurately, there is also evidence of such politics of disgruntlement and belonging underpinning some prominent migratory flows *within* the EU. Esther Bott's research, comprising qualitative interviews and survey findings amongst working-class British migrants in Tenerife, is a case in point. Attempting to illuminate these young British migrants' 'complex social psychological motivations', Bott reveals several recurring experiences and sentiments. These include attempts to escape 'an often problematic or traumatic life in the UK', 'a wider British lusting for a life in the sun as code for "having made it"' (Bott 2004, 59, 63), and – most significantly for our present purposes – views of contemporary Britain as 'crest-fallen', allegedly 'overrun' by immigrants and purportedly disadvantageous to her own citizens. The notion of a recent 'deterioration of Britain' – and its association, particularly by male research participants, with immigration – was at the heart of many an account Bott encountered. This was exemplified in claims that 'asylum-seekers … get all the jobs and houses and healthcare … all you do is pay tax to support the foreigners', that 'Britain's not British any more', that 'they're all there claiming benefits and you can't … [though] you're British citizen', that in Bradford 'you wouldn't believe how bad it's got', and that Luton is 'full of mosques' (Bott 2004, 64–65). There are further remarkable rhetorical parallels between *Krone* readers' letters and Bott's data. The latter also reveals a discursive chain linking crime, immigration and political discontent, reflected in a British migrant's claim that the government is 'responsible for the asylum-seekers, who are responsible for the drug and crime problems' (Bott 2004, 65). Similarly, the rhetorical feature of portraying other national contexts as examples worth emulating, as in *Krone* readers' support for a Swiss ban on minarets, resurfaces in a shocking statement by one of Bott's interviewees (2004, 65) that 'Britain should be more like Australia and let people die in boats off the coast'. Particularly the accounts offered by young male British migrants in Tenerife are rife with narratives of social decline:

[R]acist and anti-immigrant narratives … construct the notion that Britain is 'no longer British'. The idea that Britain is 'full' and can no longer accommodate 'true Britons' or 'true Britishness' is also important to motivations to migrate to a location that can accommodate these nationalist feelings. Thus Tenerife becomes a space where Britishness can survive threats imposed by floods of 'resource-draining illegals', from which Britain is unprotected and has therefore 'deteriorated'. (Bott 2004, 65)

It is stating the obvious to repeat that many everyday claims and interpretations analyzed above are thoroughly de-contextualized, often factually wrong, driven by self-interest, and sometimes ethically deeply problematic. That said, an understanding of some of the life-worlds, motivations, sentiments and politics that help shape contemporary Europe demand an analysis of the identity discourses examined here.

**Concluding remarks**

It has been argued that in a wider national and European context dominated by neo-liberalism the *Krone* and its readership seek to construct a stable identity by juxtaposing the idea of the 'hard-working, law-abiding and "genuine" Austrian' to various 'demonized' others: foreigners, welfare dependents, drug-addicts and criminals (Rittberger 2009, 51). This analysis has confirmed that much of the discourse encountered in Austria's most popular newspaper, particularly its readers' letters, and comparable phenomena in other parts of Europe are indeed underpinned by an oppositional 'logic' – directing sometimes fierce criticism at a range of others deemed responsible for, or symptoms of, perceived social decline. Whilst 'positive self- and negative other-presentation' (Wodak 2007, 662) thus partly characterize the discourses of national belonging and exclusion discussed in this chapter, my analysis has shown that they also display a wider range of argumentative concerns and defining rhetorical features. First, such discourses operate through *discursive chains*, which in 'tying' disparate issues to one another offer both a (simplistic) interpretative lens and particular political position on complex social realities. Second, the questions as to *which Europe* some of its citizens want and as to how far this is seen to differ from current structures lies at the heart of the everyday debates analyzed above. Importantly, EU-scepticism has been shown not to be a monolithic phenomenon but to subsume different political visions and identity discourses offering various definitions of the relationship between the nation-state and the European network state. Third, the argumentative use of contextually chosen memories – or the 'analogical' (mis)uses of history (Müller 2002, 27) – has been shown to inform everyday interpretations of perceived social decline and the articulation of a politics of disgruntlement. Significantly, such accounts do not offer synchronic comparisons across international borders, which would make European and arguably especially Austrian complaints seem at best petty[9] compared with much of the rest of the world, but diachronic comparisons with the nation's recent past. This results in a nostalgic narrative of decline, articulated through select memories and expressing common feelings that things have deteriorated.

The materials examined above echo, in part, Stuart Hall's prediction that 'we will … look back at this era in terms of the erosion of the nation-state and the national identities … associated with it'; as Hall emphasizes, however, nation-states are certainly not 'bowing off the stage of history' but going into an 'even deeper trough of defensive exclusivism' (1997, 177). This raises crucial questions about the context to the (perceived) 'decline' of nation-states and their discursive/political re-assertion. The forces of (economic) globalization, to which we turn in the next chapter, are central to such issues.

---

9   Internal inequalities notwithstanding, international comparisons have ranked Austria fourteenth-best in terms of quality of life (*Krone* 6 October 2009, 7), Vienna currently tops the global ranking for urban living standards, Austria has been ranked the world's forth-safest country (*Krone* 13 June 2010, 10) and had the lowest unemployment rates within the EU in June 2010 (*Der Standard* 31 July 2010, 1).

# Chapter 4
# Markets and Nations:
# Of Flows and Solidarities

## Introduction

E.P. Thompson's seminal analysis of eighteenth-century English food riots unearths conditions that also resonate with a dilemma defining today's era of globalization: the social costs of the ever-widening reach of market forces:

> It is possible to detect in almost every eighteenth-century crowd action some legitimising notion … men and women … were informed by the belief that they were defending traditional rights and customs … a popular consensus as to what were legitimate and … illegitimate practices in marketing, milling, baking etc. This … was grounded upon a consistent traditional view of social norms and obligations, of the proper economic functions … within the community, which … can be said to constitute the moral economy … An outrage to these moral assumptions, quite as much as actual deprivation, was the usual occasion for direct action. (Thompson 1991, 188)

Central to Thompson's argument is thus the notion of the moral economy, defined as 'confrontations in the market-place over access (or entitlement) to "necessities"' (1991, 337). In this chapter, I show that comparable tensions between economics and politics, struggles over the advocated limits to the power of markets, lie at the heart of many contemporary national identity negotiations. I illustrate this through an examination of recent Austrian debates on the environment, food, inequality, education, art, and migration, which share a common denominator: they all grapple with what one may term marketization – its ethics, extent, and expansion. Significantly, I trace these debates about the relationship between politics and economics, between the nation and markets, to the period preceding the financial crises of the last few years. As such, the following presents a record of tensions that were already felt prior to, and subsequently gathered pace with, the onset of a global financial crisis in 2008. Later parts of this analysis again broaden my empirical scope from Austria to other European contexts, whilst moving from these 'pre-crisis moments' to the current context of global financial fears and (attempted) political counter-reactions.

## Theoretical context

According to Thompson, the *longue durée* perspective needed for an understanding of English social history in the eighteenth and nineteenth centuries involved a clash between an older moral economy and newly expanding, impersonal market forces. Traditional notions of entitlement were gradually pushed aside, their widespread and 'stubborn defence' notwithstanding, by the logic of supply and demand:

> It is not easy for us to conceive … [of] a time, within a smaller and more integrated community, when it appeared 'unnatural' that any man should profit from the necessities of others, and when it was assumed that, in time of dearth, prices of 'necessities' should remain at a customary level, even though there might be less all round … [T]he death of the old moral economy of provision was … long-drawn-out. (Thompson 1991, 252–253)

Invoking a central debate in economic anthropology, one could query if this interpretation may over-romanticize the pre-modern past: the debate in question pits the *formalist* position that profit-maximization defines all economic activity, regardless of its cultural/historical context, against the *substantivists'* postulate of a fundamental discontinuity between pre-modern (socially 'embedded') economic systems and capitalist social formations, to which alone the tenets of (Western) economic theory are considered to apply. Put more simply: were pre-modern economies indeed governed by a different economic logic not driven by profit-maximization with its disregard for social norms and costs? It is not my intention to side with one historical hypothesis against the other. Yet, there is another way of reading both the historical record examined by Thompson and the contemporary materials analyzed below: social actors in these otherwise very different contexts clearly conceive(d) of economic alternatives, of systems grounded in localities and traditions, of local/national moral economies that (aim to) circumscribe the reach of market forces.

Struggles over and against the consequences of expansive markets seen to 'colonize' ever wider realms of life are a hallmark of our current historical epoch and provide my focus in this chapter. Such struggles also manifest in political reassertions of the local:

> [W]hat is happening at the margins … out there in the local? What about the people who did not go 'above' … but went underneath, to the local? The return of the local is often a response to globalization. It is what people do when, in the face of a particular form globalization … they opt out … and say: 'I don't know anything about that any more. I can't control it. I know no politics that can get hold of it. It's too big … Everything is on its side. There are some terrains in between, little interstices, the smaller spaces within which I have to work.' (Hall 1997, 183)

It is now a social scientific truism that the state no longer exercises a (territorially circumscribed) monopoly of power. Yesteryear's 'container theory' (Beck 2000, 23), which equated (most) politics with the nation-state and associated social relations with relatively self-contained localities, is of comparatively little use in a world of instant, world-wide communication, global economic actors, universally shared risks, globally distributed inequalities, and the transnational 'flow' of finances, technologies, media-images, ideologies, and – with highly variable degrees of institutional resistance – people (Appadurai 1990). In such a context, politics become multi-dimensional – concerned with the global, national, regional and local – and potentially internally ambiguous: supporting regional markets, for example, may help reproduce local or national configurations of power, whilst bolstering the forces of counter-hegemony in the global realm, its widening inequalities and dominant multinational corporations.

The data examined below needs to be seen in such contexts of multi-dimensional power relations and ideological struggles. Much of the material analyzed here circulated in Austria's public sphere in the period leading up to and following the parliamentary election on 1 October 2006.[1] This qualitative analysis examines a wide range of relevant sources: Austria's (ideologically heterogeneous) national press – daily and weekly, tabloid and broadsheet; news on the national broadcasting network ORF; regional papers and magazines; the electoral programmes by the five main parties (i.e. SPÖ, ÖVP, FPÖ, the Green Party, BZÖ), further complemented by smaller electoral campaigns (i.e. by critical MEP Hans-Peter Martin and Austria's communists respectively). Moreover, to capture as much of the ideological spectrum as possible,[2] the data also includes reflections offered by academics, newspaper columnists and public intellectuals.

This chapter further develops my over-arching argument that contemporary Austria needs to be understood to the backdrop of a succession of recent crises, including the perceived consequences of globalization, reactions to which have been highly variable, with nationalism one among several competing forces (advocating ethnic exclusion and pluralism respectively) in a strongly contested political field and increasingly lively civil society. Continuing along these lines, I here ask: *what* exactly is – in Austria and other parts of Europe – widely experienced and defined as an already existing or imminent *crisis*? Ruth Wodak has suggested (2006) that explaining nationalism as a reaction to globalization reveals little and calls for more differentiated accounts. This chapter seeks to provide such a more nuanced analysis by exploring recurring perceptions of globalization and various interpretations of its consequences.

---

1   The 2006 election results were as follows: SPÖ – 35.3 per cent of the vote, ÖVP – 34.3 per cent, Greens – 11.1 per cent, FPÖ – 11 per cent, BZÖ – 4.1 per cent (http://www.orf.at/061010-4750/4751txt_story.html).

2   What follows, however, is a qualitative analysis of recurring themes, concerns, and advocated political strategies, not a quantitative analysis concerned with the relative statistical/demographic representativeness of different discourses.

To analyze contemporary tensions between markets and moral economies, between the global and the local or national, this chapter draws on two bodies of literature: first, seminal interpretations (Jameson 1991) of the postmodern era as defined by the commodification of (almost) every aspect of life; second, the earlier-mentioned anthropological/historical debates concerning the (dis) continuities between pre-modern economies and (contemporary) markets as well as associated social transformations. Related questions concerning the perceived or advocated limits of the market recur throughout the data analyzed below, revealing three partly inter-connected concerns: with *widening commodification*; with *the relationship between economics and politics*; and *identity-negotiations informed by competing 'ideological orders'*. Through my central, Austrian case study and other European examples this chapter thus traces the impact of contemporary socio-economic transformations on biographies and everyday lives, local experiences of globalization, and contested interpretations of the market, its promises, consequences, dangers and advocated limits.

### Nature, commodification, (economic) strategies for the future

According to Fredric Jameson, late-/multinational-/consumer capitalism is partly defined by the commodification of previously extra-economic realms. He detects 'a prodigious expansion of capital into hitherto uncommodified areas', resulting in a 'new and historically original ... colonization of Nature and the Unconscious' (1991, 36). A close reading of recent and current debates in Austria reveals a widespread preoccupation with the first of these market expansions: the question as to whether natural resources should be (fully) commodified, related issues about the provision of food and energy for (Austrian) consumers, and discussions about climate change and proposed (economic) strategies for dealing with it as one of the most profound challenges of the twenty-first century.

*Water*

As discussed in chapter two, control of 'Austrian water' has been a key concern over recent years. In January 2003, the earlier-mentioned Günther Nenning contributed to this debate by articulating a protectionist discourse: Austria was, Nenning (2003c) argued, richly endowed with the most precious natural resource, which multinational corporations were keen to 'cash in on' (in times of growing water scarcity); such efforts to turn Austrian water into a commodity for the international market, he stressed, had to be resisted, ownership and user-rights had to remain in public Austrian hands; moreover, Nenning described water as a 'treasure' rather than a commodity, referring to its 'value and dignity' rather than its market-price, and thus conceptualized water in terms of its use- rather than exchange value, and access to it as a national entitlement to be protected.

The issue of 'national water' resurfaced several months later, when the *Krone* (30 August 2003, 12–13) reported local fears that four hydroelectric power stations in the Tyrolean Alps (that had hitherto provided 20 per cent of the electricity for the national rail network) might be put up for sale. A possible result of EU plans for a transnational 'water market', this was seen to entail more than the likely loss of local jobs: quoting a campaign against these possible developments, the article headline read 'Don't sell our water to foreign companies'.

These were not isolated concerns about the fate of national water supplies if transformed into market commodities. In their 2006 election campaigns most of the country's main parties commented on the 'water issue'. The SPÖ declared that it would not consider privatizing the country's water supply (SPÖ 2006, 18). In patriotic reference to the national flag, the ÖVP promised that 'our water will remain red-white-red', decisions about the use of Austrian water would remain 'in Austrian hands' (ÖVP 2006, 35) – a promise SPÖ and ÖVP subsequently reiterated in their joint governmental programme (*Regierungsprogramm* 2007, 74). The BZÖ (2006a, 9) also committed itself to protecting 'our water' from being 'sold off', and the FPÖ (2006, 6) opposed attempts to liberalize water supplies across the EU, defining water provision and hydroelectric energy as national, public responsibilities.

Whilst electoral manifestos need to be read sceptically, such inter-party agreement is noteworthy. Furthermore, the 'water issue' is only one manifestation of a more far-reaching concern with the widening commodification of natural resources. A range of current debates in – and indeed far beyond – Austria unfolds in a discursive force field around the nation-state, the environment and the market.

*Food and agriculture*

As mentioned earlier, Austria's 'scenic beauty' and 'food' emerged as key symbols of national identity in two surveys of the 1980s, with 80 per cent (Reiterer 1988, 118) and 97 per cent of respective respondents declaring their pride in the former, and 74 per cent articulating their attachment to the latter (Bruckmüller 1996, 70).[3] The 1980s were, in Austria as elsewhere, a decade of growing environmental awareness – fuelled by the Chernobyl nuclear disaster in 1986 – of the transnationally shared risks of 'late modernity'. With regard to food (Gruber and Bohacek 2006, 68, 75), Austria had – in 1975 – introduced the strictest legislation governing food production in Europe; twenty years later, the country's EU accession entailed a shift from such tight national regulation to cross-border competition on the European food market, its emphasis on consumer choice,

---

3    A recent survey (http://oesterreich.orf.at/stories/187976/) asked a sample of 1,000 Austrians to name specifically their 'greatest national treasure'/'object of pride': Austria's scenic beauty emerged as the most popular national symbol (53 per cent), and – compared to a 1975 study – the reported centrality of the country's food had increased from 13 to 23 per cent.

relative openness to new food production technologies, and its regulation by detailed pan-European legislation on hygiene and food labelling. To the backdrop of such changing legislative contexts concerns about food production have come to be widely debated. Moreover, public discourses about scenery and food – as symbols of Austrian national identity – often centre on farming and the changing conditions of agricultural production on the contemporary, international market.

Rapid post-war urbanization notwithstanding, rural Austria and a traditional, agricultural way of life continue to provide potent symbols of national identification. The 'rural space' featured in all parties' 2006 electoral programmes, where it was conceptualized as a realm of vital economic production and cultural activity (e.g. BZÖ 2006b; Bürgerliste Martin 2006, 12) and promised financial/ infrastructural support (e.g. ÖVP 2006, 38–39; SPÖ 2006, 18) to confront the challenges of technological and economic change. Such change has been analyzed by sociologist and public intellectual Roland Girtler, whose ethnographic and social historical work (1996; 2002) traces a seismic agricultural transformation over recent decades: the metamorphosis of previously self-sufficient, local farmers into highly specialized, profit-maximizing, yet struggling producers for an international market dominated by big 'agro-business' and supermarkets. Girtler's apprehension about the effects of this particular 'great transformation' (Polanyi 1944) on farmers, animals, the environment and consumers clearly resonates with wider public anxieties. The latter manifest, for example, in campaigns – parallel to similar concerns and movements across other parts Europe – appealing to consumers to opt for Austrian milk portrayed as the environmentally sustainable and socially 'fair' choice.

Animal rights, in the context of the treatment and transport of livestock across and beyond the EU, frequently featured in Nenning's *Krone* columns during 2001 (see Nenning 2002, 176–180): from the subsidized slaughter of cows ('to rescue the saturated market') to the European-wide suffering of some 'six million pigs' being kept in containers, Nenning criticized what he saw as the EU's complicity with a 'system of industrialized animal exploitation'; the latter, he argued, was driven by agricultural businesses depriving farmers of alternatives to the cost-effective but factory-like keeping of livestock in disregard of 'animal dignity'. The issue surfaced in several 2006 party-manifestos: the reduction (SPÖ 2006, 18) of live animal transports[4] was advocated, as was its complete stop across the EU and a shift away from factory-farming livestock (FPÖ 2006, 11), as well as a constitutional commitment to animal protection (e.g. BZÖ 2006a, 10). Yet more revealingly, the Greens' opposition to factory-farming (and its calls for relevant EU-standards) was based on an ethical objection to the commodification of living beings: animals, the Green programme (2006, 9) insisted, should not be regarded as 'production units'.

---

4    The government subsequently proposed legislation envisaging shorter live animal transports within Austria, better qualified personnel and clear guidelines for equipment and hygiene in the vehicles used (http://www.orf.at/ticker/254779.html).

Concerns about environmental and health-related consequences of an ever-expanding agricultural market dominated by multinational business are often voiced in relation to genetically modified (GM) imported food. Surveys have repeatedly revealed that the majority of Austrians oppose GM-food, making the country the most critical in the EU; contrary to the advocates of GM-food (who speak of production increases and cost-effectiveness), there are widespread objections and fears about possible long-term, yet-unknown effects on the environment and consumers' health; opposition climaxed in an anti-GM-food petition signed by 1.2 million Austrians in 1997 (Gruber and Bohacek 2006, 11). The issue has continued to be much debated: in their 2006 manifestos, SPÖ (2006, 16–17), ÖVP (2006, 34), Greens (2006, 8) and BZÖ (2006a, 9) all declared their commitment to continuing with Austria's GM-free approach to agriculture; they also recognized, however, the current impossibility of a wholesale stop to the cross-border circulation of certain GM-products within the common European market; the continued and EU-wide labelling of GM-products was thus advocated as imperative.[5] The FPÖ (2006, 10) went further in calling for an EU-wide ban on the production and import of any GM seeds and food.

In December 2006, Austria's then Minister of Agriculture secured Brussels' approval of the Alpine Republic's ban on imports of genetically modified corn (Zöchling 2007b, 19), which the *Kronen Zeitung* (29 January 2007) interpreted as an indication that Austria was the vanguard of a global reaction against the commercialization of GM-food by multinational agro-businesses. A more recent *Krone* report pitted Austria's GM-free farming against externally encroaching GM-crops and their increasingly dominant lobby in Brussels, appealing to the former to continue resisting the latter (Perry 2010a). Also relevant is the continually growing popularity (e.g. http://steiermark.orf.at/stories/177806/) of organically-farmed products: since 1998 Austria has had the worldwide largest proportion of organic farmers, who now cultivate 13.5 per cent of agricultural land, compared to 3.4 per cent across the rest of the EU (Gruber and Bohacek 2006, 49). Werner Lampert (2005), pioneer of Austria's organic movement, portrays the differences between organic and conventional, 'industrialized' agriculture through a series of dichotomies echoed in much public discourse: between biodiversity and monoculture, between small-scale farming and transnational corporations, between sustainability and 'rationalization', between responsibility (for the environment and consumers' health) and profit maximization; the latter, he argues, reduces natural resources and living beings to their exchange value, thus ignoring the 'dignity' of both animals and plants (Lampert 2005, 157, 98).

---

5   See Gruber and Bohacek (2006, 14) for a summary of (Austria's role in the genesis of) EU legislation concerning the labelling of GM-products, and of exemptions from such legislation as in the case of meat, milk or eggs from animals reared on GM-plants.

*Climate change and the market*

The positions examined above thus oppose the commodification of natural resources and the colonization of previously local/national systems of production, distribution and consumption by pan-European and global markets. There are, however, related contemporary challenges, such as climate change, for which prominent reactions advocate 'the market' as an appropriate measurement and a necessary response. Such *economistic* environmental discourses are by no means peculiarly Austrian: parts of the much-discussed 'Stern report', for example, emphasized the economic consequences of climate change (e.g. droughts affecting financial markets, possible market failures brought about by global warming) rather than its immediate environmental and human 'costs' (DW-TV 30 October 2006);[6] similarly, there are prominent European voices advocating the more effective liberalization of electricity markets and 'emissions trading' as key strategies for confronting climate change (http://www.dw-world.de 29 January 2007).

Whilst global warming is finally acknowledged as a key challenge of the twenty-first century, some relevant Austrian discourses reveal a distinctive tension: a still common self-understanding of Austria as providing the highest quality of life and environment in the EU and one of the highest worldwide (e.g. ÖVP 2006, 32) sits uneasily with the fact that the country lags considerably behind its obligations under the Kyoto agreement (e.g. http://www.orf.at/ticker/241559. html) and has, since 1990, produced disconcerting increases in greenhouse-gas emissions (http://oesterreich.orf.at/stories/165273/). Moreover, statistics reveal a drastic recent increase in lorry-traffic crossing the country (http://www.orf. at/070313-10121/10122txt_story.html), for which toll-increases and expansions of the rail-network have been suggested as counter-measures (http://www.orf. at/ticker/247295.html). Climate-/energy related sections of the now previous government's programme, and a subsequently released 'climate strategy' (e.g. http://www.orf.at/070218-9376/9377txt_story.html), were considered 'inadequate' by the opposition and environmental organizations, whilst criticisms of Austria's recent 'climate record'[7] also appeared in parts of the media (e.g. Enigl and Lettner 2007, 30).[8] Notwithstanding the contentiousness of the SPÖ-ÖVP coalition

---

6    Similarly, the consultancy firm McKinsey calculated (http://www.orf.at/070326-10607/10608txt_story.html) that the EU's targeted 20 per cent reduction in CO2 emissions by 2020 would incur annual costs of 60–80 billion euros; an *economistic* approach to environmental policy also underpins the prediction by the German Institute for Economic Research (DIW) that climate change will cost Germany 800 billion euros by 2050.

7    The EU commission corroborated such criticisms in further reducing Austria's 'CO2-emissions rights' (http://www.orf.at/070402-10849/10850txt_story.html).

8    There are counter-examples: following the EU's agreement on a 20 per cent reduction in CO2 emissions and a 20 per cent increase in the use of renewable energies (not including nuclear energy) by 2020, Vienna's 'energy efficiency programme' was portrayed as a 'good practice example' (DW-TV 9 March 2007). Also, thanks to hydroelectric power Austria at one point derived some 70 per cent of its electricity – the highest proportion within the EU

government's plans (e.g. http://www.orf.at/ticker/247100.html, http://www.orf.at/ticker/247206.html), there was noteworthy agreement on how climate change and possible counter-strategies were conceptualized, with the economy being widely used as a way of assessing the consequences of global warming and as a framework for trying to avert them.

The unusually warm winter of 2006/07 entailed significant losses for parts of Austria's winter-tourism sector (e.g. http://vorarlberg.orf.at/stories/164779/), causing concern about the long-term economic costs of climate change (e.g. http://ooe.orf.at/stories/165001/). A discourse interpreting global warming economically was also evoked in response to meteorological studies predicting warmer Alpine winters: such trends (i.e. lack of snow below 2000 meters altitude), it was feared, could jeopardize many Austrian skiing regions (http://www.orf.at/070116-8141/8142txt_story.html). Whilst the economic significance of Austrian winter-tourism explains such responses, it is worth noting that there were other, not primarily *economistic* interpretations emphasizing, for example, that glacial shrinking – another consequence of global warming – would entail the loss of water reserves (http://science.orf.at/science/news/146388).[9] Such co-existing discourses raise questions about the relevance of the market as both indicator and response to climate change.

The Green party's electoral programme (2006) challenged many symptoms of unconstrained market forces: it advocated a national and global fight against poverty, minimum social welfare standards, and criticized plans to partly privatize Austria's health service; it opposed the competition for foreign investment, the related reduction in tax revenue and widening inequalities between and within nation-states; its alternative approach to globalization envisaged improved social security across the EU, transnational cooperation and civil society initiatives. At the same time, the Greens' call for a 'social and ecological capitalism' insisted that the market could provide much-needed solutions: there was a recurring vision (2006, 4–6) for reconciling environmental sustainability, economic growth and employment through a uniquely Austrian market niche; her 'environmental industry', it was argued, could create jobs and deliver 'green growth' through technological innovation (particularly in the area of renewable energies) for the

---

– from renewable energy sources (*Profil* 15 January 2007, 49). The government seemed to respond to criticism in raising petrol taxes more than intended and in dedicating additional revenue to energy-/climate-related purposes (http://www.orf.at/070321-10410/10411txt_story.html). Recent country-comparisons confirm that whilst Austria does exceptionally well in terms of resource efficiency, water quality and environmental spending, the gap between her Kyoto-obligations and current $CO_2$ emissions continues to be a very serious concern (*Der Standard* 6 August 2010, 1).

9  Elsewhere, Kenyan Nobel-price-winner Wangari Maathai has formulated a comparable *non-economistic* response to global warming: her UN campaign for the planting of some 1 billion trees, each capable of absorbing 12 kilograms of $CO_2$ and providing enough oxygen for four people each year (http://www.orf.at/ticker/242197.html).

international market. This was not an isolated suggestion[10] that environmentalism makes economic sense: in their criticism of the government's 'climate strategy' (http://www.orf.at/070218-9376/9380txt_story.html), the Greens reiterated that investing in renewable energies would reduce Austria's greenhouse-gas emissions *and* create jobs. Then Chancellor Gusenbauer, an intended target of this criticism, similarly emphasized the market-compatibility of environmental responsibility soon thereafter, stressing that energy efficiency offered opportunities for economic growth and job creation (http://www.orf.at/070307-9940/9941txt_story.html).[11] Then Vice-Chancellor and Finance Minister Molterer echoed this (http://www. orf.at/070321-10410/10411txt_story.html): agreeing that tackling climate change could create employment and stimulate growth, he defended the government's 'climate strategy' and argued that it balanced ecological and economic demands.

This section has examined debates about what constitutes 'too much' or 'too little' marketization/commodification with regard to natural resources, transformations in agricultural production, and climate change. We next turn to a cluster of debates that – though superficially unrelated – similarly concern the market, its advocated limits or feared expansion, and various (formerly) extra-economic realms.

### 'Dis-/Re-embedding'

Karl Polanyi's seminal *The Great Transformation* (1944) traced a 'double movement' across the nineteenth and (early) twentieth centuries: first, the 'dis-embedding' effects of industrial capitalism that 'separated out economy from society and polity by turning labour, land and other natural resources into commodities … as though they were items produced for sale'; second, attempts to counter the 'social divisiveness' of expanding markets through various institutional and ideological means of 're-embedding economy in society'; whilst some such reactions against the social consequences of unfettered market forces were as widespread as 'unions, factory acts, agricultural tariffs, and central banking', others were ideologically as radically different as German fascism, the American New Deal and (later) welfare states (Dalton 1968, xxiv–xxvi).

A similar 'double movement' between the forces of 'pure' competition and attempts to limit the reach of commodification and 'dis-embedding' is evident in (and far beyond) contemporary Austria, albeit in the vastly different context of *liquid modernity* (Bauman 2000) – its globally 'nomadic' capital, relatively disempowered nation-states, and chronic uncertainties. Two inter-related concerns

---

10　For a journalistic account of Austrian companies successfully competing on the international market for 'environmental technologies', see *Profil* (12 March 2007, 62–70).

11　Relevant sections in the SPÖ electoral manifesto had also partly resembled some of the Greens' proposals: the SPÖ (2006, 16) had planned a reduction in 'green investments' abroad in favour of Austrian equivalents with 'job creation potential'.

define many debates across the political spectrum: the local, national consequences of an economy widely seen to be increasingly dis-embedded; and a concern with the inverse development of spheres considered 'cultural', 'educational', or 'collective' being seemingly 'colonized' by economic considerations.

*Taming the market*

In a *Profil* interview Austria's former Chancellor defined responsible politics by its creation of 'islands of solidarity' in times of 'globalization, profit-seeking and heightened selfishness' (Gusenbauer cited in Lackner 2007a, 22).[12] It has been argued that his SPÖ's narrow victory over the ÖVP in the 2006 election reflected the widespread impression that the latter over-emphasized economic- at the expense of social concerns (Linsinger 2006). In its electoral programme the ÖVP had defined its 'eco-social capitalism' as a reconciliation of economic success, social security and environmental standards and as a 'convincing answer to the challenges of globalization' (2006, 3). Following its electoral disappointment, however, the party was observed to shift to the left, discussing minimum standards of social security, following transnational trends towards 'compassionate conservatism', and advocating 'flexicurity' – a formula combining social security with a flexible labour market and full employment. The ÖVP's general secretary was quoted as saying that a 'necessary' period of market liberalization now had to be balanced by an emphasis on social safety nets (Linsinger 2006, 24). A previous Vice-Chancellor and head of the ÖVP even suggested that his party had got trapped in 'the neo-liberal *Zeitgeist*', that globalization had wrongly been portrayed as a 'natural law', and that answers for widening inequalities were required; criticizing (some) multinational corporations and off-shore tax havens, he stressed that free trade required social and ecological standards, and that politics had to regain its primacy over economics (Riegler cited in *Profil* 11 December 2006, 22–23).

Calls for a political re-embedding of the market emanate not only from within Austria's previous or current coalition governments but are also articulated, often with greater vehemence, across the country's otherwise ideologically highly heterogeneous opposition parties. The Greens' vision for a 'social Europe' and anti-poverty agenda reveal a market-scepticism they partly share – despite their profound disagreements and fundamental differences (see below) – with their main ideological 'others'. The BZÖ thus went into the 2006 election describing itself as the previous government's 'social conscience' and advocating 'social capitalism': the latter would support small-/medium-sized companies as opposed to transnational corporations, insist on social and ecological production-standards, introduce a tax on international capital transfers (*Tobin tax*), and assume responsibility for local jobs (BZÖ 2006b). Not dissimilarly, the FPÖ's party

---

12　At the time the SPÖ-ÖVP governmental programme was seen to contain both continuities with, and significant contrasts to, the previous ÖVP-BZÖ coalition government (Enigl and Lackner 2007).

programme (2005, 18–21) anticipated a 'fair capitalism' capable of reconciling a competitive economy with social responsibility, criticized the social and ecological exploitations witnessed under 'unfettered capitalism', and articulated support for Austria's small-/medium-sized companies on the international market. Significantly, Austria's communist party (KPÖ) and Hans-Peter Martin's 'citizens' initiative', whilst occupying ideological positions usually diametrically opposed to BZÖ/FPÖ, articulated partly comparable assessments of the economic status quo. The KPÖ (2006, 1) spoke of an 'unconstrained capital expansion', as a result of which health, education and pensions had been commodified. Already a decade earlier Martin had described globalization as a potentially disastrous 'trap' of growing inequalities, rising unemployment figures, dominant multinational corporations, disempowered politics, and fearful citizens susceptible to the agendas of xenophobic populists; a more democratic EU, tax reforms (including the introduction of Tobin tax), globally binding social and ecological trading-standards, and transnational civil societies were advocated as necessary counter-strategies (Martin and Schumann 2006 [1996]).

*National 'moral economies'?*

Attempts to negotiate the contradictions between global market forces and national/local sentiments and responsibilities even infuse some highly unexpected domains: in roadside- and national television advertising campaigns McDonald's – a symbol of globally 'nomadic' capital – has committed itself to using potatoes and beef only from Austrian farmers. Plausibly decoded as a multinational's concession to concerns about health and agricultural production examined above, this suggested that local consumer preferences or anxieties can impact on marketing-/business decisions by key actors on the global market (see Germann Molz 2007, 67–69). Several recent debates have similarly centred on the desirable reach of the market, the consequences of an increasingly dis-embedded economy, and on the nation-state's responsibilities. The first debate concerned what may be termed the commodification of time: suggestions to extend shop-opening-hours to Sundays were opposed by the then government-to-be (ZIB 1 21 December 2006) and by nearly two thirds of the Austrian population (http://www.kleinezeitung. at/nachrichten/wirtschaft/286159/index.do). An article in a regional monthly 'street magazine' provided a rationale for such opposition: critical of the 'neo-liberal round-the-clock shopping trend', it called on readers to dedicate Sundays to friends, families or themselves but not to consumerism (Schwentner 2007); its underlying sentiment may thus be paraphrased as resistance to the forces of seemingly all-encroaching commodification.

Other debates involve a critique of global markets through a discourse strongly reminiscent of the 'moral economies' documented amongst the European poor of the eighteenth and nineteenth centuries (Thompson 1966) and Southeast-Asian subsistence-farmers (Peletz 1983; Scott 1976).[13] Such 'moral economies' are based on a taken-for-granted 'right to survive', serving as a standard of legitimacy (applied to the performance by political elites) and outweighing economic considerations of profit maximization. As mentioned, the 2006 Austrian electoral campaigns and results were significantly shaped by discussions about the social costs of neo-liberal re-structuring and, conversely, by promises to strengthen social safety mechanisms for the most vulnerable. Whilst the BZÖ (2006b) opposed the exclusive search for profit it ascribed to global capitalism and declared that humans should not be subject to economic cost-benefit calculations, the FPÖ (2005, 21) called for social solidarity and minimum living-standards without undermining 'naturally occurring' hierarchies and differences. The Greens (2006, 11–12) defined 476,000 people living in poverty[14] and 221,000 working poor as 'unacceptable' and called for minimum social benefits amounting to 800 euros monthly. Similarly, the SPÖ (2006, 15) envisaged a fairer distribution of wealth, more adequate taxes for large (multinational) corporations, and 'needs-oriented basic benefits'. Initially, previous ÖVP Chancellor Schüssel and his Interior Minister variously criticized calls for increased and partly centralized (rather than regionally administered) benefits (http://derstandard.at 7 December 2006) or considered them 'quintessentially communist' demands (http://www.orf.at/ticker/231618.html). The extent and financing of benefit-rises constituted temporary obstacles in the negotiations between SPÖ and ÖVP (e.g. http://www.orf.at/ticker/237660.html). Following their formation of a coalition government, however, its programme received some praise for addressing poverty and for its planned harmonization of the social-benefits-system across the country's nine regions (*Profil* 22 January 2007a). After years of delay and further modifications a new minimum welfare scheme (*Mindestsicherung*) was eventually agreed to be implemented as of autumn 2010. The wider context to such developments included a near doubling of social-benefits-recipients between 1996 and 2005 (http://www.orf.at/ticker/232859.html). To this backdrop, political performance is indeed frequently assessed against a widely taken-for-granted 'right to survive' and required safety-nets for the vulnerable. As we see below, however, the boundaries of entitlement and exclusion within such moral economies are major points of ideological disagreement.

---

13   Recent anthropological literature (Tomlinson 2005, 113) challenges received wisdom on moral economies in showing that they are *not* inevitably undermined by industrialization and modernity.

14   According to a subsequent study (see http://orf.at/070430-11807/11808txt_story.html), 420,000 people living in Austria face 'manifest poverty', whilst a million people are socio-economically 'vulnerable'.

*Education, art, commodification and resistance*

If calls for a re-embedding of the economy in structures of solidarity and re-distribution are one manifestation of market-scepticism, opposition to the commodification of once extra-economic realms is another. This was shown in a series of protests and controversies surrounding university education: in early 2007, the SPÖ's failure to persuade its coalition-partner to scrap tuition fees, as declared in its electoral manifesto (SPÖ 2006, 10), triggered protests in Vienna and at other universities (e.g. http://www.orf.at/ticker/241048.html; http://oesterreich.orf.at/stories/165145/; http://ooe.orf.at/stories/165486/) and grassroots disgruntlement within the SPÖ (Horaczek 2007; http://ooe.orf.at/stories/171837/). A new system whereby students could provide 60 hours of specified voluntary work (e.g. tutoring socially disadvantaged pupils) in lieu of the 363 euro semester-fees (http://www.orf.at 27 March 2007) was interpreted differently by proponents and critics.[15] Yet, both responses invoked the market: to Chancellor Gusenbauer (Lackner 2007a, 22) this scheme offered social engagement and solidarity as an antidote to our era's 'heightened selfishness'; conversely, critics stressed that the implied hourly wage of 6 euros was half the market-rate, leading the Red Cross to fear that the scheme could inflate care-work (Wally 2007a, 33). Whilst the then Chancellor thus presented the scheme as a valuable counterweight to the widening reach of market forces, critics feared that it would further disadvantage some of those doing important but already financially under-rewarded work.

Another educational debate – between Vienna and Brussels – revealed tensions between transnational markets and 'the nation'. In 2006 Austria introduced a quota-system for medical students, reserving 75 per cent of 1,500 available places for entrants with Austrian school-leaving certificates, 20 per cent for other EU citizens, and 5 per cent for non-EU citizens. The EU-commission objected, finding the system discriminatory and in contravention of EU regulations (http://www.orf.at/ticker/242231.html), but granted Austria until May 2007 to justify her position (http://www.orf.at/070219-9432/9433txt_story.html). The government argued, ultimately successfully,[16] that quota were necessary to prevent future shortages of Austrian doctors (e.g. *Profil* 22 January 2007b, http://oe1.orf.at/inforadio/72909.html, http://oe1.orf.at/inforadio/73328.html). The debate thus reflected a perceived clash between an open educational market for mobile EU-citizens and a national infrastructure dependent upon permanent residence and enduring local ties.

The clearest clash between markets and educational philosophies opposed to commodification emerged in weeks of student protests in Vienna and other

---

15   This new system also set out to expand scholarship schemes and increase student benefits (e.g. http://www.orf.at/070115-8087/8088txt_story.html; http://www.orf.at 26 March 2007).

16   Its 500-page report to the EU commission included data from international studies showing that the majority of qualified doctors return to their country of origin following completion of their studies (http://www.orf.at/ticker/254111.html).

university cities in late 2009. Central to these protests, which included high-profile and week-long sit-ins, were calls for free access to higher education and against both a reintroduction of tuition fees and entry restrictions. The students' slogan 'Education, not job-training' (*Bildung statt Ausbildung*) reflected a general opposition to what was seen as a growing dominance of economic interests over higher education (Brodnig and Gantner 2009). Similar resentments of universities' alleged colonization by the demands of business manifested in protests against the 'Bologna-process' in March 2010: initiated in 1999, the Bologna process intended to standardize European degree structures, to facilitate greater intra-European student mobility and improve graduates' employability; to its most vocal critics, however, it had resulted in a stifling marketization of universities (http://www.orf.at/100310-48897/index.html).

The relationship between the market and the traditionally not-fully-commodified has also been debated in relation to art and cultural production. The SPÖ has stressed (2006, 24) that artists' contributions to public discourse and 'social wealth' transcend economics, with the Greens similarly emphasizing (2006, 22) that art cannot be 'reduced to economic factors'. Meanwhile, the ÖVP (2006, 80) observed in its 2006 manifesto that regional cultural initiatives were artistically *and* economically significant and creative industries 'engines' of innovation and economic growth. Subsequently, Culture Minister (and former banker) Claudia Schmied also saw potential synergies between art and business; whilst considering the former 'deeper' than the latter, she envisaged a symbiotic relationship between cultural production and economics: rather than latter merely funding the former, she argued for the potential economic benefits and spin-offs of artistic performances and cultural initiatives associated with Austria[17] (Nüchtern 2007).

These snapshots of Austrian debates echo Polanyi's 'double movement': between atomizing market relations as well as widening commodification and attempts to re-embed economic processes in political structures respectively; between economic competition and roles and responsibilities (still) widely attributed to the nation-state. Discussions about issues as varied as social welfare, higher education and art thus share a preoccupation with encroaching market forces and their perceived (socially dis-embedding) consequences. And whilst the issues are omnipresent, there is – as has also been shown – little consensus about appropriate counter-strategies. In the next section we turn to identity politics, which need to be understood in the context of the processes outlined thus far.

---

17   Schmied provided the hypothetical example of Vienna symphony orchestra concerts abroad being followed by meetings involving artists, companies and politicians.

## Markets, exclusions, identity politics

Attempting to reconcile the formalist and substantivist paradigms, Bloch and Parry (1989) argue that historically economic systems have combined two co-existing spheres: first, a 'short-term transactional order' of competition and individual acquisition; second, a 'long-term' social/moral order, to which the former is considered subordinate and which is articulated through discourses on the reproduction of the household, the community or the nation. Bloch and Parry also suggest (1989, 29–30) that contemporary capitalism may be 'entirely different' – defined by the dominance of individualized economic practice and arguably no longer able to relate it to the long-term cycle of social ('cosmic') reproduction. Austrian identity politics can be approached through, but promises to further refine, this theoretical lens: articulated in the context of market forces perceived to be increasingly all-pervading, prominent identity discourses still insist on a larger, collective order whose reproduction or achievement is considered a moral task transcending individual self-interest and economic gain. Crucially, on this level ideological contestation comes to the fore: identity politics unfold in a diverse discursive field involving *competing* notions of social/moral order.

*Profil* columnist Lingens (2006, 144) has argued that economic challenges and their proposed solutions are identical across the EU, clearly revealing the primacy of the market. Stephan Schulmeister (cited in Wolf 2007) from the Austrian Institute for Economic Research challenges this: similar to Polanyi's 'double movement', he speaks of historical cycles alternating between market dominance and political counter-reactions; within the EU, he observed prior to the recent financial crisis, there were emerging tendencies away from neo-liberalism. Another observer (Payrleitner 2004, 117–125) links the global dominance of mobile capital over national politics to local anxieties and yearnings for stability and familiarity. It is precisely in the interface between transnational economic forces and localized experiences, personal ethics and collective yet contested concerns that crucial identity negotiations occur.

*Wealth, inequality and investment*

According to former Chancellor Gusenbauer, his government's key aim was successful competition without 'capitulating to globalization' and poverty (Lackner 2007a, 22). Tensions between policies considered conducive to growth through (foreign) investment and local/national solidarities underpinned some critical episodes for the previous coalition. The above-mentioned plans for 'minimum benefits', for instance, sat uneasily with the scrapping of inheritance tax: part of the ÖVP's electoral manifesto, this was presented as an economically meaningful concession to the middle class; sections of the media took a more critical stand (e.g. Lingens 2007; Mappes-Niediek 2007; Meinhart and Zöchling 2007), arguing that social inequalities would widen and that – following the previous scrapping of wealth tax and concessions to business – Austria's tax-system favoured the rich more than any other Western industrialized nation's.

In an episode soon thereafter, national loyalties overrode transnational economic forces: when it looked likely that a large steel-manufacturer would become the second Austrian business institution – following the financial scandal around, and take-over of, the 'bank for labour and economics', or Bawag (e.g. Palme 2006) – to be sold to a foreign private-equity-fund in the space of a few months, public outcry ensued. Backed by several politicians, this 'collective hysteria' (Himmelbauer et al. 2007) was followed by a surprising turn-of-events: rather than international investors CVC Capital Partners, Austria's other major steel-manufacturer, VoestAlpine, stepped in and bought the company in question. In this context, journalist Palme (2007) detected a new, transnational and transideological *Kapitalismuskritik*. Her colleague Herbert Lackner (2007b) suggested that opposition to international investors targeting Austrian companies was not mere inward- or backward looking protectionism, but a reaction against the disempowerment of politics by international finance and the latter's uncompromising quest for profits that left no room for ethics.[18]

There are parallels between such episodes and the discussions surrounding water and food examined above: they implicate discursive negotiations of national boundaries – variously amounting to their affirmation or contestation – to the backdrop of the contemporary (global) economy and the inequalities, uncertainties, or opportunities associated with it.

*The 'other' – exclusion versus pluralism*

This analysis has revealed noticeable transideological agreement on perceived market expansions and their feared effects: thus, the commodification of water is widely defined as a problem; there are widespread ethical objections to global agro-business, and common concerns about the local consequences of transnational competition – between nation-states and regions – for investment. Conversely, there is considerable disagreement on the commodification of, for example, higher education and art. At the same time, the sentiment that the market provides appropriate measurements and counter-strategies for climate change also recurs across the ideological spectrum. Much of this can be summarized by saying that market forces that transcend national boundaries and infiltrate previously non-commodified areas are widely perceived as defining characteristics or challenges of our era. Ideological differences often manifest not on the level of 'diagnosis' but in terms of proposed counter-strategies. Thus, for example, whilst there is inter-

---

18  Such arguments echo seminal social scientific ideas, including Ulrich Beck's concept of 'denationalization shocks' (2000) or David Harvey's observation (2006) that whilst (contemporary) capitalism is driven by the compulsive re-investment of profits (or 'surplus absorption'), the scope of politics is increasingly reduced to the provision of 'good business environments'.

party agreement on the significance of rural areas, their contemporary dilemmas, and the need for appropriate financial/infrastructural support, only BZÖ (2006b) and FPÖ (2006, 11) have spoken of a 'renationalization' of agricultural politics. Ideological differences are at their most pronounced in terms of proposed responses to immigration – one of the defining transnational 'flows' (Appadurai 1990) of our time.[19] A close reading of the 2006 party manifestos and associated debates corroborates existing analyses (Karner 2007b) of Austria's political field: as strongly contested between discourses of exclusion and pluralism, advocating rigid national boundaries or multicultural diversity respectively.

Pre-election debates in 2006 utilized discursive categories and demands commonly encountered in immigration-related discussions across and indeed beyond 'fortress Europe': echoing the widely-evoked though sometimes problematic distinction (Castles 2003; Richmond 2002) between 'political refugees' and 'mere economic migrants',[20] there was far-reaching agreement that asylum- and immigration policies had to be kept strictly separate (e.g. SPÖ 2006, 23); also, there were recurring calls to privilege existing migrants' 'integration' over additional immigration (e.g. ÖVP 2006, 96), which were subsequently echoed in the coalition's governmental programme (http://www.orf.at/070116-8131/8132txt_story.html). The most glaring and predictable ideological contrasts emerged from the manifestos by BZÖ and FPÖ on one end of the spectrum, and by the Greens' on the other: both BZÖ (2006a, 2) and FPÖ (2006, 3) claimed that Austria was 'no country of immigration', they variously suggested that multiculturalism had failed (BZÖ 2006b) and declared their opposition to 'radical Islam' (FPÖ 2006, 4; 11); exclusionary demands ranged from substantial reductions in immigration (BZÖ 2006a, 2) to an 'immigration-stop' (FPÖ 2006, 3), tighter citizenship legislation (FPÖ 2006, 4), and compulsory private health-insurance for foreigners (FPÖ 2006, 10). Conversely, the Greens (2006, 18–19) demanded recognition that Austria was, in fact, a 'country of immigration' and campaigned for migrants' rights, empowerment and inclusion. On the level of social realities, parallel developments in 2006–2007 also revealed contradictory forces of exclusion and inclusion: thus, the number of reported racist incidents was higher in 2006 than in any previous year on record (http://wien.orf.at/stories/180216/). At the same time, there is evidence (Karner 2007b) of a now lively civil society, in which multicultural diversity and ethnic hybridity are celebrated – in opposition to nationalist discourses of exclusion; and whilst restrictive legislation pertaining to immigration and asylum introduced by the previous ÖVP/FPÖ-BZÖ government

---

19    Ethnic stereotyping and exclusion in Austria have – to the backdrop of the FPÖ's rise to political prominence since the 1980s – received systematic (international) attention over recent years, both in media- and academic (e.g. Camus 2002; Hainsworth 2000; Pick 2000; Reisigl and Wodak 2001; Wodak 2000) circles.

20    This distinction often fails to appreciate the complex, overlapping and inter-related causes underpinning much forced migration, ranging from political persecution to environmental degradation and economic destitution.

was widely criticized (e.g. http://www.orf.at/ticker/249907.html, http://www.orf.at/ticker/250670.html), growing numbers of local communities were campaigning to prevent the possible deportation of (socially integrated) asylum-seekers in their midst (e.g. Barth 2007; http://steiermark.orf.at/stories/193255/; Meinhart 2007). Similarly poignant was the contrast between 58 per cent of Austrians purportedly opposing Turkey's possible EU accession (http://www.orf.at/ticker/235668.html), and the Western province of Vorarlberg introducing compulsory Turkish courses for future primary school teachers to respond to ethnic diversity in schools (http://vorarlberg.orf.at/stories/73561/).

Contrasting responses to 'the stranger' relate to this analysis in two respects: first, the contemporary world is defined by a *series of movements* across increasingly permeable national boundaries; alongside the transnational 'flow' of finance, technology, ideologies and media images, migration has been described as a defining characteristic of our era (Appadurai 1990, 296). Second, and in a related vein, immigration is locally often experienced in a broadly *economistic* fashion – as intensifying competition for scarce resources (e.g. Dench et al. 2006) or advocated to meet existing market requirements. Another debate revealed the complex interplay between (un)employment, (trans)national labour markets, local anxieties, and the discursive reproduction of national boundaries. Despite widespread support for temporary employment-restrictions for citizens of recent EU accession-states (e.g. http://www.orf.at/ticker/245993.html), the previous government created a (temporary) work-permit scheme for skilled foreign workers in specific branches of industry. Highly significant were the contrasting arguments used in relation to this: critics emphasized Austrian unemployment figures, advocating training for Austrian workers to meet labour-shortages; industry, however, favoured cheaper foreign workers over expensive qualifications for subsequently more costly Austrian employees (Wally 2007b).[21] The debate resurfaced in the summer of 2010, when prominent members of the current SPÖ-ÖVP coalition renewed calls for the introduction of a 'red-white-red card', akin to the US green-card scheme, to attract highly skilled, highly qualified immigrants to safeguard the otherwise threatened future of Austria's welfare and pension systems (e.g. Pöll 2010). This was variously criticized by Austria's Chamber of Labour (Gnam 2010) and some regional (SPÖ/ÖVP) politicians (Schwaiger 2010), who argued that providing qualifications and employment for jobless Austrians should take precedence over inviting more competition through additional immigration. Meanwhile there are solitary calls – articulated from a different point on the ideological spectrum by critics of ethnic exclusion and global inequalities (e.g. Werner 2004) – for a *global* version of the European model for the free movement of capital, goods *and people*. Beneath such diverging views are contrasting definitions of the relationship between economic activity, social solidarity and group boundaries: protectionism subordinates economic practice to the perceived needs of a national

---

21   Employment restrictions for citizens of recent EU accession-states will be lifted in May 2011.

community; advocates of the free-market uphold a belief in the socially regulative and politically benevolent functions of unconstrained economic activity; some left-leaning critics oppose both the inequalities (re)produced by the market and the exclusions perpetuated by discourses of ethnic/national belonging. Importantly, however, all three ideal-typical dispositions relate economics to politics, albeit in radically different ways. Such contrasting ideological reactions partly challenge Bloch and Parry's suggestion that contemporary economic practice may no longer be considered subordinate to the 'reproduction of social and ideological systems' (1989, 1). Contemporary Austria reveals that mature capitalism is not necessarily defined by the historically atypical 'divorce' between economics and cultural beliefs/ethics;[22] instead, the material examined above reveals *competing moral/ ideological orders* mobilized and fought over in debates about the effects of the market on the environment, animal rights, food, art, social welfare, education and migration. Such key debates in contemporary Austria and her much-discussed, ideologically diverse identity politics therefore need to be understood in the context of the local effects of global market forces.

### Global markets, other European nations

Other European contexts similarly reveal different notions and understandings of moral economies: variously associated with (welfare) entitlements, ethics, sustainability, local or national traditions of, for example, food production and consumption, such moral economies are widely considered to be under threat or erosion due to the transnational flows, influences and novel configurations of power that define contemporary economic globalization and global markets.

The first highly relevant example to be mentioned here is captured in a recent analysis of 'gastronationalism' – of food acting as a boundary marker in opposition to 'globalism's homogenizing tendencies' (DeSoucey 2010, 433), as exemplified by the controversial French speciality food of *foie gras*, the liver of force-fed ducks or geese. Seen by many as a symbol of French culinary excellence and national identity, *foie gras* has also provoked widespread international criticism underpinned by concerns about animal rights and welfare. Based on her fieldwork in a range of relevant settings (including markets and production facilities) and presenting detailed analyses of parliamentary debates, media coverage and interviews with key actors in the *foie gras* industry and amongst some of its critics, DeSoucey shows that the debates surrounding this emotionally laden speciality reveal a clash between ideological forces pulling in opposite directions: a regional moral

---

22　However, contradictions between the economic and ethical principles associated with a particular ideological disposition can arise: for a relevant instance of such tension, see Menasse's interpretation (2005, 396) of Austria's crisis of 2000 (i.e. the temporary 'sanctions' following the formation of the ÖVP-FPÖ coalition) as indicative of an emerging gap 'between economics and morality'.

economy grounded in traditional systems of food production and consumption, and an international movement arguing for the universality of animal rights. The context to these debates is partly shaped by wider, pan-European tensions between a common agricultural-/food market on one hand, and EU-legislation (such as the 'Protected Designation of Origin' label) designed to help often smaller-scaled farming and to recognize regional 'authenticity claims linking food to place' (DeSoucey 2010, 437) on the other. To this backdrop, the French National Assembly and Senate defined *foie gras* as part of France's 'cultural patrimony' in 2005. Revealingly, a senator justified its 'legislative protection' as a pre-emptive defensive move against an anticipated encroachment from outside: 'because [*foie gras*] is contested ... it is necessary to inscribe it in law; otherwise the good spirits of Brussels will come and ban ... our ["taste of place"]' (quoted in DeSoucey 2010, 444).[23] A similarly protectionist discourse advocating cultural preservation 'in the face of homogenizing markets' defines the following statements by two of DeSoucey's interviewees:

> Because you came with the category of American. And, some Americans are against the production of foie gras ... I didn't want to meet someone who doesn't like foie gras. It's a question of national solidarity. I don't think I'm especially nationalist, but in this context, I defend it.
>
> I cannot imagine that foie gras could be banned in France because it's a very traditional product, consumed in this country for a long time ... It's exactly the same as in your country, at Thanksgiving you have to have your turkey ... And, we have no Christmas without foie gras. It's a ritual in our country. You have to do it. (Quoted in DeSoucey 2010, 446–447)

Significantly, both these statement reveal an awareness that the contentiousness of *foie gras* is played out across national boundaries, in disagreement with outsiders allegedly ignorant of local traditions. At the same time, there are also internal critics, such as the head of a French animal rights group who argues that the tradition in question is – at least on a wider national scale – of relatively recent origin:

> There is a recent polarization on foie gras ... Development of foie gras production is within the last 60 years, more or less. It was there, but very weak before, there was little consumption, not all that widespread. So, the foie gras industry had a lot of work to do on the image of foie gras as something from the Southwest and, later, as being part of the image of France, like the Eiffel Tower. (Quoted in DeSoucey 2010, 444–445)

---

23  Such concerns and intra-EU tensions are by no means uncommon: a recent incident, and one not surprisingly reported in Austria's EU-critical *Krone* (Perry 2010b), involved Italian protests against EU plans to impose health warnings – about its fat and sugar content – on Italy's famous chocolate spread *Nutella*.

Whilst it clearly has echoes of some of the debates examined earlier, the gastronationalism surrounding *foie gras* and the ethical objections made by its opponents do not so much reveal tensions between a particular moral economy and international markets as a clash between different moral economies. Or in Bloch and Parry's earlier-quoted terminology, this transnational controversy implicates and reveals competing moral or ideological orders, cutting across national boundaries and pitting local traditions of food production and consumption against a universal ethics of animal rights that may have originated elsewhere but is variously contested or embraced locally.

A rigid dichotomy between transnational markets and local moral economies is also complicated – albeit for different reasons – by Cristina Grasseni's anthropological study of dairy farming, cattle-breeding and cheese-making Italian farmers at the foot of the Alps. Based on long-term ethnographic immersion, Grasseni reveals complex negotiations of tradition *and* modernity by farmers who combine local, inter-generationally transmitted skills, practices and aesthetics with an acute – and necessary – sense of entrepreneurship and innovation. This is shown, for example, in the farmers' 'promot[ing] their own "local" (mainly dairy) products, selling them on international markets precisely thanks to their association with the image of the untouched and unspoilt beauty of the Alpine landscape' (Grasseni 2009, 63). Traditional skills and local products – or rather their commodified versions – and participation in larger, European and global markets thus turn out not to be incompatible alternatives but complementary parts of the strategies employed by local farmers; their economic survival and success (e.g. Grasseni 2009, 177) combines a branded image of authentic, pre-industrial food with 'artificial selection in cattle breeding, … EU and state farming support', and investments in new technologies and infrastructure (such as new stables and milking parlours):

> [T]he capacity to reinvent oneself as custodians of tradition may well become part of a set of 'local skills' to survive in the global market. This would be the capacity to … show oneself at the same time as custodians of a long and authentic traditional lifestyle in close contact with 'Nature' *and* as modern and informed entrepreneurs, well placed along the way to 'progress' … [This] maintains tradition through change: sometimes part of what is deemed 'local skill' can be the capacity to bend local patterns of production to regimented, even high-tech procedures specifically designed for the global market. (Grasseni 2009, 183; 188)

Clearly, there are economic compulsions and novel legal frameworks that guide and constrain Grasseni's Italian farmers. At the same time, their accommodations bear the in-print of local sensitivities and preferences. Put differently, these Alpine farmers meet changing market conditions with adaptability and from their particular cultural location and its distinctive *habitus*. They are not, however, able to retreat to a position of stubborn refusal or economic disengagement. This also has echoes of Seiser's analysis of farmers' politics north of the Italian-Austrian border: Seiser (2006) shows that Austrian farmers have generally not been prone to support the FPÖ's nationalism. Both this observation and Grasseni's Italian ethnography suggest that some of the concerns and moral economies examined above reflect a wider politics of nostalgia that is generally not articulated by those people – farmers – most immediately affected by, but economically forced to accommodate to, the changes brought about by international agro-business and global food markets. Put more simply, farmers simply need to adapt and tend to do so, albeit at times surely reluctantly, with skill, local knowledge and aesthetics, but also with entrepreneurialism. Meanwhile, on the level of national politics, farmers are 'being used by neo-nationalist and right-wing populist parties as a romanticising metaphor for the genuine, unadulterated … and the typically national … as a counter-image of deterritorialising globalisation' (Seiser 2006, 213). Theoretically, Grasseni's account of Italian farmers' negotiations of both local traditions *and* economic pragmatism also partly corroborates Bloch and Parry's attempted synthesis of the substantivist and formalist positions in economic anthropology: cultural embeddedness and economically rational, profit-maximizing behaviour indeed appear to co-exist and co-define this Alpine economy that is simultaneously local and part of a much wider market.

Everyday politics in the UK, or the concerns and sentiments articulated in discussions surrounding some of the necessities of daily life, including food and work, also provide periodical insights into how so-called ordinary social actors respond to – or are seen to respond to – the transnational 'flows' typical of life in the twenty-first century. As in some of the examples examined earlier, the protagonists in some such debates perceive localities as encroached upon, and disadvantaged by, external and impersonal market forces. One example was provided by growing concerns articulated in January 2009 over the difficult market position occupied by British pig farmers within the EU and vis-à-vis some of their continental counterparts. Against the background of comparatively high animal welfare standards introduced in the UK in 1999, there were fears about British farmers' competitive disadvantage in the face of cheaper pork imports from across the channel; in the words of the chairman of a group of cross-party MPs reporting on the issue: 'The English [sic] pig industry's adherence to high welfare standards has left it vulnerable to competition from European producers whose production methods do not match ours' (quoted on BBC News 19 January 2009a). Celebrity chef Jamie Oliver joined in the debate, declaring that British pig farmers' struggles had made him 'anti-EU' (BBC Morning News 19 January 2009) and, in the ensuing Channel 4 programme 'Jamie saves our bacon' (29 January 2009), arguing that 'our British farmers need our help'. This provided yet another instance of national 'deixis' (Billig 1995a) – the use of personal pronouns – underpinning a protectionist rhetoric articulated in opposition to market forces experienced as an outside imposition with detrimental local consequences.

This debate coincided with protests at British power stations and oil refineries, pitting local workers and trade unions against foreign contractors and the anticipated arrival – and resulting competition for jobs – by foreign (EU) workers. The following examples of news coverage encapsulate the tensions:

> Hundreds of union members are protesting at the site of a new power station over claims that overseas workers were being hired instead of UK staff. Unite and the GMB said vacancies for jobs at the Staythorpe site in Newark, Nottinghamshire, were being filled by Spanish and Polish workers. The unions said the decision by contractors building the plant to hire non-British workers was a scandal … Derek Simpson, joint leader of Unite, said … 'UK workers must be given a fair chance to get a cut of the action …'. (BBC News 19 January 2009b)

> Crucial talks aimed at resolving the bitter row over foreign labour resumed as workers continued to take wildcat industrial action at sites across the country … Hundreds of strikers held another protest at Lindsey Oil Refinery in North Lincolnshire, where the dispute flared after a contract was awarded to an Italian sub-contractor, who hired its own workforce from Italy and Portugal. Unofficial strike action … has sparked copycat protests from thousands of workers at power stations and other construction sites across the country … John Monks, general secretary of the European Trade Union Confederation, said the dispute was typical of problems … across the EU where workers were employed outside their home country. (http://news.uk.msn.com/uk/article.aspx?cp-documentid=13647653)

Whilst the dispute at Lindsey was eventually resolved by a deal guaranteeing 102 new jobs for UK workers (http://news.uk.msn.com/uk/article.aspx?cp-documentid=13711435), such conflicts clearly resonate with some of the Austrian debates examined earlier and condense a defining contemporary tension: between localities and the transnational flows of capital and people, giving rise to new insecurities, competitions, and a new politics of class.

Nowhere have the perceived tensions between nation-states and global market forces been more apparent than in the assessments of, and discussions surrounding, the successive, inherently transnational financial- and debt crises since 2008. Analysis of the structural and contextual causes of these far-reaching crises must of course be left to economists. However, and by way of a preliminary conclusion to this chapter, it is sociologically instructive to cast a glance at some of the discourses, applied as interpretative frames to the perceived power of financial markets, that have shaped recent public debate. Most generally, the crises of recent months and years have led to some conceptual and political questioning of the tenets of neo-classical economics and of the long hegemony of neoliberalism. Whilst calls for a reassertion of the primacy of politics over financial markets were getting louder (e.g. Bayer 2010a), acute observers – such as British economic historian Robert Skidelsky – pointed out that a much-needed Keynesianist revival was hampered by the power of the financial sector preventing such necessary reforms (Misik 2010). Obstacles to a political 're-embedding' of the economy manifested most dramatically in the Greek debt crisis in the spring of 2010.

Spiralling Greek debt, in the wider context of several EU countries' 'downgrading' by increasingly controversial financial rating agencies, led to 'the biggest bail-out in history' (Channel 4 News 10 May 2010). Yet, there were mounting criticisms that the EU had responded too slowly (e.g. Bayer 2010b). The crisis deepened with a for some time rapidly weakening Euro, whose very future was at one point questioned (Charter 2010). Ensuing debates centred on structural weaknesses inherent in the Eurozone and the EU more generally. Prominent suggestions – by critical politicians, economists and historians – for a more resilient EU called for a power shift away from unconstrained markets[24] and included ideas for more closely coordinated economic policies within the EU, a concerted fight against inequality, transnational investments in infrastructure, information technology and higher education, a separate EU tax, and a more 'social EU' to include 'European unemployment benefits' (Lahodynsky et al. 2010). However, the dilemmas faced by the EU were summarized by Austrian sociologist Rainer Münz: whilst the markets had doubted the EU's ability to manage the Greek debt crisis and although there was a strong need for closer intra-EU economic coordination, there was little willingness to push the European Union's political integration beyond changes implemented in the Lisbon Treaty (*Profil* 3 May 2010). It is therefore not surprising that EU responses to the crisis, such as new controls over European financial markets, were seen to be relatively weak – compared to newly introduced US regulation – and to reflect the dominance of national interests within the EU; critics argued that other necessary changes, such as the creation of European rating agencies, stronger regulations for hedgefonds and European taxes on the financial sector, still needed to happen (Marterbauer 2010).

The tensions between markets and nation-states examined in this chapter were indeed epitomized by the Greek debt crisis, when – in the words of an outside observer – Greeks were forced to see that 'markets are more powerful than their government' (Channel 4 News 5 May 2010). Perhaps more accurately, the crisis acted as a strong reminder that European lives in the twenty-first century are shaped not only by nation-states but also by global markets and the European network state. Shortly after activating emergency loans by the EU and the IMF, Prime Minister George Papandreou addressed his fellow Greeks as follows:

> The time that was not granted to us by the markets will be given to us by the support of the eurozone. It is a national necessity … to officially ask our partners to activate the mechanism that was created by all of us … [W]e are sending a strong message to the markets that the EU is serious about protecting its common interests and common currency. (Quoted in Smith 2010)

---

24    This was further corroborated by the HSBC chief economist detecting a 'general discontent with market solutions' (CNN 20 May 2010).

## Conclusion

Through its central Austrian case study and snapshots of other European contexts this chapter has examined national identity negotiations as manifest in debates surrounding markets, inequality, environmentalism, and a yearning to re-empower politics. Austria's relevance to such a discussion was already evident prior to the recent financial crises, when as a beneficiary of the (south)-eastwardly expanding European market and Germany's economic upturn Austria's economy performed impressively (Himmelbauer 2006; http://oesterreich.orf.at/stories/163553/), yet there were few if any political voices advocating entirely unrestricted markets. On the contrary, a wide range of debates revolve(d) around the perceived social, cultural, demographic, and environmental costs of widening commodification, encroaching market forces and politically 'dis-embedded' economics. Yet, the material examined above illustrates that market-scepticism or economic protectionism are merely two among several competing ideological reactions; indeed, and as shown by widespread *economistic* discourses about climate change, the market is also at times regarded as a measurement and solution – rather than culprit – for contemporary dilemmas. Overall, this analysis has demonstrated that markets – their contested limits, consequences and promises – are central to the debates that shape contemporary Europe.

'Dignity' – considered inherent to humans, animals, plants or natural resources – is a recurring theme emerging from the data examined above. Significantly, this asserts (the return of) an inalienable, not-to-be-commodified quality, an intrinsic value above and beyond both use and exchange. As has been shown, many associated discourses focus on inter-related questions at the heart of the contemporary world: how far are markets meant to stretch and, conversely, what should be protected from their colonizing reach? Who or what is – or is not – to be included in economic competition in local-, national- and, increasingly, global contexts and on which or whose terms?[25] This, then, is the widely-recognized terrain of crucial contemporary debates. Moreover, it is in terms of the proposed answers and the social boundaries drawn and reproduced therein that ideological diversity and 'identity-struggles' surface. In turn, the latter remind us that contemporary economics are *not* – unlike their more localized historical predecessors – subordinated to a *singular* moral/ideological order; instead, local responses to transnational market forces reveal *discursive struggles between*

---

25   An illustration of this was provided by a transnational controversy in April 2007: when Austrian gas- and oil company OMV announced plans for a major investment in Iranian gas, the US government reacted with dismay; what was seen as a 'sensible' economic investment and a way of avoiding dependency on a single supplier (i.e. Russia) by OMV and large sections of the Austrian public, was – in light of the Iranian nuclear row – considered 'badly timed' by the US; moreover, Washington indicated that it might respond to such investments by imposing sanctions on OMV (i.e. exclusion from the US financial market) (http://derstandard.at/?id=2854647; Rexer 2007).

*several such orders.* Diverging reactions to migration (as one of several global flows) show this most succinctly. As this analysis has demonstrated, debates about the relationship between economics and politics, the market and the nation, the global and the local, the individual and the collective, as well as – crucially – the contested boundaries of such a collective, cut across many of today's defining political concerns.

Contests between different ideological orders, which this analysis points towards, need considerably more elaborate discussion. In the next chapter, I explore such competing political visions as evident in civil society activities and local media discourse.

# Chapter 5

# Counter-Hegemony: Universal Human Rights Versus Exclusive Citizen Entitlements

## Introduction

> [Recent] historiography records that members of subordinated social groups – women, workers, peoples of color, and gays and lesbians – have repeatedly found it advantageous to constitute alternative publics. I propose to call these *subaltern counterpublics* in order to signal that they are parallel discursive arenas where members of subordinated social groups … circulate counterdiscourses to formulate oppositional interpretations of their identities, interests and needs. (Fraser 1992, 123)

The following analysis returns to a theme already established in chapter one: nationalism does not exercise an ideological monopoly over national identities but finds itself challenged by more inclusive conceptualizations of belonging. I have repeatedly drawn attention to the internally contested discursive fields that shape contemporary European societies. In this chapter, I explore such diversity and political disagreements in greater detail. Contests between competing blue-prints concerning the boundaries of inclusion and entitlement take place, in part, in civil society and through critical media.[1] Often galvanized by particular incidents or controversies, alternative and more inclusive notions of belonging help illuminate the ideological oppositions that shape contemporary Europe. Crucially, such counter-discourses and more open conceptualizations of national identities not only indicate ideological heterogeneity but also reflect on nationalism: articulated in opposition to social/ethnic exclusions, they bring neo-nationalist discourses and mechanisms into scrutiny and throw them into sharp relief. Once again, my analysis focuses on Austrian materials – concerning prominent nodes in the country's civil society and counter-hegemonic, regional media – before discussing other relevant European examples. Nancy Fraser's notion of a 'multiplicity of counterpublics', quoted above as a major theoretical lead informing this discussion, provides my point of departure but will also be partly refined: some of the materials examined here reveal counterpublics that are not exclusively 'inhabited' by subordinated groups, but shared by differently positioned social actors with a joint commitment to inclusive belonging and to countering neo-nationalism.

---

1 This discussion builds on an analysis I have published elsewhere (Karner 2007b).

**Contexts**

Civil society, here defined as the societal realm of 'networks and associations formed between the home and the state that allow for public forms of discussion … argument' (Stevenson 2004, 1) and mobilization, comprises crucial sites for the excavation of more open and inclusive discourses of belonging.[2] Highly relevant to this are discussions surrounding the public sphere. Jürgen Habermas's seminal work (1978, 1987, 1989) on the bourgeois public sphere of the seventeenth and eighteenth centuries and on the conditions underpinning 'ideal speech situations' has been subject to some necessary criticism and modifications. These have included several critical observations relevant to what follows: the 'remarkable absence of nationalism from Habermas's discussion of the public sphere', the 'thinness of attention to matters of culture and the construction of identities', and Habermas's 'neglect of social movements' and concomitant articulation of 'new voices' (Calhoun 1992, 34–37). Jointly, these criticisms point to the internal diversities and fissures that characterize the public spheres in stratified, pluralistic societies and pave the way for Fraser's concept of multiple, 'subaltern counterpublics'.

Crucial to such debates and the following analysis are experiences of exclusion and attempts to transform existing configurations of power (and powerlessness) through civil society activity and critical public debate. The wider structural context to such inequalities, struggles and further fortifications, to be understood against the economic backdrop discussed in the previous chapter, has been outlined as follows:

> Racism does not contradict democracy – rather, it helps to consolidate the boundaries of democratic polities by defining who does not belong and can therefore be excluded from universalistic principles … Since most major political forces support … deregulation and economic restructuring, disadvantaged groups tend to turn their anger against the most visible signs of change: old and new ethnic minorities. Racism has thus become an emblem of resistance for disempowered groups in increasingly polarized societies. (Castles 2000, 14)

This account contains both vital insights and seemingly implicit assumptions that require more nuanced discussion. Castles alerts us to a key dimension informing national politics as much as the everyday discourses examined earlier (see chapter three): nationalism is partly premised on notions of *entitlements* that are confined to members of the in-group and therefore not extended to 'the other'. Moreover, Castles reminds us that democratic nation-states invariably also draw boundaries of inclusion and exclusion, separating citizens from non-citizens. He further corroborates that growing economic uncertainty can trigger racist resentments amongst relatively disempowered 'locals'. Whilst these dimensions form important

---

2    For a more elaborate conceptual discussion of civil society, see – for example – Però (2007a, 105–117).

parts of the context to the following analysis, two more searching questions need to be put to Castles' account: first, can or should entitlement discourses of the kind alluded to here be classified as racist? Or does this, in the absence of further conceptual clarification, unhelpfully conflate very different phenomena and forms of exclusion? Second, does the association of racism with the 'disadvantaged' fearing further competition overlook 'middle-class racism' (see Grillo 2005), the exclusions and resentments perpetuated by the relatively privileged?

These questions are partly addressed, in terms relevant to this discussion, by Philomena Essed's more exact, and more clearly defined, concept of 'everyday racism'. Based on research conducted in Holland and the US, Essed conceptualizes racism as simultaneously 'ideology, structure and process' that pervade, and intersect in, everyday life: racism is shown to be a self-interested construction of human collectives in relations of hierarchy or opposition to one another; it is also a structure of 'rules, laws and regulations' that enshrine unequal access to resources, rights and entitlements; finally, racism is also 'a process because structures and ideologies do not exist outside the everyday practices through which they are created and confirmed' (Essed 1991, 43–44). It is also worth pointing out that everyday racism thus conceptualized does not presuppose conscious awareness on part of its perpetrators or victims: ideological classifications and boundaries, structural exclusions, and the processes of their enactment and perpetuation can all be deeply embedded, widely taken-for-granted and thus overlooked. It is in this context that some of the civil society activities and public debates examined below reveal their wider significance, as conscious interventions and acts of resistance by so-called ordinary social actors against some of the exclusions and forms of disadvantage or discrimination suffered by certain 'others' occupying precarious structural positions inside 'Fortress Europe'. Moreover, such alternative, inclusive discourses and attempts at structural transformation do not generally oppose or question the institutions of the nation-state, the concept of citizenship, or the general idea of boundaries and classification. They do, however, argue for more open structures and more inclusive notions of (national) belonging.

My analysis of grassroots- and civil society resistance against discursive and/or structural exclusions focuses on a range of phenomena, initiatives and organizations in Vienna and Graz, Austria's second city (and relevant examples from elsewhere), between 2002 and 2010. This is complemented by a discussion of critical local papers, and followed by an examination of in some ways comparable local struggles over inclusion encountered in other parts of Europe. What these various examples share is a position on the ideological spectrum diametrically opposed to nationalism, from where they argue for inclusivist forms of identity, citizenship and political participation. Given that their criticisms tend to be levelled against existing national or European structures of exclusion and against a seemingly dominant ideology supportive of Europe's external fortification, such politics can be described – in Gramscian terminology – as 'counter-hegemonic', as attempting to subvert a cultural commonsense and to work towards structural change.

This chapter casts light on two issues of contextual and wider theoretical significance respectively. The former relates to a widely-observed characteristic of recent Austrian history: post-war reconstruction culminated in a political system of extraordinary stability, based on consensual democracy and the systematic power-sharing in the country's large public sector between SPÖ and ÖVP (e.g. Morrow 2000; Thaler 2001). Coupled with, by Western standards, unusually high levels of political party-membership, these were the structural conditions delaying the development of a fully-fledged civil society (e.g. Bruckmüller 1996, 42–43; Pelinka 1990, 24).[3] In what follows, however, I show that the last two decades have seen not only significant reconfigurations of these older power structures but also, crucially, the emergence of a viable and lively civil society, parts of which are analyzed below. The second, more general insight relates to the discursive content of some prominent contributions to (Austrian) civil society: the dislocations of globalization provide the context and a core-target of critique for much counter-hegemonic activity; given that nationalist discourse, its main ideological opponent, also positions itself – as we saw in the previous chapter – in opposition to the local impact of global forces and flows, the question will be addressed as to what distinguishes the left from the right in their reactions to (economic) globalization.

Analysis of relevant public debates and civil society activities reveals several key dimensions:[4] first, a series of conceptual and interpretative counter-hegemonic challenges; second, examples of criticism of, and opposition to, the treatment of asylum-seekers; third, organizations campaigning for, and attempting to support, different categories of migrants; fourth, demonstrations and partly inter-related networks of mobilization and inclusive politics; fifth, building on Fraser's work, I analyze the workings of what I term 'pluralistic counterpublics'.

### Conceptual and political challenges

Inclusive identity-discourses are encountered, for example, in critical local/ regional media. I here focus on two relevant papers (also see Karner 2007b): first, the Viennese weekly *Falter*, which also circulates outside the capital – with a regional, Styrian supplement since 2005 – and has a reputation for its investigative journalism and its critical contributions to political debates; founded in 1977, it reached some 6 per cent of Vienna's population of 1.7 million in 2000 (http:// www.falter.at/anzeigen/media.php), 1.2 per cent of the national readership in 2008

---

3   More recently, historian Moritz Csáky has still detected traces of an alleged reluctance to engage in critical public discourse, the origins of which he locates in Austria's more distant past – the Catholic counter-reformation (quoted in Winkler 2010).

4   To state the obvious: what follows cannot – and does not purport to – offer a comprehensive overview of Austria's civil society and public sphere in their entirety. Instead, the following thematic, qualitative analysis offers snapshots typical of more widely recurring discursive and organizational currents.

(http://derstandard.at/1237228391907), and has become an important and vocal part of Austria's wider media landscape. The second paper in question is a monthly 'street magazine and social initiative' entitled *Megaphon*, which is published in Graz by the Caritas of the regional diocese (though Catholicism rarely, if ever, manifests explicitly in its content) and is sold by street vendors – most of them asylum-seekers – suffering social exclusion and hardship; *Megaphon* currently sells 12,000 copies a month in Graz and other cities and towns throughout the south-eastern province of Styria (http://www.megaphon.at) and is a part of the international network of street papers (INSP).

### Complex identities in context

Along with other, similarly critical media in and beyond the Alpine Republic, *Falter* and *Megaphon* regularly challenge widespread, 'commonsensical' and divisive assumptions about cultural difference and identities. Such challenges deconstruct rigid boundaries and essentializing discourses of belonging, by variously locating identity politics in their socio-economic contexts and revealing the multiple 'axes' of difference and inequality (Brah 1996) that cut across and through any 'imagined community' (Anderson 1983).

One of many relevant examples of counter-hegemonic challenge manifested in a round-table discussion published in *Falter* in April 2004 on Islam and multiculturalism (John and Klenk 2004). The discussion involved the coordinator of a Viennese 'integration association' (i.e. *Integrationsverein Echo*), a local councillor, a social worker, and a member of the 'Austrian-Islamic Society for Education and Culture'. Reflecting on their experiences of working with Muslims in Vienna, the discussants addressed issues that have defined European debates about Islam over recent years – terrorism, patriarchy, and Islam's relationship to 'the West'. Two competing accounts emerged: first, a 'clash of civilizations' narrative analogous to Samuel Huntington's (1998) much-quoted thesis and echoed in much of the everyday discourse analyzed in chapter three. In this particular discussion, however, this Manichean discourse was only advocated by the aforementioned coordinator of a local 'integrations association', who argued that political Islam hampered Muslims' integration and was irreconcilable with the 'European values' of 'tolerance, anti-racism and liberalism'. This was challenged by the other three participants' critique of neo-liberal capitalism, their repeated declarations that poverty and exclusion had alienated many (young) Muslims, for which exclusivist identities and reactionary, selective interpretations of Islam promised an antidote (John and Klenk 2004). Such reflections thus offer structural contextualization and challenge common assumptions that ethnic or religious identities are primordial determinants of attitudes and behaviours.

At other times, the multi-dimensionality of identities is recorded. One example of this was a *Falter* portrait (Ortner 2004) of a 55-year old shop-keeper from former Yugoslavia who, after 36 years in Vienna, was described as 'quite Austrianized', reading Austrian tabloids, passionate about Austrian folk music, and considering herself to be 'both Austrian and Yugoslav'. Thus offering a fluid narrative of two co-existing self-understandings, the article also quoted the shopkeeper as saying that 'deep-down' she is 'a proud Yugoslav [*sic*]' still prone to deep melancholy over Balkan music. Contrary to nationalist rigidities, ethnic identities were therefore portrayed as biographically grounded, invested with emotion, shaped by a cultural *habitus*, yet also as subject to syncretistic redefinition and re-construction. Similar complexities are captured in a regular *Megaphon* feature – portraits of individual migrants and asylum-seekers in Graz. For example, editions in 2003 and 2004 provided glimpses into the biographies of the owner of a Chinese restaurant, a Rwandan refugee and medical student, a Turkish entrepreneur, an Iranian translator, African *Megaphon* vendors, an Argentinean family, a Bosnian psychiatrist, and the Nigerian initiator of an organization working with young Austrians and migrants. While these portraits provided glimpses of hardship, exclusion and struggle, they also emphasized experiences of local support, social integration (and in some cases the acquisition of Austrian citizenship), and cultural syncretism giving rise to identities best conceptualized – in Stuart Hall's terminology (1996, 4) – as ongoing 'process[es] of becoming'. Such accounts avoid and challenge unambiguous delineations of the imputed national 'self' from ethnic minorities as permanently excluded 'others'.

Critical media discourse also de-naturalizes rigid identity-discourses by drawing attention to the inequalities and hierarchies dividing both 'self' and 'other' internally. In discussing unequal distributions of (and struggles over) power *within* ethnic or national groups, myths of homogenous national collectives are challenged and transnational solidarities encouraged. Importantly, criticism of – for example – gendered inequalities are frequently directed at the dominant majority: a critique of (Austrian) patriarchy thus emerged, for instance, from a *Megaphon* article (Windisch 2004a) on local women's struggle to balance work and family life; the article criticized the continuing construction of children's nurturing as largely a maternal 'responsibility', which reproduced gender-specific pressures further compounded by the decline of the welfare state. Such awareness of power differentials within national 'communities' is complemented by attempts to forge transnational networks of solidarity. A narrative of support for persecuted or marginalized ethnic minorities outside the (Austrian) 'nation-state container' (Beck 2000) was articulated, for example, in *Megaphon* articles on the Roma communities of Slovakia. The articles (Windisch 2004b, 2004c) criticized controversial benefit cuts as further exacerbating the poverty, chronic unemployment and social exclusion endured by many Slovakian Romanies.

*Recording the workings of power*

The second, more directly political feature of parts of Austria's public sphere and critical media consists of its acting as a check upon the workings of state power. This has involved drawing public attention to cases of misuses of power and/or brutality.[5] A key event in this context was the tragic death of the Nigerian Marcus Omofuma in May 1999, who – whilst being deported from Austria to Bulgaria – was tied and gagged by three accompanying officers and subsequently suffocated; the fall-out to Omofuma's death included the setting up of a human rights commission in Austria's Interior Ministry (http://wien.orf.at/stories/357514/).

Two recent cases of misuses of power with tragic consequences captured and reported by *Falter* need to be mentioned in particular (see Karner 2007b). The first incident concerned the death of Cheibani Wague, a 33-year old Mauritanian physicist, in Vienna's central park on 15 July 2003. The police and ambulance were called to restrain Cheibani who had become enraged in the course of an argument. According to the initially circulating version of events, Cheibani died of heart failure following the administration of a sedative. A week after this tragic incident, however, *Falter* published an article revealing that a video recording by a local resident suggested that the force employed by police and paramedics involved had been excessive, with one paramedic shown standing on top of a motionless Cheibani whilst a doctor – instead of checking the patient's vital functions – was standing by (Klenk 2003). The *Falter*'s revelations significantly contributed to the calling of an enquiry (http://derStandard.at 18 November 2003) and, subsequently, the decision to prosecute ten people involved in the tragedy (http://wien.orf.at/oesterreich.orf?read=detail&channel=1&id=375633).

The second revelation emerged through investigative journalism (Horaczek and Weissensteiner 2003) on a group of Chechnyans, who had fled from violence and persecution at the hands of the Russian police, awaiting their possible deportation in an asylum-seeker reception centre 160 kilometres east of Prague. Less than two weeks previously they had attempted to cross the Czech-Austrian border where, the Chechnyans claimed, the Austrian border guards had ignored their pleas for asylum before 'returning' them to the Czech authorities. A spokesperson for Austria's Ministry of Interior contradicted this, saying that the group had decided not to claim asylum having been told that there were no more available places in federal accommodation (Horaczek and Weissensteiner 2003). Such conflicting accounts notwithstanding, *Falter* coverage once again fuelled public discussion. Amnesty International called for clarification of what had occurred on the Czech-Austrian border and *SOS Mitmensch*, an Austrian NGO, was considering taking legal action against the local authority in question. Final clarification of the incident was only reached six-and-a-half years later, when it was confirmed that the Chechnyans had indeed been denied their right to apply for asylum (Horaczek 2010d).

As with the conceptual challenges examined above, such critical and investigative journalism also looks beyond Austria's borders. Parts of the country's

---

5   The nature and causes of such incidents have been subject to much controversy: when Amnesty International detected forms of institutional racism in parts of Austria's police in a report published in April 2009, the Interior Ministry and Vienna's police denied this, speaking of 'isolated cases' of racism instead (*Der Standard* 10 April 2009, 1).

quality press have also taken a vocal stance in transnational debates concerning the fate of asylum-seekers in different parts of Europe. For example, the weekly *Profil* recently reported and criticized cases of police brutality against, and the destitution suffered by, asylum-seekers in Greece (Lackner 2010e).

*Critiquing neo-liberalism*

Further challenges formulated in the specific niches of Austrian civil society and public sphere examined here are directed against the dislocations associated with globalization and neo-liberal deregulation.

In May 2003, against the backdrop of the Austrian Trade Union Association's strike-action against reforms of the pension system, a *Falter* article compared government policies to Margaret Thatcher's neo-liberalism of the 1980s. They shared, it argued, an ideological commitment to privatization and their (likely) consequences were also similar: rising unemployment, the emergence of the 'working poor', heightened social inequalities and the dismantling – euphemistically presented as 'necessary reforms' – of the welfare state (John and Weissensteiner 2003). Similar assessments of globalization and privatization, which share a transnational consciousness reflected in their criticisms of 'late capitalism' across different contexts, are regularly encountered in *Megaphon*. Relevant coverage has included articles sympathetic with the political opposition articulated by social movements at the fourth world social forum in Mumbai (Reithofer 2004), the portrait of a street magazine in Buenos Aires and its battle against Argentina's economic crisis (Schmied 2002a), and support for the protest by developing countries and anti-globalization activists against the 'ideological myths of neo-liberalism' at the World Trade Organization's 2003 conference (Schmied 2003a). A recurring interpretative schema targets the economic dominance of multinational corporations, neo-liberal hegemony leading to a decline in public spending, the poverty endured by a large proportion of the world's population and exacerbated by their economic and political exclusion, and a politically stifling and atomizing consumerism (e.g. Coudenhove-Kalergi 2003) as its main objects of criticism. Such counter-hegemonic discourses also at times inform *Megaphon*'s opposition to ethnic exclusion. For example, one of the above-mentioned articles on Roma communities in Slovakia argued that their exclusion was the joint product of widespread ethnic prejudice and programmes of uncompromising de-regulation in the post-communist era. However, the author did not advocate a return to an over-romanticized past, arguing for the provision of social welfare and of culturally inclusive educational policies for Roma children – deemed necessary for their successful future participation in the information age – instead (Truger 2004).

Similarly, the above-mentioned sensitivity to patriarchal domination informs *Megaphon*'s intersection with other civil society initiatives and their critical stance on globalization. The gender-specific effects of multinational capitalism and deregulation were the focus of a conference organized by feministATTAC, a transnational network, in Graz in September 2003. This international conference involved activists and academics attempting to increase public awareness of countless women's contemporary plight. Interviewed by *Megaphon*, its local organizers summarized the gender-specific consequences of globalization as including the global sex trade and human trafficking, associations of care with femininity exacerbating women's domestic burden in a post-welfare age, widening gaps in the distribution of wealth, and the disproportionate effects of companies' 'downsizing' on women (Wolf 2003). Two months later, *Megaphon* published a summary of a study, which had – in the footsteps of *The Weight of the World* (Bourdieu et al. 1999) – investigated the local consequences of globalization and neo-liberalism through a series of interviews conducted in Graz: 23 informants had reflected on biographies shaped by experiences as diverse as migration and asylum-seeking, unemployment, making a living as journalists, teachers and artists, yet their life-histories revealed recurring themes: economic uncertainty, existential anxiety, and the absence of political help (Wolkinger 2003).

Thus we begin to see the contours of a public sphere critical of existing power structures and their ideologies of legitimation (Karner 2007b). Moreover, such challenges work across a range of scales, from the local, to the pan-European and the global. Other nodes in Austria's civil society are more directly focused on their more immediate 'surroundings' and, particularly, on the fate of asylum-seekers in Austria.

## In support of asylum-seekers

As shown in chapter three, the issue of asylum is very much at the forefront of public debate and a key target of criticism and complaint for the populist right (Gärtner 2009, 151–156). At the same time, asylum and the fate of individual asylum-seekers divide Austrian public opinion, pitting discourses of nationalist exclusion against inclusivist self-understandings and initiatives. All this needs to be put into context: as also mentioned earlier, Austria's post-1950 record of welcoming refugees, from Hungary and later from Czechoslovakia, was in many ways exemplary (see Weigl 2009, 60, 82–83). Starting in the 1990s, however, and against the backdrop of a rapid increase in forced migration across the world (Richmond 2002), much public opinion began to swing against asylum-seekers who increasingly came to be constructed as a threat and unmanageable burden. Politics followed suit with a succession of increasingly restrictive asylum- and immigration acts (Krzyżanowski and Wodak 2009).

According to the Interior Ministry, in April 2004 it was accommodating 11,000 asylum-seekers (i.e. five times as many as four years previously) awaiting decisions on their claims (http://www.noe.orf.at 29 April 2004). At the same time, NGOs – first and foremost Caritas Austria – were criticizing the Ministry over the plight of homeless asylum-seekers and what the Caritas considered a lack of political will to provide the infrastructure and finances to deal with ever increasing numbers of people and families escaping persecution and poverty. On 1 May

2004, a controversial new asylum act came into force (http://derStandard.at 29 April 2004), which stipulated that, following a period of preliminary assessments in a reception centre, asylum-seekers would henceforth either be accommodated in one of Austria's nine provinces (according to a quota system proportional to regional population size) whilst awaiting the decision on their claim, or – if they were declined in the first instance – be faced with deportation. The FPÖ's initial satisfaction with this legislation (http://www.orf.at 4 May 2004) may be read as indicative of wider European sentiments: shortly before the EU's enlargement, its then fifteen Interior Ministers had agreed to work towards a common asylum law, which (is yet to materialize and) would incorporate the idea pioneered in Austria's new act that claims made by citizens of states deemed to be 'safe' could be turned down instantly (http://www.orf.at 30 April 2004).

An asylum-system widely considered to be enormously complex saw further changes in 2009, which various institutions and critical NGOs in particular anticipated would translate into additional hardships, obstacles and injustices (http://oe1.orf.at/inforadio/110322.html).[6] Controversial recent proposals and changes have included increased detention of asylum-seekers awaiting deportation to another EU country (http://www.orf.at/ticker/331137.html), the use of x-ray to estimate asylum-seekers' age (http://orf.at/090915-42579/?href…), and restrictions confining asylum-seekers in the early stages of their application to the area of the local authority where their claim was submitted (Schmaus 2009). All of this needs to be seen in its wider European context and, more exactly, in the EU's increased fortification, as most clearly epitomized by the many tragedies of lives lost at sea whilst attempting to reach European shores, by often hopelessly overcrowded reception centres, by asylum-seekers forced to spend years awaiting decisions on their applications, and by EU member-states systematically deporting those whose hopes for a safer life inside 'Fortress Europe' come to nothing. European comparisons show that asylum-seekers' fate varies enormously depending on where and when their claims are processed. Whilst in 2008 Austria ranked amongst the EU countries with the highest rates of positive decisions on claims for asylum (http://www.orf.at 8 December 2009), this changed significantly in 2009 when the Austrian acceptance rate dropped from 61.6 per cent to 21.7 per cent (http://www.orf.at 18 June 2010). As infamously demonstrated by chronic destitution and cases of police violence reported in Greece (Lackner 2010e), for example, conditions 'on the ground' also vary markedly across the EU. In the Austrian context, recent reports have painted a mixed picture: whilst the European Commission against Racism and Intolerance has commended some recent Austrian anti-discrimination measures (http://www.orf.at 2 March 2010), national reports by the Interior Ministry's above-mentioned human rights commission and anti-racism NGO Zara documented a lack of legal support for detained asylum-seekers

6    Alongside NGOs and the Green party, Austria's Ecumenical Council of Churches has been particularly vocal in its criticisms of these changes (http://religion.orf.at/project03/news/0910/ne091019_asyl_fr.htm).

awaiting deportation and a rise in racist incidents in 2009 respectively (*Falter* 24 March 2010, 9). Most recently, in the autumn of 2010, controversial deportations – including that of a family with eight-year-old twins subsequently allowed to return – led to heated debates, protests and concessions by the Interior Minister that some 'old' asylum-applications would be re-examined and that deportations of families needed to be handled more sensitively.

Against this backdrop, numerous recent initiatives, campaigns and publicly circulating counter-discourses are noteworthy as examples of inclusivist identity-politics articulated in support of asylum-seekers and against existing structures of power and exclusion. A recent edition of the newsletter of Vienna's 'house of integration', a local civil society node working with and for forced migrants to be discussed in more detail in the next section, summarized some such initiatives and their importance:

> Few topics have triggered as much recent resistance as these new restrictions on asylum and migration: hundreds of small and large demonstrations, vigils, processions of light in many cities and towns have spoken out against the detention of asylum-seekers … against deportations and ever more restrictive measures … Success has been limited to a few cases, though. Is it worth persevering with the protests then? The answer was given by Dr Martin Luther King …: 'No more proof is needed that we are all equal! I have a dream that one day the entire nation will rise and convey this credo!' (Stranig 2009, my translation)

From amongst the many cases of hardship, tragedy and local solidarity alluded to here a few particular instances that are paradigmatic of both some of the struggles and sources of support endured and experienced by forced migrants need to be discussed in more detail, for they condense different types of dilemmas and outcomes.

One instance demonstrating the possibility of migrants falling into the cracks of a complex legal system was that of a Bosnian family in Vienna who had fled the Balkan wars in the early 1990s but unfortunately failed to comply with existing asylum-legislation at the time. As a consequence they settled in Austria without valid residence permit. Only in 2007 did the family's four children obtain humanitarian right of residence, whilst the parents found themselves in a legal catch-22: though not subject to (imminent) deportation, they did not have humanitarian right of residence and hence no work permit; a lack of income in turn prevented the possibility their obtaining (humanitarian) right of residence; the family was reported to be getting by on the studentships of its highly talented 16-year-old daughter, whose teachers, friends and headmaster were campaigning for the family; at the same time, the local authority was asking for humanitarian right of residence to be granted to the whole family (http://oesterreich.orf.at/wien/stories/206542).

A similar situation emerged in the spring of 2009 in Schruns, in Austria's western-most province of Vorarlberg (Berger 2009). Five years previously a 'hotel' accommodating refugees had opened in Schruns – to considerable local scepticism. However, and thanks to a local initiative facilitating dialogue and language courses, good neighbourly relationships between long-established 'locals' and more recently arrived forced migrants were established. These manifested particularly after a new and much-debated law came into force in April 2009, providing a potential loophole for some otherwise 'failed' asylum-seekers to apply for humanitarian right of residence under a series of conditions including continuous residence in Austria since 1 May 2004 (Reithofer-Haidacher 2009a). In Schruns this meant that twenty asylum-seekers, including families with children, who had arrived after that date were faced with potential deportation, against which a local civil society platform entitled 'We need those children' protested; supported by local politicians, teachers and dignitaries, the platform argued – in a discursive move symptomatic of much counter-hegemonic practice – by invoking a set of universal values: deporting the children in question, it was argued, would expose them to heightened insecurity, which would in turn deprive them of the 'best possible conditions for development' enshrined in the UN convention for the rights of children (Berger 2009). At the exact same time, in the Styrian town of Peggau, a Chechnyan family of nine were battling illness, post-traumatic stress and the threat of deportation to Poland under the Dublin agreement, according to which asylum-claims are to be processed by the EU member-state where the person in question first entered the EU. This case also condensed the role of NGOs – including an organization called *Asyl in Not* – in fighting individuals' and their families' corner and in articulating a counter-hegemony willing to point at potential injustices created by existing laws and regulations: a spokesperson for Amnesty International thus argued that all 'Dublin-transfers' posed considerable problems as the EU could not control the quality of the asylum-process in particular member-states and that Chechnyans in Poland were particularly disadvantaged and much more likely than in Austria to have their claims rejected (Möseneder and Schmidt 2009).

Several other recent and widely-discussed incidents revealed both the precariousness endured by asylum-seekers and the willingness of some local communities to fight their deportation. One such example, where resistance and interventions by friends, the local mayor, the local authority and even the provincial governor proved futile, was that of a 25 year-old Nigerian asylum-seeker. Despite all these efforts and much evidence of his 'full integration' after eight years in the village of Leogang in the province of Salzburg, his application for humanitarian right of residence was trumped by a rejected asylum-claim and he was deported in June 2009 (http://salzburg.orf.at/stories/366036/). The following February, in Röthis in Vorarlberg, a group of neighbours and friends physically prevented the planned deportation of a family from Kosovo (http://vorarlberg. orf.at/stories/425369/). On Austria's opposite geographical end, in the village of Wolfau in the eastern-most province of Burgenland, friends, neighbours, the local mayor, church and branch of the NGO *SOS Mitmensch* spent many months supporting a well-integrated Kosovan family of six and campaigning to prevent –

ultimately unsuccessfully – their deportation (Zöchling 2010).[7] In the spring 2010 a training match by a football team of asylum-seekers called *FC Sans Papiers* was interrupted by a police squad seeking to detain two of its – subsequently deported – Nigerian players (Heshmatpour and Zwander 2010). This triggered a road blockage by 250 demonstrators seeking to prevent the two 'failed' asylum-seekers' detention and deportation (http://wien.orf.at/stories/439586) and a series of subsequent protests and demonstrations (http://wien.orf.at/stories/440909/). And when a Kosovan family who had spent five years living in the Lower Austrian village of Winzendorf-Muthmansdorf was deported in February 2010, parents involved in the local football-club one of the Kosovan boys had played for responded by starting an initiative (see http://www.freundeschuetzen.at), which calls for well-integrated families of refugees to be granted right of residence (Apfl 2010d). Writing in *Profil*, Elfriede Hammerl (2010) saw this case as paradigmatic of similar acts of resistance witnessed across the country, which do not argue for 'unrestricted immigration' but against such deportations and indifference towards forced migrants.

Many disputes involving local resistance against the enactment and consequences of existing asylum-legislation pit universalist understandings of human rights against laws and entitlements (or exclusion) tied to (non)citizenship. Put differently, such disputes condense a clash between universalist ethics and a politics of inclusion on one hand, and dominant definitions of rights and entitlements as largely and decisively defined by citizenship on the other. In this context it is worth returning to *Falter* and *Megaphon* as two amongst several voices criticizing various facets of the asylum-system: their criticisms have targeted, for example, the perplexing details of the earlier-mentioned regulations concerning humanitarian right of residence (Reithofer-Haidacher 2009a), the detention of 'failed' asylum-seekers (Reithofer-Haidacher 2010), or their systematic deportations by 'Fortress Europe' (Sawerthal 2010). The most heated national asylum-debate, however, concerned a 'case' mentioned earlier: that of Arigona Zogaj, a teenaged girl of Kosovo-Albanian descent, whose plight and future occupied much of Austria for three years between her temporary disappearance in the autumn of 2007 following her family's unsuccessful asylum-application, their enforced departure to Kosovo in the summer of 2010 and subsequent permission to return to Austria a few months later. In that period Arigona polarized the Austrian public: supported by a list of politicians (and the Green party in its entirety), artists, intellectuals, celebrities, friends and a local priest, and voted 'person of the year' 2009 by the weekly *Profil* (Meinhart 2010a); and simultaneously vilified by many on the populist right, to whom the letter of the law had to take precedence over sentiments or biographical circumstances (Arigona clearly self-defines as Austrian and was as integrated as anyone could be, by any imaginable measurement of teenage-integration).

---

7   The uneasy coexistence of such inclusivist and rigidly exclusivist responses to asylum-seekers was demonstrated by widespread opposition to the earlier-mentioned and subsequently shelved plans for a reception centre in the town of Eberau in Burgenland.

## Organizations of solidarity

The parts of Austria's civil society and public sphere where a politics of inclusion is advocated and neo-nationalism is challenged also of course include more formal organizations and associations. As in the previous section constraints of space only allow for a presentation of snapshots of select organizations working for and with asylum-seekers and other migrants in Austria's two main cities, Vienna and Graz.

Among the critics of the asylum-system few have been as outspoken as *Frau Bock*, a former Viennese social worker who has dedicated her retirement to the organization of flats accommodating asylum-seekers (Karner 2007b). For example, in March 2003 the backlog of asylum-seekers awaiting decisions on their claims reached a high-point, among them hundreds – often those not in possession of the required documents – who were not in 'federal care' and hence, unless accommodated by NGOs, facing possible homelessness (http://fm4.orf.at/connected/119977/main). *Frau Bock*'s flats constituted a last safety-net for some of those homeless, providing them with shelter, one meal a day and, crucially (also for many others not actually living in the flats), a registered postal address whilst awaiting a decision on their asylum-claims. The project has been funded by *Frau Bock*'s pension and savings, donations and awards, and various initiatives including some 70 bars and restaurants in Vienna, Graz and Linz donating ten cents of every beer sold in the summer of 2003 to the continuing running of the flats (http://clandestino.at). Frau Bock's initiatives and project have received considerable media attention. Whilst admired and praised for her self-sacrificing work, she has also been confronted by some of the earlier-mentioned – and, we might add, pan-European – populist objections: by a 'topos of finances' and 'limited resources' (Krzyżanowski and Wodak 2009, 112) and by xenophobic discourses about cultural otherness and alleged 'criminal tendencies' (contained in discursive chains connecting asylum-seekers to drugs, for example). In a newspaper interview (http://derstandard.at/standard.asp?id=1444272) and in response to listeners on a radio programme (http://www.orf.at/030814-65875/index.html), Frau Bock fervently rejected such prejudicial discourses by emphasizing the structural marginalization and resulting despair experienced by many asylum-seekers. In light of lengthy asylum-procedures and the fact that most asylum-seekers are not allowed to work (also see Bloch 2002, 60), Frau Bock queried how these people were expected to survive, if not adequately supported by the state. Since then, Frau Bock's work has continued and has become a symbol of civil society solidarity with 'the other'.[8]

Similarly committed to supporting forced migrants is Vienna's earlier-mentioned 'house of integration' (*Integrationshaus*). Founded in 1995 to house families of refugees, it has become a 'nationally and internationally recognized' centre offering accommodation, support and advice for asylum-seekers, running

---

8    There has been a recent film made about Frau Bock's work entitled 'Bock for President' (Philipp 2010).

numerous educational and cultural projects, and campaigning for forced migrants; in 2005 the house of integration opened an asylum-seeker advice-centre that ran nearly 40,000 appointments over the following five years, it offers legal advice (supported by donations), many and varied training opportunities and a multi-lingual nursery, as well as two living units and counselling for unaccompanied under-aged asylum-seekers (Eraslan-Weninger 2010). Reflecting on its origins, co-founder and musician Willi Resetarits portrays the house of integration as an institution jointly created and run by marginalized outsiders and compassionate (as well as historically reflexive) citizens:

> Instead of the usual moans and lamentations that 'nothing can be done about this', we've taken things on. We, that is refugees who bravely stepped into an uncertain future. And 'we' also includes Austrians, whose ancestors were [often] also migrants, and who say – let's do this. (Resetarits 2010, my translation)

These insights into the motivations driving Vienna's house of integration are also theoretically significant: they suggest a modification of Fraser's concept of counterpublics as 'subaltern', since institutions and initiatives of the kind discussed here involve not only members of 'subordinated' groups but a diverse network of social actors occupying very different structural positions of relative exclusion and security respectively, but with a shared commitment to a politics of inclusion and solidarity (see below).

Also highly relevant in this context is another street magazine: published quarterly in Vienna and sold throughout Austria, it was founded as *Die Bunte Zeitung* ('The multicoloured paper') in 2000 by Congolese-born Di-Tutu Bukasa who also initiated the earlier-mentioned football team *FC Sans Papiers* for asylum-seekers in 2002 (Heshmatpour and Zwander 2010). Subsequently renamed as *The Global Player*, the magazine defines itself as a '(European) medium for dignity, justice and democracy' and includes contributions by a diverse range of people reflecting on local, national, European and global inequalities and exclusions. A recent edition, for example, contained a letter written by asylum-seekers in Austria's largest asylum-seeker reception centre:

> Out of Traiskirchen: Most respectfully we would like to share our problems with you people! ... Most of the ... asylum seekers in Austria living in the Traiskirchen camp have left their finger prints in Greece and Hungary ... you all know the situation in Greece ... life is not save. Like in our own country, Afghanistan. In Greece ... we were sleeping in the parks without any shelter ... The guys in Traiskirchen are ready to kill themselves, but not to go back to Greece or Hungary! And the Austrian law is too difficult nowadays ... keeping us waiting here, means that they are wasting our time and will finally deport us! Why? ... And Hungary is a poor country, they cannot even feed themselves ... The camps in Hungary are too dirty ... most of us had different diseases ... At last we would like to say: No border, no nation! Stop deportation! You people

must help us ... you must take our voices to the public ... We are very thankful
if you could do this. Yours sincerely, All the people of the Traiskirchen camp
(The Global Player 2010)

Reflecting profound difficulties and despair, this extract provides a glimpse of a
'subaltern counterpublic' articulating its needs, sharing its history, and seeking to
speak to – and establish links with – the public at large. It also shockingly reflects
the very different and disconcerting conditions faced by asylum-seekers in different
parts of the EU. Finally it contains traces of a more radically counter-hegemonic,
post-national politics, of a utopia of a world beyond national boundaries.

Perhaps less utopian, but enormously committed to working towards inclusion
and against inequality is an organization active in Graz and throughout the south-
eastern province of Styria called ISOP ('Innovative social projects'). Summarizing
its wide-ranging activities in 2008 as the creation of 'islands of solidarity in
times of crisis', two leading figures in ISOP identified the wider context to their
organization's work as including global poverty, growing unemployment and job-
insecurity, and widening inequalities both within and across nation-states:

> This is the context to the difficult work done by NGOs like ISOP. The need for
> alternatives to a socio-economic system based on greed, relentless competition,
> deepening social inequalities, gender discrimination and racist practices is
> particularly apparent in the everyday workings of social- and educational
> institutions. The existential need for social changes based on solidarity follows.
> (Reithofer and Brand 2009, my translation)

ISOP's inclusive politics, and everyday commitment to pluralism and solidarity,
manifest in its many projects and initiatives. In 2008 alone, these included a long
list of (multi)cultural events and inter-cultural encounters, numerous employment-
related projects, job-advice and training, qualifications for migrants and job-related
German language courses, collaborations with other civil society organizations,
a new regional centre offering advice on integration and anti-discrimination,
numerous youth projects and afternoon-clubs for children (*Isotopia* 2009).

The local network of civil society organizations – regularly documented in
*Megaphon* – that operate in and around Graz and articulate inclusive identity-
discourses and a counter-hegemonic politics of solidarity and social change
has become vibrant and far-reaching. Its many 'nodes' include an initiative
campaigning for right of residence for socially integrated asylum-seekers (Maier
2009); inter-cultural allotments (Schweiger 2008); culturally diverse migrants'
organizations dedicated to facilitating integration (e.g. Reithofer-Haidacher
2008a), as well as particular ethnic associations committed to cultural dialogue
(e.g. Aigner 2009a; Alber 2009) and a migrants' committee working with the local
authority (Reithofer-Haidacher 2008b); open-access lectures jointly organized by
academics and social workers (Joschika and Wrann 2009); various organizations
working with traumatized refugees (Reithofer-Haidacher 2009b), linking teenaged

refugees with local families (Schweiger 2010), and organizing football matches between Africans and policemen (Wietheger 2010).

## Demonstrating (for) inclusion

Another cluster of counter-hegemonic activity has included a number of recent protests and demonstrations articulating opposition to exclusionary structures, mechanisms and ideologies. Their assessments, rhetoric and demands throw both the neo-nationalism they are opposing and their own alternative politics of inclusion and solidarity into sharp relief. In this context a defining feature of (neo-) nationalist discourse needs to be recalled – an emphasis on citizens' entitlements, outsiders' access to which is denied and blocked. Not surprisingly, there is now a long tradition of such 'citizens-entitlement-thinking' in the FPÖ's politics. It manifested most clearly in the 1992–1993 'Austria First' petition, 'allowing the party to become the main "articulator" of the (old) social fears of "the other" in general, and of migrants as "default scapegoats" in particular' (Krzyżanowski and Wodak 2009, 116). However, and highly relevant to this discussion, this also led to the largest demonstration in the history of the Second Republic, a 'sea of light' (*Lichtermeer*) in Vienna in January 1993, attended by some 350,000 people firmly opposed to the FPÖ's exclusionary demands (e.g. Weigl 2009, 85). Recent manifestations of a divisive entitlement-logic have included FPÖ-head Heinz-Christian Strache calling for new support-mechanisms for Austrian parents in the realms of employment and welfare and for separate social security systems for citizens and foreigners (http://www.orf.at/ticker/344496.html), and FPÖ-plans for a 2011 petition on immigration, asylum and non-citizens' employment (http://www.orf.at 14 July 2010).

Another crucial part of the wider context against which inclusive identity-politics have reacted is the highly disconcerting, increased prominence of extreme rightwing activity, which has been partly attributed to the recent economic crisis and which has revealed cross-border connections between the extreme right sub-cultures of Germany and Austria (http://orf.at/090513-38250/38251txt_story.html). Parts of Austria's civil society, including some 50 organizations, responded by forming an 'alliance against the right' and with 'processions of light' in Linz and Vienna in May 2009 (http://derstandard.at/druck/?id=1240550310779). At about the same time, and following an earlier-mentioned and deeply troubling incident involving four teenagers violently interrupting a commemoration of the liberation of the former concentration camp in Ebensee (Upper Austria), the town responded with a gathering and a demonstration – involving residents and (local) civil society organizations – against rightwing extremism (http://ooe.orf.at/stories/363974/; http://ooe.orf.at/stories/362658/).

Ideological polarization has arguably been at its most pronounced over issues of religious diversity. This became evident in Vienna's district of Brigittenau in May 2009, when the planned expansion of a local Islamic centre was opposed by a 'citizens' initiative' (see Kübel 2009) and a demonstration it organized involving 700 people and parts of the FPÖ clashed with a counter-demonstration of similar size (http://oesterreich.orf.at/wien/stories/362107). The campaigns for the EU-election in 2009 also saw the FPÖ's highly controversial instrumentalization of religion – articulated in claims to 'keep the Occident in Christian hands' – strongly opposed by numerous politicians, Austria's churches and Islamic- as well as Jewish communities (http://salzburg.orf.at/stories/364666/).

Responses to the polarizing and exclusionary tone of parts of the 2009 EU-election campaigns included an impressive initiative by two Viennese students who utilized the internet to organize a 'chain of light' (*Lichterkette*) around Austria's Parliament in June 2009; supported by several thousand internet signatories and public intellectuals Robert Menasse and Doron Rabinovici, the initiative called for respect, responsibility and a celebration of diversity (http://wien.orf.at/stories/369218/). The event also inspired a parallel demonstration for respect and dignity in Graz, supported by a number of civil society bodies including religious organizations and an inter-cultural 'advice-centre' (http://steiermark.orf.at/stories/369249/). Similar calls for solidarity and demands for structural transformations were articulated by two other demonstrations a year later, both of which involved networks of individuals, NGOs, celebrities and political actors: the first demonstration in July 2010 called for right of residence to be granted to Arigona Zogaj and her family and, more generally, for more inclusive asylum-legislation; the second demonstration also took place in Vienna's historical centre two months later and similarly demanded an overhaul of Austria's asylum- and immigration laws, as well as educational reforms and a fairer distribution of wealth and employment (*Falter* 30 June 2010, 11).

Much of this discussion has centred on ideological polarizations over issues of asylum. Such tensions also emerged in relation to two controversies in the southern province of Carinthia. The first revolved around a highly controversial centre for asylum-seekers – who were alleged to have broken the law – in the remote, mountainous *Saualm* region; when it was announced that the centre would close in April 2009, the Green party welcomed these news as 'a civil society victory', especially given that several allegations against asylum-seekers there had turned out to be false and that some of them were seriously ill (http://kaernten.orf.at/stories/343252/). Diametrically opposed reactions to asylum-seekers also manifested in another dispute over a possible reception centre in Carinthia; whilst the dominant response to this possibility was one of opposition, often articulated by arguing that such a centre would be detrimental to the local tourist industry, an initiative countered this by committing its members to holidaying in the very locality that might house an asylum-seeker reception centre (http://oesterreich.orf.at/stories/373686/).

## Pluralistic counterpublics

This discussion has provided snapshots of counter-hegemony encountered in parts of Austria's civil society. Manifest in the magazines, papers, associations, networks and initiatives discussed above, inclusive discourses of identity and opposition to neo-nationalism arguably found its most prominent articulation in demonstrations against the ÖVP-FPÖ coalition in February 2000, followed by a large-scale day of protest in Vienna several weeks later, and many months of continued 'resistance' (*Widerstand*) through weekly 'Thursday-night demonstrations' thereafter. Also relevant, as another example of public criticism of the effects of increasingly restrictive legislation on asylum-seekers, was a public reading of homeless asylum-seekers' names outside the Interior Ministry in December 2003 (http://derStandard.at 19 December 2003). In these and the examples discussed above, the protagonists' ideological opposition to, and organizational distance from, populist neo-nationalism are easily discernible. In other instances of civil society activism, however, parts of the left and right have found themselves – their usual and defining opposition to one another notwithstanding – temporarily sharing a space of critique. Examples of such partial and topic-specific convergence have included environmental protests and, most famously, protests against the EU's Lisbon Treaty in 2008. Calls for a referendum and criticisms of the Treaty's ratification by the Austrian Parliament and Federal President emanated from what are otherwise diametrically opposed ends of the ideological spectrum. For example, in November 2007 Jörg Haider, then BZÖ governor of Carinthia, started a regional campaign for a referendum under the banner of, loosely translated, 'Us patriots against EU Chaos' (Steiner 2007). At the same time, calls for a referendum also galvanized numerous organizations including peace-, anti-nuclear-, pro-democracy-, anti-globalization- and civil liberty movements as well as various public intellectuals on the left (Budin 2008). Such shared opposition to the Lisbon Treaty amongst individuals and groups otherwise positioned and defined in outright opposition to one another points to widespread scepticism of the current workings of the European network state. It also echoes an observation offered in chapter four: the political left and right at times share *diagnoses* as to what are defining contemporary issues. However, this then obviously calls for more nuanced analysis of how the left and right differ in their respective *reactions* to such widely perceived challenges.

The material examined above, and the opposition to neo-nationalism it contains, allows for such analysis. The initiatives and contributions to public debate discussed in this chapter simultaneously corroborate and partly qualify Fraser's notion of 'counterpublics': critical (local) media such as *Falter* and *Megaphon* consistently address multiple axes of differentiation and inequality – gender, 'race'/ethnicity, nationality, and class – and their complex 'intersections' (Brah 1996) in the everyday lives of ordinary social actors living through times profoundly shaped by the logic and workings of global capitalism. And as this analysis has also shown, the rationale guiding (some of) the discourses and initiatives examined includes the creation of spaces where previously and otherwise silenced voices of some among the structurally marginalized, disadvantaged and excluded can be articulated and heard; critique of existing, national as well as global, configurations of power, in part voiced by those most immediately affected and most acutely disadvantaged, informs the discursive practices and social activism examined above. At the same time, however, the critical media examined above are neither owned, nor written or read exclusively by 'subordinated groups'. Instead, they constitute a *pluralistic counterpublic* shared and jointly shaped by social actors positioned in profoundly different structural locations: by EU citizens and others struggling to negotiate access to the political space of (relative) privilege and opportunity that is 'Fortress Europe' respectively. In this shared realm of counter-hegemonic critique the discursive and institutional boundaries constructed, reproduced and 'naturalized' by rigid and exclusive discourses of national/ethnic belonging are subjected to scrutiny and deconstruction, whilst cultural syncretism and multi-dimensional identities are embraced. And whilst not everyone participating in these pluralistic counterpublics is part of a subordinated group,[9] there is a shared commitment to working and arguing for the subordinated.

This connects with the earlier-anticipated question: how to conceptualize the difference between two ideologically contrasting reactions, epitomized by the pluralist civil society discourses examined above and exclusivist ideologies of national identity respectively, against a common set of conditions – the dislocations of globalization. As I have shown, the counterpublics discussed here are critical of the human and local consequences of globalization and neo-liberal politics *as well as* of the strategies of exclusion typical of neo-nationalist discourses of belonging. In criticizing globalization, however, pluralist counter-hegemony shares an ideological 'other' with its other ideological 'other' (i.e. neo-nationalism). This emerged, albeit inadvertently, from Jörg Haider's assessment that Austria needed a 'new movement, which would address people's [social- and employment-related] anxieties' and 'counteract the negative consequences of globalization' (http://www.orf.at 9 March 2005). To distinguish, then, the critical analyses of globalization characteristic of the counter-hegemonic realm analyzed above from neo-nationalist anti-globalization, we may turn to Zygmunt Bauman:

> [Nationalism] selects the securely habitual reality, spreading all around, well-founded, mirrored in scores of reciprocally reinforcing events, predictable and unobtrusively obvious, as the only tolerable (or, indeed, the only habitable) universe. It is ... short of any project side-tracking from the well-trodden routes;

---

9    There are, however, other Austrian media (and organizations) that correspond more closely to Fraser's definition of 'subaltern counterpublics' in more exclusive association with 'members of subordinated social groups': Vienna's migrants' magazine *Biber* (http://www.dasbiber.at) and a magazine 'by and for minorities' entitled *Stimme* (http://minderheiten.at/stat/stimme/zeitschr.htm) are cases in point.

it is, in fact, motivated … by its … fear of the unusual, the strange, the not-yet-materialized, the unknown. (1999, 121)

Nationalism thus exhibits a distinctive attitude towards discursively constructed and reified notions of 'cultural tradition' and 'the nation's past'. In times of far-reaching change, it seeks solace in an advocated 'return' to older certainties, no longer taken-for-granted (Karner 2005b), but consciously debated and asserted against its perceived ideological 'others'. In an Austrian context, the 'return' advocated by populism has always been selective, given its widely-appealing insistence on the reconfiguration of some entrenched political structures. It is, however, in terms of their contrasting constructions and responses to 'otherness', formulated to the same socio-economic backdrop, that nation-centred reactions to globalization differ from the counter-hegemonic discourses examined above: while the former seek to reify and protect rigidly defined and exclusive identities, the latter acknowledge and celebrate the ambivalence and syncretism of lived identifications.

## Other European contexts

Providing an insight into another European national context, a recent overview of Czech civil society resonates with the thematic analysis presented above. As in the Austrian case, the Czech Republic's critical public sphere is thus shown to include the following types of organizations and activism: help for Holocaust-survivors; documentation of, and opposition to, the extreme right; NGOs supporting migrants and refugees (Roubalová and Kostlán 2009, 157).

Other literature on European civil societies returns the discussion to particular localities. Also paralleling the direction of my analysis, such work locates attempted counter-hegemonic politics of inclusion in the life-worlds of particular towns and cities. Two examples are particularly relevant to this analysis, for they both echo my earlier discussion and offer additional insights into the dynamics and dilemmas of civil society activity inside 'Fortress Europe'. The first is a study of diametrically opposed local reactions to asylum-seekers in the white-collar, seaside town of Saltdean, a suburb to Brighton on the southern English coast (Grillo 2005). The context to this was shaped by the UK's 2002 National Asylum and Immigration Act, whose provisions included the creation of nationally dispersed 'induction centres' for asylum-seekers' 'preliminary processing and health checks'. Ralph Grillo offers a detailed analysis of local reactions to rumoured proposals to turn Saltdean's Grand Ocean Hotel into one such induction centre. As in some of the Austrian examples discussed earlier, local reactions in Saltdean were both strong and highly varied. To illuminate their rhetorical and organizational manifestations, Grillo provides a 'discursive analysis of … local materials found in letters, emails, newspapers, newsletters, Websites, leaflets, speeches and a television talk-show, paying special attention to vocabularies, phrases, tropes, and instances used in argument' (2005, 245). Saltdean residents' responses to the possible arrival of asylum-seekers in their midst are thus shown to have fallen – broadly – into two mutually opposed groups, articulating an 'anti-' and 'pro-discourse' respectively. The former was mobilized by a newly created 'Saltdean Residents Action Group' (SRAG), whose discourse Grillo describes as 'localist'. Its arguments against a local asylum-seeker induction centre, resembling several of the discursive chains brought to play in some of the everyday populism analyzed in chapter three of this book, centred on claims that Saltdean could not 'cope': more accurately, the anti-discourse postulated that the local infrastructure was ill-equipped to deal with an influx of outsiders, there were recurring concerns about safety and security and a fear of rising crime, and postulated 'threats to community values and ways of life'; moreover, it was claimed that even if in the first instance only a few asylum-seekers were housed locally, this would subsequently result in the locality being 'swamped' or 'overrun' by much larger numbers (Grillo 2005, 244; 246). By contrast, and in opposition to this reactionary localism (that defined itself as 'merely realist'), an inclusive 'pro-camp' formed an alternative organizational vehicle – 'Saltdean for Tolerance and Respect' (STAR). It articulated a 'cosmopolitan discourse' and sought to dispel the negative myths surrounding asylum through an 'intercultural … globally-oriented, compassionate and humanitarian' vision. Its arguments against the 'anti-discourse' were premised on a sense of responsibility for 'the other' and also saw asylum-seekers' potential arrival as bringing benefits to the locality – through their cultural and linguistic diversity and, if they were allowed to work, by supporting and working for local businesses (Grillo 2005, 247).

There are important parallels between Grillo's analysis of the Saltdean-dispute and parts of my earlier analysis. Most obviously, Grillo draws attention – in another context – to similar ideological polarizations over asylum. Also, his analysis resonates with my discussions in unearthing the 'topoi' (e.g. of scarcity, entitlements and threats or, conversely, of responsibility) and discursive chains at work in such diametrically opposed reactions to a defining transnational 'flow' of our time. Furthermore, Grillo addresses the difficult question as to what to make of localists' claims 'not to be racist, merely realist'. Grillo assesses such denials of racism amongst a group of relatively privileged, middle-class residents by comparing their discourse with that of the extreme right British National Party. This comparison shows that whilst the two discourses partly intersect, they are not identical: Saltdean residents opposed to a local induction centre are thus shown to share the BNP's concern with scarcity and nationals' entitlements – a 'concern that … much is spent on asylum-seekers while schools and hospitals lack resources' – without, however, invoking the BNP's 'anti-multiculturalism', its 'language of culture, race and "our people"' (Grillo 2005, 252–253). Yet, as Grillo goes on to show, the question is more complex: such distancing from key parts of the extreme right's xenophobic populism does not explain why a possible influx of asylum-seekers gives rise to fears about falling house prices or rising crime in the first instance; invoking Solomos and Back's notion of 'racism's "metonymic elaborations", the way it may be articulated through a "variety of coded signifiers"',[10] Grillo points at the (arguably unconsciously imported) 'historical baggage' of 'racist and culturalist, e.g. orientalist, assumptions' resonant in at least some localist discourse (2005, 256–257).

A second body of work that further illuminates the contemporary workings of Europe's civil societies in particular localities is contained in Davide Però's research (2007a, b) in two of Southern Europe's 'progressive' cities – Bologna and Barcelona. Conducted in a wider Western European context he defines as 'pervaded by a hegemonic ethno-nationalist discourse' (2007a, 4), Però's ethnographic studies of local councils and NGOs working with, and responding to, migrants makes a point also important to chapter six in the present book: differences and polarizations between the right and the left's respective responses to 'the other' are real, significant and far-reaching, yet they do not tell the full story. In Però's work this translates into a discussion of some of the (perhaps unintended) consequences of contemporary leftwing policies on migrants' life-worlds and chances.

In his ethnography of Bologna, Però examines contemporary, 'postsocialist' left party politics – particularly its discourses on immigration and multiculturalism – as well as a series of local and 'progressive civil societal organisations' including committees, NGOs and cooperatives (2007a, 16). The resulting analyses throw light on the sometimes contradictory effects of local initiatives designed as channels of solidarity and support. For example, a 'pro-refugee civic committee' comprising a range of NGOs and associations and set up to 'facilitate the implementation of the … decision by the Bologna City Council to locate a group of undocumented Rom refugees in the nearby velodrome … for the period of their regularization' (Però 2007a, 108) is shown – due to its entanglements with political parties and the city government – to have been ambivalent in its effects on migrants:

> Despite its positive contribution to the deflation of racism … at the grassroots level and … the temporary acceptance of the refugees in the district, the Velodrome Committee remained an integral part of a … political establishment characterized by policy practices that were in significant ways paternalistic, authoritarian and oppressive of the Rom refugees they targeted … [T]hese policy practices were … based on surveillance, invisibilization, separation and marginalization of the refugees, especially after the latter had been relocated in the 'permanent' camp situated in the middle of the countryside … and in physical as well as social isolation. (Però 2007a, 112)

Such insights lead Però to formulate a general critique of the postsocialist left. Having exchanged its historical commitment to 'class justice and social change' for an essentially neo-liberal 'politics of order and conflict avoidance', the contemporary left – Però argues – often fails migrants; the latter have come to be 'seen in ethnocultural rather than socioeconomic terms and from a perspective of

---

10    There is some conceptual overlap between such 'coded signifiers' and what were earlier analyzed as 'discursive chains'.

... unconditional support for the market economy rather than from one of struggle for the egalitarian transformation of such economy ... and society' (Però 2007a, 138).

Però develops this critique further in a second ethnographic study conducted in Barcelona (2007b). Through analyses of consultative institutions, particularly the city's *Consell Municipal d'Immigració* (comprising various organizations, representatives of the local authority, of employers and of immigrant groups by origin), and of 'immigrants-allied organizations' that are 'contracted as service providers', Però argues that governance – the 'governmental form typical of late modernity resulting from [such] collaboration between government and civil society' – benefits the already powerful considerably more than those it purportedly sets out to empower (2007b, 271). Consultative bodies are thus interpreted as largely 'token institutions' that help legitimize political elites but further enshrine migrants' status as 'second-class political subjects' without voting rights. At the same time, those NGOs that become part of the system of governance are shown to be, at least partly, 'co-opted':

> The non-profit organisations gain from governance by being hired and funded ... [and] being elevated to the role of public interlocutor by the political elites ... [T]hese NGOs constitute a booming sector that has been referred to as an 'industry' because of the economic dimension involved ... [T]his NGO sector has carved out for itself the role of institutional mediator of migrants' interests when this is often not the case ... (Però 2007b, 282)

As shown by some of the more far-reaching and searching forms of counter-hegemony examined earlier, Però's sobering conclusion (2007a, 142) that 'even the so-called "progressive" forces are largely operating within an exclusionary logic and failing to extend ... universalist principles beyond the narrow boundaries of their own national "imagined community"' does not apply to, or capture, many of the Austrian materials analyzed in this chapter. Yet, other parts of his work undoubtedly resonate more widely, for they alert us to the (potential) discrepancies between ideology and practice, between (professed) ideals and some of the (perhaps unintended) consequences of their implementation.

## Concluding remarks

This chapter has focused on select voices and initiatives in Austria's and other European civil societies. Whilst one should not assume too much ideological homogeneity within and across these, the analysis presented here has revealed a range of recurring phenomena and thematic areas: the articulation of a counter-hegemony critical of both ethnic/national exclusions and of neo-liberalism; initiatives against the exclusion or deportation of asylum-seekers; organizations working for and with various groups of migrants; networks and demonstrations of inclusion and, jointly, the existence of what I have termed – in modification of Nancy Fraser's terminology – *pluralistic counterpublics*. As has been shown, relevant civil society 'nodes' and contributions to critical public debate combine local engagement with a distinctly transnational consciousness and a politics of wide-reaching, ethnically inclusive solidarity. As such, the material examined here bears witness to the vitality of European civil societies and to the contested terrain of public debates on ethnicity, multiculturalism, national identities and (economic) globalization. Such vitality notwithstanding, voices of pessimism also emanate from within the (counter-)public spheres examined above. For example, Armin Thurnher, co-founder and editor of *Falter*, routinely presents more sobering verdicts on the state of the (mainstream-/tabloid) Austrian media and the extent of political debate facilitated therein (e.g. Thurnher 2004). Occupying a different vantage point, that of academic meta-discourse, this analysis has taken the critical media (including the papers examined above) and relevant local initiatives and organizations as important manifestations of a public sphere of debate and activism. However, and as shown by Però's studies (2007a, b) of Bologna and Barcelona for example, the mere existence of such civil society activity does not automatically translate into empowerment for those most in need of it.

Qualitative in nature, this has of course not been an analysis of numbers but an attempt to document and examine the distinctive and politically significant presence of critical discourses that constitute a part of (Austrian) civil society and play important roles in the articulation of counter-hegemonic, inclusive national identities. The wider context of national and European structures of power and exclusion is, of course, vital and inescapable. The up-hill battle faced by the counter-hegemonic politics examined here was reflected, for example, when the earlier mentioned recent changes to Austria's asylum-system were debated: according to a survey reported in the *Krone*, 62 per cent of Austrians supported more restrictive asylum legislation (Gnam 2009).

In the next chapter, I argue that the picture is yet more complex and cannot be reduced to a straightforward dichotomy pitting dominant discourses of exclusion against a counter-hegemony of inclusion and pluralism: first, because there are also other types of discourses offering alternative definitions of the relationship between self and other in circulation; and second, because there are questions about the relationship between discourse and subjectivity, and thus the debatable (in-)stability of political 'convictions' and ideological *interpellations*, to be raised.

# Chapter 6

# Everyday Politics: Self–Other Relationships and Lived Ambivalences

## Introduction

In a searching critique Paul Gilroy depicts contemporary Europe as shaped by contradictory forces: on one hand, by exclusive identity politics, enduring racisms, and 'melancholic', backward-looking nationalist narratives of loss and alleged decline; and, on the other hand, by an emerging everyday culture of 'conviviality', encountered in urban settings and various artistic and cultural genres, that takes pluralism, cultural syncretism, boundary-crossings and multi-dimensional identities for granted. Or in his own words:

> Europe stands today militarized once again … against its proliferating enemies, within and without … identity, belonging, and … the imperiled integrity of national states are being communicated through the language and symbols of absolute ethnicity and *racialized* difference. (Gilroy 2004, 155)

> [S]pontaneous, convivial culture … its ability to live with alterity without becoming anxious, fearful or violent … refer[s] to the processes of cohabitation and interaction that have made multiculture an ordinary feature of social life in … urban areas … The radical openness that brings conviviality alive makes nonsense of closed, fixed and reified identity. (Gilroy 2004, xi)

This aptly sets the stage for the discussion presented in this chapter and its juxtaposition of ideologies pertaining to self-other relationships to the messy complexities of the everyday.[1] In the first part of this analysis, however, I argue for a partial modification of Gilroy's framework in revealing a broader range of discourses delineating 'self' and 'other' and defining their inter-relationships differently. Put another way, whilst rigid exclusions are indeed rife, contemporary identity discourses vary noticeably in their constructions of boundaries, their demands of the other, and their respective political 'visions'. The second part of the analysis examines instances of discursive ambivalence: political commitments and their ideological 'orderliness' notwithstanding, everyday practices and lived realities are thus shown to exhibit (sometimes surprising) contradictions and

---

1   Parts of this chapter draw on discussions I have presented elsewhere (Karner 2009; 2010a).

negotiations. As always, the crux of this chapter focuses on Austrian materials, before turning to other relevant European settings.

## Theoretical leads

Repeating a social scientific maxim, identities require 'otherness', the self presupposes 'others' and defines itself by the delineation from 'them'. This, however, can only be a starting-point for a more far-reaching discussion. As has been emphasized throughout this book, and as illustrated particularly in chapter five, different identity-discourses vary enormously in the types of self-other boundaries and relationships they draw and advocate, ranging from rigidly exclusionary nationalisms to a politics of inter-ethnic solidarity and inclusion. The first part of this analysis argues that sociological analysis of national identity negotiations must pay attention to the different kinds of *self-other category relations* assumed and advocated by the various discourses on offer. Put differently, whilst the delineation of boundaries between 'in-' and 'out-groups' is indeed common to all identity politics, there is ideological variation in how the relationship between self and other is understood. Theoretically relevant to this is Gerd Baumann and André Gingrich's notion (2004) of 'grammars of identity'. Invoking key contributions to cultural/anthropological theory, Baumann and Gingrich differentiate between three grammars based on distinct ways of conceptualizing self-other relationships: first, an 'orientalizing' grammar that constructs 'us' and 'them' as mutually exclusive categories and negative mirror images of each other; second, a 'grammar of segmentation', according to which a local 'enemy' can become an ally against a common regional other, who in turn may join an emerging national 'ingroup' in opposition to outsiders on such a higher scale of identification; third, a 'grammar of encompassment' that constructs and hierarchically subsumes others – in a model of concentric circles – as 'really part of us', albeit 'not quite like' those arguing from the powerful 'centre' (Baumann and Gingrich 2004). In what follows, I selectively draw on the concept of 'grammars of identity' in an analysis of several different, and prominent, ways of conceptualizing the actual or advocated relationships between 'the national majority' and various others in circulation in Austria and other parts of Europe. Whilst 'orientalizing' grammars are common, the 'logic' of other relevant discourses does not quite conform to 'segmentation' and 'encompassment', thus suggesting that there are other 'grammars' at work.

The second part of this analysis examines different forms of ambivalence as encountered on the level of 'messy', everyday social realities. The first set of lived complexities hardly comes as a surprise: revealing diversities within and between social categories, they cut across and therefore problematize stereotypes, dominant discourses and clichés, as well as statistical 'reductions' that associate particular collectives with significant though never all-subsuming characteristics. Everyday solidarities and practices are thus shown to belie and subvert simplistic ideological 'orderliness' (Karner 2010a). One obvious example of such complexities is that of 'richness and diversity … [being] at odds with nationalist attempts to create uniform cultures and citizens' (Smith 2008, 188). The second set of ambivalences poses more of a theoretical (and arguably also political) challenge: they reveal contextual variations, discursive shifts and ideological contradictions performed and lived by particular social actors. Invoking Michael Billig's notion of 'ideological dilemmas', Heer et al. (2008, 11) make an observation relevant to this when they describe 'utterances and texts, and … above all, *everyday* interactions and discursive practices [that] almost necessarily contain contradictions and inconsistencies, reflecting ambivalence on the part of the speaker or writer'. Some such dilemmas and contradictions were recorded in Billig's analysis of everyday talk about the British royal family. Talk about an institution seemingly out of sink with 'outwardly egalitarian times' involves, Billig shows (1992, 14), a 'complicated consciousness, composed of cross-cutting themes'. In this chapter we encounter comparable instances of inconsistencies and individuals' 'complicated consciousness' with regard to identity-discourses and lived self-other relations. Analysis of such ambivalence, I suggest, can fruitfully proceed along the theoretical lines drawn by Billig and others:

> Discourse analysts have stressed that people do not typically possess a single 'attitude' on an issue, which is to be repeated unchangingly … Instead, there is variability, as different common-sense repertoires … [are] used on different conversational occasions. (Billig 1992, 149)

## Contexts

In 2007 16.3 per cent of Austria's population had a 'migration background' (Lebhart and Marik-Lebeck 2007, 168–170), which amounts to one of the highest percentages of first or second generation migrants in the EU (Fassmann 2007, 394) and among industrialized nations more generally (http://www.orf.at/071115-18687/18688txt_story.html). Austria has thus manifestly become a country of immigration over recent decades, though much public discourse – particularly on the populist right – has yet to acknowledge this. There is, however, growing official recognition of many migrants' structural disadvantages: much higher unemployment rates (Biffl 2007, 265), persisting educational disadvantages (Weiss and Unterwurzacher 2007), higher proportions of people living in poverty or at risk of poverty (Heitzmann and Förster 2007, 291–293), and particular disadvantages – lower wages and high unemployment – faced by a substantial proportion of female migrants (http://www.orf.at/100528-51724/51725txt_story.html). Moreover, a pan-European study by the British Council and the Migration Integration Policy Group suggested that Slovakia, Greece, Cyprus, Latvia and Austria provided the structural conditions least conducive to migrants' integration (e.g. http://oe1.orf.at/inforadio/82242.html; http://www.orf.at/071016-17681/index.html). Along similar lines there are growing concerns and criticisms of the large incidence of 'dequalification' experienced by many non-Austrians, whose prior training and education are not recognized and who therefore find themselves employed below their skills and levels of qualification (e.g. Meinhart 2010b; Gächter 2010). Migrants' disadvantages can become particularly apparent in specific localities: thus, a recent report revealed that 44 per cent of Vienna's population were either born abroad, do not hold Austrian citizenship, or have at least one parent of foreign origin, which therefore does not automatically include the grandchildren of the 'classic guest-worker' who migrated to Austria in the 1960s; the study in question reported noticeable disadvantages in education, employment and health faced by very significant proportions of Vienna's migrants (Stemmer 2010).

Political debate, for example in the run-up to elections in 2006 and 2008, generally reflects both pan-European tendencies and the internally contrasting attitudes towards immigration that define Austrian politics. As was shown in chapter four, this tends to manifest in some of the categories used and demands made, which are symptomatic of contemporary immigration-related discussions across 'Fortress Europe' and variously insist on the sometimes problematic distinction (e.g. Castles 2003) between 'political refugees' and 'mere economic migrants' or on giving priority to existing migrants' 'integration' over new immigration. In the Austrian context, as also shown earlier, the deepest ideological disagreements over immigration and pluralism define the contrasting leanings and programmes of FPÖ and BZÖ on one hand, and the Greens on the other: whilst the former have claimed – in apparent denial of the above-quoted demographic realities – that Austria is 'no country of immigration' (BZÖ 2006a, 2; FPÖ 2006, 3) and made various exclusionary demands and policy suggestions (e.g. BZÖ 2006a, 2; FPÖ 2006, 3, 4, 10), the latter demand migrants' rights and inclusion and recognition of the fact that Austria is a 'country of immigration' (e.g. Green Party 2006, 18–19). Similarly part of the context to the following analysis are the discursive polarizations and debates concerning ethnic pluralism, immigration and asylum evident in Austria's media and civil society examined earlier (chapters three and five).

Recent developments have also included a decline in the number of naturalizations following the introduction of more restrictive legislation pertaining to the acquisition of Austrian citizenship in 2006 (http://oesterreich. orf.at/stories/403669/), and a noticeable change in the relative size of different migrant communities in Austria brought about by intra-EU mobility: in 2009/2010 Germans thus constituted, for the first time, the largest grouping of immigrants in Austria, ahead of citizens of the former Yugoslav states and Turkey (http:// oesterreich.orf.at/stories/443726/). Discursively, many current debates focus on the effects of migration on local life-worlds. One prominent response, with obvious parallels across the European Union, has declared the 'end of multiculturalism'. Its main premise has also been captured by Dutch sociologist Paul Scheffer who argues that the notion of migration as enriching local lives is detached from reality; on the contrary, he postulates, migration entails likely losses – with both migrants and members of the ethnic majority losing a previously familiar world, in their countries of origin and their local neighbourhoods respectively (Charim

2009). With some councils observing that integration poses challenges yet to be met successfully (http://oe1.orf.at/inforadio/101220.html), many debates centre on religious differences, particularly Islam – now the second largest religious community in Austria, with some 500,000 Muslims and approximately 200 prayer rooms (http://oesterreich.orf.at/stories/464689/). Adding to examples of local conflict mentioned earlier, recent controversies focused on religious difference have included a debate triggered by the president of the Islamic Faith community in Austria: in the long-term, he suggested, each of Austria's nine regional capitals would ideally have a mosque with a minaret; predictably, both FPÖ and BZÖ reacted with angry opposition (http://oe1.orf.at/artikel/256868). Other recurring debates centre on children's linguistic competence and the pedagogical challenges confronting schools with large percentages of children from migrant families whose mother tongue and language of education differ (e.g. Brühl 2009; Jungwirth 2010). Alongside all this, migrants and 'neo-Austrians' are increasingly recognized as important audiences across the political parties, albeit in very different ways, resulting in an 'ethnicization of politics' that – seen critically – can perpetuate stereotypes instead of capturing diversities and differences within cultural communities (Apfl and Tóth 2010). The wider context to the analysis below also included the creation of a 'national action plan for integration' in early 2010, according to which – and following the examples set by Germany, Sweden and Denmark – non-asylum-seeking, non-EU migrants intending to join family members in Austria will have to demonstrate some German language competence at the time of immigration (http://www.orf.at/100119-47046/index.html).

The data analyzed below include recent materials drawn from a wide variety of sources, including Austria's ideologically heterogeneous media – the public broadcasting network, daily tabloids and broadsheets, weekly and monthly papers (both national and regional). Other literature and materials include public documents and reflections offered by intellectuals and literary figures. All these materials were selected on the basis of their relevance to the questions examined in this chapter: they offer insights, first, into the workings and 'grammars' of competing ideological blue-prints for self-other relationships; and, second, they reveal – albeit sometimes inadvertently – lived complexities, ambivalences and discrepancies between discourse and practice, between ideological 'orderliness' and 'messy' everyday negotiations.

## Orientalizing discourses

A first, recurring and in some ideological/argumentative contexts undoubtedly dominant 'grammar of identity' broadly corresponds to one of Baumann and Gingrich's ideal types – that of 'orientalization'. It defines several discourses and their characteristic topoi examined in chapter three, namely those premised on notions of threats and alleged 'invasions', which construct the discursive building blocks of self and other in oppositional terms, as mutually exclusive, diametrically opposed categories.[2] Examples of orientalizing identity discourses are encountered across numerous contemporary debates and in many contexts. They are particularly prominent in hostilities towards the perceived dangers of Islam and in other nationalist 'discursive chains' discussed earlier, such as the ideological conflation of asylum-seekers with crime and a concomitant opposition to a universal ethics of human rights.

Exclusivist/orientalist identity discourses underpin, for example, some scepticism about immigration and opposition to multiculturalism. Such sentiments emerged from the findings of a public opinion survey in 2004, where 65 per cent of some 1,300 Austrian respondents defined recently arrived migrants as a 'drain' rather than a 'benefit';[3] and whilst most respondents expected 'outsiders' to adapt, a large majority also declared that migrants generally, Asian and sub-Saharan African migrants allegedly in particular, failed to integrate (http://www.orf.at/ticker/158514.html?tmp=9339). Even more clearly exclusivist was a recent, highly controversial suggestion made in an upper Austrian town with a large migrant population to henceforth prohibit non-EU citizens from acquiring property in the area (http://ooe.orf.at/stories/454626/): evidently, such suggested exclusions are hardly conducive to closer relationships between, or integration of, 'self' and 'other', effecting the latter's *anthropoemic* (Bauman 1990) segregation instead.

Distinctly orientalist, offering 'positive self- and negative other presentation' (Wodak 2007, 662), are portrayals of forced marriage and horrific cases of patriarchal violence in Austria's Turkish community as not only affecting individual women but as allegedly representative of many (e.g. Richter 2009) or even most Turkish girls' lives. High-profile versions of orientalist and Islamophobic thought[4] have emerged in examples of FPÖ (pre-election) rhetoric. One instance, the party's claimed intention in their 2009 EU-election campaign to 'keep the Occident in Christian hands', which drew strong criticisms from across Austria's

---

2  Baumann stresses (2004, 20) that orientalizing grammars are not exhausted by a binary opposition of 'us' (e.g. the West) to 'them' (e.g. the Orient); instead, they offer a 'binary opposition subject to reversal': whilst the other is primarily 'denigrated', parts of it (i.e. the Orient constructed as 'spontaneous, luxuriant and mystical') are also 'desired', as repositories of that, which 'we' have allegedly lost. Space does not allow for a (psychodynamic) investigation of the motivational forces driving the orientalizing discourses mentioned below and I therefore focus the present discussion on their primary impetus – the construction of rigid us-them dichotomies. However, see chapters two, three and four for analyses of the contexts, sentiments and perceptions giving rise to nationalist/populist discourses as well as their contestation.

3  The framing of responses to migration in cost-benefit terms is noteworthy and problematic, as it allows little, if any, space for human rights considerations and imposes an instrumentalist framework (see below) instead.

4  For analyses of Islamophobic sentiments, discourses and practices in and beyond Austrian right-wing populism, see Gärtner (2009, 135–150) and Bunzl and Hafez (2009). Islamophobia is here defined as 'fear and hatred towards Islam and Muslims' (Allen 2009, 23), frequently articulated through reifying misconstructions and in power-struggles.

political spectrum, civil society initiatives and religious institutions (http://orf. at/090519-38489/?href=http%...), has already been mentioned. Islamophobia also surfaced in January 2008 in Graz, shortly before local elections, when the FPÖ's main candidate 'achieved' (inter)national notoriety with widely-reported, highly offensive statements delivered at a party gathering (e.g. Lackner 2008b). Similarly infamous was an internet 'game' involving players 'stopping' mosques, minarets and muezzins per click of their mouse, which the Styrian FPÖ displayed on its homepage in the run-up to regional elections in September 2010 prior to being forced by court order to remove the game (e.g. http://www.krone.at/Oesterreich/ Richter_stoppt_Anti-Minarett-Spiel...). Discursively, there are parallels to the Swiss campaign and referendum against minarets in late 2009 discussed in chapter three, as well as to other high-profile hostility towards Islam in other European contexts: most recently, this included a controversial book by German banker and Social Democrat Thilo Sarrazin warning that Germany was threatened by Islamization (e.g. Gepp 2010a).

Moving further towards the far end of the political spectrum, there are – worryingly – also extremist versions of oppositional identity-discourses, which not only allow for no meaningful relationships between self and other but which also at times 'translate' their radical discursive binarism into physical violence. Whilst this is a large and complex terrain covered by existing, specialist literature (e.g. Aftenberger 2007; Ryan 2004), some recent examples of right-wing extremism and violence need to be mentioned in the context of the present discussion. Between 2006 and 2008 Austria saw a worrying rise in right-wing extremist[5], xenophobic and anti-Semitic crimes reported to the police – a near-doubling from 419 to 831 incidents; whilst one suggested explanation saw this as partly reflecting heightened preparedness on part of the public to report such crime, other responses rightly called for further educational programmes and security measures to fight extremism (http://www.orf.at/ticker/318332.html). More recently, racist attacks have included xenophobic graffiti, threatening letters and attempted arson attacks on a migrants' residential block in Vienna (Bandion and Bernold 2010) and an asylum-seekers' home in Graz (http://steiermark.orf.at/stories/469174).

These different forms of discourse, mobilization and social action must certainly not be conflated, for political sentiments, rhetoric and acts of physical violence are clearly different kinds of phenomena. Yet, there is arguably a common ideological current running through these otherwise very different phenomena: a discursive 'ordering' of the world broadly based on an 'orientalist grammar of identity', according to which someone part of 'them' cannot be, or become, part of 'us' and vice versa. In- and out-groups are constructed as essentialized, mutually and perpetually opposed categories, with no in-between spaces or overlaps being acknowledged, and no boundary-crossing movements deemed legitimate.

---

5    Important to note in this context is the growing significance of the internet to such extremist organizations and networks (Horaczek 2010a).

**Integrationist discourses**

There are grounds for arguing that – overall – the discursive 'logic' of advocated self–other relationships currently hegemonic across (and beyond) the EU is one of expected or more or less enforced integration: the other's difference is defined as in need of partial or total transformation; such metamorphosis is seen as desirable or even necessary, turning 'them' into a recognizable part of 'us'. However, examination of relevant discursive materials shows that there are different integrationist discourses at work and in ideological competition with one another. On one end of the spectrum there are aggressive versions, which demand the other's more or less complete assimilation, thereby resembling what Zygmunt Bauman describes – following the anthropologist Claude Lévi-Strauss – as *anthropophagic* responses to otherness: modern nation-states, Bauman argues (1990; 1993, 163), have combined such *anthropophagic*, or ingestive, reactions to 'the stranger' with *anthropoemic* strategies of segregation and exclusion (that resonate in orientalizing discourses). Arguably, political proposals currently debated in several European countries including Belgium, France and the Netherlands to outlaw the public wearing of the 'full' Islamic veil constitute examples of such strong *anthropophagic* thought and suggested practice. More locally, a recent example of *anthropophagic* practice surfaced in a school in the region of Salzburg, which now encourages pupils only to communicate in German whilst at school; interestingly, all major political parties other than the Greens voiced their support for such measures (http://salzburg.orf.at/stories/449716/). Elsewhere, parts of ÖVP youth-branch have recently demanded that German be spoken in Austrian mosques and sermons be delivered in German (http://www.orf. at 12 August 2010). Other integrationist discourses, however, are more moderate, benign and 'fashionable': their various versions of advocated integration see it as a form of necessary accommodation between ethnic majorities and migrants, or as a collective search for *cohesive*, pluralistic communities.

*Integrationisms: versions and effects*

A recent publication by Austria's Interior Ministry, to which migration experts from within and outside the ministry contributed, focused on various facets and dimensions important to successful (future) integration: education and linguistic competence; employment and living quality; political participation; inter-cultural dialogue; responsible, fair, diverse and balanced media, and a general commitment to inclusive identities based on respect for diversity (Bundesministerium für Inneres 2008).[6] Austria's then Interior Minister stressed that integration was not a 'one-

---

6    In terms of its reception, the report was initially praised as a much-needed official acknowledgement of the difficulties faced by migrants, whilst receiving some criticism for focussing on settled migrants and overlooking asylum-seekers, the most vulnerable category of migrants, and thereby leaving Austria's asylum-legislation largely unexamined

way street' but combined the rights enjoyed by the national majority to security, belonging and roots with understanding and compassion for migrants and their descendents; mutual respect, it was argued, was key to integration (Platter 2008). Another contribution to this report also defined integration as a 'two-way process', distinguishing it clearly from *anthropophagic* forms of full assimilation:

> Integration clearly differs from assimilation, which would demand the other's complete adaptation to existing circumstances, whilst permitting the local status-quo to continue without adjustment. Integration, by contrast, does not force others to abandon their cultural and social identities, nor to fully submerge in the host-society. However, they do have to acknowledge and work around local values, and existing laws must be adhered to … Politically, integration lies between assimilation and pluralistic multiculturalism, whilst being premised on freedom, the rule of law and human dignity (Vogl and Matscher 2008, 15–16, my translation).

Yet, one version of integrationism, based predominantly on a one-way process of accommodation, is premised on a clear local hegemony of cultural values and symbols of identity, which migrants are expected to respect and adopt. Examples of this have included suggestions made by Austria's previous Interior Minister: those have included the idea that naturalizations should entail an oath sworn on the Austrian flag, a clear and unsurprising rejection of some Muslims' wish to have elements of the shari'a considered in Austrian law (http://www.orf.at/091026-44023/index.html), or the intention articulated after the setting-up of an experts' 'commission on integration' that a 'clear picture' of things desirable or undesirable – examples given were patriarchal violence or an emphasis on family honour over and above human dignity – be communicated to migrants (Ortner 2010). Meanwhile, however, other publicly circulating and debated proposals for a more successfully integrated, culturally heterogeneous society incorporate clear and important elements of self-criticism and suggested structural changes. Some of Austria's best-known critical journalists have variously taken issue with the 'weaknesses' of the Austrian educational system and its role in the reproduction of social disadvantages for many amongst the descendents of the Turkish 'guest workers' who started arriving in the 1960s (Lingens 2010a), or called 'for mosques with minarets' but 'against Christian crucifixes in Austrian classrooms' (Rainer 2009). Also, the city of Vienna has set up an 'immigration commission' including migration-experts and representatives of NGOs, whose task is to identify key problems and make policy suggestions (http://oesterreich.orf.at/wien/stories/364032/). There have also been intra-party SPÖ debates and disagreements over whether the party needs to do more to address migrants' educational disadvantages (http://steiermark.orf.at/stories/391803) or whether asylum-seekers' exclusion from the job-market should be ended (http://orf.at/090828-41940/?href=http%3A…). Also worth mentioning

---

(Ortner 2008a, b). For later and other criticisms, see http://oe1.orf.at/inforadio/101382.html and Permoser et al. (2010, 10).

are suggestions by German migration-expert Mark Terkessidis who challenges the dominant understanding of integration with an alternative notion of 'inter-culture' (*Interkultur*): this includes, he argues, an acknowledgement that migrants are a permanent part of European societies, a deconstruction of the ideologically 'fixed "us"' to which migrants are expected to assimilate, alternative self-understandings premised on hybridity, and greater institutional willingness to include migrants, to define diversity as the new norm and migration as a chance to work towards positive change (Charim 2010; Wolkinger 2010). The introduction in 2010 of an 'Austrian Integration Price' to be awarded to 'people and projects' contributing to such changes and to societal appreciation of diversity arguably constitutes a step in this direction (http://wien.orf.at/stories/431398/).

In a critical vein, research by Permoser et al. (2010) examines the changing role of the religious organizations representing Islam and Orthodox Christianity in Austria in the context of concerns and at times heated debates about integration. Against this backdrop, they show that the established roles for these organizations – the Islamic Faith Community in Austria and the Greek Oriental Metropolis of Austria – as 'institutional partners of the state' in religious matters has grown to their being seen as representatives of entire (and internally heterogeneous) migrant communities. The effects of this have included more 'fluid and uncertain form[s] of symbolic cooperation' with other political actors, in which religious organizations assume the role of mediators on a wider range of issues without necessarily being able to shape policy directions (Permoser et al. 2010, 4, 10). Moreover, religious leaders have become increasingly involved in party politics and a host of issues pertaining to migrants' integration is now viewed by growing sections of the public – sometimes unhelpfully – through a religious prism. Furthermore, Permoser et al. record how intra- and inter-religious tensions have ensued. All of this points at some of the wider, seemingly unintended consequences of the now dominant integrationist discourse, including a sometimes counter-productive interpretative privileging of (assumed) religious solidarities, a new public prominence of particular organizations and concomitant power struggles within and between the immigrant communities they purportedly represent.

*'Bridging' capital and (the search for) 'community cohesion'*

A related discourse draws on the notion of 'community cohesion' as a new framework for defining desirable relationships between culturally and socio-economically heterogeneous groups that has become increasingly prominent across Europe. One of its main advocates in the British context outlines it thus:

> The term 'community cohesion' was … adopted for the British context, based principally on race and faith and used to underline the necessity to develop shared values across ethnic divisions, as a response to community conflict and unrest … [and] to emphasise that changing attitudes and values were crucial to repairing the fractures between communities. (Cantle 2008, 50–51).

Community cohesion discourse emphasizes the need for 'meaningful interactions' and relationships spanning across ethnic divisions – often referred to under Putnam's concept (2000) of 'bridging' social capital – and the urgency to address social inequalities and exclusions. The afore-mentioned report by Austria's Interior Ministry included elements of this community cohesion discourse. It acknowledged that there was a need both for 'new approaches to integration able to redress migrants' structural disadvantages and barriers' (Stock and Rümmele 2008, 120, my translation) and for 'improved inter-ethnic relations … [and] forms of cooperation' (Hutter and Perchinig 2008, 150, my translation). Similar two-way definitions of integration underpin the local initiatives and policies by the Viennese SPÖ: since 2008 it has combined clear opposition to xenophobia, introductory (language) courses, advice and help for migrants, with an insistence that the latter have both rights and obligations to abide by local rules and conventions (Ortner 2009b).[7] The at least partial success of the Viennese model has been reported for particular areas with high proportions of migrants, where interaction across ethnic boundaries has become part of everyday life; whilst local residents have stressed the importance of a shared language and migrants' German language competence, outside observers have commented positively on the fact that Viennese districts where migrants constitute more than 40 per cent of the local population show – in contrast to other European cities – no discernible signs of 'ghettoization' (Radio Wien Internet 30 September 2010).

Political participation and representation are clearly crucial to working towards cohesive communities. This was indirectly communicated by a regional Green politician of Turkish ancestry who saw her own work in Vorarlberg's regional assembly as a 'sign of lived integration' enabling dialogue and 'bridge-building' between migrants and the ethnic majority (http://vorarlberg.orf.at/stories/391829/). Other aspects include everyday interactions with 'the other' who – it may be postulated – will cease to be seen as other in the course of time. This hope was recently articulated by the president of the Islamic Faith Community of Austria: alongside the earlier-mentioned hope for mosques with minarets in each of Austria's nine regional capitals, he expressed his intention to combat clichéd understandings[8] of Islam and the need for fostering interaction across religious boundaries (http://www.orf.at/stories/2010293/2010296/). The importance of inter-group contacts, networks and organizations has also been documented in particular localities. In the Upper Austrian city of Steyr, for example, a local integration-centre organizes women's groups, city walks, trips to museums, school projects

---

7   A similar understanding was articulated by the German Federal President on the occasion of the twentieth anniversary of German reunification: he argued that Germany had to strive for better integration, that Islam was now part of Germany, and that disregard for Germany and her values – whether by religious fundamentalists or political extremists on the right or left – would not be tolerated (http://www.orf.at/stories/2018028/2018024/).

8   The theme of clichéd portrayals – and their contestation – of the other is explored in chapter seven.

and an 'integration party' to help develop 'bridges' between locals and migrants (Möseneder 2010). There is growing recognition of the importance of generally agreed upon rules and frameworks for integration (*Integrationsleitbilder*), which involve all sides, recognize migrants' potentials and difficulties, as well as the hardships suffered across different sections of local communities (Haar 2009). The city of Dornbirn, in Austria's western-most region of Vorarlberg, was the first to design such a framework in 2001: this resulted in numerous institutional changes and innovative projects to combat social exclusion and facilitate 'bridging capital'; whilst their assessments have been largely positive, there is also local awareness that meaningful relationships between sections of the local Turkish population and long-established residents need to be developed further (Özkan 2009). Elsewhere, in Graz, some local politicians have called for a comparable local framework to specify the rights, needs and obligations for the city's heterogeneous residents, some fifteen per cent of whom are migrants (Winter 2010).

## Instrumentalism

An alternative, in some debates across Europe increasingly dominant discourse regards self-other relations differently: through a cost-benefit prism, which defines desirable immigration as bringing benefits (e.g. skills, competitive advantages on the global market, tax revenue) to the nation. As with some of the argumentative patterns characteristic of everyday populist nationalism examined in chapter three, what is also significant about such instrumentalist approaches to the other is what is not being said: reducing immigration to considerations of likely benefits or disadvantages to the so-called 'host-society' leaves little room for ethical considerations based on a universalist understanding of human rights. Put differently, in a system of global inter-dependencies and enormous inequalities it can certainly be argued that the relatively affluent parts of the world bear certain responsibilities for those less privileged and fortunate; further, it may be insisted that at least some of those escaping (economic) destitution, disadvantage and hopelessness should be welcomed – regardless of what they have to offer – by the comparatively rich. Instrumentalist discourses, however, allow for no such ethical considerations, favouring a 'rational-choice' approach to managing migratory flows. At the same time, instrumentalism also differs from the two grammars of identity examined above: it is neither overly preoccupied with (*anthropoemic*) orientalization effecting forms of discursive exclusion, nor with demanding – in more or less all-subsuming *anthropophagic* fashion and at least not primarily – the other's full cultural integration. What matters most, in this alternative discursive framework, is a (potential) migrant's (economic) utility.

In June 2007 parts of the ÖVP announced that it would formulate a new programme of integration premised on the understanding that the job market and economic prosperity needed migration or, more importantly, particular migrants with certain qualifications (http://oe1.orf.at/inforadio/77388.html). Not dissimilar were the recommendations made in a report by the above-mentioned integration commission, which argued – with regard to Vienna – that economic growth, affluence and employment relied upon attracting well-qualified migrants who would keep the city economically/internationally competitive: (local) SPÖ, ÖVP and Green politicians agreed with such a pragmatic approach informed by immigration 'criteria' (http://wien.orf.at/stories/419286/). Austria's Industrial Partners (*Industriellenvereinigung*) have argued for some time that immigration – if managed by clear criteria and a 'transparent point system' – was a source of economic growth and competitiveness as well as of enriching diversity (Spinka 2009). A possible 'paradigm-shift' in this direction began to unfold in 2009 when the SPÖ-ÖVP coalition government started debating a new, 'criteria-led' immigration model, centred on a 'red-white-red card' granting residence and work permits only to potential (non-EU) immigrants with linguistic competence, qualifications and skills needed on the Austrian job market; promising fairness, transparency and potentially quicker naturalization and integration, the proposed model presented Canada and its point-system (with publicly accessible criteria and the minimum-points required of potential immigrants adjusted to the state of the job market) as the example to be emulated (Ortner 2009c). The perhaps surprisingly widespread appeal of such pragmatism[9] emerged when parts of the BZÖ, and hence sections of the populist right, voiced their support for attracting 'only the best migrants' – as measured by Austrian economic needs and interests (http://www.orf.at 3 March 2010). Calls for a catalogue of criteria to structure future immigration and a 'red-white-red card' took centre-stage again in August 2010, when prominent politicians and ministers called for economically opportune immigration (*Der Standard* 31 July 2010, 1), arguing that a strategic approach to attracting migrants (for specific sections of the job market) was necessary to guarantee the long-term viability of Austria's social welfare- and health care systems (Pöll 2010).

Two other observations need to be made of instrumentalist discourses and reactions to them. First, they also – albeit sometimes inadvertently – contain a commentary on, and implicit criticism of, previous migratory flows to Austria, particularly that of the classic (Turkish) 'guest-workers' of the 1960s, who often arrived with little social and educational capital and whose structural disadvantages have often been 'inherited' by the following generation(s) (see Lingens 2010b). Second, there have been critical voices contesting the 'logic' of instrumentalism. *Profil* editor Christian Rainer, for example, has argued that 'outside all utility considerations a rich, industrialized nation such as Austria has the moral obligation

---

9   The success of an instrumentalist line of argumentation also surfaced in another context: in December 2009 the Styrian town of Vordernberg voted convincingly for the local opening of a 'deportation centre' for 'failed' asylum-seekers. This followed the SPÖ mayor's campaigning for such a centre, which he successfully portrayed as a much-needed opportunity (i.e. jobs, infrastructure, investment) in an economically struggling and demographically shrinking area (e.g. Schwaiger et al. 2009).

to welcome people attempting to escape poverty' (2010b, my translation). Another critical journalist has commented as follows:

> The principle of economic usefulness is dominant, whilst values like human rights and dignity are being sidelined. 'Useful' human beings are wanted. (Wrann 2009, my translation)

## Conviviality and syncretism

A very different understanding of self-other relationships resembles what Paul Gilroy terms 'spontaneous and ordinary hybridity' (2004, 132) and describes as a 'convivial' counter-culture defined by taken-for-granted proximity to – and engagement with – diversity and boundary-crossings; the result is an 'ordinary, spontaneous anti-racism' (2004, 161) that offers hope:

> [T]here are other stories about 'race' and racism … apart from the endless narrative of immigration as invasion and the melancholic blend of guilt, denial, laughter and homogenizing violence that it has precipitated. Those emancipatory interruptions can perhaps be defined by a liberating sense of the banality of intermixture and the subversive ordinariness of … convivial cultures in which 'race' is stripped of meaning … The version of multiculturalism that takes shape at this point is not then a lifestyle option. Its dissident value is confirmed everywhere in the chaotic pleasures of the convivial postcolonial urban world. (Gilroy 2004, 166–167)

Conviviality negotiates and crosses boundaries with ease, creating pockets and realms of dialogue, pluralism and inclusion in and through everyday life. It manifests in countless examples and yet remains – as far as public attention and discourse go – often overlooked. The following are a mere selection of everyday convivial encounters, settings and (emerging) institutions, discussion of which could have substituted them with any number of similar instances. In any case, they illustrate the potential of an alternative response to otherness premised on an appreciation of diversity and a commitment to creating more inclusive political structures.

One example of lived inclusion is provided by a number of inter-cultural allotments in different Austrian cities and parts of the country. Inspired by the US community-gardens of the 1970s, their aim is to use gardens as a means of connecting people (Pölsler 2010). One such project, Innsbruck's inter-cultural garden, involved some 150 people in the autumn of 2009 and has been described as follows

> What our people have in common: they come from many different countries. 'We've got people from Turkey, Argentina, Austria, Mexico, Bosnia and many other places', the project leader … explains. Our aim is not just to garden, but to

> get to know one another. The main target audience are recently arrived migrants, the aim is to facilitate language-learning and friendship-building through gardening, where people … meet and cooperate. (20er 2009, 4, my translation)

Other institutions and initiatives intending to build bridges between communities and ethnically diverse individuals include inter-faith groups, such as the Group for Christian-Muslim Dialogue in Innsbruck (http://oehinfo.uibk.ac.at/theo/dialog/) and a recent Muslim-Jewish conference in Vienna (Bandion 2010), or multilingual nurseries in several Austrian cities. Amongst the latter are a recently opened German-Turkish nursery in Vienna in which children learn both languages (Horaczek 2010b), or a long-established inter-cultural, multilingual kindergarten in Graz, which in 2008 looked after children of 21 different nationalities (Motter 2008). Education is of course, and contrary to some of the populist 'fears' about declining educational standards allegedly due to multilingual classrooms, potentially crucial to integration and to developing conviviality. This was recently shown by a Viennese secondary school awarded an integration prize by Austria's public broadcasting network: with a large majority of pupils with migration backgrounds, the school has defined linguistic heterogeneity not as a burden but as a positive challenge and teaches some subjects in three languages – German, Turkish and Bosnian/Croatian/Serbian, thus providing first- and second language tuition (Brodnig 2010). At the same time, conviviality-building need not be confined to local or national contexts: the Upper Austrian village of Kirchheim is part of a pan-European 'network of villages of culture' connecting twelve rural areas across the EU and organizing regular week-long exchange visits between them; such direct contacts and immersions in other parts of Europe have helped combat EU-scepticism locally with a form of lived cosmopolitanism (Lahodynsky 2010). Another form of conviviality has been lived at the margins of Austrian society and near the geographical boundaries of Vienna for more than fifty years. It is a settlement of refugees, which has housed individuals and families from most of the world's major crises, war zones and civil wars – from Hungary and Czechoslovakia to Chile, Vietnam, Somalia, Chechnya and Afghanistan – over the last six decades. Known locally as 'Macondo', it was until recently supported by an 'integration-centre' offering social work support and is home to some 3,000 refugees from 22 different countries (Brugner 2009; Niederndorfer and Wolf 2009). Hardship and some inevitable conflicts notwithstanding, the settlement also shows how proximity to many 'others' and conviviality define some life-worlds.

Conviviality also manifests in positive evaluations of cultural 'intermixture', as in this journalistic case for more historically grounded and self-aware appreciation of diversity:

> Immigration brings dynamism, mixing provides strength. Vienna experienced its historical high-points whenever different peoples mixed along the Danube. One may deny or forget this and lament about so-called parallel societies and

problems of integration. But the fact is: intermixture not only defined the city's
past, it is also its future. (Hoffmann-Ostenhof 2010a, my translation)

Similar openness – and open-mindedness – defined the following reader's letter in
a regional daily newspaper, which challenged the kinds of prejudicial discourses
about Islam and Muslims analyzed in chapter three:

> A survey showed that 50 per cent of Austrians fear Islam … Very few are
> likely to actually have had bad experiences with Muslims. Their fear can only
> be due to negative media coverage of Islam … I am not an expert, which is
> why I would like to see Muslim journalists describe their faith … This is not
> about establishing which religion is 'right' or 'better', I simply would like to
> learn about Muslims' everyday lives. Only then can I form an opinion on its
> compatibility with Western values. Globalization makes us all part of one life-
> world. It's impossible to retreat to a little corner from which the unfamiliar,
> including Islam, is barred. (*Kleine Zeitung* 10 April 2010, 46, my translation)

'Intermixture' does not just happen on an aggregate, societal level but infuses the
biographies of individuals and families who experience and embody hybridity as
part of their daily lives. Once again, examples of such taken-for-granted blurring
of boundaries and lived cultural syncretism of course abound across and beyond
contemporary Europe. They include the practices and self-understandings of
many (first-generation) migrants and their families. Parts of the Austrian media
have drawn attention to the ease with which some migrants and 'neo-Austrians'
combine, switch (see Ballard 1994) and navigate between diverse cultural registers,
practices and symbols:

> On October 17 the family celebrate Diwali … But Christmas is also celebrated.
> It is a mixture of India and Austria. The boundaries blur. (Oster 2009, my
> translation)
>
> Some Muslims celebrate Christmas, often for their children and although it
> has no religious significance for them … Karim was brought up as a Catholic
> and as a Muslim, his Egyptian father would take him to the mosque, his Austrian
> mother to church … Whilst family Abadi no longer celebrates Christmas, the
> Turkish-Kurdish family Fidan can't get enough … daughter Begüm started
> it, when she learned about Christmas at school … Their Austrian neighbour
> realized this and suggested they celebrate together … their Christmas tree and
> celebrations are now distinctly multicultural … Begüm: 'We are growing up in
> two cultures, this enables us to look in more than one direction simultaneously.'
> (Berangy 2009, my translation)

## Ambivalences

It is in the realm of local lives that difference is encountered, identities are negotiated, exclusions are endured or transcended, and the political struggles of the quotidian are fought. In this section I turn to everyday lives and particular localities to examine if and how the different discursive patterns and political blueprints examined above are appropriated, born out or contradicted by everyday practices and solidarities. In doing so, we encounter divergences from the respective 'logics' and self-other category relations proposed and imposed by the discourses analyzed in the first part of this chapter. In re-appropriation of Homi Bhabha's terminology (1990b, 297), we may therefore speak of a 'tension' between the discursive (or 'pedagogical' in Bhabha's formulation) and the 'performative'. Put differently, lived realities often stubbornly refuse to conform to the ideological orderliness expected of – and projected onto – them. The following discussion focuses, broadly, on two forms of such divergences: first, an examination of shared local realities and complexities that challenge simplistic narratives about the 'other' and self-other relationships; second, ambivalences on the individual level, which show that social actors can display remarkably little consistency in their discursive leanings and, instead, contextually switch 'interpretative repertoires' (Wetherell and Potter 1992) or occasionally contradict, through practice, their professed ideological positions.

### Islamic presences: Image versus realities

Key sections of the analyses presented in this book have shown the prominence of Islam and Muslim migrations in the discourses and debates that contribute to the continual (re)making and (re)negotiating of national identities in Austria and, more generally, across the European Union. Many such debates bear the imprint of both long-established, often deeply orientalist European 'memories' and homogenizing (mis)constructions of Islam and, particularly since the terrorist atrocities of 9/11, of an equally reifying contemporary Islamophobia. A sociological response to such discourses and their underlying sentiments needs to insist on contextualization and on closer examination of historical and contemporary realities that are, of course, far more complex, multi-dimensional and contradictory than monolithic stereotypes and narratives acknowledge.

In the Austrian context there are frequent, laudable attempts by the quality press to counter populist clichés of Muslims and migrants – reflected in the discursive chains and claims about an alleged lack of integration, criminality, future demographics, education or welfare state dependency discussed in chapter three – with statistical facts and contextualizing accounts that draw attention to structural inequalities and exclusions suffered by many migrants (e.g. Lackner 2009; Staudinger and Treichler 2009; Hacker and Kern 2010). A study of migrants' integration into Austrian society commissioned by the Interior Ministry revealed what it described as a 'complex picture' that challenges monolithic stereotypes, reveals heterogeneity within migrant communities and draws attention to widespread experiences and feelings of marginalization amongst them:

> The large majority (83 per cent) of [migrants] feel entirely or largely integrated and agree with Austria's way of life and values (70 per cent). The Turkish population in Austria also shows large levels of agreement with democratic values … On the other hand, there are socio-economic problems for a relevant minority amongst the less educated … a relatively large section of religiously-politically oriented Muslims have reservations about certain elements of Austrian society, especially regarding family, gender roles … This is particularly true of migrants with Turkish descent, 45 per cent of whom object to aspects of the Austrian way of life … and only 26 per cent of whom feel integrated. Amongst Bosnian Muslims these percentages are much smaller … Many migrants perceive themselves to be facing disadvantages … 57 per cent criticize racism and xenophobia, 46 per cent a lack of opportunities for migrants, 53 per cent of Turkish migrants see Muslims as disadvantaged in Austria and nearly two thirds report negative experiences with the dominant majority. (Ulram 2009, 4–5, my translation)

Comparable complexities emerged from a study across different communities by sociologist Hilde Weiss: structural disadvantages rooted, partly, in large proportions of first-generation migrants – 65 to 70 per cent among Turkish migrants – with no occupational training, whose marginalization is inherited by one third of the next generation; little, if any, 'bridging capital' amongst those living in ethnically homogeneous areas; strong preferences for ethnic endogamy and concerns about 'Westernization' among large parts of the Turkish community, but 40 per cent of Turkish youths also professed to feeling at home neither in Austria nor in Turkey; at the same time, two thirds of youngsters with migration backgrounds understandably resented questions about belonging being framed in such either-or terms; and whilst second-generation migrants showed no significant differences when compared to the dominant majority in their willingness to participate politically, the future role of schools in enabling successful integration also emerged clearly (http://diepresse.com/home/panorama/oesterreich/441873/print.do). Such studies thus throw diversities within migrant communities into sharp relief. Moreover, they draw much-needed attention to the lived effects of structural and discursive exclusions,[10] whilst contextualizing disadvantages both in Austrian structures and in migrants' biographies and original social positions/marginality in their countries of origin.

Everyday struggles and antagonisms often revolve around cultural practices and around reifying misconstructions of the 'other'. Recent examples of conflict

---

10  According to a recent OECD study second-generation migrants are clearly disadvantaged on the job market compared to Austrians with similar qualifications (see Höller and Noormofidi 2009).

have centred on language and religious symbols. For instance, when there were isolated calls for Turkish schools in Vienna and Linz, political reactions were largely negative and dismissive (http://ooe.orf.at/stories/439146). Whilst concerns about the impact of such linguistic 'separatism' on community cohesion may be plausible, especially in light of some of the issues and sentiments summarized above, it is also worth noting that other, existing 'foreign language schools' (e.g. English, Czech, Slovenian) generally evoke no such integration concerns (see Sertl 2009, 127–128). Assumed lack of integration tends to be associated with Turkish (working-class) migrants in particular. Put differently, the dominant interpretative prism clearly distinguishes between different categories of 'the other', only some of which are discursively linked to anxieties about integration and community cohesion. Debates about minarets, which often echo and invoke the earlier-mentioned Swiss referendum controversy, also reflect widespread orientalizing definitions of Islam as an 'other' irreconcilable with local or Western values and traditions. At present, only four Austrian mosques have minarets – including ones in Vienna, the Tyrolean town of Telfs, and Bad Vöslau in Lower Austria respectively: in each of these contexts, local complaints or opposition led to changes to local Muslims' practice or plans, variously including calls for prayer performed less loudly or minarets being built to a lower height than initially planned (http://oesterreich.orf.at/stories/406575). Meanwhile, the regions of Carinthia and Vorarlberg have changed planning-permission legislation, now effectively obstructing the construction of minarets (Hafez and Potz 2009). In this context, there are occasional journalistic contributions that reveal real complexities where populist reductions paint vastly oversimplified pictures. Such nuanced commentaries avoid Manichean dichotomies, they realize that stereotypes fail to capture the ambivalences of cultural traditions and individuals' life-histories. At the same time they know that behind the above-mentioned controversies and populist caricatures there are real issues and real conflicts, and that resolutions may indeed be hard to come by, for at stake are at times competing value systems that may indeed be difficult to reconcile. One such example was provided by an article on women's role in Islam in Austria's weekly *Profil* (Hager and Meinhart 2007). Where much everyday discourse projects shocking examples of patriarchal violence onto Islam and Muslims in their entirety, the article emphasized contradictions, competing understandings and different frameworks of scriptural interpretation amongst Muslims; gender inequalities and oppression were criticized, whilst cultural change within Muslim communities and women's agency in *negotiating* different structural and cultural pushes and pulls took centre-stage:

> In this force-field between religious-patriarchal worldviews … and Western ways of life Muslim women living in Austria are trying to find their way … The taboos are beginning to lift. Progressive imams are arguing against genital mutilation and forced marriage. (Hager and Meinhart 2007, 25, my translation)

At first sight this account perhaps reproduces elements of an orientalizing 'clash of civilizations' narrative. At closer inspection, however, it – crucially – moves the discussion from the realm of discourse to the domain of everyday practice: it acknowledges that Muslim women live lives constrained by – and at the intersection of (see Brah 1996) – different structures, cultural traditions and values. In emphasizing their *negotiations* of the power and various ideologies exercised on them, ambivalences and contradictions on the level of the individual and cultural change within communities are revealed.

*Rarely acknowledged complexities*

What I propose to call 'lived ambivalences' refuse to, or cannot, conform to the rigid *either-or* decisions and allegiances demanded of them by much populist discourse. Questions of solidarity, identity, belonging and integration turn out to evoke more complex *both-and* answers. Rather than exclusive self-definitions as either part of 'us' or 'them', some lived identities are decidedly liminal. Integration and community cohesion, it may have to be conceded, may not be the absolute properties they are widely assumed to be (i.e. either a person/community is or is not integrated) but context-specific accomplishments that co-exist with feelings of alienation and disenfranchisement. In a world of transnational connections and biographies people's solidarities are likely to be multi-dimensional. Identity politics implicate not only the ethnic majority vis-à-vis 'the other', but also complex negotiations between and within different ethnic/religious communities. Returning to the crucial issue of individuals' negotiations of the structural constraints and cultural traditions they find themselves in, everyday politics is likely to reveal the significance of individual agency and the ubiquity of social change.

One form of ambivalence surrounds the politics and impact of Austria's largest 'mosque-association'. *Atib* has been active in Austria for twenty years, it now operates 60 prayer-rooms and Islamic centres, catering for some 25,000 families (Apfl 2010a). The organization acquired considerable public profile in the course of local controversies in Vienna surrounding plans to expand one of Atib's centres (see Kübel 2009) and the planned opening of another one. Its most vocal critics accuse it of fostering 'parallel lives' in the name of Turkey, which sends and pays for its 60 imams; Atib's self-definition, however, is that of a force for integration with an open-door policy for anyone regardless of their religious, ethnic or national backgrounds. Meanwhile, local (expert) observers suggest that Atib's politics and practices are more complex than either its aggressive critics or its defensive self-portrayal allow: whilst there is recurring scepticism about Turkey's involvement and the organization's historical thrust towards intra-group 'bonding' (rather than inter-communal 'bridging'), there is also positive acknowledgement that its imams are moderate, that Atib is now actively seeking dialogue and arguably constitutes a much-needed vehicle for 'neo-Austrians' of Turkish descent and their multi-dimensional identities (Apfl 2010a).

Other lived complexities are embodied by sections of ethnic communities that contradict stereotypes of 'the other' and are therefore rarely acknowledged in populist narratives and reifying portrayals of, for example, 'the' low-skilled, working-class Turkish 'guest-worker' who passes his alleged unwillingness to integrate and social exclusion to the next generation. It is of course obvious, and corroborated by the statistics and studies quoted above, that such stereotypes inevitably reduce and distort considerably more complex and varied social realities. Parts of the media have therefore begun to draw attention to sections within communities entirely overlooked by monolithic narratives. There have been portrayals of individuals within a growing but rarely acknowledged Turkish middle-class in Austria that is estimated to include some 30,000 people (Gepp 2009), Vienna's migrant magazine *Biber* has reported on some Austrian Turks' middle-class suburbanization or move to the countryside (Yildiran 2010), and ethnic communities are increasingly recognized and targeted as opening important and growing market niches for local economies (Apfl and Bernold 2009).

Ambivalence may be at its most apparent in the identity politics and self-understandings of some second-generation migrants acutely affected by structural disadvantages, exclusion, and what has been described as a 'double alienation' from both Austria and their families' countries of origin:

> [Austrian Turks] are accused of lacking loyalty towards their new home and of clinging to their old traditions, of using the state they actually reject. Integration is believed to have failed, Islamization … is feared … Volkan (29) says 'yes, there is a little truth behind these charges, yet they are also nonsense'. What does an Austrian know about what it's like being a Turk in Vienna? One carries two hearts, lives in two worlds and remains a stranger in both. (Zwander 2010, my translation)

'Volkan's' account of how some Turkish parents have passed their disappointment (about lack of social mobility and xenophobia encountered in the course of their settlement in Austria) onto their children and seek solace in an 'inner immigration' clearly captures common experiences.[11] Yet, the above-mentioned heterogeneities and the following account remind us that there is no single narrative able to subsume all life-histories and self-understandings:

> My father arrived in Austria in 1967 as a guest-worker … My friends know that my origins are Turkish, I like showing them that I am Austrian. This is why I've got our flag on my car. Why shouldn't I be proud of Austria? I went to school here and work here. At the European football championship I – of course – supported our country, not Turkey. (Construction-worker quoted in Brodnig 2008, my translation)

---

11    For a (historical) overview of Turkish migrations to, and experiences in, Austria, see Hinsch (2009).

Integration-debates take place not only between the dominant majority and (a specific category of) the perceived 'other'. Instead, discussions about mutual obligations in an ethnically/religiously diverse society with regard to community cohesion also unfold within and between minority communities. Some of these, in the Austrian and German contexts, have pitted an organization of former Muslims, now atheists, against (traditionalists within) Muslim communities in sometimes hostile confrontations over religion and democracy (Apfl 2010b). Another dimension to current integration-debates emerged when the president of Vienna's Jewish community called for a 'respectful discussion about Islam', supporting calls for more mosques in Austria but also arguing that these did not need minarets; further, he stressed that there was no room in Austria for 'people unwilling to integrate', though these were only a very small minority (http://diepresse.com/home/panorama/religion/592978/print.do). This illustrated that integration-related discourses are not just communicated by the dominant majority in the direction of migrant communities, but that such discourses have acquired a wider prevalence and also surface in negotiations amidst (different) religious groups.

Other forms of lived ambivalence define particular localities, including some widely associated with assumed lack of community cohesion. However, a closer look at such presumed 'problem areas', such as that taken by journalist Joseph Gepp (2010b) at an allegedly conflict-ridden part of the Viennese district of Favoriten, can reveal a more ambivalent picture of occasional tensions *and* much ordinariness and relative conviviality. Contrasts between externally held, negative stereotypes and lived realities of some successful integration also emerge from some of the multilingual, multi-ethnic classrooms frequently vilified in populist discourse (Hasewend 2009; Horaczek 2010c).

By way of a preliminary conclusion it is worth noting a snapshot illustrating how the lived ambivalences of pluralism can manifest. On 8 April 2010, the regional daily *Kleine Zeitung* captured the co-existence of both profound challenges and partial successes of multi-ethnic urban life: it reported conflicts between long-established residents and recently arrived migrants in a block of flats in Graz; critical responses to a survey in which 72 per cent of respondents thought Muslims failed to integrate and 54 per cent thought of Islam as a threat; but there were also reports of a multicultural prom celebrating diversity and of a local 'Africa-centre' dedicated to building bridging capital.

*Individual negotiations*

The above ambivalences cut across and partly define certain life-worlds. As such, they of course also manifest in individuals' biographies and daily lives. In this section, I pay closer attention to this individual level and focus, in particular, on social actors' discursive manoeuvres in the contexts of ideological diversity and everyday politics discussed earlier.

The individual level lies at the heart of a collection of eighteen portraits of elderly women migrants in Graz, including recently arrived refugees as well as long-established, naturalized migrants, whose experiences reveal the significance of both 'bonding' and 'bridging' capital, of exclusion and help, of isolation as much as of conviviality. Such contradictory yet co-existing facets have defined, for instance, Joy's – a South African's – biography:

> She met her future husband, an Austrian, in Durban when she was 31 … In 1971 they arrived in Graz with their son. Joy recalls with resignation: 'Because of the colour of my skin I couldn't find work as a nurse in Austria' … After a while she made good friends with Austrians, she has Austrian citizenship, feels at home here and eventually found work … She thinks that migrants in Austria are well-supported [now]. (Bacher et al. 2008, 106–107, my translation)

Painful memories and experiences of discrimination here sit alongside feelings of local belonging and a largely positive account of the local situation now faced by migrants. Whilst this adds more weight to the earlier argument that exclusions and conviviality can co-exist (rather than singularly defining a given context), it tells us little about how individuals – whether members of the dominant majority or of ethnic minority communities – respond to the ideologically heterogeneous and contested social fields they inhabit. Clearly, this question matters in most contemporary contexts. A first indication that ambivalence also surfaces in individuals' discursive leanings is provided by Amal Treacher's psychoanalytical reading of her 'mixed-race/mixed-class/mixed-religion' (i.e. Egyptian-English) family history, which alerts us to the possibility – or perhaps likelihood – of individual social actors holding, switching and moving between contradictory positions:

> My father was a complex man and he held contradictory positions for he had a deep and fierce pride and loyalty to Egypt and to being Egyptian while simultaneously he positioned himself as being more like a Westerner. Longing and pride … is a lethal mix as it produces longing to be the other and pride to be who one is. (Treacher 2007, 353)

Returning to the Austrian context, and focusing on individual members of the ethnic majority, there is evidence of (sometimes surprising) discursive flexibility and of divergences between everyday practices and professed ideological positions.[12]

---

12   Though not discussed here, electoral decisions also reflect political repositionings – including some radical shifts from the left to the right or vice versa – as manifest in individuals' changing voting preferences over time (for such changes at recent local elections in Vienna, for example, see Lettner 2010a). Further, it needs to be stressed that whilst the following examples show discursive switches on the political right, the left is certainly not immune from similar inconsistencies. For example, more research is needed on (potential) discrepancies between discursive commitments to multiculturalism and practices of exclusion (see Però 2007a, b). Taking this further: racism on the left is – of course – not an inevitable oxymoron.

One example was reported in Graz after local elections in January 2008, at which FPÖ and BZÖ campaigned with populist slogans and promises, and the earlier-mentioned manifestation of Islamophobia. Following media reports of violence between Austrian and Albanian youths in one of the city's most deprived areas, a council estate located in an electoral ward where 24 per cent of votes had gone to either the FPÖ or BZÖ (as opposed to 15 per cent across the city), *Falter* journalist Gerlinde Pölsler visited the area. The resulting article, however, captured social marginalization alongside feelings of disempowerment and an acute sense of local identity *cutting across* ethnic boundaries. Most unexpected was an encounter with a local BZÖ-activist:

> Edith ... lives with her 14-year old daughter in a council flat. In their living room, there are 14 kids ... Some Kosovo-Albanians, one Bosnian, another one is Kurdish, there is a girl from Romania, a few Austrians ... So what happened about the fight? ... 'Just fun.' ... 'We were bored.' ... Edith's flat is a last resort for the kids. She has [protected] several of them when their situations at home escalated ... There is an ambivalence about Edith ... She says: 'We really need programmes for integration, with all the xenophobia around.' She explains why she is also a BZÖ-functionary: she likes those [foreigners] 'who work' but says that many exploit the welfare system. And she'll protect all children. (Pölsler 2008, 5, my translation)

This captures parts of the local interface of ethnic pluralism and social deprivation, depicting an everyday culture defined by shared marginalization *and* conviviality. With election results also testifying to the local salience of nationalist sentiments, however, ideological ambivalence is not only encountered in the locality but also on the level of individual dispositions and responses. 'Edith' is, at least when queried, aware of the seeming tension between her BZÖ-activism and her commitment to lived integration.

A similar example of perhaps unexpected everyday accommodation to some 'others' alongside staunch opposition to – and negative portrayals of – other others has been captured with a local FPÖ-activist in a Viennese district:

> When Fozzy arrives at his local pub ... people call him over ... 'This is my power base', he says proudly. Most of them vote FPÖ because of him, the Chinese waitress, the Iranian businessman, the Serbian regular ... 'I am no xenophob', he says. In his block of flats he harmoniously shares a floor with Bosnians, Albanians and Asians. 'It works very well, the only ones causing problems are the Turks in the council estates. Their arrogance is unbelievable ... They're the only one who hate us.' (Gantner 2009, my translation)

Whilst this echoes the FPÖ's current delineation of the allegedly 'hostile', 'unintegrated' Turkish Muslim 'other' as its central scapegoat, 'Fozzy's' rhetoric also contains another key tenet of right-wing populist discourse – a focus on citizens' entitlements and the concomitant insistence that foreigners' access to social welfare/ health care is unaffordable and should be stopped: 'Fozzy's' suggested solution to a wide range of issues is that of 'Austrians first' (Gantner 2009).

'Edith's' and 'Fozzy's' ambivalences thus include strong elements of nationalist anxieties about competition for scarce public resources (e.g. Dench et al. 2006). Other, high-profile, populist discursive manoeuvres seem to constitute primarily forms of 'impression management'. For example, and in light of the FPÖ's repeatedly hostile campaigning against 'the Turkish other', it seems impossible to read Heinz-Christian Strache's following account as anything other than a strategic attempt to deflect charges of xenophobia:

> Decades ago the first people from Turkey arrived and were hard-working. Generally, there were no integration-problems. Today, there are problems with the third generation … Because the media unfortunately often distort, I would like to clarify a few things: I respect every culture, particularly Turkish culture … A great country and culture and proud people … Whilst we think the process of European integration has now reached its geographical, cultural and historical limits, we certainly want a far-reaching partnership with Turkey … Islam is one of the world's great religions and deserves the greatest of respect. I've also got Muslim friends, this isn't a question of religion… (quoted in Apfl 2010c, my translation)

A final snapshot of discursive ambivalence to be mentioned differs from the examples above. Unlike 'Edith', 'Fozzy' and the FPÖ's head, all of whom manoeuvre amongst (at least slightly) diverging positions – or between discourse and practice – self-consciously, the following example opens the possibility that tensions between professed ideology and lived reality need not always be noticed. The instance, reported by author Peter Turrini (2001, 68–69), was a confrontation in a pub in Carinthia, a region with a long history of ethnic-territorial disputes: Turrini and a friend were conversing in Slovenian, when they were verbally attacked by a farmer declaring that Austria was 'German-speaking land', yet doing so in Slovenian. This reveals the hybridity of lived identities as a challenge to the artificial rigidity of exclusivist identity discourses. It also raises the question if the farmer was deliberately ignoring his own bilingualism or, conversely, if he had inadvertently slipped into Slovenian. Either way, the farmer reveals a discrepancy between the 'messiness' of everyday life and the artificial 'orderliness' of (nationalist) discourse (Karner 2010a).

Whatever the motivations or degree of consciousness involved, such examples raise conceptually challenging questions about the stability and coherence of social actors' ethical and political positions. Returning to the theoretical lead outlined earlier, discourse analysis offers a framework for making sense of ambivalence, contextual negotiations and variations. Wetherell and Potter's research on everyday racism in New Zealand, for example, presents evidence of Billig's notion of the 'kaleidoscope of common sense':

[W]e do not find ... the neat organization which might be expected from a person [with] a consistent set of beliefs and attitudes or a single model of the world ... shifts are fluidly made ... 'liberal and egalitarian values' are selectively ... reworked, sometimes to racist and authoritarian effect ... it was typical ... for respondents to move between ... claims that might be described as racist and others that could be thought anti-racist ... How should these ... interviewees be classified? ... What is a methodological problem for attitude theory is all grist to the mill of discourse analysis, for [our] analytical goal is not to classify people but to reveal the discursive practices through which race categories are constructed and exploitation legitimated. We do not expect individuals to be consistent in their discourse – indeed, it would be very surprising if they were. (Wetherell and Potter 1992, 92, 102)

## Ambivalently cohesive British communities

Debates about the relationships between dominant national majorities and various 'others' are taking place across Europe. As in the Austrian case, social realities cannot be read off any of the co-existing and competing discourses concerning self-other relationships in a straightforward manner. Three major British cities, each of relevance to the now dominant community-cohesion agenda and to this chapter, illustrate this with particular clarity.

Ambivalences resonating with the analysis above are revealed by Michael Keith's reflections on his political involvement in, and research on, the London Borough of Tower Hamlets and Barking and Dagenham. The multifaceted character of these locales is captured by several uneasy juxtapositions: between, on one hand, the area's long history of inward migrations and its self-portrayal – also in London's bid for the 2012 Olympics – through 'the interplay of regeneration and multicultural diversity of the East End'; and, on the other, the large local inroads made by the British National Party at local elections in 2006 (i.e. the BNP's most substantial gains in the city) and conflicts between 'strands of political Islam and secular Bangladeshis, new EC [sic] accession country migrants and black and white East Enders' (Keith 2008, 2.7). Keith shows that recent local changes have included substantial population growth, concomitant pressures on public services, and serious decline of a manufacturing economy that formerly provided reliable and much-needed employment. This problematic mix has played into the hands of the BNP's calls for a 'prioritisation' of long-established 'locals' over more recently arrived residents. Such calls for unequal distribution of resources and entitlements have acquired growing appeal in the context of 'three strands of competition': over 'access to social goods' (e.g. education, social housing, health care), 'access to private goods' (i.e. the housing market) and over employment (Keith 2008, 3.22–3.24). Struggles over scarce resources and the resulting instrumentalist use of ethnic/national solidarities (see Cohen 1969) echo key parts of the earlier analyses and the findings of another study of London's East End: Dench et al. (2006)

argue that local racial conflict reflects, in large part, the alleged marginalization of the white working-class by the British welfare system. Yet, Keith argues, local realities are too complex to be reduced to a conflict pitting a long-established, local working-class against 'incomers':

> [A] downbeat narrative of racial antagonism squares oddly with the absence of milltown disorders … (as witnessed in northern UK towns in … 2001), the diverse solidarities that faced down seven East End bombings since 1990 by the Irish Republican Army, the Nazi nail bomber on Brick Lane and the '7/7' Islamist bombings … The emphasis on state failure likewise sits awkwardly alongside unrivalled improvements in Tower Hamlet schools, the recognition of a social services department … as the best in the country, and an award by the local government watchdog … for 'community cohesion' … None of this is to gainsay the historical legacy of poverty in the East End … social polarization that juxtapose the Docklands' new wealth with reproduced patterns of social disadvantage or the massive pressures on limited welfare resources. (Keith 2008, 2.2).

At stake in local and everyday politics are two competing models of belonging and entitlement: 'languages of rights … and concepts of identity … that draw on the tension between … obligations to those we know and love … [as opposed to] a sense of justice that … treats with indifference a sense of belonging locally, preferring to privilege the … rights of all' (Keith 2008, 4.1). These tensions in London's East End resonate with my analysis in chapter five of two competing politics that privilege (exclusive) citizen entitlements and (universal) human rights respectively. Moreover, Keith's observations relate to key debates about immigration and integration currently unfolding across large parts of continental Europe, including Austria, Germany and Switzerland: whether social welfare entitlements should be extended to all migrants, particularly in the context of family-reunifications with former 'guest-workers', or, alternatively, if participation in the job-market should become – arguably in emulation of the US – the primary or even exclusive means of migrants' social integration (e.g. Club 2 13 October 2010).

Further similarities between the ambivalences discussed above and the wider literature emerge from a study by John Clayton, who also speaks of 'negotiating national identities' (2009, 494), of young people's inter-ethnic relations in Leicester. Crucially, Clayton insists that an understanding of the lived realities of urban pluralism needs to penetrate behind rhetoric about community cohesion to illuminate individuals' everyday practices and solidarities in their localities. What is significant about Leicester is its self-portrayal as a 'successful multicultural city'. Through interviews and a focus on various places, institutions and practices that shape youngsters' life-worlds (e.g. parks, public spaces, sub-cultures, work, education) Clayton shows that local realities are more multi-dimensional and ambivalent: there is evidence of 'everyday racism' (Essed 1991) and of 'articulations of white defensiveness and loss' (Clayton 2009, 488) by some living on marginalized estates; rhetoric of entitlements, exclusions and political disillusionment also recurs in parts of Leicester, and neighbourhoods are 'coded' in terms of class and 'race', making them relatively (un)safe for differently positioned individuals; alongside, however, there are shared spaces of multicultural interaction, conviviality, and a growing, self-confident ordinariness 'attached to' transnational identities and religious diversity. Clayton summarizes the ambivalences, 'challenges, complexities and possibilities' of the everyday:

> [R]acial exclusion and inter-cultural collaboration ... co-exist in this city ... Experiences of ... spaces can be both progressive and divisive, depending upon the manner in which engagement is facilitated and the weight of past experience ... making a straightforward distinction between those places which 'work' in terms of positive inter-ethnic relations and those which do not, a misleading binary. (Clayton 2009, 487, 490, 494)

Similar complexities have been captured in an even more localized setting – a specific part of inner-city Birmingham with a particularly bad external reputation – where I have been co-conducting research with David Parker over several years. An area with a South Asian Muslim majority, Alum Rock suffers from chronic structural disadvantages and has, especially since a series of terror-related arrests, come to be externally portrayed as a place of Islamically-underpinned 'parallel lives' and as a 'no-go-area' for non-Muslim outsiders. However, local realities are far more complex: acute infrastructural deprivation sits alongside local 'bridging' initiatives aimed at fostering inter-faith dialogue and community building (Karner and Parker 2008); the area's bad external reputation is challenged by local networks, individuals and initiatives attempting to counteract social exclusion and displaying deeply-felt commitments to the locality, its diverse residents and future (Parker and Karner 2010). At the same time, everyday life in Alum Rock displays a series of ambivalences – conflicts and conviviality, bridging capital and ethnic exclusions, political activism and entrenched, sometimes stifling structures of decision-making all co-exist, making it impossible to designate the area categorically as either lacking or displaying community cohesion; Alum Rock *both* possesses *and* lacks community cohesion, to different degrees and in different contexts (Karner and Parker forthcoming).

### Concluding remarks

This chapter has developed the overall analysis in two inter-related directions: first, and drawing on the notion of 'grammars of identity', I have examined ideologically diverse responses to ethnic pluralism as manifest in competing discourses on the relationships between dominant majorities and various 'others'. Second, this discussion has fore-grounded the realm of the everyday and presented a series of snapshots of lived complexities and ambivalences, including discrepancies between social actors' professed ideological dispositions and everyday practices/ relationships. Overall, this analysis has corroborated and added to observations (Weigl 2009, 99) of the 'far-reaching societal changes' that have taken place – in Austria as elsewhere – over recent decades, creating migrant communities that are 'internally split', belie 'simplistic categorization' and challenge 'linear models of integration'. As this discussion has also shown, 'local' reactions have been similarly diverse and ambivalent, adding further dimensions and complexities to ethnically plural and politically contested social fields.

In the next and final chapter I turn to questions of cultural/symbolic representation and, in doing so, shift the focus from discourses about 'the other' to discourses by the othered. Put differently, we now turn to an examination of cultural agency by migrants and their descendents as manifest in various forms and genres of self-definition, self-portrayal and self-assertion.

# Chapter 7
# 'The Other': Representations *Of* and *By*

## Introduction

> [I]f you feel you have been denied the chance to speak your piece, you will try extremely hard to get that chance. For indeed, the subaltern can speak ... (Said 1995, 335)

> [T]here emerges a more instantaneous and subaltern voice of the people, a minority discourse that speaks betwixt and between times and places. (Bhabha 1990b, 309)

Most of the analyses presented thus far have focused on different perspectives amongst 'ethnic majorities' directed, in part, towards some of those considered, constructed and positioned as 'others'. For all my emphasis on the diversity of, and antagonisms between, competing political positions, the emphasis has so far been on the various discursive, organizational and lived responses generated from within dominant national majorities to migratory flows and ethnic pluralism. Voices and self-portrayals of those 'others' have been relatively few and far between. This final chapter goes some way towards redressing this relative imbalance. Through an analysis of the representational politics, dynamics and struggles unfolding around various 'others', their political and cultural agency – captured by the quotations opening this chapter – now takes centre-stage. In keeping with previous chapters, I again focus on my main, Austrian case study before turning to other European contexts. Two preliminary points need to be made. First, what follows is inevitably provisional and tentative, even more so than the discussions of the previous chapters, all of which call for further research. The realm of cultural representation, though, is in any geographical setting and particularly in our 'information age' (Castells 1996), enormous and continually expanding. Inevitably, the following therefore focuses on a mere selection of snapshots. Second, the discussion invited below is by definition inter-disciplinary: questions of representation implicate sociology and cultural studies as much as the arts, literary theory and academic analyses of any and all forms of cultural signification and expression.

**Contexts**

The English verb 'to represent' subsumes two processes that other languages, including German, separate: first, one of 'acting on behalf of' someone else; second, a process (and its results) of 'depicting' someone or something (e.g. Littler 2010, 1). Whilst the former refers to formal, political representation, the latter captures processes of cultural signification. Though distinct, we also know – at least since Edward Said's seminal *Orientalism* – that cultural representations are intrinsically political, that depictions of 'the other' are part and parcel of the power-relationship between self and other. There are at least two key threads deriving from Said's work, discussed in his afterword to the 1995-edition of *Orientalism*, that are of direct relevance to the analysis below. First, his objection to Orientalism as a 'system of thought [that] approaches a heterogeneous, dynamic, and complex human reality from an uncritically essentialist standpoint', thus obscuring historical change and 'the *interests* of the Orientalist' (Said 1995, 333–334, italics in the original). Equally relevant, and captured by Said's observation quoted at the beginning of this chapter, is one of the new (sub-) disciplines his work helped develop – *Subaltern Studies*, or a 'revolution in historiography, the immediate goal being to rescue the writing of … history from the domination of the nationalist elite and restore to it the important role of the urban poor and the rural masses' (Said 1995, 352).

   Enormously significant shifts in the politics of (cultural) representation have of course also been recorded in Europe's post-colonial, multicultural cities. Philip Cohen (1992, 85), for example, mentions the 'autonomous space[s] of representation', in which otherwise 'silenced or marginalized' ethnic minorities 'find their own political voice'. Stuart Hall (1997, 183) goes even further in speaking of 'the most profound cultural revolution' of the late twentieth century as having come about 'as a consequence of the margins coming into representation – in art, in painting, in film, in music, in literature, in the modern arts everywhere, in politics, and in social life generally'. Cultural/symbolic representation thus defines not only artistic activity but also everyday life. More exactly, everyday cultures are, in part, realms of signification and – as such – subject to ideological negotiation and struggle. Who is empowered to speak on whose behalf, who can represent whom, themselves or others, how categories of 'self' and 'other' are constructed, reproduced or challenged, where and when discourses and images about collectivities and individuals are articulated – these are defining questions in the sociology of culture and in the politics of the quotidian. Projected onto this analysis, this raises questions about everyday representations of groups considered/ constructed as ethnically 'other' in relevant Austrian and other European discursive realms; these are questions about *representations of the other* by members of a self-defining 'ethnic majority'. Secondly, this needs to be counter-balanced with (the beginnings of) a discussion of the politically inverse process of *representations by the 'othered'* of their own experiences, life-worlds and self-understandings. In what follows, I examine select instances of 'the new discourses of subjects who have been marginalized coming into representation' (Hall 1989, 25) in Austria and other parts of Europe. Such a discussion reveals contested cultural fields, in which (often orientalist) *representations of* 'the other' are challenged by *representations by* the other. However, the resulting representational struggles and dynamics are yet more complex and multi-dimensional: neither representations of nor representations by the other are monolithic, but they can reveal internal disagreements and struggles or be potentially ambivalent in their ideological motivations and results; further, there are types of *co-representations* based on dialogue and solidarities between members of the dominant majority and some amongst the marginalized; finally, some representations by the subaltern 'reverse the gaze', thus offering critical insights into the structures that have effected their subordination.

Both processes – the representing *of* and the self-representing *by* 'the other' – take place, certainly in ethnically diverse societies of the twenty-first century, literally every day, in countless formats, genres and settings. A discussion of these continually unfolding processes thus has to be highly selective and is bound to remain tentative, consisting of highly specific and localized snapshots at best. It needs to be stressed that such snapshots are selected from a staggering variety of artistic genres and media, including – in addition to the ones mentioned by Hall – community newspapers, magazines and newsletters, radio stations, TV channels and programmes, street art, photography, theatre, and the internet in all its facets. Representations of and by 'the other' occur in all these and many other settings and formats.[1] The following discussion could have selected from any of these, and future research has, assuming that 'the other's' cultural self-portrayals and self-expressions are given the attention they deserve, much to do. Moreover, contextualization of the following snapshots demands a reminder of the wide range of very different 'categories of the other' – each with its distinctive histories and experiences in relation to the dominant majority – this discussion of relevant Austrian materials has selected from: autochthonous ethnic groups (i.e. Slovenian, Croat, Czech, Hungarian, Slovak, Roma and Sinti),[2] religious communities (e.g. Jewish, Muslim, Protestant or Orthodox Christian), former 'guest-workers' from former Yugoslavia and Turkey and their descendants, different groups of long-established refugees as well as more recently arrived asylum-seekers, and the structurally very differently positioned, often highly qualified migrants from within

---

1   The ubiquity and ordinariness of 'hyphenated identities' in the artistic community, uneasily juxtaposed to experiences of exclusion, was recently stressed in a round-table discussion about 'integration' involving a writer, a musician and a film-makers with 'migration background' (currently) residing in Vienna (Dusini and Kralicek 2010).

2   For a descriptive overview of print- and broadcast media and some publishing houses for and by Austria's autochthonous minorities (and some critical comments on their current funding and limited reach), see Purkarthofer et al. (2005). For a brief summary of various media for different ethnic communities in Austria, see Sandrisser and Winkler (2008, 201), and for African voices on the radio and the internet, see Markom and Weinhäupl (2007, 152).

the EU and other industrialized parts of the world are – of course – *all* implicated in representational dynamics and formats of the kinds mentioned below. Again: the following is merely a step and future research has much to examine, not least given the ongoing, unceasing and continually expanding nature of the cultural fields and processed involved.

Overall, the following snapshots of self- and other-representations, and most importantly of the others' self-representations, illustrate one of Homi Bhabha's key arguments:

> The 'locality' of national culture is neither unified nor unitary … the problem of outside/inside must always itself be a process of hybridity, incorporating new 'people' … generating other sites of meaning and … producing … political antagonism and unpredictable forces for political representation … The 'other' is never outside or beyond us; it emerges forcefully, within cultural discourse, when we think we speak most intimately and indigenously 'between ourselves'. (Bhabha 1990a, 4)

This is of crucial relevance to this book in general, and this chapter in particular. National cultures turn out to be intrinsically heterogeneous, multi-vocal and – especially in times of global flows – inevitably hybrid. At the same time, they are ideologically contested, with a complex politics of (cultural) representation unfolding around the competing discourses of inclusion and exclusivity discussed earlier. In what follows, then, I pay specific attention to some of the 'subaltern voices' in what Bhabha calls (1990a, 5) – drawing on Sneja Gunew's reading of Australia's diverse literary genres – a 'multiculturalist counter-public sphere', where 'the excluded voices of migrants and the marginalized' acquire space, get articulated and heard. In the first instance, however, some of the countless and daily depictions of various 'others' emanating from within an 'ethnic majority' need discussion.

### Representations of …

Given that, as stressed above, power and representation are mutually implicated and closely enmeshed, the manifestations of (hegemonic) power in and through prominent representational modes and 'regimes' (Hall 1997, 174) form an obvious starting-point to this discussion. Yet, continuing with the earlier theme of a critical 'counter-public' shared by differently positioned social actors, later sections of this chapter illustrate that not all representations of others aim at, or inadvertently contribute to, their continuing othering or marginalization. In a subsequent analytical step we thus discover emancipatory representations based on inter-ethnic dialogue and inclusive politics. To begin with, however, our focus needs to be on a variety of representational genres that reflect, legitimate and help perpetuate existing structures of inequality.

Constructions and portrayals of 'the other' reflect configurations and workings of power. Continuing with Said, and given the preoccupation with Islam and Muslims common to many contemporary debates about multiculturalism and integration across Europe, an analysis of such representations of the other needs to be alert to the enduring prevalence of orientalist assumptions and depictions. Defined as a 'system of representation' that 'act[s] towards bringing "the Orient" into "Western" consciousness ... and under Western dominion', Orientalism constructs 'the Orient' as 'separate, different, conservative or archaic or barbarian' (Richardson 2004, 5). Applied to some of the examples below, Orientalism consists of self-interested, (largely) negative reifications of 'the other', with whom a similarly reified 'self' is – or perceives itself to be – engaged in a power struggle. As shown earlier, recent years have seen a proliferation of (local) tensions over religious difference and their instrumentalization by discourses and political manifestos premised on populist stereotypes of, and opposition to, 'the other' as scapegoat, alleged 'intruder' and threat. In the Austrian context, critics of these developments have observed a predominance of 'largely negatively connoted' public representations of Islam (Bunzl and Hafez 2009, 8). My analysis of readers' letters to Austria's largest newspaper in chapter three revealed some such negative representations and their close association of Islam with a variety of alleged dangers. Other recent research (Saad 2009, Sonnleitner 2009) has shown that *some* broadsheet coverage transports less explicit, but nonetheless monolithic pictures of Islam – as, for example, in the context of the infamous 'Danish-caricatures-controversy' of 2005 – or a 'latent scenario of fear' attached to Islam. Put differently, versions of the 'discursive chains' examined earlier have also featured in some broadsheet commentaries, as, for instance, in *Profil*'s engagement with the caricatures-controversy:

> Intra-Islamic disagreements about the caricatures are ignored and the conflict emerges as seemingly absolute and civilizational ... The controversy over the caricatures is discursively linked to the terrorist attacks of 9/11, the wars in Afghanistan and Iraq, Islam is closely associated with war and violence. (Sonnleitner 2009, 194, my translation)

Similarly relevant are analyses of the portrayals of Islam and Christianity contained in some of Austria's school textbooks. Such work shows that alongside some very positive examples of balanced representations that offer nuanced, critical engagement with (the histories of) both 'self' and 'other', there are also continuing clichés, generalizations, and anachronistic, lop-sided comparisons that, for example, contrast contemporary Christianity with medieval Islam (Heine 2009, 60). Among the monolithic, orientalizing clichés thus reproduced in some textbooks are generic associations of Islam with war and of Christianity with peacefulness (Pratl 2009, 64–69). Importantly, it has been pointed out that in Austria and other parts of central Europe Orientalism often takes a slightly different form shaped by the region's history: a 'frontier orientalism' that constructs a 'bad, aggressive

Muslim', associated with the history of Ottoman attacks and frequently projected onto today's Turkish migrants; this is simultaneously contrasted to the notion of a 'controlled' (and often Bosnian), 'domesticated' and thus 'good Oriental' (Gingrich quoted in Markom and Weinhäupl 2009, 89–90). The topos of *'the' violent, male Muslim* also recurs in some of the interpretations offered by parts of the public of shocking cases of patriarchal violence and forced marriage. As shown by Gamze Ongan (2009), head of an advice centre for women migrants in Vienna, prominent and in many ways problematic accounts attribute such violence unequivocally to Islam, instead of offering a critical examination of the structural contexts in which forced marriages and what has come to be called 'tradition-bound violence' occur. In offering such 'culturalist' interpretations, statistically more common experiences among migrants, such as poverty, are sidelined and structural factors exacerbating some women's vulnerability, such as a precarious residence status that is – in the context of family reunifications – often tied to the husband's or father's, remain un-scrutinized. Ongan elaborates:

> How come everyone seems keen to contribute to changing scandalized gender-relations, whilst interest in equality quickly wanes when it comes to access to employment, education or social mobility? … Depictions of forced marriage as a general, Islamic rule or practice or as that of a 'backward' culture denigrate a large group of migrants and exacerbate those families' exclusion … What's needed are measures that protect the women affected without providing new arguments for … Islamophobia. (Ongan 2009, 74–75, my translation)

Stating an obvious and sad truth, crude depictions, racist stereotypes and decontextualized, reductive and derogatory 'discursive chains' attached to many 'others' still abound across and far beyond contemporary Europe. Speaking in 2002, Araba Evelyn Johnston-Arthur, founder of the 'the movement of the young African diaspora in Austria', described key dimensions of the representational politics or, more accurately, of the enduring symbolic exclusion and stigmatization suffered by many Africans: first, Johnston-Arthur summarized new forms of racism that construct Africans no longer, as in the colonial era, as 'savages' but – in the Austrian context – as 'drug-dealers'; second, she observed a 'glaring discrepancy' between Africans as 'visible objects' frequently viewed through pejorative topoi and their relative 'invisibility as subjects' (Schmied 2002b). More recently, in the context of the football world-cup in South Africa, there was some critical debate about the global media's role in perpetuating a system of representations and portrayals that have silenced, stereotyped and depersonalized Africans; its narrative structure is as dichotomous as it is predictable:

> A specific role-distribution defines the picture of the entire continent: Africans are substitutable, nameless, helpless, without history. The whites, by contrast, are defined as acting subjects, with names and faces. Whilst the former silently

look into the camera and suffer, the latter speak and we identify with them.
(Hamann 2010, 20, my translation)

At the same time, of course not all representations of others originating within
an ethnic majority at the heart of Europe are easily classified in terms of their
motivations and effects. There is, instead, scope for considerable ambivalence,
such as is encountered in representations that are aware of the workings of
orientalism and aim for a critical distance from discriminatory discourses, yet –
inadvertently – reproduce some tacit and problematic assumptions and depictions
of 'the other'. One such form of ambivalence has been revealed by a recent study
of Austrian secondary school textbooks that provides insights into more complex
*representations of the other* as encountered in Austrian educational settings.
Echoing the discourse analytical understanding of language and social realities as
mutually constitutive, the authors (Markom and Weinhäupl 2007, 200, 4) consider
school textbooks to simultaneously reflect and help shape cultural assumptions.
In wider conceptual terms, the study examines the relevance of everyday cultures
of signification to processes of ideological reproduction or social change. More
accurately, Markom and Weinhäupl examine the representation of racism, anti-
Semitism, gender, sexuality, and various 'others' (i.e. Islam, 'the developing
world', non-Western indigenous peoples) in the history, geography and biology
textbooks most widely used in Austrian secondary schools. Asking whether these
textbooks challenge discrimination or, conversely, whether existing stereotypes
are perpetuated, the authors reveal a multi-dimensional and ambivalent picture:

> Open discrimination was widely avoided and racism rejected. Similarly, fixed
> gender roles were being questioned … and homosexuality is now mentioned.
> Particularly the new editions show much good will. However, our analysis …
> shows that engagement with racism, sexism and other 'isms' is often somewhat
> superficial. On a deeper level … partly derogatory discourses sometimes reappear:
> about Europe's superiority and 'Indians' threatened by extinction, about Islam as
> an allegedly totalizing force and associations of Africa with hunger … The most
> diverse … social contexts are homogenized, political hierarchies overlooked,
> and sharp delineations from 'the others' drawn … Structural and individual
> discrimination are at times forgotten … [and] power hierarchies disguised.
> (Markom and Weinhäupl 2007, 1, my translation)

Undoubtedly well-intentioned though such *representations of the other* are,
Markom and Weinhäupl reveal the inadvertent persistence of discourses of
rigid 'othering' and uncritical 'hierarchizing' in school books widely used in the
classrooms of contemporary, multi-ethnic Austria.

  If these are snapshots of some of the countless representations, forms of
symbolic marginalizations, and types of ambivalences encountered across various
everyday cultures, a second and crucial question follows: how do some individuals

'othered', hierarchized and reified by such discourses represent themselves and their assumed 'communities'?

## Representations by ...

One of the contributions to the earlier-mentioned collection of papers on integration published by Austria's Interior Ministry in 2008 stresses the crucial role played by the media. More accurately, it argues that the media's responsibilities and scope for contributing to successful integration and community cohesion consist of three distinctive dimensions: first, the types of depictions of migrants and their problems as well as endeavours to facilitate integration offered by the 'host-society's' media; second, specific media *for and by* migrants and their contributions to integration; third, the visibility of people with 'migration background' in the public and private media of the dominant majority (Sandrisser and Winkler 2008, 196). The first of these dimensions has of course been the focus of extensive analyses throughout this book; the crux of the resulting discussions can be summarized under the heading of *heterogeneity* – there is no singular representational system but an ideologically diverse, internally contested social and cultural field, in which discourses of neo-nationalist belonging, on one end of the spectrum, and inclusive politics of inter-group solidarity and dialogue, on the other, compete. Moreover, and as shown both in the previous section and in chapter six, particular individuals or discursive appropriations can display considerable ambivalence, spanning or switching ideological orientations. The third of the three media-dimensions emphasized by Sandrisser and Winkler warrants a separate analysis, which would exceed the scope of the present chapter and is therefore here mainly just underlined as an important area for future research. It is the second dimension, various media for and by migrants and their contribution to – or take on – integration, that lies at the heart of the remainder of this chapter. This having been said, the materials examined below are taken from a considerably wider range of realms of signification and types of cultural representations than simply that of the print and broadcast media. We thus return to Stuart Hall's earlier-quoted observations (1997, 179) of a veritable 'explosion of ... new forms of cultural communication and ... representation' that has arguably amounted to the 'most profound cultural revolution' of our era:

> Our lives have been transformed by the struggle of the margins to come into representation – not just to be placed by a dominant imperializing regime but to reclaim some form of representation for themselves. Paradoxically, marginality has become a powerful space. It is a space of weak power, but it is a space of power, nonetheless. Anybody who cares for what is creatively emergent in the contemporary arts will find that it has something to do with the languages of the margin ... New subjects, new genders, new ethnicities, new regions, and new communities – all hitherto excluded from the major forms of cultural representation ... – have emerged and have acquired through struggle, sometimes

in very marginalized ways, the means to speak for themselves for the first time.
(Hall 1997, 183)

In what follows, and through a discussion of relevant, select snapshots, we examine the workings of some of the 'languages of the margin' and its 'spaces of weak power' in a little more detail. Such voices of various 'others' are crucial for an enhanced understanding of the lived experiences of ethnic pluralism, social inequality, integration, and national identity politics.

*'Subaltern counterpublics'*

As already discussed, various Austrian media constitute examples of Nancy Fraser's notion of 'subaltern counterpublics', or 'parallel discursive arenas where members of subordinated social groups ... circulate counterdiscourses to formulate oppositional interpretations of their identities, interests and needs' (1992, 123). Such subaltern counterpublics thereby exemplify the politics of cultural representation touched upon earlier: they depict and formulate the 'identities, interests and needs' of the subordinated *and*, in the process, critically – or, in Gramscian terminology, counter-hegemonically – engage with those very structures and configurations of power that effect and perpetuate their subordination. Signification thereby emerges, yet again, to be profoundly political. However, and as some of the following examples show, subaltern counterpublics should not be thought of as entirely separate, necessarily parallel discursive universes, as they often aim for and at times achieve a discursive presence amongst 'the mainstream'.

One of the Austrian subaltern counterpublics briefly mentioned in chapter five is a magazine called *Stimme*, German for 'voice', which was founded in 1991 and is published quarterly 'by and for minorities'. Available online, contributors identify with or support various minority communities, and its thematic issues offer critical reflections on the status-quo. This is illustrated by the wide range of foci of previous issues, which have included critical examinations of discourses about 'parallel societies', 'minority literatures', the history of 'guest-workers' in Austria, 'fractured identities', the impact of globalization on minority communities, anti-discrimination-, anti-racism and legislation pertaining to autochthonous ethnic groups (http://minderheiten.at/stat/stimme/zeitschr.htm). Also relevant here is the previously mentioned Viennese magazine *Biber*. Published since 2006, and in contrast to papers and magazines – such as the Austro-Turkish *Yeni Vatan* or *Polonika*, the monthly magazine 'for Poles in Austria' – for particular ethnic communities, *Biber* self-defines as 'trans-culturally' speaking to and across all Viennese with (and without) 'migration backgrounds'. It aims to deconstruct stereotypes and negative clichés of migrants, to portray pluralism as a positive challenge and opportunity, to represent those who do not feel spoken to in the mainstream media, but to also encourage (self)critical debate within migrant communities:

> Biber's main aim is to provide a medium in which other groups can feel
> represented. Of course, there is also a critical dimension. We want to portray
> other ways of life, whilst also questioning them – both at the same time. (http://
> www.wieninternational.at/de/node/6341?SESS88d391…., my translation)

Other relevant media outlets providing representational space for those relatively
marginalized, 'invisible' or 'inaudible' elsewhere include local radio stations
offering multi-lingual programmes and 'constructive engagement' with the
'chances and challenges' of multiculturalism (Aigner 2008a), or the Viennese
'community TV-channel' *Okto*: the latter has operated since 2005 and invites
contributions by anyone with programme-ideas and a commitment to human
dignity; by November 2009 Okto had produced 110 programmes, including
regular, multi-lingual contributions by 'Africans in the diaspora', programmes on
Roma communities, on poverty, homelessness, social exclusion and integration, as
well as on sexual orientations and identities (Aigner 2009b).

As already implied, the boundaries between some mainstream media and
certain counterpublics are beginning to get more porous, with some individuals
of various 'migration backgrounds' finally achieving wider visibility and thus
countering a discrepancy that has been described (Dempfer 2009a, 54) as migrants
being the object of much journalistic interest, whilst rarely (other than in niche-
media for and by migrants) featuring amongst the producers of journalistic
accounts. Recent initiatives by several Austrian broadsheets (i.e. *Wiener Zeitung*,
*Die Presse*, *Der Standard*) for regular pages or sections specifically by journalists
with 'migration backgrounds' (Gantner 2010) can thus be read as signs of some
'others' belatedly 'coming into mainstream representation'. A key actor in this
respect is Simon Inou, refugee from Cameroon and head of an organization that
aims to place 'migrant-journalists' in mainstream media:

> What is unique about Inou is the determination with which he has worked his way
> from the margins into the centre of the Austrian public: 'Radio Africa', which he
> co-founded, was still directed at the African community. The monthly section on
> Africa he wrote for the *Wiener Zeitung* already aimed at local audiences … With
> his organization M-Media he has clearly arrived at the heart of Austrian society,
> which he hopes to encourage to face its own diversity more honestly. (Hamann
> 2009, 20, my translation)

Other examples of the subaltern acquiring some self-representational space that is
noticed by at least parts of the wider, dominant public include specific artistic or
journalistic initiatives and creations. One such recent example was a documentary
entitled *Little Alien* by Bosnian-born film-maker Nina Kusturica, who followed
six under-aged refugees in Austria, capturing their everyday (bureaucratic) trials
and tribulations, their experiences of exclusion, their painful memories, fears and
hopes for a better life, as well as some of their more ordinary, teenaged problems
that they have in common with those more fortunate than themselves (*Megaphon*

169, 13). The documentary was also shown at various Austrian schools, providing 'local' youngsters with the opportunity to discuss it with Nina Kusturica and the documentary's protagonists themselves:

> It is usually only in the media that Austrian teenagers may hear of the kinds of lives lived by these youngsters from Afghanistan and Africa. Kusturica wanted to tell their individual stories … First love, education, choosing a future career: some of the issues faced by these under-aged asylum-seekers barely differ from those familiar to their Austrian counterparts. In terms of opportunities and prospects, however, the differences couldn't be greater. (http://www.orf. at/091020-43862/index.html, my translation)

Other, though very different histories of exclusion and suffering lie at the heart of the annual 'Jewish Echo' (*Das Jüdische Echo*), founded in 1951 by Holocaust survivor Leon Zelman. Its 58th edition, published in 2009, was entitled 'At home in Europe' (*Zuhause in Europa*) and contained – alongside its Austrian emphasis – country-specific case studies of Europe's diverse Jewish communities. The overarching theme was an exploration of Judaism and Jewish identities as deeply embedded in, and intrinsically part of, European societies, thereby deconstructing representations of Jewish communities as an 'exotic other' (Pelinka 2009). In addition to essays on anti-Roma racism, Islamophobia and anti-Semitism, this edition of the Jewish Echo also offered depictions of civil society activity in different parts of Europe. With the Shoah as the omnipresent and inescapable backdrop, this wide-ranging collection (*Das Jüdische Echo* 2009) thus showed glimpses of various groups that – their deep historical roots in Europe notwithstanding – continue to be 'othered', marginalized and excluded by narrow discourses and politics of nationalist belonging.

*Self-assertion*

As stressed throughout this discussion, self- and other-representations through cultural means are intrinsically political insofar as they variously help legitimate or critically examine existing structures of power and exclusion. Relevant examples of the latter, of critical, subaltern self-representations, indeed proliferate – not only, but arguably especially in our era of new technologies and the novel modes, realms and registers of self-expression and self-articulation facilitated by them. Whilst the politics of self-representation occurring on the internet can only here be highlighted as warranting the attention of extensive future research, there are also noteworthy examples of ideological contestation directed at discourses of nationalist belonging and exclusion to be encountered in more 'traditional' representational formats. The following snapshot is a case in point.

Ideological opposition and critique can be at their most compelling if they side-step, deconstruct and refuse the central categories that define dominant discourses. This is illustrated, for example, by Seher Çakir, an award-winning

Austro-Turkish writer and poet, who rejects others' re-telling of her life-story as allegedly epitomizing a 'good Turk's successful integration':

> This interpretation enrages Seher, because there is another, less clichéd way of telling her story, which highlights the universal search for a good life. Origin, language struggles, anachronistic traditions, are only some of the possible obstacles, other people happen to confront others, but no one is spared their own challenges. She already knew when she was sixteen that her life was hers ... and she was not going to conform to others' stereotypes ... Her dream was to be recognized as an author, not as an Austrian or Turkish author, nor as an author 'with migration background', but just as an author ... She chose and fought for it. But that, she says, everyone has to do anyway, regardless of whether they are 'long-term or short-term Austrians'. (Dempfer 2009b, 6–7, my translation)

Categories of ascription, stereotypes as well as the very delineation of 'self' and 'other' are here challenged by an alternative interpretative framework, one which asserts the individual's rights over and above 'traditional' demands and expectations, which seeks to overcome discursive and structural exclusions and emphasizes what is common to all of us: the challenge of living a self-defined life.

Yet more direct was the self-assertion and political critique offered by a young Austro-Serb, whose family had escaped from the war in former Yugoslavia to Innsbruck in 1991. Stirred by the presidential candidacy of the highly controversial Barbara Rosenkranz in 2010 (see chapter one) and strongly opposed to the FPÖ's nationalism more generally, he wrote a reader's letter to *Profil*, which triggered hundreds of congratulatory emails and comments on facebook, was reposted online and commented on across various internet blogs (Lettner 2010b). His letter epitomized the contested terrain that is 'the nation', challenging nationalist exclusions and defining belonging inclusively:

> I would like to comment on something often claimed by Barbara Rosenkranz and her party ...: the homeland ... I was born in a country that no longer exists, because it was torn apart in a brutal war ... I am 22 years old and have lived, for as long as I can remember, in my city, in my Innsbruck. I am Austrian and Serb. This is no contradiction, no sign of unwillingness to integrate, this is my life ... I have the same right to love the mountains around Innsbruck, just as I will continue to moan about the Austrian national football team. You do not own our homeland. There are others here too. We have the same right to consider the scenery, Kafka, the mentality 'ours'. We also exercise our right to hate the traces of the Nazi past, because we love this country – without flags, without false pride, without nostalgia, and without racism. (quoted in Lettner 2010b, 34–35, my translation)

What we encounter here is of central significance to a key argument made in this book: an alternative, non-nationalist 'deixis' (Billig 1995a), which 'rhetorically points at', and hence delineates, an inclusive, internally heterogeneous, culturally hybrid, and critically self-reflexive national identity. As argued particularly in chapter one, nationalism does not exercise an ideological monopoly over the forms national identities can take; the latter clearly assume very different forms, ranging from the rigidly and narrowly exclusivist on one end of the spectrum, to the much more self-consciously diverse and positively inclusivist on the other.

*More ambivalence*

It is stating the obvious to emphasize that there is of course much ideological diversity and contestation *within* the cultural representations emerging from among the historically silenced and marginalized. Their (self-)representations reflect internal conflicts and heterogeneities, conceptualizing – and responding to – 'the other's' own delineations and experiences of 'self' and 'other' in a wide variety of different ways. Whilst this also remains an area for further research, the following snapshot illustrates some of the complexities and contestations that reflect a multiplicity of voices and fissures amongst and between various 'others'.

The snapshot in question was provided by an article by Sedat Pero, a Turkish-born Kurdish teacher and award-winning author who has lived in Austria since 1997, addressing the question currently debated across Europe: the extent to which multiculturalism has or has not 'worked' and which factors help or hinder migrants' social, political and cultural integration. Pero's response (2008) is thought-provoking: he provides a *critical representation by the othered*, speaking from the vantage point of a (former) migrant but not on a presumed community's behalf. Instead, he writes as an individual, critical of the multiple, intersecting 'axes' of difference and exclusion (Brah 1996) that constrain migrants' life-worlds, but not as a spokesperson for a collectivity reified in the dominant discourses of the ethnic majority. Pero challenges all parties implicated in contemporary discussions surrounding integration, which – he claims – has thus far failed in Austria yet must take place to avoid French scenarios of ghettoization. Equally concerned by what he describes as ethnic segregation taking place in some of Vienna's schools, whereby migrants' social marginalization is inherited by the next generation, by xenophobia, and by the self-separation he detects amongst some migrant communities, Pero defines structural/educational reforms, German language competence, and a universal commitment to 'Western values' as pre-requisites for a successful future. He casts his critical eye far and wide:

> Integration is not about having … cultural associations or sports groups … to keep the outside world at bay. Integration is not about having Turkish or Greek food every now and then … Both sides are implicated … Problematically, many intellectuals … position themselves, mechanically, in opposition to rightist populism … It is bizarre to see the generally secular left support calls for more mosques just because the radical right opposes [them] … In opposing racism, they may support certain Islamists who misuse Western democracy and Islam …

> In their countries of origin some 'mosque builders' ... condone systems that seek
> to write minorities out of their histories ... Do those on the left know how some
> [such Islamists] treat their wives at home? (Pero 2008, 14, my translation)

Whatever one's response to Pero's assessment, it seems clear that it cannot
be reduced to his own structural and ethnic positioning, nor to the diasporic
manifestations of Turko-Kurdish hostilities. Instead, it provides evidence of a
representational struggle over ethnic/religious boundaries and the exercise of
power and political agency *both across and within* them.

Other forms of ambivalence partly question the linearity and absoluteness of
the historical schema – a movement from representations of the other towards
representations by the historically 'othered' and concomitant opposition against
the former by the latter – explored thus far: we next discover that some important
representational realms involve 'self' and 'other' in productive and inclusive
processes of co-production.

## Inclusive dialogues and co-representations

Close attention to some of the many products and genres of representation generated
by what Stuart Hall terms (1997, 183–184) the 'cultural revolution' of the historical
'margins coming into representation' and 'recovering their own hidden histories'
reveals another category of signification: forms of co-representation, wherein
very differently positioned social actors – members of historically dominant and
subordinated groups respectively – cooperate to jointly capture and articulate the
memories, histories and experiences of those 'othered' and marginalized.

One such co-production and co-representation was a recent Austrian-Nigerian
film-project, which combined cultural and distinctly political ambitions in seeking
to address transnational audiences. Entitled *Hope & Nightmares*, the film is set
both in Austria and in Nigeria, it was initiated by young film-maker Fritz Aigner
from Graz, who met with Nigerians on a weekly basis to engage in 'lively debate
between and about cultures':

> Heavenson Osbourne, Nigerian asylum-seeker in Graz, is the film's main
> character ... 'Our own problems and experiences are in the script', say Okezie
> Agba Okeke and Ike-Benson Nkwocha, two of the six Nigerians in the team
> ... The main aim is to challenge prejudice: 'The film can show the Austrian
> audience that migration can have many reasons, and that it's very difficult', says
> Okeke, a long-standing asylum-seeker. As *Hopes & Nightmares* will also be
> shown in Nigeria, there is another opportunity. 'Another key aim is to challenge
> the false hopes many Africans attach to Europe ...', says Samson Ogiamien.
> (Schweiger 2009, my translation)

Inclusive dialogue across ethnic and structural divides thus here enabled powerful political messages to be conveyed to European and African audiences.

Similar initiatives and co-representations of migrants' life-worlds defined a series of cultural projects in the Styrian city of Feldbach in 2008. With twelve per cent of the local population – many of them of Kurdish origin – of foreign nationality, one of the projects involved migrants as city-guides, throwing light on their experiences of, and views on, the locality (Zierler 2008). Another project, which resulted in local exhibitions and a collection of essays and photographic and textual portraits (Krese et al. 2008), involved two sisters – writer Maruša and photographer Meta Krese – tracing some of Feldbach's migrants' trajectories 'backwards', to their families and places of birth in central Anatolia. The preface to the resulting collection, whose title translates as 'Being different without fear', is worth quoting at length:

> To listen to the voices of migrants … *about* whom mostly others talk and on whom they act, implies a transformation of their status – as objects and people turned into strangers – into subjects with the right to a language, a home and the right to tell their stories. Maruša and Meta Krese's work is all about deconstructing existing pictures of the stranger and about replacing them with the stories of real people. On their journey the two artists traced the transnational connections of migrants from Turkey. Over several weeks they visited families in Feldbach, which then resulted in contacts and visits to these families' relatives in Turkey … This is not about nationalist connotations of roots but – on the contrary – about routes. (Reithofer 2008, 8, my translation, italics in the original)

Inadvertently or otherwise, this framing of Maruša and Meta Krese's project draws on two central – and to the present discussion crucially significant – tenets of Stuart Hall's cultural theory: first, the representational empowerment that turns 'objects' of classification, depiction and exclusion into agents of their own self-representation and self-portrayal (albeit here in collaboration with 'others'); and second, an understanding of *all* identities (Hall 1996) as 'ongoing routes of becoming' shaped both by the institutional and discursive parameters within which they are lived and by individuals' own, context-specific investments in, detachment from, and negotiations of, their various ideological interpellations. Highly relevant to this discussion overall was the ethos of the overarching, earlier-mentioned series of cultural initiatives in Feldbach in 2008 and the concomitant opening of a migrants' advice-centre: one of the key organizers described this ethos as an 'anti-Orientalism' that deconstructs Western discourses of exclusion, acknowledges that 'the other' is part of 'us', and empowers migrants not only to take part in but to actively shape local cultural practices and representations (Aigner 2008b).

One of the Styrian organizations mentioned in chapter five, ISOP (or 'Innovative Social Projects'), played a vital role in coordinating both these social/cultural initiatives in 2008 and Maruša and Meta Krese's follow-on project. Once again, the sisters met with migrant families in Feldbach, recording their stories, photographically capturing their everyday lives, and 'making their otherwise hidden life-histories visible' (Reithofer 2010, 4). The resulting portraits, again photographic and textual, were further examples of *co-representations of and by* artists and some of those conventionally positioned as 'others', who jointly reveal complexities in place of simplistic narratives and depictions: different reasons and trajectories of migration; experiences of exclusion, everyday racism and de-qualification alongside examples of inter-ethnic friendship and 'bridging capital'; intergenerational differences and some tensions; enduring transnational connections and feelings of loss (Krese et al. 2010). The complexities and ambivalences captured by Maruša and Meta Krese's work in collaboration with their participants and artistic co-producers have been summarized as follows:

> Many of them came here for work, others for political reasons. They are confronted by others' prejudices every day, and they also hold prejudices of their own ... They have problems not only with Austrians, but also between themselves. Their opinions on politics, religion and tradition vary. And they are actually only united by one thing: the hope for a happy life. (Schaffer 2009, my translation)

Maruša and Meta Krese's portraits of – and encouraged self-representations by – Turkish migrants found one other outlet. An exhibition, again coordinated by ISOP, entitled 'We are here' (*Wir sind da*) displayed a series of migrants' portraits right at the heart of regional power: it was held between April and August 2010 in the inner courtyard of the building housing Styria's political representatives, where the pictures aimed to convey self-confidence and to challenge existing clichés (Motter 2010a). Framing the exhibition, a sign by Robert Reithofer from ISOP read as follows (my translation):

> 'We are here', we have long been part of Styrian society, this is what these women, men and youngsters of Turkish origin are articulating ... We are proud members of this society ... 'Being here' is also a question about new homes, which are also internally somewhat split. They always also contain memories of Turkish landscapes, shown here alongside the portraits. Making new homes underlines how necessary it is for us to work on a new understanding of social solidarity beyond nationalist boundaries.

Representations such as these provide powerful illustrations of what Homi Bhabha terms (1990b, 300) 'counter-narratives of the nation' that subvert essentialist identities. We next turn to a series of cultural representations that develop challenges against established boundaries and hegemonic definitions of belonging further.

## 'Reversing the gaze'

Stuart Hall has pointed out that the colonial relationship between the centre of power and the colonized 'margins' was significantly shaped by a one-way vision, a one-directional gaze that helped fix, define and exercise power over the subordinated:

> [T]he colonized other was constituted within the regimes of representation of …
> a metropolitan center. Those colonized persons were placed in their otherness,
> in their marginality, by the nature of the 'English eye'. The 'English eye' sees
> everything else but is not so good at recognizing that it is actually looking at
> something. It becomes coterminous with sight itself. (Hall 1997, 174)

What was a feature of (British) colonialism also defines other relationships of power and inequality in other contexts. The starting-point to the present discussion was that power manifests in symbolic representations. To this we now add that processes and products of cultural signification are not only inherently political but presuppose acts of looking. Moreover, the gaze of the powerful carries definitional weight, it can – in Hall's terminology – 'place' and thereby help to constitute 'the other', without necessarily being conscious of it. At the same time, however, the 'cultural revolution' Hall associates with the 'margins coming into representation' also, as we discover below, entails new, subaltern visions that partly reverse (Göttsche 2010) the gaze of power and cast critical glances in the direction of the historically dominant.

In the Austrian context an example of such counter-hegemonic visions is contained in a recent collection of essays (Niemann 2009) by Viennese residents of various 'migration backgrounds'. In addition to providing an overview of the diverse migratory histories that have shaped Vienna over the centuries – Czech, Serbian, Croatian, Slovenian, Bosnian, Macedonian, Hungarian, Jewish, Polish, Turkish, Chinese, American, African, Italian, German, and others – this 'intercultural anthology' contains what has been summarized as an 'aesthetic of diversity': its first- and second-generation migrant authors offer their perceptions of Vienna, they describe experiences of arriving in the city, feelings of 'alienation at home', linguistic barriers, multidimensional identities, and an enduring sense of longing for plurality and for another home now left behind (Menasse 2009, my translation). Employing different literary styles and genres, the collection offers insights into its contributors' complex life-histories, it thereby deconstructs stereotypes and cuts across rigid categories of belonging. Its defining themes include what one contributor describes as her 'changing identities', the 'fractures of exile', and a deep concern about 'the insurmountable divisiveness of the populists' language' (Rabinowich 2009, 58, my translation). Arguably most relevant to our discussions is another contribution that captures some of the unresolved ambivalences of contemporary multiculturalism, whilst arguing for much-needed structural changes and articulating a vision that also seems to incorporate elements of the community cohesion discourse mentioned in chapter six:

> The 'host-society' acts with ambivalence, and yet we're moving in a direction of growing urban diversity ... what's needed are long and thorough processes of reflection and debate about contemporary realities ... There must be more than an ethos of mere co-existence, of 'live and let live' ... After 40 years of immigration to Austria there are new generations who are not just 'guests' any more but citizens ... tolerance is not enough, respect for other cultures is required ... The art of politics is to provide educational resources and opportunities for social mobility for everyone ... [which requires] common aims and values that need to apply universally ... Values should no longer be associated with nationality and origin but need to relate to chances given to everyone. We need a modern society that defines difference as normality ... and enables voluntary cultural hybridization. (Öztoplu 2009, 111–113, my translation)

What we encounter here is a political vision for the future that, simultaneously, offers critical reflections on the present, calling for more openness both structurally and culturally.

A critical perspective on the dominant majority from another subaltern position also emerges from a short text by a school-child of Turkish origin published in both German and Turkish in a recent collection of essays:

> Austrians don't want to know the Turks living here, they don't want to see us as we are, but only through their stereotypes ... If they took the time to get to know us, I'm sure they would like us. And we would then surely be paid fair wages and there would be no hostility. I suggest we get to know one another better, only then will we understand each other. (Quoted in Bardakçi et al. 2009, 128, my translation)

Stereotypes often invite counter-stereotypes and especially in light of its author's age the metonymical tone of this assessment is understandable. At the same time, and crucially, behind its own stereotypical representation of the dominant other, this text captures painful memories, whether personally experienced or relayed by family and friends, profound and enduring structural inequalities and a timely appeal for more 'bridging capital'.

The difficulty of arriving at non-stereotypical self- and other portrayals, especially when the boundaries and groups represented are historically significant and politically charged, is captured – though perhaps inadvertently – by another recent collection of essays. A compilation of reflections by Germans in Austria (and Austrians who grew up in Germany before moving to Austria) that also includes a 'counter-depiction' by an Austrian author residing in Berlin, its title translates as 'We have arrived in order to stay' (*Wir sind gekommen, um zu bleiben*) and it describes various dimensions of what its editor terms the 'unique feeling of being German in Austria' (Steffen 2009, 10–11, my translation). Like all cultural representations these pictures of Austria by a small sample of some of her 120,000 current German residents need careful contextualization: first, in the historically complex identity negotiations by Austrians vis-à-vis Germans discussed in chapter one, which in the course of the twentieth century underwent successive paradigmatic shifts – from Austria's once dominant (pan-)Germanic self-understanding, to the post-war construction of her 'big German neighbour' as the Alpine Republic's main identity-bestowing 'other', to a more recent national self-definition less reliant upon and concerned with Germany as a point of reference and contrast (Lackner 2010d). Second, recent and large German migratory flows to, and experiences of, Austria are of course very different from those discussed above. Germans in Austria 'speak' and 'look', by and large, from structural positions of relative privilege, having migrated as EU-citizens, many as students, many others attracted by Austria's comparatively low unemployment-rates; considerably higher percentages of Germans in Austria are highly qualified and/or university graduates than their Austrian counterparts (Wurmdobler 2009, 17). Put differently, (these) German self/other representations of and in Austria also need to be read from their particular vantage points, their ideological and structural histories, and their respective positions of class and status. Within these contexts, the collection of German reflections on Austria in question is remarkable for several reasons. First, several contributions (e.g. Reiter 2009, Körtner 2009) return to long-established clichés of Austria and Austrians as, for example, hierarchically consensual rather than committed to political debate, status conscious, embedded in nepotistic networks, and as allegedly to this day less prepared to confront the Nazi past than Germans. Whilst, as emphasized in the introduction to this book, such depictions indeed capture significant phenomena and legacies of, for example, the histories of the Habsburg Empire and the counter-reformation, they cannot metonymically stand in for social realities that are now considerably more multi-dimensional, internally contested and contradictory. It may also be objected that accounts such as the following simplify – and selectively interpret realities that are more complex on both sides of the Austrian-German border – in the service of a binary identity construction of its own:

> [I]f one has spent most of one's youth debating rather than learning, one has internalized democratic values and critical consciousness to such an extent that the Austrian engagement with the past makes one want to leave again straight away. (Steffen 2009, 10, my translation)

Second, this collection returns, time and again (e.g. Fenderl 2009), to what outsiders often perceive as a paradox: the importance attached by many Austrians to country-specific variations within a (largely) shared language as boundary markers between Austria and Germany.[3] Third, some of the contributors to this volume depict an ambivalence in their relationship to Austria and Germany that is highly relevant to this discussion:

> After many years in Vienna … I would probably also in Berlin be inhabiting what … Homi Bhabha terms the 'third space', a cultural liminality; in a pitiful 'neither here nor there' but also in an enviable and enriching 'both here and there'. (Hartnack 2009, 143, my translation)

Returning to the historically subordinated and oppressed, there are also two other snapshots – of particular subaltern histories 'coming into representation' and of the hegemonic gaze being temporarily reversed – to be mentioned here. The first was a powerful series of exhibitions in 2006, part of Vienna's commemoration of Mozart's 250th anniversary, entitled 'Hidden Histories' (*Verborgene Geschichte/n: Remapping Mozart*). Its four 'configurations' contained a variety of formats and genres of representation, they were co-ordinated by an impressive list of curators including the earlier-mentioned Araba Evelyn Johnston-Arthur, and its unifying rationale was to uncover and trace the voices of the historically silenced and to thereby present their 'counter-histories'. Taking a longue durée perspective, the exhibits critically examined a variety of historical contexts and struggles, operating on various geographical scales, stretching from Mozart's life-time to the here and now, from racist oppression to feminist struggles against patriarchy, from the history of slavery and Western Orientalism to the fate of asylum-seekers in contemporary Europe. The exhibitions' main focal point, however, was Austria or, more accurately, the various and successive systems of profound structural inequalities that have shaped Central Europe more generally since the eighteenth century. Put differently, the critical historiography offered by 'Hidden Histories' documented the fate and suffering of the many 'others' constructed, oppressed and marginalized by a multitude of mechanisms in the course of Western history since the enlightenment. Through previously overlooked historical documents and a variety of artistic genres the exhibits captured the life-histories of, for example, an eighteenth century African servant in Vienna, the workings of an organization by Black women founded in Vienna in 2004, the instrumentalism that defines contemporary European preoccupations with migrants' 'economic utility', instances of police violence against Africans, or the history of anti-Semitism and its effects on one particular family from the late eighteenth century to the Holocaust and beyond. The following account of an installation on the African diaspora in Austria also contains the wider theoretical framework that gave coherence to 'Hidden Histories' wide-ranging examinations of such diverse contexts:

---

3   This echoes Wodak et al.'s findings (1999, 193) that their Austrian research participants stressed 'Austrian German … in particular contexts as an important criterion of difference between Austria and Germany'.

> An installation on emancipatory perspectives on the past and present of the
> African diaspora in Austria ... [it] is a fragmentary search for traces of the
> hitherto invisible histories of life and survival of an African diaspora at the
> time of Mozart ... [It is also based on] bell hook's notion of 'talking back' ...
> [to] make these histories visible and to thematize realities that have thus far
> been ignored ... thereby confronting established distortions ... This is part of
> a process of writing Black Austrian counter-histories. (Johnston-Arthur and
> Sternfeld 2006, my translation)

The 'Hidden Histories' projects clearly transcended the particularities of the
African diaspora in Austria and offered a much wider space for the exploration of
multiple 'subjugated knowledges' (Foucault 1980). In doing so, they powerfully
articulated several 'subaltern histories' that throw what Duncan Bell describes
(2003, 66) as an inherently contested and ideologically diverse 'mythscape' into
sharp relief. This, in turn, testifies to the contestability of hegemonic definitions of
national 'belonging'.

Another example of the historically 'othered' 'looking' and 'talking back'
was provided by a more recent cultural project in July 2010 involving fourteen
international artists of different 'migration backgrounds' spending fourteen days
in various (rural) localities in the north of Styria, reversing the usual gaze of the
dominant onto 'the stranger', replacing it with their own glimpses from their
vantage-points as outsiders and, simultaneously, attempting to build new 'bridges'
(Motter 2010b). In addition to local presentations of their resulting reflections the
artists also published their thoughts and impressions on an internet blog (www.
fremdsehen.at). Their diverse responses to their rural immersions included
ethnographic listings of words unknown to people not familiar with the local
dialect, confrontations with painful memories and feelings of loss, reflections
on cross-cultural miscues, on a conversation with a local FPÖ politician, and
on moments and encounters of 'conviviality' (Regionale10, 2010). There were
also more critical reflections, as the following instance of everyday ethnocentric
stereotyping encountered earlier in Vienna and the artist's resistance against it:

| | |
|---|---|
| Driving instructor: | You drive well, you could become a taxi-driver ... |
| My thoughts: | Why is it so widely assumed that foreigners want to drive taxis? Probably because there are many foreign taxi-drivers in Vienna. Don't people wonder why the percentage of highly educated taxi-drivers is so large? ... |
| Driving instructor: | Careful, there are railways in Europe ... |
| My thoughts: | ... Is he trying to say that Europe is the only industrialized continent? After 30 minutes I got out of the car, angrily ... This was too much for a day, I've since changed driving instructors. (Bobadilla 2010, my translation) |

## Other European snapshots: British Asian voices and African-German literature

As emphasized throughout this chapter, this discussion has been inevitably selective, choosing from a very wide range of (continually expanding) realms of signification and presenting a mere selection of snapshots that condense important and recurring features of the cultural politics of self-/other representation. Furthermore, it could certainly be argued that a national focus and a discussion cutting across a variety of artistic genres and media of expression are too wide: indeed, more locally-focused research (e.g. Parker and Karner forthcoming) reveals multi-dimensional and complex representational struggles and spheres – including, amongst others, poetry, the internet, photography and street art – in the much more narrowly delineated localities of particular cities or even neighbourhoods. This having been said, the national focus guiding the present discussion of course fits my analytical concerns in this book overall and, along with the diversity of means and modes of self-/other representations examined above, it is best-suited to an illustration and examination of Austria's and other European countries' internally contested 'national mythscapes', in the ongoing construction and negotiation of which numerous groups participate and have a stake. With this is mind I now turn – once again – to other European contexts to examine recent research highly relevant to the above analysis. And, once again stating the obvious, the remainder of this discussion is also inevitably and highly selective. The politics of cultural representation constitute a vast and growing terrain across and far beyond Europe, within nation-states and, as just mentioned, even within particular localities. However, the following two snapshots, contained in recent analysis of relevant forms of cultural production in the UK and Germany respectively, are highly germane to this chapter for two reasons. First, they reflect representational forms and dynamics that resonate strongly with key insights emerging from my analysis of Austrian materials. Second, they provide further insights into the diasporic connections and their cultural manifestations that are part and parcel of European societies.

The first set of insights is provided by Yasmin Hussain's analysis (2005) of some of the best-known works of British Asian women's writing and film-making, including Monica Ali's controversial novel *Brick Lane*, Meena Syal's earlier *Anita and Me*, and Gurinder Chadha's influential films *Bhaji on the Beach* and *Bend it like Beckham*. Importantly, Hussain (2005, 3, 45) provides an epistemological rationale for treating cultural texts – whether fiction, cinema or poetry – as 'entirely relevant to the sociology of culture': not as straightforward 'mirrors' of the social world but as critical reflections and perspectives on them, as 'in a real sense eyewitness accounts … not literal autobiographies, but representations of … the lived experience and preoccupations of each author which she recogni[zes] as relevant to lives other than her own'. An appreciation of the political and cultural significance of such works of course requires contextualization – in the post-war history of successive phases of South Asian migration to and settlement in the UK, as well as in the internal diversities (i.e. national, regional, linguistic, religious, devotional, in terms of caste hierarchies and varied migratory trajectories) that make, Hussain reminds us, 'British South Asian' an 'umbrella term' containing much heterogeneity. To this one must add the continuing and in some cases widening socio-economic gaps between different segments of the British Asian communities, reflected in continuing social marginalization suffered by some and considerable upward social mobility experienced by others (Modood et al. 1997). It is within these historical and structural contexts, Hussain shows, that the novels and films listed above critically reflect upon, condense and illuminate key dimensions of British South Asian lives since the 1960s: experiences of everyday racism, inter-generational changes and tensions, and also complex individual negotiations of the multiple expectations and power relations British Asian women have found themselves in; moreover, 'stereotypical images and ethnocentric perceptions' of South Asian women on part of the 'majority culture' (Hussain 2005, 1) are challenged by more nuanced depictions of their women protagonists' complex roles, their struggles, agency and resilience. This also includes engagements with the significance of cultural syncretism, hybridity and the ability to navigate different cultural registers and 'codes' in the everyday lives of (especially second- and third generation) British Asian women. Overall, Hussain's analyses offer two insights of particular significance to this chapter. First, she shows that creative works by British South Asian women reflect 'differences and conflicts … not only between but also within cultural groups' and that this 'plurality of identities … demolish[es] … monolithic stereotypes of South Asian womanhood and of South Asian communities in general' (Hussain 2005, 10). In addition to reflecting (on) individual agency and negotiations of multiple hierarchies and structures of power, British Asian cultural production testifies to the fact that the 'cultural majority' has also been transformed by the presence of, and encounters with, 'the other'. This is perhaps most clearly demonstrated by what Hussain terms (2005, 16) the 'desification' of British cinema, its enrichment by the introduction of South Asian 'themes, music and language' that has effected a broadening and re-definition of British identities:

> Films … by British South Asian women … [now constitute] a distinctive genre … that manages to be both authentic and popular. The experience of life in the diaspora is central to Gurinder Chadha's films … The protagonists, their motivations, the themes, the use of music, and the very language of the dialogue mark this cinema as characteristically South Asian and British … [H]er films take various icons … of 'White Britain', for instance football, David Beckham and the seaside holiday, and redefine them as … open to many cultural claims, so that David Beckham can be as inspirational to a South Asian girl … Chadha's cinema has redefined what it means to be British, it has opened up the cultural space of Britishness to alternative identifications. (Hussain 2005, 132)

The second set of conceptually and empirically relevant insights emerges from Dirk Göttsche's analysis (2010) of African diasporic writing in German(y) since the 1980s. Göttsche traces an important shift in this growing literary genre that consists of often autobiographical accounts of their authors' memories of Africa and their subsequent, frequently very difficult or traumatizing experiences in Germany: this shift entailed a move away from earlier works that, combining critique of racism with 'African self-assertion', tended to 'operate with clear-cut oppositions between Europe and Africa, often leaving the African migrant torn between two irreconcilable worlds' towards a more distinctly post-colonial literature reflecting Africans' subsequent identity re-negotiations and more or less successfully claiming a space in German society (Göttsche 2010, 57–58). This is reflected in a series of novels and autobiographies by African migrants published since the 1990s, which are defined by 'cross-cultural self-assertion' and their authors' 'embracing [of] the postcolonial condition as a dynamic "Third Space"'. As Göttsche goes on to show (2010, 59), however, such African diasporic writing in German does not offer an uncritical celebration of 'happy hybridity' but testifies to their authors' ongoing struggles and resilience. Moreover, this literary genre continues to be eminently political – committed to 'African causes' such as the fights against female genital mutilation and the use of child soldiers, whilst also critically engaging with bureaucratic hurdles and exclusions, xenophobic prejudice and post-unification racism encountered in Germany. As significantly, African-German literature now reflects 'richness and diversification of the African voice', thus 'undercutting the colonial binary "Africa" vs. "Europe", which continues to inform stereotypical German perceptions of Africa' (Göttsche 2010, 70, 61). Key themes of my earlier discussion – the political significance of 'the other's' self-assertion and 'looking back' in the cultural realms of an internally/ethnically diverse nation – resonate in Göttsche's summary (2010, 55–56):

> Contributing to the transcultural diversification of contemporary German literature, African migrants' writing can … be read both as African literature in German and as German literature by writers with an African background. It illustrates how postcolonial literatures and diasporic writing undercut the traditional notion of national literatures, operating at the 'interstices' … of two or more cultures. Reversing the traditional German gaze at the African Other … African migrants' writing reflects and promotes significant changes in German society and culture itself. Since the late 1990s, much of the autobiographical writing in this tradition combines … cross-cultural self-assertion in the face of often traumatic experience with an explicit agenda in cultural politics, raising the African voice in both German and transnational debates.

Writing about specific genres of cultural production in Britain and Germany respectively, Hussain and Göttsche add to my analysis of Austrian materials and provide further empirical corroboration of key observations Avtar Brah (1996) has made of diasporas: first, representational genres of the kinds discussed here can help throw the 'intersecting', 'multi-axial' power structures (e.g. gender, ethnicity, nationality, religion, class) shaping diasporas into sharp relief. Second, cultural representations are powerful testimony to the fact that 'diaspora spaces' (Brah 1996, 209) jointly 'inhabited' by migrants *and* those positioned as 'indigenous' have indeed transformed the lives of both the dominant 'self' and subaltern 'others'. The latter are not only 'here' and part of 'us', but they have also evidently found 'their' voice, whether or not local nationalists like or even acknowledge it.

## Concluding remarks

Stuart Hall argues (1997, 184) that the cultural revolution of 'the margins ... com[ing] into representation' involves, by necessity, a recovery of 'their own hidden histories' and a 're-tell[ing of] their stor[ies] from the bottom up'; this applies, Hall shows, to anti-colonial struggles as much as to feminism or the civil rights movement, all of which involved a rediscovery of 'a past that previously had no language'. In this chapter I have traced the recovery of some such previously hidden and silenced histories in select cultural representations by various subaltern groups in Austria and other parts of Europe. Large parts of this discussion thus focused on cultural articulations of what Krzyżanowski and Wodak term (2009, 4) the 'insider perspective' by 'the marginalized and vulnerable'. However, this analysis has also shown that broader contextualization is needed, particularly in the dominant histories and representational 'regimes', against which subaltern voices react. Moreover, and in keeping with the crux of previous analyses in this book, there is evidence of plurality, discursive contestation and ambivalence in both spheres of signification – within the realms of *representations of* the other and in *representations by* 'the othered'. Finally, the politics of cultural representation also implicate acts of 'looking' and of 'reversing' the dominant gaze, as well as emancipatory co-representations, in which 'self' and 'other' co-operate in forms of dialogue and jointly tell 'the others'' histories 'from the bottom up'. Seen in its wider context, this chapter has made an argument crucial to this book in its entirety: the sphere of cultural representations powerfully testifies to the internal heterogeneity and ideological contestability of (contemporary) nations.

# Conclusion

On 22 September 2010 *The New York Times* offered a series of observations, concerning what it described as a rising tide of European 'right-wing sentiment', worth quoting at length:

> As anti-immigrant sentiment continues to sweep across Europe, generating a right-wing populist wave from the shores of the Mediterranean to the chilly reaches of Scandinavia, there is growing concern that such politics could take root [in Germany] too, in the fertile ground of financial uncertainty, rising anti-Muslim sentiment and a widening political vacuum left by the misfortunes of the once mighty Christian Democratic Union. While the Swedes this week elected an anti-immigrant party to Parliament for the first time, and the French are busy repatriating Roma, Germans continue to debate a best-selling book blaming Muslim immigrants for 'dumbing down society' and have heard a prominent conservative ally of the chancellor … suggest that Poland helped to instigate World War II. 'Uncertainty is widespread over German society,' said Gero Neugebauer, a political scientist at the Free University of Berlin. (Slackman 2010)

This account is enormously pertinent to the analyses contained in the present book. First, it corroborates, if further confirmation is needed, that the kinds of identity politics and negotiations examined above, and particularly right-wing populism as a key force, are indeed pan-European phenomena and, one may add, similarly prominent far beyond the current boundaries of the European Union. Second, we are reminded of some of the manifestations of narrow and exclusivist discourses of belonging, as encountered, for instance, in growing Islamophobic sentiments and the earlier-mentioned controversy triggered by Thilo Sarrazin or in shifts to the right in parts of Europe considered bastions of inclusivism until not long ago. Third, the three main dimensions to the national identity negotiations examined in this book – globalization (and the insecurities generated by it), the past (and 'memory politics'), and 'the other' – all re-appear in Slackman's account. Fourth, *The New York Times* contextualizes right-wing populism in wider feelings of insecurity and disenchantment with established political parties, thereby echoing important and recurring themes emerging from the above analyses. Less than a month later German Chancellor Angela Merkel declared that the 'old model of mere multi-cultural co-existence has absolutely failed' (*Zeit im Bild* 16 October 2010, my translation), thus articulating what is now Europe's seemingly hegemonic response to 'the other': a discourse of integrationism that, whilst assuming different forms, is premised on a sense of crisis widely associated with immigration and ethnic/religious pluralism.

This book has offered a series of qualitative analyses of a wide range of publicly circulating data to capture some of the interpretative frames, perceptions, sentiments, experiences and claims that underpin both the neo-nationalist, populist right-wing politics summarized above and the inclusive alternatives formulated to contest them. In the process we have uncovered a wide spectrum of co-existing and competing answers to some of the key preoccupations of contemporary (European) politics: questions as to how far nations – as well as the supra-national 'network state' of the EU – stretches or ought to stretch, as to who is or is not to be included (and on whose terms), and as to how porous national boundaries are permitted to be. The wider context to these questions includes, as we have seen, some of the changes and perceived dislocations brought about by, or widely associated with, economic globalization. Moreover, the varied responses to these issues of course do not appear out of a historical vacuum but are informed by historical memories that are themselves subject to ideological contestation in what Bell (2003) describes as a heterogeneous 'national mythscape'.

In terms of its empirical foci, this book has attempted to not only illuminate contemporary Austria as its central case study but to also relate it to, and contextualize it within, other European examples and settings throughout. Such a broad approach is by definition ambitious, demanding appreciation of Austrian particularities – such as comparatively restrictive legislation pertaining to naturalization or the country's nationalists' unclear relationship to Austria's darkest historical chapter (see Gärtner 2009, 58–59) – alongside an extrapolation of themes, sentiments and dynamics encountered across Europe. The preceding chapters have uncovered such pan-European common ground in a range of areas: competing discursive frameworks – and their respective histories – that go into the continuing negotiation of national identities; perceived crises affecting established symbols and narratives of national identity as well as different reactions to such crises; the politics of everyday argumentation that attempts to make sense of a range of current affairs by selectively (mis-)using various historical points of reference; a pre-occupation and struggles with the question as to how far (global) markets and 'flows' stretch, or should stretch, and what, if anything, ought to be protected from their reach and 'logic'; civil societies, in which competing definitions of rights clash – a nation-centred 'citizens-entitlements-discourse' with a universalist human rights ethos respectively; everyday experiences of living with pluralism that are more complex and multi-dimensional than any of the publicly available discursive blueprints concerning the relationship between 'self' and 'other' acknowledge; and, finally, the importance of cultural representations of and by 'the other' to the ongoing negotiation of national identities and the articulation of experiences of inequality and exclusion.

National identity negotiations have thus been shown to relate very closely to a variety of phenomena and questions that define the early twenty-first century, particularly the relationship between the local and the global, the ethics of living with '(super-)diversity', and the challenges of confronting persisting as well as 'multi-axial' inequalities. Put another way, national identities are major cognitive, discursive and experiential categories of our era, despite or arguably because of its globalizing tendencies. The politics and negotiations of national belonging and exclusion manifest not only in debates about immigration and the future of multiculturalism, but in the rights, responsibilities and entitlements enshrined in citizenship legislation and human rights discourses respectively, in discussions surrounding the local or regional effects of global markets and the ever more encompassing forces of commodification, as well as in the realms of civil society activity and cultural production. In documenting competing responses to these diverse issues, I have concentrated on widely circulating, public discourses. One of the 'calls for further research' emanating from this book would be a possible return to what Wodak et al. (1999) describe as 'semi-public' and 'semi-private' understandings, to be recorded through focus-groups and interviews, in which so-called 'ordinary social actors' appropriate or variously respond to public discourse. It can indeed be hoped that the themes and findings contained in this book will help trigger future research on such 'semi-public' and 'semi-private' responses in Austria and other parts of Europe (and beyond).

Right-wing populism has been described in the Austrian context as a 'politics of emotions' (Haslinger 1995) or, more recently by *Profil* columnist Sven Gächter (2010, my translation), as the 'production and distribution of agitation' – descriptions that also capture the wider European picture contained in the above-quoted article in *The New York Times*. The present book has applied a three-fold strategy to illuminate such right-wing sentiments, resulting exclusions as well as inclusive counter-discourses further: first, and most centrally, thorough contextualization; second, in order to record relevant public experiences and debates in their many facets and dimensions, I have cast my sociological eye in many directions and documented national identity negotiations across a variety of political, social and cultural realms; third, the analyses contained here have drawn upon a range of relevant theoretical frameworks. Put differently, an understanding of contemporary European societies, in which right-wing populism plays a – though, as we have seen, not the only – prominent role, requires engagement with the diversity of European histories and memories and with politics that are simultaneously local, regional, national, pan-European and global. Moreover, an accurate portrayal of the forces shaping contemporary Europe also demands that social and political fields are captured in their multi-dimensionality and ideological diversity. And as the various theoretical leads informing the preceding chapters have aimed to demonstrate, we need to pose wide-ranging conceptual questions about ongoing discursive identity negotiations; about the (cultural) effects of perceived crises; about everyday (memory-) politics and the use of historical analogies; about the relationship between economics, politics and competing 'moral orders'; about the workings of civil societies and the public sphere; about the relationship – and potential discrepancies – between ideological, interpretative positions and everyday life; and about the 'subaltern' in the sphere of cultural production.

So what next? The local effects of globalizing pressures, transnational 'flows' and transformations are as far-reaching and real as the challenges of living with diversity and diverse inequalities. As we have seen, there is no shortage of simplistic 'answers' and alleged 'solutions' on offer, circulated from different points on the ideological spectrum. The analyses contained in this book, by contrast, do not translate into yet another simple blue-print or set of purported 'policy recommendations'. If anything, we have seen that we need to look beyond deceptively simple binaries and distorting caricatures, whoever articulates them, to capture lived realities that are often considerably more nuanced and complex. That having been said, it is of course self-evident that some positions and political frameworks are far more conducive than others to working towards a more just, more inclusive, more peaceful and more humane future. Also, and this is a suggestion that does flow rather easily from the earlier analyses, such hopes for the future are likely to require – in Austria, across Europe and beyond – more 'bridging capital', more willingness to speak across boundaries and to interrogate those boundaries, coupled with the realization that such self-other interactions and dialogues involve people speaking and acting from very different structural positions.

A recurring theme in this book has been that of ambivalence. Ambivalence and hence contradictions have been revealed in place of monolithic depictions of entire groups, localities, histories or national contexts, thus challenging portrayals that unhelpfully take one very real and important facet as a metonym for a much larger, multi-faceted entity. At other times, ambivalence has turned out to also feature on the individual level – in particular social actors' identity negotiations and interpellations, thus revealing significant (and, one may add, potentially empowering) divergences between people's life-worlds and the artificial ideological orderliness various discourses seek to impose on them. Might it be that we need to do more to acknowledge and celebrate such divergences, if only to draw attention to the ubiquity of boundary-crossings and convivial hybridity? In other contexts it is likely to be objected, of course, that revealing or insisting upon ambivalence stands in the way of taking a clear position or may even generate a nihilistic relativism at a time when urgent and principled social action are needed. There is, however, another reading of and response to ambivalence: as an invitation to collective and individual self-reflection, and as perhaps conducive to the kind of humility and willingness to listen to all 'others', in all their complexity, that the urgency and enormity of the challenges facing all of us demand.

I still wake up to the same song every morning. After all, questions about rapid and far-reaching social change, about 'marketization' and commodification, about memory, about our shared humanity and the various boundaries we draw amongst and between ourselves seem timelier than ever.

# References

Abts, K. et al. (2009), 'Sources of Euroscepticism', *World Political Science Review* 5:1(article 3), http://www.bepress.com/wpsr/vol5/iss1/art3/.

Adunka, E. (2002), 'Antisemitismus in der Zweiten Republik', in H. Wassermann (ed.), *Antisemitismus in Österreich nach 1945* (Innsbruck: Studienverlag).

Aftenberger, I. (2007), *Die neue Rechte und der Neorassismus* (Graz: Leykam).

Aigner, F. (2008a), 'Dialoge im Sprachrohr', *Megaphon* 156, p. 11.

―――― (2008b), 'Regionale Chancen', *Megaphon* 153, p. 29.

―――― (2009a), 'Brasilianisches Beben', *Megaphon* 167, p. 15.

―――― (2009b), 'Eine Frage der Einstellung', *Megaphon* 170. p. 17.

Alber, M. (2009), 'Ein neues Bild von Ruanda', *Megaphon* 167, p. 26.

Alexander, R. (2008), 'So österreichisch war Österreich noch nie', *Welt am Sonntag* 3 August, p. 8.

Allen, C. (2009), 'Das erste Jahrzehnt der Islamophobie', in J. Bunzl and F. Hafez (eds.), *Islamophobie in Österreich* (Innsbruck: Studienverlag).

Amesberger, H. and Halbmayr, B. (2002), 'Frauen und Rechtsextreme Parteien' in W. Eismann (ed.), *Rechtspopulismus* (Vienna: Czernin).

Anderson, B. (1983), *Imagined Communities* (London: Verso).

Apfl, S. (2009), 'Die Islamlehrer', *Falter* 5, pp. 10–12.

―――― (2010a), 'Die Islam-Macher', *Falter* 25, pp. 18–19.

―――― (2010b), '"Ich habe abgeschworen"', *Falter* 9, pp. 9–11.

―――― (2010c), 'Rüsünkrünz für HüCü', *Falter* 12, p. 13.

―――― (2010d), 'Eine Elterninitiative engagiert sich für humanitäres Bleiberecht', *Falter* 12, p. 18.

Apfl, S. and Bernold, M. (2009), 'Kauf das!', *Falter* 43, pp. 10–12.

Apfl, S. and Klenk, F. (2009), 'Von Opfern und Tätern', *Falter* 33, p. 12.

Apfl, S. and Tóth, B. (2010), 'Der Kampf ums Kreuzerl', *Falter* 37, pp. 11–12.

Appadurai, A. (1990), 'Disjuncture and Difference in the Global Cultural Economy', in M. Featherstone (ed.), *Global Culture* (London: Sage).

Augoustinos, M. (1998), 'Social Representations and Ideology', in U. Flick (ed.), *The Psychology of the Social* (Cambridge: Cambridge University Press).

Auinger, H. (2000), *Haider – Nachrede auf einen bürgerlichen Politiker* (Vienna: Promedia).

Back, L. (2007), *The Art of Listening* (Oxford/New York: Berg).

Bacher, H. et al. (2008), *Ältere Migrantinnen in Graz berichten aus ihrem Leben* (Graz: SeniorInnenbüro).

Baier, W. (2009), 'Tiroler Parolen gegen Hemmschwellen', *Der Standard* 10 August, p. 19.

Ballard, R. (ed.) (1994), *Desh Pardesh* (London: Hurst).

Bandion, V. (2010), 'Eine verrückte Idee wird Realität', *Falter* 32, p. 18.

Bandion, V. and Bernold, M. (2010), 'Kritzeln, zündeln, flüchten', *Falter* 28, p. 13.

Bardakçi, S. et al. (eds.) (2009), *Dazugehören oder nicht?* (Innsbruck: Studienverlag).

Barth, J. (2007), 'Die Abschiebung des Tigers', *Profil* 1, pp. 28–29.

Bauman, Z. (1990), 'Modernity and Ambivalence', in M. Featherstone (ed.), *Global Culture* (London: Sage).

——— (1992), *Intimations of Postmodernity* (London: Routledge).

——— (1993), *Postmodern Ethics* (Oxford: Blackwell).

——— (1998), *Globalization* (Cambridge: Polity).

——— (1999 [1973]), *Culture as Praxis* (London: Sage).

——— (2000), *Liquid Modernity* (Cambridge: Polity).

Baumann, G. (1999), *The Multicultural Riddle* (London: Routledge).

——— (2004) 'Grammars of identity/alterity: A structural approach', in G. Baumann and A. Gingrich (eds.), *Grammars of Identity* (Oxford: Berghahn).

Baumann, G. and Gingrich, A. (eds.) (2004), *Grammars of Identity* (Oxford: Berghahn).

Bayer, K. (2010a), 'Die Brandstifter, sie schreien jetzt Feuer', *Falter* 19, pp. 6–7.

——— (2010b), 'Der Ausverkauf Europas', *Falter* 18, pp. 18–19.

BBC News (19 January 2009a), 'Standards fears over pork imports', http://newsvote.bbc.co.uk/mpappspagetools/print/news.bbc.co.uk/1/hi/uk/7825519.stm?a …, accessed 19 January 2009.

——— (19 January 2009b), 'Protest over power station jobs', http://newsvote.bbc.co.uk/mpapps/pagetools/print/news.bbc.co.uk/1/hi/england/nottingha …, accessed 19 January 2009.

Beattie, A. (2006), 'The victims of totalitarianism and the centrality of the Nazi genocide', in B. Niven (ed.), *Germans as Victims* (Basingstoke: Palgrave Macmillan).

Beck, U. (1992), *Risk Society* (London: Sage).

——— (2000), *What is Globalization?* (Cambridge: Polity).

Bell, D. (1973), *The Coming of Post-Industrial Society* (New York: Basic Books).

Bell, D. S. A. (2003), 'Mythscapes: Memory, mythology, and national identity', *British Journal of Sociology* 54:1, 63–81.

Berangy, N. (2009), 'Die, die trotzdem feiern', *Die Presse* 23 December, p. 11.

Berger, S. (2006), 'On taboos, traumas and other myths', in B. Niven (ed.), *Germans as Victims* (Basingstoke: Palgrave Macmillan).

Berger, J. (2009), 'Bleiberecht kontra Kinderrechte', *Der Standard* 9 April, p. 8.

Bering, D. (2002), 'Gutachten über den antisemitischen Charakter einer namenpolemischen Passage aus der Rede Jörg Haiders vom 28. Februar 2001', in A. Pelinka and R. Wodak (eds.), *"Dreck am Stecken"* (Vienna: Czernin).

Bernhard, T. (1988), *Heldenplatz* (Frankfurt: Suhrkamp).

Bet-El, I. R. (2002), 'Unimagined communities: The power of memory and the conflict in the former Yugoslavia', in J-W Müller (ed.), *Memory & Power in Post-War Europe* (Cambridge: Cambridge University Press).

Biffl, G. (2007), 'Erwerbstätigkeit und Arbeitslosigkeit', in H. Fassmann (ed.), *2. Österreichischer Migrations- und Integrationsbericht, 2001–2006* (Klagenfurt: Drave).

Billig, M. (1992), *Talking of the Royal Family* (London/New York: Routledge).

——— (1995a), *Banal Nationalism* (London: Sage).

——— (1995b), 'Socio-psychological aspects of nationalism', in K. v. Benda-Beckman and M. Verkuyten (eds.), *Nationalism, Ethnicity and Cultural Identity in Europe*, Utrecht: European Research Centre on Migration and Ethnic Relations.

Bischof, G. (1993), 'Die Instrumentalisierung der Moskauer Erklärung nach dem Zweiten Weltkrieg', *Zeitgeschichte* 20:11, 345–366.

Bhabha, H. (1990a), 'Introduction', in H. Bhabha (ed.), *Nation and Narration* (London/New York: Routledge).

——— (1990b), 'DissemiNation', in H. Bhabha (ed.), *Nation and Narration,* (London/New York: Routledge).

Bieler, A. (2000), *Globalisation and Enlargement of the European Union* (London: Routledge).

Black, I. and Connolly, K. (2000), 'Europe in turmoil over far right pact in Austria', *The Guardian* 3 February, p. 1.

Bloch, A. (2002), *The Migration and Settlement of Refugees in Britain* (New York: Palgrave).

Bloch, M. and Parry, J. (1989), 'Introduction', in J. Parry and M. Bloch (eds.), *Money and the Morality of Exchange* (Cambridge: Cambridge University Press).

Bobadilla, C. (2010), 'Freitagvormittag: Fahrstunde in Wien', *Megaphon* 178, p. 17.

Bott, E. (2004), 'Working a working-class utopia: Marking young Britons in Tenerife on the new map of European migration', *Journal of Contemporary European Studies* 12:1, 57–70.

Botz, G. and Sprengnagel, G. (1994), *Kontroversen um Österreichs Zeitgeschichte* (Frankfurt/New York: Campus).

Bourdieu, P. (1977), *Outline of a Theory of Practice* (Cambridge: Cambridge University Press).

Bourdieu, P. et al. (1999), *The Weight of the World* (Cambridge: Polity).

Boyes, R. (2008), 'Austria: "We have to ask what's going wrong?', *The Times* 29 April, http://www.timesonline.co.uk/tol/news/world/europe/article3835616.ece? print=yes&r…, accessed 30 April 2008.

Brah, A. (1996), *Cartographies of Diaspora* (London/New York: Routledge).

Braun, S. E. (2010), 'Sie fühlen sich unsicher', *Falter Heureka* 1, p. 9.

Brodnig, I. (2008), 'Patriotismus', *Falter* 24, p. 71.

——— (2010), 'Eine Schule feiert', *Falter* 24, p. 19.

Brodnig, I. and Gantner, M. (2009), 'Interview: "Ich habe es satt"', *Falter* 45, pp. 10–13.

Brook-Shepherd, G. (1997), *The Austrians* (London: HarperCollins).

Brubaker, R. (2001), 'The return of assimilation? Changing perspectives on immigration and its sequels in France, Germany, and the United States', *Ethnic and Racial Studies* 24:4, 531–548.

Bruckmüller, E. (1992), 'Das Österreichbewußtsein', in W. Mantl (ed.), *Politik in Österreich* (Vienna: Böhlau).

——— (1996 [1984]), *Nation Österreich* (Vienna: Böhlau).

Brugner, P. (2009), 'Fünfzig Jahre am Rande der Stadt', *Jungle World* 28.

Brühl, U. (2009), 'Sprachlos in Österreich', *Kurier* 10 August, p. 10.

Budin, C. (2003), 'Gen-Essen kommt auf den Teller', *Kronen Zeitung* 3 September, p. 9.

——— (2008), 'Neuer Protest gegen EU-Diktat', *Kronen Zeitung* 26 January, p. 23.

Bukey, E. B. (2000), *Hitler's Austria* (Chapel Hill: The University of North Carolina Press).

Bundesministerium für Inneres (2008), *Gemeinsam kommen wir zusammen* (Vienna: Bundesministerium für Inneres).

Bunzl, J. (2002), 'Who the hell is Jörg Haider', in R. Wodak and A. Pelinka (eds.), *The Haider Phenomenon in Austria* (New Brunswick: Transaction).

Bunzl, J. and Hafez, F. (2009), 'Ein interdisziplinärer Sammelband zum stereotypen Umgang mit dem Islam/den MuslimInnen in Österreich', in J. Bunzl and F. Hafez (eds.), *Islamophobie in Österreich* (Innsbruck: Studienverlag).

Bürgerliste Martin (2006), 'Perspective 2030', http://www.weisse.at/fieleadmin/user_upload/pdf/DKG-Grundsätze.pdf, accessed 8 September 2006.

Burke, J. (2008), 'Haider, Austria's notorious far-right politician, is killed in road crash', *The Observer* 12 October, p. 31.

Busek, E. (2001), 'Abstammung allein kann es nicht sein', in B. Coudenhove-Calergi (ed.), *Meine Wurzeln sind anderswo* (Vienna: Czernin).

——— (2008), *Eine Seele für Europa* (Vienna: Kremayr & Scheriau).

BZÖ (2006a), 'Positionen für ein modernes, soziales, leistungsfähiges und sicheres Österreich', http://www.bzoe.at, accessed 8 September 2006.

——— (2006b), 'Bündnispositionen', http://www.bzoe.at, accessed 8 September 2006.

Calhoun, C (1992), 'Introduction: Habermas and the public sphere', in C. Calhoun (ed.), *Habermas and the Public Sphere* (Cambridge, Massachusetts: MIT Press).

Camus, J-Y. (2002), 'Die radikale Rechte in Westeuropa', in W. Eismann (ed.), *Rechtspopulismus* (Vienna: Czernin).

Cantle, T. (2008), *Community Cohesion* (Basingstoke: Palgrave Macmillan).

Castells, M. (1996), *The Rise of the Network Society* (Oxford: Blackwell).

——— (1997), *The Power of Identity* (Oxford: Blackwell).

——— (2000), *End of Millennium* (Oxford: Blackwell).

Castles, S. (2000), *Ethnicity and Globalization* (London: Sage).

——— (2003), 'Towards a sociology of forced migration and social transformation', *Sociology* 37:1, 13–34.

Chalmers, M. (ed.) (2002), *Beneath Black Stars* (London: Serpent's Tail).

Charim, I. (2009), '"Mit Verlusten ist zu rechnen"', *Falter* 39, p. 13.

——— (2010), 'Ein Schlachtruf gegen Multikulti und Integration', *Falter* 18, p. 13.

Charim, I. and Rabinovici, D. (eds.) (2000), *Österreich – Berichte aus Quarantanien* (Frankfurt: Suhrkamp).

Charter, D. (2010), '"The Euro is in danger"', *The Times* 20 May, p. 1.

Clayton, J. (2009), 'Thinking spatially: Towards an everyday understanding of inter-ethnic relations', *Social & Cultural Geography* 10:4, 481–498.

Cohen, A. (1969), *Custom and Politics in Urban Africa* (London: Routledge & Kegan).

Cohen, P. (1992), '"It's racism what dunnit": Hidden narratives in theories of racism', in J. Donald and A. Rattansi (eds.), *'Race', Culture and Difference* (London, Sage).

Condor, S. (2000), 'Pride and prejudice: Identity management in English people's talk about "this country"', *Discourse & Society* 11:2, 175–205.

Coudenhove-Kalergi, B. (2003), 'Touristen', *Megaphon* 96, p. 5.

Cram, L. (2009), 'Introduction: Banal Europeanism: European Union identity and national identities in synergy', *Nations and Nationalism* 15:1, 101–108.

Crossley, N. (2004), 'On systematically distorted communication', in N. Crossley and J. M. Roberts (eds.), *After Habermas* (Oxford: Blackwell).

Dalton, G. (1968), 'Introduction', in *Karl Polanyi: Primitive, Archaic and Modern Economics* (Boston: Beacon Press).

*Das Jüdische Echo* (2009), 'Zuhause in Europa', 58.

De Cillia, R. et al. (1999), 'The discursive construction of national identities', *Discourse and Society* 10:2, 149–173.

Dempfer, R. (2009a), 'Medien mit scharf', *Henri* 7, pp. 54–55.

——— (2009b), 'Die "gute Türkin"', *Henri* 7, pp. 6–7.

Dench, G. et al. (2006), *The New East End* (London: Profile).

DeSoucey, M. (2010), 'Gastronationalism: Food traditions and authenticity politics in the European Union', *American Sociological Review* 75:3, 432–455

Dusini, M. and Kralicek, W. (2010), '"Ich habe ein Problem mit dem Wort Integration"', *Falter* 40, pp. 30–32.

Edensor, T. (2002), *National Identity, Popular Culture and Everyday Life* (Oxford/ New York: Berg).

Eisman, W. (ed.) (2002), *Rechtspopulismus* (Vienna: Czernin).

Embacher, H. et al. (1999), *Umkämpfte Erinnerung* (Salzburg: Residenz).

Enigl, M. (2010), 'Unbehagen in der Idylle', *Profil* 25, pp. 36–37.

Enigl, M. and Lackner, H. (2007), 'Wende nach der Wende', *Profil* 4, pp. 12–18.

Enigl, M. and Lettner, M. (2007), 'Dicke Luft', *Profil* 5, pp. 30–33.

Eraslan-Weninger, A. (2010), '15 Jahre Integrationshaus', *Die Gute Zeitung – Sonderausgabe*, p. 4.

Essed, P. (1991), *Understanding Everyday Racism* (London: Sage).

Fairclough, N. (1989), *Language and Power* (London: Longman).

―――― (1992), *Discourse and Social Change* (Cambridge: Polity).

Fassmann, H. (2007), 'Zusammenfassung', in H. Fassmann (ed.), *2. Österreichischer Migrations- und Integrationsbericht, 2001–2006* (Klagenfurt: Drave).

Fenderl, B. (2009), 'Von Quarktaschen und Topfengolatschen', in E. Steffen (ed.), *Wir sind gekommen, um zu bleiben* (Vienna: Czernin).

Fillitz, T. (2006), '"Being the native's friend does not make you the foreigner's enemy!"', in A. Gingrich and M. Banks (eds.), *Neo-Nationalism in Europe and Beyond* (New York: Berghahn).

Fitzmaurice, J. (1991), *Austrian Politics and Society Today* (London: Macmillan).

Fliedl, K. (ed.) (1998), *Das andere Österreich* (Munich: dtv).

Flynn, B. (2008), 'Soaking up atmosphere, the Nazi who sent 100s to death camps', *The Sun* 16 June, pp. 4–5.

Flynn, B. et al. (2008), 'I lusted after my mother', *The Sun* 9 May, pp. 6–7.

Fogu, C. and Kansteiner, W. (2006), 'The politics of memory and the poetics of history', in R. N. Lebow et al. (eds.), *The Politics of Memory in Postwar Europe* (Durham: Duke University Press).

Foucault, M. (1980), *Power/Knowledge* (Brighton: Harvester).

FPÖ (2005), 'Das Parteiprogramm der Freiheitlichen Partei Österreichs', http://www.fpoe.at, accessed 8 September 2006.

―――― (2006), 'Wahlprogramm der Freiheitlichen Partei Österreichs, FPÖ', http://www.fpoe.at, accessed 8 September 2006.

Fraser, N. (1992), 'Rethinking the public sphere', in C. Calhoun (ed.), *Habermas and the Public Sphere* (Cambridge, Massachusetts: MIT Press).

Fukuyama, F. (1992), *The End of History and the Last Man* (London: Hamish Hamilton).

Gächter, A. (2010), 'Bildung ist super – aber nicht für alle!', *Megaphon* 179, p. 4.

Gächter, S. (2010), 'Niedertrachtenfest', *Profil* 40, p. 15.

Gantner, M. (2009), 'Fozzys Tour', *Falter* 48, pp. 10–11.

―――― (2010), '"Wir sind hier und wir werden mehr"', *Falter* 15, pp. 21–22.

Gärtner, R. (2009), *Politik der Feindbilder* (Vienna: Kremayr & Scheriau).

Gellner, E. (1983), *Nations and Nationalism* (Oxford: Blackwell).

―――― (1998), *Language and Solitude: Wittgenstein, Malinowski and the Habsburg Dilemma* (Cambridge: Cambridge University Press).

Gepp, J. (2009), 'Generation Aufstieg, *Falter* 28, pp. 31–33.

―――― (2010a), 'Thilo Sarrazin schafft sich ab', *Falter* 35, p. 16.

―――― (2010b), 'Ein ¾ Kilometer Wien', *Falter* 34, pp. 31–33.

Germann Molz, J. (2007), 'Guilty pleasures of the golden arches', in J. Davidson et al. (eds.), *Emotional Geographies* (Aldershot: Ashgate).

Gilroy, P. (2004), *After Empire* (Abingdon: Routledge).

Gingrich, A. (2002), 'A man for all seasons: An anthropological perspective on public representation and cultural politics of the Austrian Freedom Party', in R. Wodak and A. Pelinka (eds.), *The Haider Phenomenon in Austria* (New Brunswick: Transaction).

———— (2006) 'Nation, status and gender in trouble?', in A. Gingrich and M. Banks (eds.), *Neo-Nationalism in Europe and Beyond* (New York: Berghahn).

Girtler, R. (1996), *Sommergetreide* (Vienna: Böhlau).

———— (2002), *Echte Bauern* (Vienna: Böhlau).

Gnam, P. (2002), '"Kernenergie" ist das Unwort des Jahres', *Kronen Zeitung* 9 January, pp. 2–3.

———— (2009), 'Mehrheit befürwortet Ministerin Fekters strengere Asylgesetze', *Kronen Zeitung* 29 July, p. 3.

———— (2010), 'Die Arbeiterkammer lehnt mehr Zuwanderung entschieden ab!', *Kronen Zeitung* 28 July, p. 3.

Goslan, R. (2006), 'The legacy of World War II in France', in R. N. Lebow et al. (eds.), *The Politics of Memory in Postwar Europe* (Durham: Duke University Press).

Göttsche, D. (2010), 'Cross-cultural self-assertion and cultural politics: African migrants' writing in German since the late 1990s', *German Life and Letters* 63:1, 54–70.

Grasseni. C. (2009), *Developing Skill, Developing Vision* (New York: Berghahn).

Green Party (2006), 'Zeit für Grün: Das Grüne Programm', http://www.gruene.at/uploads/media/GrünesWahlprogramm2006_04pdf, accessed 8 September 2006.

Griffin, L. J. and Bollen, K. A. (2009), 'What do these memories do? Civil rights remembrance and racial attitudes', *American Sociological Review* 74:4, 594–614.

Grillo, R. (2005), '"Saltdean can't cope": Protests against asylum-seekers in an English seaside suburb', *Ethnic and Racial Studies* 28:2, 235–260.

Gruber, A. and Bohacek, H. (2006), *Lebensmittel heute* (Graz: Kammer für Arbeiter und Angestellte für Steiermark).

Grunwald, H. (2010), 'Nothing more cosmopolitan than the camps? Holocaust remembrance and (de-)Europeanization', in M. Conway and K. Kiran Patel (eds.), *Europeanization in the Twentieth Century* (New York: Palgrave Macmillan).

Guibernau, M. (2007), *The Identity of Nations* (Cambridge: Polity).

Haar, A. (2009), 'Kein "Fairplay" bei der Integration', *Die Presse* 8 April, p. 9.

Habermas, J. (1978), *Knowledge and Human Interests* (London: Heinemann).

———— (1987), *The Theory of Communicative Action: Vol. II.* (Boston: Beacon Press).

———— (1989), *The Structural Transformation of the Public Sphere* (Cambridge, Massachusetts: MIT Press).

Hacker, P. and Kern, M. (2010), 'Blick hinter den Schleier', *Kurier* 9 April, p. 3.

Hafez, F. (2009), 'Zwischen Islamophobie und Islamophilie: Die FPÖ und der Islam', in J. Bunzl and F. Hafez (eds.), *Islamophobie in Österreich* (Innsbruck: Studienverlag).

Hafez, F. and Potz, R. (2009), 'Moschee- und Minarettbauverbote in Kärnten und Vorarlberg', in J. Bunzl and F. Hafez (eds.), *Islamophobie in Österreich* (Innsbruck: Studienverlag).

Hager, A. and Meinhart, E. (2007), 'Menschen zweiter Klasse', *Profil* 45, pp. 20–27.

Hainsworth, P. (2000), 'Introduction: the extreme right', in P. Hainsworth (ed.), *The Politics of the Extreme Right* (London: Pinter).

Hall, S. (1989), 'Ethnicity: Identity and difference', http://www.csus.edu/indiv/l/ leekellerh/Hall,%20Ethnicity_Identity_and_Difference.pdf, accessed 25 November 2009.

———— (1996), 'Who needs identity?, in S. Hall and P. duGay (eds.), *Questions of Cultural Identity* (London: Sage).

———— (1997), 'The local and the global: Globalization and ethnicity', in A. McClintock et al. (eds.), *Dangerous Liaisons* (Minneapolis: University of Minnesota Press).

Haller, M. (ed.) (1996), *Identität und Nationalstolz der Österreicher* (Vienna: Böhlau).

Hamann, S. (2009), 'Prinz, Tellerwäscher, Journalist', *Falter* 37, pp. 19–20.

———— (2010), 'Weiße Engel, schwarze Massen', *Falter* 23, pp. 19–20.

Hammerl, E. (2010), 'Nicht in unserem Namen', *Profil* 13, p. 33.

Hanisch, E. (1994), *Der lange Schatten des Staates* (Vienna: Ueberreuter).

Hansen, T. B. (1999), *The Saffron Wave* (Princeton: Princeton University Press).

Hartnack, C. (2009), 'Im dritten Raum', in E. Steffen (ed.), *Wir sind gekommen, um zu bleiben* (Vienna: Czernin).

Harvey, D. (2006), 'Social justice and the city', Public Lecture, University of Nottingham, 7 December.

Hasewend, S. (2009), 'Die Kinder hinter den Zahlen', *Kleine Zeitung* (Steiermark) 5 April, pp. 34–35.

Haslinger, J. (1995), *Politik der Gefühle* (Frankfurt: Fischer).

Haupt, W. (2005), 'EU-skeptisch und trotzdem treu', *Kleine Zeitung* 11 August, p. 5.

Heer, H. et al. (eds.) (2008), *The Discursive Construction of History: Remembering the Wehrmacht's War of Annihilation* (Basingstoke: Palgrave Macmillan).

Heine, S. (2009), 'Auf holprigen Wegen: die Darstellung des Islams in österreichischen Schulbüchern, Fach Geschichte, 5.-8. Schulstufe', in J. Bunzl and F. Hafez (eds.), *Islamophobie in Österreich* (Innsbruck: Studienverlag).

Heitzmann, K. and Förster, M. (2007), 'Armutsgefährdung, manifeste Armut und Einkommenschancen von MigrantInnen in Österreich', in H. Fassmann (ed.), *2. Österreichischer Migrations- und Integrationsbericht, 2001–2006* (Klagenfurt: Drave).

Herf, J. (2002), 'The emergence and legacies of divided memory: Germany and the Holocaust since 1945', in J-W. Müller (ed.), *Memory & Power in Post-War Europe* (Cambridge: Cambridge University Press).

Herzog-Punzenberger, B. (2009), 'Dazugehören oder nicht?', in S. Bardakçi et al. (eds.), *Dazugehören oder nicht?* (Innsbruck: Studienverlag).

Heshmatpour, C. and Zwander, W. (2010), 'Papierlt in Wien', *Falter* 19, pp. 38–40.

Himmelbauer, M. (2006), 'Pluskorrektur', *Profil* 49, pp. 52–55.

Himmelbauer, M. et al. (2007), 'Operation Europaplatz', *Profil* 14, pp. 36–42.

Hinsch, S. (2009), 'Zur Situation türkischer MigrantInnen in Österreich', in S. Bardakçi et al. (eds.), *Dazugehören oder nicht?* (Innsbruck: Studienverlag).

Hintze, C. I. (2003), 'Den Konfitüreknechten den Kampf ansagen', http://derstandard.at, accessed 23 October.

Hoffmann-Ostenhof, G. (2007), 'Der Pendelschlag', *Profil* 5, pp. 80–81.

——— (2010a), 'Gemischter Satz', *Profil* 16, p. 81.

——— (2010b), 'EU-Bundesstaat – jetzt!', *Profil* 21, p. 67.

Hoffmann-Ostenhof, G. and Müller, G. (2009), 'Der schwarze Kontinent', *Profil* 25, pp. 60–66.

Höller, H. and Noormofidi, D. (2009), 'Willkommen in "Little Istanbul"', *Falter* 43, pp. 46–48.

Horaczek, N. (2007), 'Zu ebener Erde und 1.Stock', *Falter* 3, pp. 12–15.

——— (2008), 'Souverän ins Out', *Falter* 25, p. 6.

——— (2010a), 'Was kann die Kuh dafür, dass sie so braun ist?', *Falter* 35, pp. 19–20.

——— (2010b), 'Wenn das Puppenhaus im Kindergarten auch bebek evi heißen kann', *Falter* 37, p. 20.

——— (2010c), 'Keine Panik im Pausenraum', *Falter* 36, pp. 11–12.

——— (2010d), 'Strassers Tschetschenenlüge', *Falter* 28, pp. 10–12.

Horaczek, N. and Weissensteiner, N. (2003), 'Eine nette Einladung', *Falter* 46, http://www.falter.at/print/F2003_46_1.php, accessed 27 April 2004.

http://derstandard.at/standard.asp?id=1444272, 'Ute Bock: "Bin ja nicht von der Polizei" – die Nachlese zum Chat', accessed 9 October 2003.

http://derstandard.at/standard.asp?id=1725913, 'Österreicher sehen EU-Mitgliedschaft so negativ wie noch nie', accessed 13 July 2004.

http://derstandard.at/?id=2854647, 'Breite Front gegen US-Einmischung', accessed 25 April 2007.

http://derstandard.at/druck/?id=3395006, 'Kommentar der anderen', accessed 8 July 2008.

http://derstandard.at/druck/id=1240297879283, 'Schlechte Noten für Strafverfolgung von NS-Tätern in Österreich', accessed 11 May 2009.

http://derstandard.at/druck/?id=1240550310779, '2000 Teilnehmer in Linz', accessed 11 May 2009.

http://derstandard.at/1237228391907, 'Standard steigert Reichweite auf 5,5 Prozent', accessed 23 August 2010.

http://diepresse.com/home/panorama/oesterreich/441873/print.do, 'Junge Migranten zwischen zwei Welten', accessed 9 January 2009.

http://diepresse.com/home/panorama/oesterreich/478066/print.do, 'Tirol: Kein Hotelzimmer für jüdische Familie', accessed 11 May 2009.

http://diepresse.com/home/panorama/religion/592978/print.do, 'Muzicant fordert mehr Moscheen – aber ohne Minarette', accessed 14 September 2010.

http://fm4.orf.at/connected/119977/main, 'So macht Bier trinken Sinn', accessed 18 August 2003.

http://kaernten.orf.at/stories/343252/, 'Asylwerberheim auf der Saualm sperrt zu', accessed 18 February 2009.

http://news.uk.msn.com/uk/article.aspx?cp-documentid=13647653, 'Foreign labour dispute talks resume', accessed 3 February 2009.

http://news.uk.msn.com/uk/article.aspx?cp-documentid=13711435, 'Refinery workers accept jobs deal', accessed 5 February 2009.

http://oe1.orf.at/inforadio/72909.html, 'Gusenbauer bei Merkel, Regelung der Medizinerquoten?', accessed 7 February 2007.

http://oe1.orf.at/inforadio/73328.html, 'Medizinstudium: Hahn erklärt Brüssel die Quotenregelung', accessed 19 February 2007.

http://oe1.orf.at/inforadio/77388.html, 'ÖVP-Kehrtwende in der Integrationspolitik?', accessed 18 June 2007.

http://oe1.orf.at/inforadio/82242.html, 'Österreich in Sachen Integration EU-Drittletzter', accessed 16 October 2007).

http://oe1.orf.at/inforadio/101382.html, 'Jahresbilanz: Breite Kritik an "Integrationsdialog"', accessed 21 January 2009.

http://oe1.orf.at/inforadio/101220.html, 'Zuwanderung Beispiel Wels: Integration überfordert Gemeinden', accessed 26 January 2009.

http://oe1.orf.at/inforadio/110322.html, 'Begutachtung: Breite Kritik an neuem Fremdenecht', accessed 22 July 2009.

http://oe1.orf.at/inforadio/112625.html, 'Eurobarometer: Krise dämpft EU-Skepsis der Österreicher', accessed 10 September 2009.

http://oe1.orf.at/artikel/256868, 'Moscheendebatte: Länder zurückhaltend', accessed 23 August 2010.

http://oesterreich.orf.at/stories/163553/, 'Exporte erstmals über 100 Mrd. Euro', accessed 10 January 2007.

http://oesterreich.orf.at/stories/165145/, 'Studenten gehen weiter auf die Straße', accessed 17 January 2007.

http://oesterreich.orf.at/stories/165273/, 'Klimabilanz noch weit von Kyoto-Ziel entfernt', accessed 22 January 2007.

http://oesterreich.orf.at/stories/187976/, 'Der größte Stolz der Österreicher', accessed 24 April 2007.

http://oesterreich.orf.at/stories/373686/, '"Urlaub mit Freunden" für Asyldebatte', accessed 17 May 2009.

http://oesterreich.orf.at/stories/403669/, 'Zahl der Einbürgerungen stark rückläufig', accessed 17 November 2009).

http://oesterreich.orf.at/stories/406575/, 'Bau von Minaretten umstritten', accessed 30 November 2009.

http://oesterreich.orf.at/stories/443726/, 'Deutsche erstmals größte Ausländergruppe', accessed 19 May 2010.

http://oesterreich.orf.at/stories/464689/, '200 Gebetsräume für 500,000 Muslime', accessed 23 August 2010.

http://oesterreich.orf.at/wien/stories/206542/, 'Wiener Familie droht Ausweisung', accessed 23 July 2007.

http://oesterreich.orf.at/wien/stories/362107/, 'Sechs Verletzte und ein Nazi-Sager', accessed 15 May 2009.

http://oesterreich.orf.at/wien/stories/364032/, 'Zuwandererkommission nimmt Arbeit auf', accessed 25 June 2009.

http://ooe.orf.at/stories/165001/, 'Winter ohne Schnee: Hoteliers rufen um Hilfe', accessed 16 January 2007.

http://ooe.orf.at/stories/165486/, 'Studiengebühren: Friedliche Demo in Linz', accessed 18 January 2007.

http://ooe.orf.at/stories/171837/, 'SPÖ Ebensee verlost Studiengebühren', accessed 14 February 2007.

http://ooe.orf.at/stories/363974/, 'Demonstration in Ebensee', accessed 06 May 2009.

http://ooe.orf.at/stories/362658/, 'Peinliche Erkenntnis in Ebensee', accessed 18 May 2009.

http://ooe.orf.at/stories/439146/, 'Türkische Schulen auch für Linz gefordert', accessed 29 April 2010.

http://ooe.orf.at/stories/441047/, 'Keine Videoüberwachung für Gedenkstätte', accessed 6 May 2010.

http://ooe.orf.at/stories/454626/, 'Diskussion über Zuwanderungsstopp in Traun', accessed 8 July 2010.

http://orf.at/070430-11807/11808txt_story.html, '27 Prozent armutsgefährdet', accessed 1 May 2007.

http://orf.at/090513-38250/38251txt_story.html, 'Besorgniserregende Zahlen', accessed 14 May 2009.

http://orf.at/090519-38489/?href=http%…, 'Auch Kirche kritisiert FPÖ-Kampagne', accessed 20 May 2009.

http://orf.at/090828-41940/?href=http%3A…, '"Grundsätzlich neue Überlegungen" nötig', accessed 7 July 2009.

http://orf.at/090915-42579/?href…, 'Kritik in vielen Punkten', accessed 16 September 2009.

http://religion.orf.at/project03/news/0910/ne091019_asyl_fr.htm, 'Kirchen protestieren gegen Veschärfung des Fremdenrechts', accessed 19 October 2009.

http://salzburg.orf.at/stories/364666/, 'Religionsvertreter: "Verhetzung durch FPÖ"', accessed 27 May 2009.

http://salzburg.orf.at/stories/366036/, 'Abschiebung: Kritik am Innenministerium', accessed 3 June 2009.

http://salzburg.orf.at/stories/449716/, 'HBLA: Parteien für Deutschpflicht an Schule' accessed 15 June 2010.

http://science.orf.at/science/news/146388, 'Klimawandel: Kein Skispaß mehr unter 2,000 Meter', accessed 16 January 2007.

http://steiermark.orf.at/stories/177806/, 'Bio-Lebensmittel für den Klimaschutz', accessed 12 March 2007.

http://steiermark.orf.at/stories/193255/, 'Iranische Flüchtlingsfamilie darf bleiben', accessed 16 May 2007.

http://steiermark.orf.at/stories/369249/, 'Lichterkette für Respekt und Menschenwürde', accessed 18 June 2009.

http://steiermark.orf.at/stories/391803/, 'Flecker kritisiert Faymanns Ausländerpolitik', accessed 23 September 2009.

http://steiermark.orf.at/stories/469174, 'Asylwohnheim-Anschlag: Zeugen gesucht', accessed 12 September 2010.

http://vorarlberg.orf.at/stories/73561/, 'Volksschullehrer müssen Türkisch lernen', accessed 30 November 2005.

http://vorarlberg.orf.at/stories/164779/, 'Massive Verluste für manche Liftbetreiber', accessed 16 January 2007.

http://vorarlberg.orf.at/stories/391829/, 'Aydin zieht als erste Migrantin in Landtag ein', accessed 23 September 2009.

http://vorarlberg.orf.at/stories/425369/, 'Protest: Bürger verhindern Abschiebung', accessed 25 February 2010.

http://wien.orf.at/oesterreich.orf?read=detail&channel=1&id=375633, 'Anklage in der Cause Cheibani Wague', accessed 12 April 2005.

http://wien.orf.at/stories/180216/, 'So viele Übergriffe wie noch nie', accessed 21 March 2007.

http://wien.orf.at/stories/357514/, 'Causa Omofuma jährt sich zum zehnten Mal', accessed 18 March 2009.

http://wien.orf.at/stories/369218/, 'Lichterkette als Zeichen für Zivilcourage', accessed 18 June 2009.

http://wien.orf.at/stories/419286/, 'Migrations-Debatte läuft an Realität vorbei', accessed 6 January 2010).

http://wien.orf.at/stories/431398/, 'Einreichfrist für Integrationspreis startet', accessed 24 March 2010.

http://wien.orf.at/stories/439586, 'Blockade für Einwanderer: 42 Anzeigen', accessed 5 May 2010.

http://wien.orf.at/stories/440909/, 'Wieder Demo gegen Abschiebung', accessed 6 May 2010.

http://www.diepresse.at/default.asp?channel=k&ressort=k&id=370338, 'Österreicher empört: Mozart kein Deutscher', accessed 8 August 2003.

http://www.diepresse.at/Artikel.aspx?channel=p&ressort=eu&id=381404, 'Jeder Dritte fühlt sich bedroht', accessed 8 October 2003.

http://www.diepresse.at/Artikel.aspx?channel=c&ressort=w&id=392950, 'Kriminalität ist größtes Ärgernis', accessed 12 December 2003.

http://www.kleinezeitung.at/nachrichten/wirtschaft/286159/index.do, 'Österreicher mehrheitlich gegen Sonntagsöffnung', accessed 7 December 2006.

http://www.krone.at/Oesterreich/Richter_stoppt_Anti-Minarett-Spiel….., 'Richter stoppt "Anti-Minarett-Spiel" der FPÖ', accessed 14 September 2010.

http://www.orf.at/030814-65875/index.html, 'Ute Bock im Porträt', accessed 18 August 2003.

http://www.orf.at/ticker/158514.html?tmp=9339, 'Umfrage: Zuwanderer "mehr Belastung als Nutzen"', accessed 16 September 2004.

http://www.orf.at/ticker/231618.html, 'Grundsicherung für Prokop "urkommunistische Forderung"', accessed 4 October 2006.

http://www.orf.at/061010-4750/4751txt_story.html, 'Ein Mandat von BZÖ zu Grünen', accessed 10 October 2006.

http://www.orf.at/ticker/232859.html, 'Zahl der Sozialhilfeempfänger steigt weiter', accessed 17 October 2006.

http://www.orf.at/ticker/235668.html, 'Umfrage: Mehrheit gegen EU-Beitritt der Türkei', accessed 15 November 2006.

http://www.orf.at/ticker/237660.html, 'SPÖ drängt auf gesetzlichen Mindestlohn von 1,000 Euro', accessed 5 December 2006.

http://www.orf.at/ticker/241048.html, 'ÖH kündigt weitere Studentenproteste an', accessed 12 January 2007.

http://www.orf.at/070115-8087/8088txt_story.html, '"Valorisierung sämtlicher Gebühren"', accessed 15 January 2007.

http://www.orf.at/070116-8141/8142txt_story.html, 'Wintertourismus massiv gefährdet', accessed 16 January 2007.

http://www.orf.at/070116-8131/8132txt_story.html, 'Von Studiengebühren bis Integration', accessed 16 January 2007.

http://www.orf.at/ticker/241559.html, 'Heimische Klimabilanz meilenweit von Kyoto-Ziel entfernt', accessed 17 January 2007.

http://www.orf.at/ticker/242197.html, 'Klimawandel: UNO forciert globale Aufforstung', accessed 24 January 2007.

http://www.orf.at/ticker/242231.html, 'Medizinerquote: EU-Verfahren gegen Österreich', accessed 24 January 2007.

http://www.orf.at/070218-9376/9380txt_story.html, 'Heftige Ablehnung von Grünen und Greenpeace', accessed 19 February 2007.

http://www.orf.at/070218-9376/9377txt_story.html, 'Persilschein für neun Mio. Tonnen CO2', accessed 19 February 2007.

http://www.orf.at/070219-9432/9433txt_story.html, 'Starke Argumente gefordert', accessed 20 February 2007.

http://www.orf.at/ticker/245671.html, 'Mindestsicherung: Erstes Modell soll im Juni stehen', accessed 26 February 2007.

http://www.orf.at/ticker/245993.html, 'ÖGB und AK: Weiter Veto gegen ausländische Fachkräfte', accessed 1 March 2007.

http://www.orf.at/070307-9940/9941txt_story.html, 'Roter Hoffnungsträger in EU?', accessed 8 March 2007.

http://www.orf.at/ticker/247100.html, 'Grüne wollen höhere Steuer auf "Benzinfresser"', accessed 12 March 2007.

http://www.orf.at/070313-10121/10122txt_story.html, 'Transitwelle in und um Wien', accessed 13 March 2007.

http://www.orf.at/ticker/247206.html, 'Klimapolitik: Einigkeit bei SPÖ und ÖVP', accessed 13 March 2007.

http://www.orf.at/ticker/247295.html, 'Transit: Faymann setzt auf Schienenausbau', accessed 14 March 2007.

http://www.orf.at/070321-10410/10411txt_story.html, 'Anhebung höher als geplant', accessed 21 March 2007.

http://www.orf.at/070326-10607/10608txt_story.html, 'Nur das Minimalziel', accessed 27 March 2007.

http://www.orf.at/070402-10849/10850txt_story.html, 'CO2-Verschmutzungsrechte gekürzt', accessed 3 April 2007.

http://www.orf.at/ticker/249907.html, 'Fremdenrecht: Prammer fordert sofortige Überprüfung', accessed 11 April 2007.

http://www.orf.at/ticker/250670.html, 'Fremdenrecht: VfGH Präsident wünscht sich Reparatur', accessed 19 April 2007.

http://www.orf.at/ticker/254111.html, 'Regierung: 500-Seiten-Bericht zu Medizinerquote', accessed 23 May 2007.

http://www.orf.at/ticker/254779.html, 'Ministerrat: Neues Tiertransportgesetz', accessed 30 May 2007.

http://www.orf.at/071016-17681/index.html, 'Platter "steht dazu"', accessed 16 October 2007.

http://www.orf.at/071115-18687/18688txt_story.html, 'Viele Zuwanderer aus der EU', accessed 15 November 2007.

http://www.orf.at/ticker/318332.html, 'Rechtsextremismus: Zahl der Anzeigen fast verdoppelt', accessed 18 February 2009.

http://www.orf.at/ticker/331137.html, 'UNHCR kritisiert Fekters Asylpläne', accessed 14 June 2009.

http://www.orf.at/ticker/338265.html, 'Ortstafeln: Bandion-Ortner pocht auf politische Lösung', accessed 18 August 2009.

http://www.orf.at/ticker/338499.html, 'Zahl der Einbürgerungen weiter stark rückläugig', accessed 20 August 2009.

http://www.orf.at/ticker/344496.html, 'NR-Sondersitzung zur Sozial- und Arbeitsmarktpolitik', accessed 15 October 2009.

http://www.orf.at/091020-43862/index.html, 'Warten auf eine planbare Zukunft', accessed 22 October 2009.

http://www.orf.at/091026-44023/index.html, 'Ritual zur Identitätsstiftung', accessed 26 October 2009.

http://www.orf.at/100119-47046/index.html, 'Verpflichtende Sprachkenntnisse fix', accessed 19 January 2010.

http://www.orf.at/100308-48803/index.html, '"Persönlich sehr betroffen"', accessed 8 March 2010.

http://www.orf.at/100310-48897/index.html, 'Ziele nie erreicht?', accessed 11 March 2010.

http://www.orf.at/100528-51724/51725txt_story.html, 'Niedriger Verdienst, höhere Arbeitslosigkeit', accessed 28 May 2010.

http://www.orf.at/stories/2010293/2010296/, 'Hoffen auf "Normalität"', accessed 22 August 2010.

http://www.orf.at/stories/2018028/2018024/, 'Gegen "Zementierung von Vorurteilen"', accessed 3 October 2010.

http://www.wieninternational.at/de/node/6341?SESS88d391…, '"Biber" – Stadt-magazin "mit scharf" die Dritte', accessed 18 February 2009.

Huntington, S. (1998), *The Clash of Civilizations and the Remaking of World Order* (London: Touchstone).

Hussain, Y. (2005), *Writing Diaspora* (Aldershot: Ashgate).

Hutter, K. and Perchinig, B. (2008), 'Partizipation braucht Voraussetzungen', in Bundesministerium für Inneres, *Gemeinsam kommen wir zusammen* (Vienna: Bundesministerium für Inneres).

Ingrao, C. W. (2001), 'Foreword' in P. Thaler, *The Ambivalence of Identity* (West Lafayette: Purdue University Press).

*Isotopia* (2009), 'ISOP-Tätigkeitsbericht 08', 66, Graz.

Jameson, F. (1991), *Postmodernism, or, The Cultural Logic of Late Capitalism* (London/New York: Verso).

Jarausch, K. (2010), 'Nightmares or daydreams?' in M. Pakier and B. Stråth (eds.), *A European Memory?* (New York/Oxford: Berghahn).

Jelinek, E. (1985), *Die Ausgesperrten* (Reinbek: Rowohlt).

John, G. and Klenk, F. (2004), '"Der Islam entfremdet"', *Falter* 15, http://www.falter.at/print/F2004_15_1.php, accessed 27 April 2004.

John, G. and Weissensteiner, N. (2003), 'Maggie mag er eben', *Falter* 20, http://www.falter.at/print/F2003_20_1.php, accessed 27 April 2004.

John, M. and Marschik, M. (2002), 'Ortswechsel: Antisemitismus im österreichischen Sport nach 1945', in H. Wassermann (ed.), *Antisemitismus in Österreich nach 1945* (Innsbruck: Studienverlag).

Joschika, R. and Wrann, G. (2009), 'Mit Elan im fünften Jahr', *Megaphon* 166, pp. 30–31.

Judt, T. (2002), 'The past is another country: myth and memory in post-war Europe', in J-W. Müller (ed.), *Memory & Power in Post-War Europe* (Cambridge: Cambridge University Press).

Jungwirth, M. (2010), 'Ganztagsschule für Türken', *Kleine Zeitung* 14 April, pp. 4–5.

Kaloianov, R. (2008), *Affirmative Action für MigrantInnen? Am Beispiel Österreichs* (Vienna: Braumüller).

Kansteiner, W. (2006), 'Losing the war, winning the memory battle', in N. Lebow et al. (eds.), *The Politics of Memory in Postwar Europe* (Durham: Duke University Press).

Karlsson, K-G. (2010), 'The uses of history and the third wave of Europeanisation', in M. Pakier and B. Stråth (eds.), *A European Memory?* (New York/Oxford: Berghahn).

Karner, C. (2002), 'Austro-Pop since the 1980s: Two case studies of cultural critique and counter-hegemonic resistance', *Sociological Research Online* 6:4, http://www.socresonline.org/6/4/karner.html.

——— (2005a), 'The "Habsburg Dilemma" today: Competing discourses of national identity in contemporary Austria', *National Identities* 7:4, 411–434.

——— (2005b), 'National *doxa*, crises and ideological contestation in contemporary Austria', *Nationalism and Ethnic Politics* 11:2, 221–263.

——— (2007a), *Ethnicity and Everyday Life* (London/New York: Routledge).

——— (2007b), 'Austrian counter-hegemony: critiquing ethnic exclusion and globalization', *Ethnicities* 7:1, 82–115.

——— (2009), 'Everyday globalization, resistance and ambivalence: Austrian snapshots', ICMiC Working Paper (number 6), http://www.nottingham.ac.uk/shared/shared_icmic/PDFs/Karner-ICMiC-WP-09-06.pdf.

——— (2010a), 'Hybridity and the politics of the everyday in contemporary Austria', *German Life and Letters* 63:1, 71–87.

——— (2010b), 'The uses of the past and European integration: Austria between Lisbon, Ireland and EURO 08', *Identities: Global Studies in Culture and Power* 17:4, 387–410.

Karner, C. and Parker, D. (2008), 'Religion versus rubbish: Deprivation and social capital in inner-city Birmingham', *Social Compass* 55:4, 517–531.

——— (forthcoming), 'Conviviality and conflict: Pluralism, resilience and hope in inner-city Birmingham', *Journal of Ethnic and Migration Studies*.

Kaschuba, W. (2010), 'Iconic remembering and religious icons', in M. Pakier and B. Stråth (eds.), *A European Memory?* (New York/Oxford: Berghahn).

Keith, M. (2008), 'Between being and becoming? Rights, responsibilities and the politics of multiculture in the New East End', *Sociological Research Online* 13:5, http://www.socresonline.org.uk/13/5/11.html.

Kleindel, W. (1984), *Die Chronik Österreichs* (Dortmund: Chronik Verlag).

Klenk, F. (2003), '"Den Tobenden verpackt"', *Falter* 35, http://www.falter.at/print/F2003_35_1.php, accessed 27 April 2004.

——— (2009), 'Fall eins: die Cause Ortstafel', *Falter* 33, p. 10.

Kindermann, D. (2004), 'Rückkehr zur alten Schreibweise', *Kronen Zeitung* 12 August, p. 3.

Kopt, R. (2003), 'Na so was! Seit wann ist Mozart Deutscher?', *Kronen Zeitung* 7 August, pp. 10–11.

Kornprobst, M. (2005), 'Episteme, nation-builders and national identity: The re-construction of Irishness', *Nations and Nationalism* 11:3, 403–421.

Körtner, U. (2009), 'Ein Westfale in Wien', in E. Steffen (ed.), *Wir sind gekommen, um zu bleiben* (Vienna: Czernin).

Kosta, B. (2003), 'Murderous Boundaries: Nation, Memory and Austria's Fascist Past in Elfriede Jelinek's *Stecken, Stab und Stangl*', in B. Kosta and H. Kraft (eds.), *Writing Against Boundaries* (Amsterdam/New York: Rodopi).

Kovács, É. (2009), 'Anerkennen oder erkennen', *Jüdisches Echo* 58, 96–100.

KPÖ (2006), 'Ändere die Welt, sie braucht es!', http://www.kpoe.at, accessed 8 September 2006.

Krese, M. et al. (eds.) (2008), *Ohne Angst verschieden sein* (Graz: Leykam).

—— (eds.) (2010), *Neue Heimaten?* (Graz: CLIO).

Krzyżanowski, M. and Wodak, R. (2009), *The Politics of Exclusion* (New Brunswick: Transaction).

Kübel, J. (2009), '"moschee.ade oder moschee.at": Eine Konfliktanalyse auf der Such nach Islamophobie in Österreich', in J. Bunzl and F. Hafez (eds), *Islamophobie in Österreich*, (Innsbruck: Studienverlag).

Kunovich, R. M. (2009), 'The sources and consequences of national identification', *American Sociological Review* 74:4, 573–593.

Lackner, H. (2007a), '"Ein Wechsel bringt immer Turbulenzen"', *Profil* 3, pp. 20–22.

—— (2007b), 'Die lieben Heuschrecken', *Profil* 13, p. 13.

—— (2008a), 'Der falsche Mann? '*Profil* 29, p. 11.

—— (2008b), 'Politik im Dschungel-Camp', *Profil* 39, pp. 30–31.

—— (2009), 'Die etwas anderen Österreicher', *Profil* 43, pp. 32–35.

—— (2010a), 'Die neue Schamlosigkeit', *Profil* 3, pp. 16–21

—— (2010b), 'Der eiskalte Engel', *Profil* 10, pp. 16–22.

—— (2010c), 'Gegenwind am Donaukanal', *Profil* 11, pp. 14–18.

—— (2010d), 'Liebe und Waschtrog', *Profil* 16, pp. 33–38.

—— (2010e), 'Aktion "Malaka"', *Profil* 8, p. 29.

Lahodynsky, O. (2010), 'Klein-Bonum Kirchheim', *Profil* 30, p. 25.

Lahodynsky, O. et al. (2010), 'Brüssler Spritzen', *Profil* 20, pp. 16–21.

Lakoff, G. (1987), *Women, Fire, and Dangerous Things* (Chicago: The University of Chicago Press).

Lamb-Faffelberger, M. (1992), *Valie Export und Elfriede Jelinek im Spiegel der Presse* (New York: Peter Lang).

Lampert, W. (2005), *Schemckt's noch?* (Salzburg: ecowin).

Langer, J. (1996), 'Nation – schwindende Basis für soziale Identität? Eine Studie über 17–19 jährige Schüler und Schülerinnen', in M. Haller (ed.), *Identität und Nationalstolz der Österreicher* (Vienna: Böhlau).

Lebhart, G. and Marik-Lebeck, S. (2007), 'Bevölkerung mit Migrationshintergrund', in H. Fassmann (ed.), *2. Österreichischer Migrations- und Integrationsbericht, 2001–2006* (Klagenfurt: Drave).

Lebow, R. N. et al. (eds.) (2006), *The Politics of Memory in Postwar Europe* (Durham: Duke University Press).

Lettner, M. (2010a), 'Wohin & woher?', *Profil* 41, p. 26.

———— (2010b), 'Patriot 2.0', *Profil* 12, pp. 34–35.

Levy, D. and Dierkes, J. (2002), 'Institutionalising the past: Shifting memories of nationhood in German education and immigration legislation', in J-W. Müller (ed.), *Memory & Power in Post-War Europe* (Cambridge: Cambridge University Press).

Lichtmann, T. (ed*.) (1993), Nicht (aus, is, über, von) Österreich: Zur österreichischen Literatur, zu Celan, Bachmann, Bernhard und anderen* (Frankfurt: Peter Lang).

Liessmann, K. P. (2005), *Die Insel der Seligen* (Innsbruck: Studienverlag).

Lingens, P.M. (2006), 'Ende der Auseinandersetzung', *Profil* 48, p. 144.

———— (2007), 'Die "Kleinen" bezahlen die Rechnung', *Profil* 12, p. 128.

———— (2008), 'Diese SPÖ ist unwählbar', *Profil* 28, p. 112.

———— (2010a), 'Das Inländer-Problem', *Profil* 4, p. 105.

———— (2010b), 'Das Jahr(zehnt) der FPÖ', *Profil* 2, p. 97.

Linsinger, E. (2006), 'Linkswende', *Profil* 50, pp. 22–24.

Linsinger, E. and Zöchling, C. (2009), 'Die Banalität des Bösen', *Profil* 24, pp. 16–22.

Littler, M. (2010), 'Negotiating difference in contemporary German-language culture', *German Life and Letters* 63:1, 1–5.

Loitfellner, S. (2008), '"The appalling toll in Austrian lives": The Wehrmacht and its soldiers in Austrian school books', in H. Heer et al. (eds.), *The Discursive Construction of History* (Basingstoke: Palgrave Macmillan).

Lödén, H. (2008), 'Swedish: Being or becoming? Immigration, national identity and the democratic state', *International Journal of Social Science* 3:4, 257–264.

Löw, R. (2010a), 'Warum es an der Zeit ist für die Vereinigten Staaten von Europa', *Falter* 20, p. 7.

———— (2010b), 'Von der Spitze des Olymp hin zum möglichen Ende des Euro', *Falter* 18, p. 7.

Lukes, S. (1998), 'Foreword', in E. Gellner, *Language and Solitude* (Cambridge: Cambridge University Press).

Lynn, N. and Lea, S. (2003), '"A phantom menace and the new apartheid": The social construction of asylum-seekers in the United Kingdom', *Discourse & Society* 14:4, 425–452.

Maier, C. (2009), '"Die Regierung hat Angst vor den Fremden"', *Megaphon* 162, p. 11.

Male, E. (2003), 'Was sagt uns der Marmelade-Krieg?', http://www.diepresse.at, accessed 31 October.

Mann, R. and Fenton, S. (2006), 'Everyday articulations of national identity: methodological considerations', http://www.bristol.ac.uk/sociology/leverhulme/conference/conferencepapers/mann.pfdf, accessed 29 May 2008.

———— (2009), 'The personal context of national sentiments', *Journal of Ethnic and Migration Studies* 35:4, 517–534.

Mappes-Niedik, N. (2002), *Österreich für Deutsche* (Berlin: Ch. Links).

—— (2007), 'Spielverderber', *Megaphon* 139, p. 5.

Markom, C. and Weinhäupl, H. (2007), *Die Anderen im Schulbuch* (Vienna: Braumüller).

—— (2009), '"Der Islam" im Schulbuch', in J. Bunzl and F. Hafez (eds.), *Islamophobie in Österreich* (Innsbruck: Studienverlag).

Marterbauer, M. (2010), 'Reförmchen, das den Eliten nicht wehtut', *Falter* 29, pp. 6–7.

Martin, H-P. and Schumann, H. (2006 [1996]), *Die Globalisierungsfalle* (Reinbek: Rowohlt).

McCrone, D. (1998), *The Sociology of Nationalism* (London: Routledge)

*Megaphon* 169 (October 2009), 'Kleiner Fremder', p. 13.

Meinhart, E. (2007), 'Hier geblieben!', *Profil* 6, pp. 34–36.

—— (2010a), 'Das Mädchen für alles', *Profil* 1, pp. 16–23.

—— (2010b), 'Gescheit gescheitert', *Profil* 32, pp. 23–26.

Meinhart, E. and Zöchling, C. (2007), 'Wer hat, dem wird gegeben', *Profil* 12, pp. 16–20.

Menasse, P. (2009), 'Der Blick der Fremden auf ihre Wiener Heimat', *Falter* 41, p. 18.

Menasse, R. (2000), *Erklär mir Österreich* (Frankfurt: Suhrkamp).

—— (2005), *Das war Österreich* (Frankfurt: Suhrkamp).

Merlingen, M. et al. (2001), 'The Right and the Righteous? European Norms, Domestic Politics and the Sanctions Against Austria', *Journal of Common Market Studies* 39:1, 59–77.

Misik, R. (2010), '"Keynes wird im Kleiderschrank verräumt"', *Falter* 16, p. 13.

Mitten, R. (1992), *The Politics of Antisemitic Prejudice* (Oxford: Westview Press).

—— (2002), 'Die Juden, die er meint …', in A. Pelinka and R. Wodak (eds.), *"Dreck am Stecken"* (Vienna: Czernin).

Modood, T. et al. (eds.) (1997), *Ethnic Minorities in Britain* (London: Policy Studies Institute).

Morehead, C. (2005), *Human Cargo* (London: Chatto & Windus).

Morrow, D. (2000), 'Jörg Haider and the new FPÖ', in P. Hainsworth (ed.), *The Politics of the Extreme Right* (London: Pinter).

Möseneder, M. (2010), 'Stadtführungen als Integrationsmaßnahme', *Der Standard* 6 August, p. 8.

Möseneder, M. and Schmidt, C. (2009), 'Flüchtlingskinder im Gefängnis oder ohne Betreuung', *Der Standard* 10 April, p. 12.

Motter, M. (2008), 'Guten Tag, Welt!', *Megaphon* 156, pp. 8–9.

—— (2010a), 'Außensichten und Innenleben', *Megaphon* 177, p. 16.

—— (2010b), 'Die Neuen im Dorf', *Falter* 28, p. 43.

Muñoz, J. (2009), 'From national-Catholicism to democratic patriotism? Democratization and reconstruction of national pride: The case of Spain (1981–2000)', *Ethnic and Racial Studies* 32:4, 616–639.

Müller, J-W. (2002), 'Introduction: The power of memory, the memory of power and the power over memory', in J-W Müller (ed.), *Memory & Power in Post-War Europe* (Cambridge: Cambridge University Press).

—— (2010), 'On "European Memory"', in M. Pakier and B. Stråth (eds.), *A European Memory?* (New York/Oxford: Berghahn).

Nenning, G. (2002a), 'Mutterleib', *Kronen Zeitung* 21 August, p. 16.

—— (2002b), *Anders gesehen* (Vienna: Ueberreuter).

—— (2002c), 'Wir sind unschuldig', *Kronen Zeitung* 18 August, p. 6.

—— (2002d), 'Ausplünderung', *Kronen Zeitung* 4 September, p. 10.

—— (2003a), 'Blunzngröstl', *Kronen Zeitung* 8 January, p. 4.

—— (2003b), 'Restrisiko', *Kronen Zeitung* 15 July, p. 10.

—— (2003c), 'Unser Wasser', *Kronen Zeitung* 29 January, p. 4

—— (2003d), 'Blockade!!!', *Kronen Zeitung* 3 November, p. 4.

—— (2004a), 'Mut zur Neutralität', *Kronen Zeitung* 8 January, p. 6.

—— (2004b), 'Nur Mut, ihr Ösis', *Kronen Zeitung* 18 August, p. 6.

*News* (2003), 'Best of Österreich', 28 August, p. 45.

Niederndorfer, F. and Wolf, T. (2009), 'Die Stadt, die es nicht gibt', *Falter* 16, pp. 36–37.

Niemann, F. (ed.) (2009), *Wienzeilen* (Weitra: Bibliothek der Provinz).

Niven, B. (2006), 'Introduction', in B. Niven (ed.), *Germans as Victims* (Basingstoke: Palgrave Macmillan).

—— (ed.) (2006), *Germans as Victims* (Basingstoke: Palgrave Macmillan).

Nowak, R. (2009), 'Graf fordert Volksabstimmung zur Rückkehr Südtirols zu Österreich', *Die Presse* 26 July, p. 7.

Nüchtern, K. (2007), '"Kultur geht tiefer"', *Falter* 3, pp. 56–57.

Obid, V. et al. (2002), *Haiders Exerzierfeld: Kärntens SlowenInnen in der deutschen Volksgemeinschaft* (Vienna: Promedia).

Ongan, G. (2009), 'Zuschreiben oder ernsthaftes Bekämpfen?', in S. Bardakçi et al. (eds.), *Dazugehören oder nicht?* (Innsbruck: Studienverlag).

Ortner, J. (2004), 'Augen zu und durch', *Falter* 3, http://www.falter.at/print/F2004_04_3.php, accessed 27 April 2004.

—— (2008a), 'Mag Platter Ausländer?', *Falter* 5, p. 6.

—— (2008b), 'Integrier mich!' *Falter* 5, p. 13.

—— (2009a), 'Das Prinzip Hohenems: Der Lohn der Provokation', *Falter* 39, p. 14.

—— (2009b), 'Hat Faymann Angst vor Ausländern?', *Falter* 41, pp. 6–7.

—— (2009c), 'Gesucht: jung, weiß und christlich', *Falter* 7, pp. 10–11.

—— (2010), 'Leiten, aber ohne Kultur', *Falter* 23, p. 13.

Oster, C. (2009), 'Die neuen Österreicher', *Kleine Zeitung* (Steiermark) 25 October, pp. 6–7.

ÖVP (2006), 'Kursbuch Zukunft: modern, sicher, menschlich', http://www.oevp.at/download/Kursbuch_lang_web_pdf, accessed 8 September 2006.

Özkan, D. (2009), 'Dornbirn: Zwischenbilanz der Pioniers', *Die Presse* 8 April, p. 9.

Özkirimli, U. (2000), *Theories of Nationalism* (London: Macmillan).

Öztoplu, B. (2009), 'Kulturen der neuen Generationen', in F. Niemann (ed.), *Wienzeilen*, (Weitra: Bibliothek der Provinz).

Pakier, M. and Stråth, B. (eds.) (2010), *A European Memory* (New York: Berghahn).

Palme, L. (2006), 'Benya wäre einverstanden', *Profil* 51/52, pp. 24–27.

—— (2007), 'Die neuen Barbaren', *Profil* 13, pp. 56–57.

Parker, D. and Karner, C. (2010), 'Reputational geographies and urban social cohesion', *Ethnic and Racial Studies* 33:8, 1451–1470.

—— (forthcoming), 'Remembering the Alum Rock Road: Reputational geographies and spatial biographies', *Midlands History*.

Payrleitner, A. (2004), 'Die Ratlosigkeit der Intellektuellen vor der Welt der Zahlen', in E. Breisach and J. Rauchenberger (eds.), *Wohin steuert Österreich?* (Vienna: Czernin).

Peletz, M. (1983), 'Moral and political economies in rural Southeast Asia', *Comparative Studies in Society and History* 25:4, 731–739.

Pelinka, A. (1990), *Zur Österreichischen Identität* (Vienna: Ueberreuter).

—— (1998), *Austria: Out of the Shadow of the Past* (Boulder: Westview Press).

—— (2000), 'Die rechte Versuchung', in H-H. Scharsach (ed.), *Haider — Österreich und die rechte Versuchung* (Reinbek: Rowohlt).

—— (2002), 'Struktur und Funktion der "Aschermittwochrede" Jörg Haiders', in A. Pelinka and R. Wodak (eds.), *"Dreck am Stecken"* (Vienna: Czernin).

—— (2009), 'Wie das Echo nach Leon Zelmans Tod weiterhallt', *Falter* 50, p. 20.

—— (2010), 'Wie Rechtsextreme östlich von Wien aufmarschieren', *Falter* 12, p. 16.

Pelinka, A. and Weinzierl, E. (eds.) (1987), *Das Grosse Tabu* (Österreichische Staatsdruckerei: edition S).

Pelinka, A. and Wodak, R. (eds.) (2002), *"Dreck am Stecken"* (Vienna: Czernin).

Pelinka, P. (2004), 'Ein neuer Schildbürgerstreich', *News* 19 August, p. 40.

Permoser, J. M. et al. (2010), 'Religious organisations as political actors in the context of migration: Islam and Orthodoxy in Austria', *Journal of Ethnic and Migration Studies*, iFirst article, 1–19.

Però, D. (2007a), *Inclusionary Rhetoric/Exclusionary Practices* (New York: Berghahn).

—— (2007b), 'Migrants and the politics of governance: The case of Barcelona', *Social Anthropology* 15:3, 271–286.

Pero, S. (2008), '"Ihr Linken seid naiv"', *Falter* 5, p. 14.

Perry, M. (2010a), 'Bollwerk gegen die Gentechnik', *Kronen Zeitung* 4 August, pp. 24–25.

—— (2010b), 'EU will uns Appetit auf das ach so köstliche Nutella verderben', *Kronen Zeitung* (Steiermark) 1 August, p. 20.

Philipp, C. (2010), 'Ohne Blödeln hält man das nicht aus', *Megaphon* 173, pp. 8–9.

Pick, H. (2000), *Guilty Victim: Austria from the Holocaust to Haider* (London/ New York: I.B. Tauris).

Platter, G. (2008), 'Integration gestalten', in Bundesministerium für Inneres, *Gemeinsam kommen wir zusammen: Expertenbeiträge zur Integration* (Vienna: Bundesministerium für Inneres).

Pohl, W. (2003), 'Schlechte Verlierer', *Kronen Zeitung* 04 January, p. 18.

Polanyi, K. (1944), *The Great Transformation* (New York: Rinehart).

Pöll, R. (2010), 'Koalition will um Migranten werben', *Die Presse* 27 July, p. 1.

Pollak, A. (2008), 'The myth of the "untainted Wehrmacht"', in H. Heer et al. (eds.), *The Discursive Construction of History* (Basingstoke: Palgrave Macmillan).

Pollak, A. and Eger, N. (2002), 'Antisemitismus mit Anspielungscharakter', in A. Pelinka and R. Wodak (eds.), *"Dreck am Stecken"* (Vienna: Czernin).

Pölsler, G. (2008), 'Wo die Wut wächst', *Falter Steiermark* 8, pp. 4–5.

——— (2010), '"Unsere Gärten"', *Falter* 26, pp. 41–42.

Pommer, M. (2001), 'Das TV-Deutsch ruiniert unsere Sprache', *Kronen Zeitung* 5 September, pp. 8–9.

Portisch, H. (1996), *Jahre des Aufbruchs, Jahre des Umbruchs* (Vienna: Kremayr & Scheriau).

Potter, J. and Wetherell, M. (1998), 'Social representations, discourse analysis and racism', in U. Flick (ed.), *The Psychology of the Social* (Cambridge: Cambridge University Press).

Pratl, M. (2009), 'Analyse der Schulbücher', in J. Bunzl and F. Hafez (eds.), *Islamophobie in Österreich* (Innsbruck: Studienverlag).

*Profil* (11 December 2006), '"ÖVP ist in der Falle des neoliberalen Zeitgeistes"', 50, pp. 22–23.

——— (15 January 2007), 'Teure Umwelt', 3, p. 49.

——— (22 January 2007a), 'War das die Wende nach der Wende?', 4, p. 18.

——— (22 January 2007b), 'Wissenschaftsminister Hahn über…', 4, p. 29.

——— (12 March 2007), 'Energie & Umwelt extra', 11, pp. 62–72.

——— (29 May 2009), 'Lieber gemeinsam als einsam', 23, p. 36.

——— (22 March 2010), 'Interview mit Geert Wilders', 12, pp. 80–85.

——— (3 May 2010), '"Der Euro wird bestehen bleiben"', 18, pp. 22–23

Purkarthofer, J. et al. (2005), 'Medienlandschaft der autochthonen Minderheiten in Österreich', *Wiener Linguistische Gazette* 72, http://www.univie.ac.at/ linguistics/publications/wlg/722005/PurkarthoferRainerRappl/WLG72.pdf, accessed 27 October 2010.

Putnam, R. (2000), *Bowling Alone* (New York: Simon and Schuster).

Rabinovici, D. (2000), 'Wohin mit Österreich? Oder: Zwischen Tracht und Niedertracht. Gedanken zu einer neuen Koalition', in I. Charim and D. Rabinovici (eds.), *Österreich: Berichte aus Quarantanien* (Frankfurt: Suhrkamp).

Rabinowich, J. (2009), 'Janus in Babylon', in F. Niemann (ed.), *Wienzeilen* (Weitra: Bibliothek der Provinz).

Rainer, C. (2009), 'Für Minarette. Gegen Kreuze', *Profil* 50, p. 15.

―――― (2010a), 'Ausländer ist nicht Ausländer', *Profil* 3, p. 13.

―――― (2010b), 'Fekter und die Analphabeten', *Profil* 31, p. 13.

Rathkolb, O. (2005), *Die paradoxe Republik* (Vienna: Paul Zsolnay).

Rauscher, H. (2000), 'Eine geschlossene Verdrängungskette', in H-H. Scharsach (ed.), *Haider – Österreich und die rechte Versuchung* (Reinbek: Rohwolt).

Regierungsprogramm (2007), http://www.spoe.at/bilder/d255/regierungsprogramm _09012007.pdf, accessed 9 January 2007.

Regionale10 (2010), *Fremdsehen.At*, Graz.

Reisigl, M. (2002), 'Dem Volk aufs Maul schauen, nach dem Mund reden und Angst und Bange machen', in W. Eismann (ed.), *Rechtspopulismus* (Vienna: Czernin).

Reisigl, M. and Wodak, R. (2001), *Discourse and Discrimination* (London: Routledge).

Reiter, B. (2009), 'Das geht sich aus', in E. Steffen (ed.), *Wir sind gekommen, um zu bleiben* (Vienna: Czernin).

Reiter, M. (2002), 'Antisemitismus von Links? Traditionen, Kontinuitäten, Ambivalenzen', in H. Wassermann (ed.), *Antisemitismus in Österreich nach 1945* (Innsbruck: Studienverlag).

Reiterer, A. (ed.) (1988), *Nation und Nationalbewußtsein in Österreich* (Vienna: Verband der wissenschaftlichen Gesellschaften Österreichs).

―――― (1996), 'Intellektuelle und politische Eliten in der Nationswerdung Österreichs', in M. Haller (ed.), *Identität und Nationalstolz der Österreicher* (Vienna/Cologne: Böhlau).

Reithofer, R. (2004), 'Wider die Gefrässigkeit des Kapitalismus', *Megaphon* 102, pp. 10–11.

―――― (2008), 'Vorwort', in M. Krese et al. (eds.), *Ohne Angst verschieden sein* (Graz: Leykam).

―――― (2010), 'Verborgene Lebensgeschichten erzählen', in M. Krese et al. (eds.), *Neue Heimaten?* (Graz: CLIO).

Reithofer, R. and Brand, B. (2009), 'Inseln der Solidarität in Zeiten der Krise', *Isotopia: Forum für gesellschaftspolitische Alternativen* 66, p. 1.

Reithofer-Haidacher, E. (2008a), 'Sieg nach Punkten', *Megaphon* 153, pp. 6–7.

―――― (2008b), 'Frauen vor!', *Megaphon* 153, p. 12.

―――― (2009a), 'Das Gnadenrecht lebt weiter', *Megaphon* 166, p. 13.

―――― (2009b), 'Wo die Sprache vesagt', *Megaphon* 164, pp. 6–7.

―――― (2010), 'Eldards Traum', *Megaphon* 173, p. 10.

Resetarits, W. (2010), 'Des moch ma!', *Die Gute Zeitung – Sonderausgabe*, p. 2.

Reuters (2009), 'Austria's Graf gets grief over "united Tyrol"', http://blogs.reuters. com/global/2009/07/29/austrias-graf-gets-grief-over-united-tyrol/, accessed 19 August 2009.

Rexer, A. (2007), 'Kühl kalkuliert', *Profil* 18, pp. 54–55.

Richardson, J. E. (2004), *(Mis)Representing Islam* (Amsterdam: John Benjamins).

Richmond, A. H. (2002), 'Globalization: Implications for immigrants and refugees', *Ethnic and Racial Studies* 25:5, 707–727.

Richter, G. (2009), 'Die Wahrheit muss ans Licht!', *Kronen Zeitung* (Steiermark) 22 November, p. 20.

Ringel, A. (ed.) (2005), *Österreichs verwundete Seele 20 Jahre nach Erwin Ringel* (Vienna: Kremayr & Scheriau).

Rittberger, M. (2009), 'Wie kommt die Ausländerfeindlichkeit in die Kronen Zeitung?', in S. Bardakçi et al. (eds.), *Dazugehören oder nicht?* (Innsbruck: Studienverlag).

Ritterband, C. E. (2008), 'Missbrauch: Wegschauen und hinschauen', *Der Standard* 29 April, http://derstandard.at/?id=3320530, accessed 30 April 2008.

Roth, G. (1996), *Das doppelköpfige Österreich* (Frankfurt: Fischer).

Roubalová, V. and Kostlán, F. (2009), 'Die unerschrockene Zivilgesellschaft', *Das Jüdische Echo* 58, 157–160.

Ryan, N. (2004), *Homeland* (Edinburgh/London: Mainstream Publishing).

Saad, K. (2009), 'Islamophobie in österreichischen Tageszeitungen', in J. Bunzl and F. Hafez (eds.), *Islamophobie in Österreich* (Innsbruck: Studienverlag).

Said, E. (1995 [1978]), *Orientalism* (London: Penguin).

Salzmann, S. (2003), '"Unser Wasser nicht in das Ausland verkaufen"', *Kronen Zeitung* 30 August, pp. 12–13.

Sandrisser, W. and Winkler, H. (2008), 'Die Stärke der kulturellen Vielfalt', in Bundesministerium für Inneres, *Gemeinsam kommen wir zusammen* (Vienna: Bundesministerium für Inneres).

Saville, M. (1999), *'Das geliebte, genauso gehasste Österreich'* (University of Nottingham: PhD Thesis).

Sawerthal, A. (2010), 'Europas Schub', *Falter* 19, p. 13.

Schaffer, T. (2009), 'Maruša und Meta Krese dokumentieren die Situation von Zuwanderern im oststeirischen Feldbach', *Falter* 52, p. 58.

Schiedel, H. and Neugebauer, W. (2002), 'Jörg Haider, die FPÖ und der Antisemitismus', in A. Pelinka and R. Wodak (eds.), *"Dreck am Stecken"* (Vienna: Czernin).

Schmaus, C. (2009), 'Flüchtlinge haben Rechte', *Die Gute Zeitung* 14c, p. 3.

Schmied, H. (2002a), 'Tango Neoliberal', *Megaphon* 82, pp. 26–27.

―――― (2002b), '"Vom Buschneger zum Drogendealer"', *Megaphon* 82, p. 10.

―――― (2003a), 'Iron Bartenstein', *Megaphon* 97, p. 4.

―――― (2003b), '"Der Washington Consensus ist gescheitert"', *Megaphon* 97, pp. 8–9.

Schönauer, E. (2003), 'Ost-Lkw verpesten die Luft', *Kronen Zeitung* 16 January, p. 8.

Schrems, T. (2002), 'Deutsch-Deutsch ist uns Powidl', *Kronen Zeitung* 30 July, p. 9.

Schwaiger, G. (2010), 'Aufregung um mehr Zuwanderer', *Kronen Zeitung* (Steiermark) 29 July, p. 12.

Schwaiger, G. et al. (2009), '70 Prozent für Schubhaftzentrum', *Kronen Zeitung* (Steiermark) 21 December, p. 11.

Schweiger, B. (2008), 'Wurzeln schlagen', *Megaphon* 152, p. 11.

——— (2009), 'Falsche Träume in neuem Licht', *Megaphon* 170, p. 16.

——— (2010), 'Halt in einer fremden Welt', *Megaphon* 175, pp. 8–9.

Schwentner, J. (2007), 'Konsumpausen auf Rezept', *Megaphon* 136, p. 4.

Scott, J. (1976), *The Moral Economy of the Peasant* (New Haven: Yale University Press).

Seiser, G. (2006), '"Healthy native soil" versus common agricultural policy', in A. Gingrich and M. Banks (eds.), *Neo-Nationalism in Europe & Beyond* (New York: Berghahn).

Sertl, M. (2009), 'Ungehobene Schätze', in Bardakçi, S. et al. (eds.), *Dazugehören oder nicht?* (Innsbruck: Studienverlag).

Sickinger, H. (2008), 'Jörg Haider', in A. Pelinka et al. (eds.), *Kreisky – Haider: Bruchlinien österreichischer Identitäten* (Vienna: Braumüller).

Slackman, M. (2010), 'Right-wing sentiment collects, ready to burst its dam', *The New York Times* 22 September, p. 8.

Smith, A. D. (1986), *The Ethnic Origins of Nations* (Oxford: Blackwell).

——— (2008), *The Cultural Foundations of Nations* (Oxford: Blackwell).

Smith, H. (2010), 'Greece buckles under pressure from markets and asks for €45bn bailout to fund huge deficit', *The Guardian* 24 April, p. 46.

Snyder, T. (2002), 'Memory of sovereignty and sovereignty over memory: Poland, Lithuania and Ukraine, 1939–1999', in J-W. Müller (ed.), *Memory & Power in Post-War Europe* (Cambridge: Cambridge University Press).

Sonnleitner, B. (2009), 'Der Karikaturenstreit in den österreichischen Printmedien am Beispiel des Nachrichtenmagazins *profil*', in J. Bunzl and F. Hafez (eds.), *Islamophobie in Österreich* (Innsbruck: Studienverlag).

Spillman, L. (1997), *Nation and Commemoration* (Cambridge: Cambridge University Press).

Spinka, A. (2009), 'Zuwanderung als Chance', *Megaphon* 171, p. 4.

SPÖ (2006), 'Den Wohlstand gerecht verteilen: 20 Projekte für mehr Fairness in Österreich', http://www.spoe.at/bilder/d253/wahlprogramm06_internet_inkl_cover1.pdf?101422, accessed 8 September 2006.

Spudich, H. (2004), 'Der Transitvertrag: 1991–2003', http://derstandard.at, accessed 9 January.

Stadler, F. (ed.) (2004), *Österreichs Umgang mit dem Nationalsozialismus* (Vienna/New York: Springer).

Staudinger, M. and Treichler, R. (2009), 'Daham im Islam', *Profil* 49, pp. 56–61.

Steffen, E. (2009), 'Vorwort', in E. Steffen (ed.), *Wir sind gekommen, um zu bleiben* (Vienna: Czernin).

Steiner, E. (2007), 'Mit Löwen und Runen gegen die EU', *Der Standard* 19 December, p. 8.

Stemmer, M. (2010), 'Systembedingte Bildungslücken bei Migranten', *Der Standard* 10 April, p. 10.

Stevenson, N. (2004), 'The possibility of a European civil society', paper presented at the *Civil Societies, Violence and Reconciliation Conference*, Oxford, 26 April.

Stiegnitz, P. (2000), *Heimat zum Nulltarif* (Vienna: edition va bene)

Stock, C. and Rümmele, W. (2008), 'Kommunales Engagement als Integrationsfaktor', in Bundesministerium für Inneres, *Gemeinsam kommen wir zusammen* (Vienna: Bundesministerium für Inneres).

Stranig, S. (2009), 'Nützen Proteste?', *Die Gute Zeitung* 14c, p. 1.

Stroeken, K. (2002), 'Why the world loves watching football', *Anthropology Today* 18:3, 9–13.

Sully, M. (1990), *A Contemporary History of Austria* (London: Routledge).

Tanzer, O. (2003), 'Österreich versäumte Einsprüche', http://oesterreich.orf.at, accessed 22 October.

Thaler, P. (2001), *The Ambivalence of Identity: The Austrian Experience of Nation-Building in a Modern Society* (West Lafayette: Purdue University Press).

The Global Player (2010), 'Out of Traiskirchen', 2, p. 7.

Theiss, L. (2009), 'Interview: "Strache ist eine schlechte Kopie meines Bruders …"', *Krone Bunt* 12 July, pp. 32–33.

Thompson, E. P. (1966), *The Making of the English Working Class* (New York: Vintage Books).

———— (1971), 'The moral economy of the English crowd in the eighteenth century', *Past and Present* 50, 76–136.

———— (1991), *Customs in Common* (London: Merlin).

Thurnher, A. (2004), 'Doppeltes Versagen – Österreichs Medien und Österreichs Eliten', in E. Breisach and J. Rauchenberger (eds.), *Wohin steuert Österreich? Kritische Analysen und unorthodoxe Konzepte* (Vienna: Czernin).

———— (2008), 'Hans Dichand und die Macht. *Falter* 27, p. 10.

———— (2010), 'König der Könige', *Falter* 25, pp. 10–14.

Tomlinson, K. (2005), '"Bread is before everything"', in N. Redclift (ed.), *Contesting Moralities* (London: UCL Press).

Treacher, A. (2007), 'Circulating emotions, beliefs and fantasies: The Middle East and the West', *Psychodynamic Practice* 13:4, 345–360.

Truger, A. (2004), 'Keine Lösung in Sicht?', *Megaphon* 103, p. 4.

Turrini, P. (2001), *Ich liebe dieses Land* (Frankfurt: Suhrkamp).

Uhl, H. (2006), 'From victim myth to co-responsibility thesis: Nazi rule, World War II and the Holocaust in Austrian memory', in R. N. Lebow et al. (eds.), *The Politics of Memory in Postwar Europe* (Durham: Duke University Press).

———— (2008), 'Interpreting the "War of Annihilation"', in H. Heer et al. (eds.), *The Discursive Construction of History* (Basingstoke: Palgrave Macmillan).

Ulram, P. (2009), *Integration in Österreich* (Vienna: GfK Austria and Bundesministerium für Inneres).

Ulram, P. and Tributsch, S. (2004), *Kleine Nation mit Eigenschaften* (Vienna: Molden).

Unverdorben, M. (2003), 'Adler flogen aufs Podest', *Salzburger Nachrichten* 30 December, p. 21.

van den Berghe, P. (1995), 'Does race matter?', *Nations and Nationalism* 1:3, 357–368.

——— (2005), 'Ethnies and nations: Genealogies indeed', in A. Ichijo and G. Uzelac (eds.), *When is the Nation? Towards an Understanding of Theories of Nationalism* (London/New York: Routledge).

Vertovec, S. (2000), *The Hindu Diaspora* (London: Routledge).

——— (2007), 'Super-diversity and its implications', *Ethnic and Racial Studies* 30:6, 1024–1054.

Vogl, M. and Matscher, F. (2008), 'Integration: zwischen Assimilation und pluralistischer Multikultur', in Bundesministerium für Inneres, *Gemeinsam kommen wir zusammen: Expertenbeiträge zur Integration* (Vienna: Bundesministerium für Inneres).

Vranitzky, F. (2008), 'Eine Lanze für die EU', *Kronen Zeitung* 29 July, pp. 4–6.

Wally, M. (2007a), 'Schöne Ideen', *Profil* 6, pp. 32–33.

——— (2007b), 'Schweißen, drehen, fräsen', *Profil* 10, p. 26.

Wassermann, H. P. (ed.) (2002), *Antisemitismus in Österreich nach 1945* (Innsbruck: Studienverlag).

Weigl, A. (2009), *Migration und Integration* (Innsbruck: Studienverlag).

Weiss, G. and Wodak, R. (2003), 'Introduction', in G. Weiss and R. Wodak (eds.), *Critical Discourse Analysis* (Basingstoke: Palgrave Macmillan).

Weiss H. and Unterwurzacher, A. (2007), 'Soziale Mobilität durch Bildung?', in H. Fassmann (ed.), *2. Österreichischer Migrations- und Integrationsbericht, 2001–2006* (Klagenfurt: Drave).

Werner, K. (2004), 'Norderweiterung', *Megaphon* 100, p. 5.

Wetherell, M. and Potter, J. (1992), *Mapping the Language of Racism* (New York: Harvester Wheatsheaf).

Wietheger, H. (2010), 'Stanglpass gegen Fremdenhass', *Megaphon* 178, pp. 8–9.

Windisch, C. (2004a), 'Kinderbetreuung im Kreuzfeuer', *Megaphon* 102, pp. 6–7.

——— (2004b), 'Zu Besuch bei den Bettlern', *Megaphon* 103, pp. 6–7.

——— (2004c), 'Leben im Ghetto', *Megaphon* 103, pp. 8–9.

Winkler, S. (2010), 'Die Republik der Tabus', *Kleine Zeitung* (Steiermark) 8 August, pp. 4–5.

Winter, G. (2010), '"Es fehlt ein Konzept zur Integration"', *Kleine Zeitung* (Steiermark) 07 April, p. 23.

Wittlinger, R. (2006), 'Taboo or tradition?', in B. Niven (ed.), *Germans as Victims* (Basingstoke: Palgrave Macmillan).

Wodak, R. (2000), 'Echt, anständig und ordentlich', in H-H. Scharsach (ed.), *Haider – Österreich und die rechte Versuchung* (Reinbek: Rowohlt).

——— (2006), 'Right-wing populist rhetoric: Local answers to global questions', Seminar given at Loughborough University, 1 February.

———— (2007), 'Discourse in European Union organizations: Aspects of access, participation, and exclusion', *Text & Talk* 27:5–6, 655–680.

Wodak, R. et al. (1999), *The Discursive Construction of National Identity* (Edinburgh: Edinburgh University Press).

Wodak, R. and Pelinka, A. (eds.) (2002), *The Haider Phenomenon in Austria* (New Brunswick: Transaction).

Wodak, R. and Reisigl, M. (2002), '"…Wenn einer Ariel heisst…"', in A. Pelinka and R. Wodak (eds.), *"Dreck am Stecken"* (Vienna: Czernin).

Wolf, B. (2003), 'Frauen macht sichtbar', *Megaphon* 96, pp. 6–7.

———— (2007), 'Verzerrte Welt', *Megaphon* 137, pp. 8–9.

Wolkinger, T. (2003), 'Was das Leben schwer macht', *Megaphon* 99, p. 9.

———— (2010), '"In Österreich ist die Fiktion noch intakt"', *Falter* 25, p. 51.

Wrann, G. (2009), 'Saualpe, Hundsheim & Co', *Megaphon* 162, p. 4.

Wurmdobler, C. (2009), 'Jetzt bloß nicht ausrasten!', in E. Steffen (ed.), *Wir sind gekommen, um zu bleiben* (Vienna: Czernin).

Yadgar, Y. (2002), 'From the particularistic to the universalistic: national narratives in Israel's mainstream press, 1967–1997', *Nations and Nationalism* 8:1, 58–72.

Yildiran, E. (2010), 'Türkenverlagerung', *Biber* 8, http://www.dasbiber.at/content/t%C3%BCrkenverlagerung, accessed 2 September 2010.

Zierler, A. (2008), 'Ohne Angst verschieden sein', *Megaphon* 153, pp. 26–27.

Zinggl, W. (2002), 'Was ist eine Kulturnation?', *Der Standard* 13 April, p. 6.

Žižek, S. (1989), *The Sublime Object of Ideology* (London: Verso).

Zöchling, C. (2007a), 'Ikone der Rechten', *Profil* 45, pp. 34–35.

———— (2007b), 'Es pröllt', *Profil* 1, pp. 18–19.

———— (2009a), 'Im Dienste der Wehrmacht', *Profil* 33, pp. 14–21.

———— (2009b), 'Ist der Ruf erst ruiniert…', *Profil* 37, pp. 32–34.

———— (2010), 'Wer strebend sich bemüht…', *Profil* 30, pp. 22–24.

Zwander, W. (2010), 'Im Käfig von Ottakring', *Die Zeit* 22 July, p. 8.

*20er (Die Tiroler Straßenzeitung)* (2009), 'Gemeinsam garteln', 10, p. 4.

**CD-ROM**

Johnston-Arthur, A. E. and Sternfeld, N. (2006), 'Was aller Welt unmöglich erscheint', Third configuration in P. Marboe et al., *Verborgene Geschichte/n: Remapping Mozart*, (Wiener Mozartjahr).

**Music**

STS (2000), 'I bin aus Österreich', *STS & Band Live*, amadeo: 157 829-2 [CD].

## Newspapers and magazines

*Der Standard*, various dates and page numbers as given in text.
*Die Presse*, various dates and page numbers as given in text.
*Falter*, various dates and page numbers as given in text.
*Kleine Zeitung* (Steiermark), various dates and page numbers as given in text.
*Kronen Zeitung* (or *Krone*), various dates and page numbers as given in text.
*Le Nouvel Observateur*, date as given in text.
*National Zeitung*, date as given in text.
*Profil*, various dates and page numbers as given in text.
*The Guardian*, date as given in text.
*TV Woche*, date as given in text.

## Radio

Radio Wien Internet, http://wien.orf.at/magazin/popup?skin=liveradio2&width=3 20&height=260&opions=undefined, date as given in text.

## Television

BBC Morning News, dates as given in text.
Channel 4 (29 January 2009), 'Jamie saves our bacon'.
Channel 4 News, dates as given in text.
Club 2 (13 October 2010), 'Ruck nach rechts', ORF 2.
CNN (20 May 2010), 'Quest means business'.
DW-TV (30 October 2006), 'Journal'.
——— (9 March 2007), 'Journal'.
——— (25 April 2007), 'Made in Germany'.
Euronews, dates as given in text.
*Zeit im Bild*, dates as given in text, ORF 2.
ZIB 1, dates as given in text, ORF 1.

## Websites

http://clandestino.at, website providing information on *Frau Bock* and other civil society initiatives, accessed 28 August 2003.
http://dieStandard.at, gender-related news/headlines on the website of *Der Standard*, dates accessed as given in text.
http://derStandard.at, news/headlines on the website of *Der Standard*, daily newspaper, various dates accessed as given in text.

http://minderheiten.at/stat/stimme/zeitschr.htm, website and archive for *Stimme*, a magazine 'for and by minorities', accessed 24 August 2010.

http://oehinfo.uibk.ac.at/theo/dialog/, website of the Group for Christian-Muslim Dialogue, Innsbruck, accessed 17 September 2009.

http://sport.orf.at, sports-related news/headlines on the website of Austria's public broadcasting network, dates accessed as given in text.

http://tirol.ORF.at, regional news/headlines on Tyrol on the website of Austria's public broadcasting network, dates accessed as given in text.

http://wien.ORF.at, regional news/headlines on Vienna on the website of Austria's public broadcasting network, dates accessed as given in text.

http://wcm.krone.at, http://wcw.krone.at, news/headlines on the website of *Kronen Zeitung*, daily newspaper, various dates accessed as given in text.

http://www.bzoe.at, BZÖ website.

http://www.dasbiber.at, website and archive for Vienna's migrants' magazine *Biber*, accessed 24 August 2010.

http://www.diepresse.at, news/headlines on the website of *Die Presse*, daily newspaper, various dates accessed as given in text.

http://www.dw-world.de, 'Projekt Zukunft' on the website of Deutsche Welle, date accessed as given in text.

http://www.falter.at/anzeigen/media.php, *Falter* website, information on readership, circulation etc., accessed 4 May 2004.

http://www.fpoe.at, FPÖ website.

http://www.fremdsehen.at, website of a Styrian cultural initiative involving international artists spending a fortnight in rural localities and reflecting on their experiences.

http://www.freundeschuetzen.at, website and petition for an initiative calling for humanitarian right of residence for well-integrated (families of) asylum-seekers, accessed 7 September 2010.

http://www.gruene.at, *Die Grünen* (Austria's Green party) website.

http://www.megaphon.at, *Megaphon* website, accessed 23 August 2010.

http://www.noe.orf.at, regional news/headlines on Lower Austria on the website of Austria's public broadcasting network, dates accessed as given in text.

http://www.oevp.at, ÖVP website.

http://www.orf.at, news/headlines on the website of Austria's public broadcasting network, various dates accessed as given in text.

http://www.spoe.at, SPÖ website.

# Index